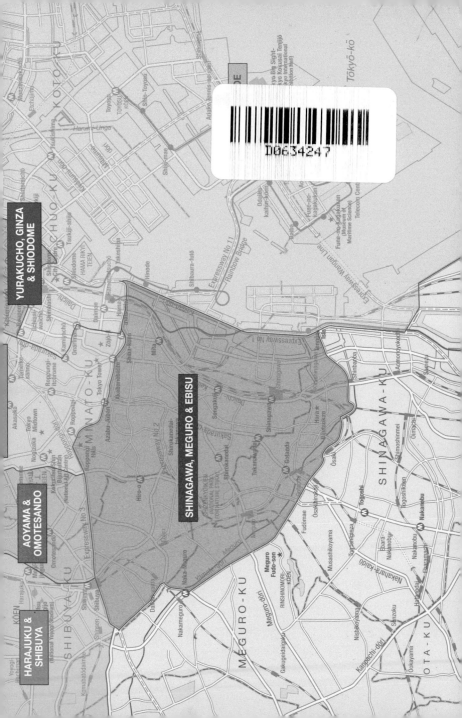

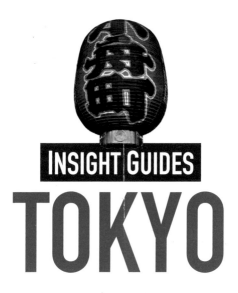

INSIGHT GUIDES
TOKYO

APA PUBLICATIONS

L

Part of the Langenscheidt Publishing Group

HOW TO USE THIS BOOK

This book is carefully structured both to convey an understanding of the city and its culture and to guide readers through its attractions and activities:

◆ The Best Of section at the front of the book helps you to prioritize. The first spread contains all the Top Sights, while the Editor's Choice details unique experiences, the best buys or other recommendations.

◆ To understand Tokyo, you need to know something of its past. The city's history and culture are described in

authoritative essays written by specialists in their fields who have lived in and documented the city for many years.

◆ The Places section details all the attractions worth seeing. The main places of interest are coordinated by number with the maps.

◆ Each chapter includes lists of recommended shops, restaurants, bars and cafes.

◆ Photographs throughout the book are chosen not only to illustrate geography and buildings, but also to convey

the moods of the city and the life of its people.

◆ The Travel Tips section includes all the practical information you will need, divided into five key sections: transport, accommodation, activities (including nightlife, events, tours and sports), an A-Z of practical tips and a handy Japanese phrasebook.

◆ A detailed street atlas is included at the back of the book, with all hotels, restaurants, bars and cafes plotted for your convenience.

PLACES AND SIGHTS

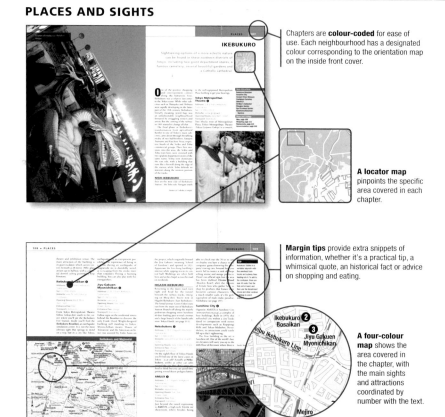

Chapters are **colour-coded** for ease of use. Each neighbourhood has a designated colour corresponding to the orientation map on the inside front cover.

A locator map pinpoints the specific area covered in each chapter.

Margin tips provide extra snippets of information, whether it's a practical tip, a whimsical quote, an historical fact or advice on shopping and eating.

A four-colour map shows the area covered in the chapter, with the main sights and attractions coordinated by number with the text.

PHOTO FEATURES

Photo features offer visual coverage of major sights or unusual attractions. Where relevant, there is a map showing the location and essential information on opening times, entrance charges, transport and contact details.

SHOPPING AND RESTAURANT LISTINGS

Shopping listings provide details of the best shops in each area. **Restaurant listings** give the establishment's contact details, opening times and price category, followed by a useful review. Bars and cafés are also covered here. The coloured dot and grid reference refers to the atlas section at the back of the book.

TRAVEL TIPS

Travel Tips provide all the practical knowledge you'll need before and during your trip: how to get there, getting around, where to stay and what to do. The A–Z section is a handy summary of practical information, arranged alphabetically.

THE BEST OF TOKYO: TOP ATTRACTIONS

At a glance, the Tokyo sights and activities you can't afford to miss, from traditional Asakusa and fashionable Omotesando to relaxing in one of the city's *onsen* baths or admiring nature in Shinjuku Gyoen.

◁ **Omotesando.** Parading down tree-lined Omotesando, Tokyo's most fashionable shopping avenue, is a must; many of the boutiques are housed in striking modern buildings designed by the world's top architects. See page 133.

△ **Onsen.** Join throngs of locals enjoying a soothing *onsen* dip at Odaiba's Oedo Onsen Monogatari, a giant modern bathhouse with a nostalgic design, or the more contemporary-styled Spa La-Qua. See pages 219 and 192.

◁ **Senso-ji.** Resplendent in red and gold is Senso-ji, the Buddhist temple that's the spiritual core of Asakusa, one of Tokyo's most venerable areas packed with craft shops and lovely ryokan (traditional Japanese inns). See page 183.

△ **Shinjuku Gyoen.** Tokyo has several beautiful traditional parks and gardens, among which the extensive Shinjuku Gyoen is a standout, combining French, English and Japanese styles of landscaping. See page 120.

▷ **Shibuya.** Be dazzled by the massed crowds and mega-wattage of neon pulsing through Shibuya, the shopping district that's the front of a million-and-one consumer crazes. See page 141.

◁ **Roppongi.** Still a raucous nightlife district, Roppongi has recently evolved into a daytime hub for art and high-class shopping at the Roppongi Hills and Tokyo Midtown complexes. See page 150.

▽ **Tsukiji.** Seafood does not come any fresher than at the vast wholesale fish and fresh produce market known as Tsukiji, where you can enjoy a breakfast of top-class sushi. See page 213.

◁ **Meiji Shrine.** Note the barrels of sake donat-edw to Meiji Shrine and be sure to visit a sake bar to sample the best. See page 139.

▽ **Imperial Palace.** You can't go inside, but making a circuit of the gardens surrounding the Imperial Palace, home to the world's oldest monarchy, provides a green escape at the heart of the city. See page 81.

▷ **River bus.** Take a river bus down the Sumida River or across Tokyo Bay towards the man-made island of Odaiba for a different perspective on this port city. See page 243.

THE BEST OF TOKYO: EDITOR'S CHOICE

Setting priorities, saving money, unique attractions... here, at a glance, are our recommendations, plus some tips and tricks even the locals won't always know.

BEST TOKYO VIEWS

Bar Six. The wide balcony outside the sixth-floor bar at the Amuse Museum provides a grand circle view across the temple compound of Asakusa's Senso-ji and beyond to Tokyo Skytree. See page 189.

Mori Tower. Not only do you get to stand on the roof of this 54-storey tower to enjoy heart-stopping 360-degree views of the city, but there's also one of the city's best galleries up here. See page 153.

Tokyo Metropolitan Government Office. The free observatory on the 45th floor has splendid views of city landmarks, the bay and – if the weather plays ball – Mount Fuji. See page 115.

Tokyo Skytree. This vertiginous communications tower and complex, opened in spring 2012, provides the city's highest observation platform. See page 202.

Yebisu Garden Place. The restaurant plaza on the 38th floor offers great views of the bay and westwards towards Shibuya and Shinjuku. See page 165.

BEST TEMPLES AND SHRINES

Asakusa Kannon (Senso-ji). Tokyo's most visited temple hosts dozens of annual events and festivals. See page 182.

Gokoku-ji. Off the beaten path, this magnificent 17th-century temple has survived earthquakes and fires. See page 111.

Kanda Myojin. This shrine is especially lively on Saturdays when weddings, rituals and festivals are held. See page 194.

Meiji-jingu. An amazing setting in the centre

Statue at Gokoku-ji, one of the few surviving Edo temples.

of a forest in the middle of Tokyo. Gravel paths lead to the shrine, an example of pure Shinto design. See page 139.

Tsukiji Hongan-ji. An architectural curiosity, this large and imposing temple is based on the ancient Buddhist monuments of South India. See page 213.

Yushima Tenjin. Associated with learning and wisdom, and known for its annual plum and chrysanthemum festivals. See page 194.

Breathtaking views from Mori Tower observation deck.

BEST FOR FAMILIES

Ghibli Museum, Mitaka. Fans of the animated Studio Ghibli movies will not want to miss this charming inventive complex. See page 25.

Origami Center. Learn about this fun and creative paper folding craft at the place it was invented. See page 193.

Kiddyland. Five floors stuffed with a vast array of toys and cute characters like Hello Kitty and Pokemon. See page 132.

Mega Web. Part of Odaiba's Palette Town complex; enjoy a giant Ferris wheel, the Toyota City Showcase and a car museum. See page 219.

Tokyo Disney Resort. Mickey and co. are all present at this replica theme park, which also includes the separate water-themed DisneySea Park. See page 223.

Tokyo Dome City. A hyperactive amusement park in the heart of the city with a giant roller-coaster, a Ferris wheel and a play area packed with toys. See page 191.

Ueno Zoo. Children will enjoy getting close to small animals in the petting zoo. See page 174.

A mind-boggling array of toys at Kiddyland.

BEST MUSEUMS AND GALLERIES

Edo-Tokyo Museum. The giant exhibition space in Ryogoku recreates Old Tokyo and documents its evolution into the modern metropolis. See page 203.

Japan Folk Crafts Museum. A beautiful wood and stone building that is home to an exemplary collection of folk crafts. See page 147.

Kiyosumi Complex. A cutting-edge enclave of galleries near Kiyosumi Gardens that show top and up-and-coming international and local artists. See page 206.

Miraikan. Tokyo's best science museum, explaining cutting-edge technology in a way that's accessible to all ages, is appropriately located in futuristic Odaiba. See page 218.

Mori Art Museum. Superior quality art exhibitions, which change every three months or so, are mounted in this massive gallery in Roppongi Hills. See page 153.

Nezu Museum. As if the elegant collection of Japanese and Chinese arts and crafts isn't sufficient, this lovely museum also has one of Tokyo's best gardens. See page 131.

Tokyo Museum of Contemporary Art. On the east side of the Sumida River this mammoth gallery is a great place to get to grips with the contemporary art scene. See page 208.

The Edo-Tokyo Museum.

BEST WALKS

Strolling along Cat Street.

Cat Street. A river long since filled in provides a traffic-free amble from Harajuku to Shibuya past cafés, boutiques and a few old houses. See page 134.

Imperial Palace Gardens. Cut through the heart of the city via the parkland that surrounds its enigmatic palace. See page 81.

Omotesando. Head to Tokyo's premier shopping avenue to admire its collection of modern architecture. At Christmas, the zelkova trees are also strung with twinkling lights. See page 133.

Tsukiji to Tsukuda-jima. This bayside stroll takes you from the frantic fish market to a tiny enclave of the city that evokes the Tokyo of centuries ago. See page 212.

Yanaka's back streets. Start anywhere among the maze of narrow, winding streets that take you through one of the oldest surviving districts of Tokyo – speckled with a cemetery, temples and old houses. See page 176.

Impressive changing sky of über-elegant Venus Fort.

ONLY IN TOKYO

Cat Petting Lounge. Nekobukero in Ikebukuro's Tokyu Hands allows you quality time with a room packed with pedigree kitties. See page 109.

Design Festa Gallery. A visual explosion of colourful art in the backstreets of Harajuku that has taken over a series of old apartment blocks. See page 134.

Maid Cafés. Roleplaying waitresses dress up in wacky costumes to serve besotted geeks and curious tourists in Akihabara. See page 198.

Meguro Parasitological Museum. A museum dedicated to those creepy body invaders; the highlight is an 8.8-metre (29ft) tapeworm removed from a human intestine. See page 164.

Oedo Onsen Monogatari. A giant, fun bathhouse complex in Odaiba, where you can soak in authentic thermal spring water. See page 219.

Find cats galore at the Cat Petting Lounge in Nekobukuro.

BEST SHOPPING

AsoBit City. One of Akihabara's largest character goods retail stores is packed with plastic models and figures. See page 196.

Don Quixote. Crammed pellmell with character goods, toys, kitchenware, lifestyle goods and booze. See page 123.

Isetan. Shinjuku's top-class department store is a reminder that shopping can be a pleasurable experience – it also has one of Tokyo's best food floors. See page 123.

Isetatsu. Specialises in *chiyogami* – printed paper products – in traditional and modern designs. See page 178.

Tokyo Midtown. Hyper-elegant shopping complex with a great selection of luxe fashions and an interior design and homewares floor stocking great local products. See page 153.

Tokyu Hands. A fun hardware and DIY store stocked with an endless array of goods. See page 111.

Venus Fort. Designed to resemble an elegant old European city, this mall in Odaiba even has an artificial sky that changes from sunrise to sunlight. See page 219.

Picnic in Yoyogi Park, a favourite with rockabilly devotees.

BEST PARKS AND GARDENS

Hama Rikyu Detached Garden. An Edo-Period stroll garden with a salt-water tidal pond and ancient pine and cherry trees, not to mention a spectacular high-rise cityscape backdrop. See page 216.

Happo-en. Gently sloping down to an ornamental pond, this pocket of greenery is a beautiful backdrop to a famous wedding hall. See page 161.

Kiyosumi Garden. Famous for its extraordinarily beautiful rocks from all over Japan. See page 207.

Koishikawa Korakuen Garden. Although landscaped, the grounds of this Edo-Period green haven have a natural feel. See page 190.

National Park for Nature Study. This peaceful park recreates the unspoiled habitat of the Musashino Plain, long before Tokyo was built. See page 161.

National Park for Nature Study Rikugien. A serene stroll garden with a teahouse, pond and wooded sections of zelkova, cherry and camphor. See page 112.

Yoyogi Park. A generous swathe of greenery popular with families and couples. See page 140.

BEST ARCHITECTURE

Fuji TV Building. One of Kenzo Tange's works, this TV studio and its suspended dome is one of the city's most futuristic-looking structures. See page 218.

The National Art Center. Metabolist architect Kisho Kurokawa's amazing gallery is a monumental work that plays with basic geometrical forms, its facade billowing like a giant curtain. See page 154.

Prada Aoyoma. Fluid and luminous, the tinted, diamond-shaped outer panels of this store allow you to peer through the stylish interior. See page 132.

St Mary's Cathedral. This early Kenzo Tange masterpiece is covered in dazzling stainless steel to symbolise the light of Christ. See page 111.

Tokyo International Forum. An imaginative building: Rafael Vinoly's glass chrysalis seems to levitate. See page 98.

21_21 Design Sight. Tadao Ando turns concrete into elegant geometry in this angular exhibition space behind Tokyo Midtown. See page 153.

The stark interior of St Mary's Cathedral.

MONEY-SAVING TIPS

Cheap Food and Drink. Many bars have a 'happy hour' that in some cases lasts for as long as two hours. Set lunches and buffets in restaurants can be very cheap, often ¥1,000 or less. You can fill up for comfortably under ¥1,000 at dinner or lunch at local fast food joints like Yoshinoya (for *gyu-don*), Matsuya (for *teishoku* and the like) and others.

Cinema Tickets. These usually cost in the region of ¥1,800, but on the first Monday of every month, cinema entrance is ¥1,000. Every Wednesday is also 'women's day' when tickets for women are ¥1,000.

Free Views. Take in sky-high panoramas of the city for free at the Tokyo Metropolitan Government Office building in West Shinjuku (see page 115) and from the top of the Yebisu Garden Place (see page 165) in Ebisu.

Grutt Pass. This ¥2,000 pass, valid for two months after being issued, provides free or discounted entry at 75 attractions, including all Tokyo's major museums; see www.museum.or.jp/grutto.

Shopping Refunds. Some department stores and major home electronics stores offer a 5 percent discount (equivalent to the Japanese consumption tax) on purchases that cost over ¥10,000. Check at the information desk before making a purchase. You will need to show your passport.

Shibuya Crossing.

Senso-ji, Asakusa.

Children in Tokyo being cared for by nursery staff.

TOKYO ENIGMAS

Tokyo pulsates with an unremitting energy that stems from a tradition of constant change and reinvention. And while this sprawling metropolis is also crowded and seemingly chaotic – even ugly – many visitors find the city strangely addictive.

In submitting itself to repeated sessions of radical urban surgery and reconstruction, Tokyo's remodelled surfaces always seem fresh, managing to escape the rigor mortis that envelops many European capitals. Tokyoites are the ultimate early adaptors, their city a virtual Petri dish for testing the latest in fashion, art and technology. With its attention firmly on the here and now, Tokyo can seem like a city with a short-term memory. Tokyo novelist Masahiko Shimada expressed this preference for the present when he wrote: 'Things that happened yesterday are already covered with shifting sand. And last month's events are completely hidden. The year before is twenty metres under, and things that happened five years ago are fossils.'

The Tokyoite generation in Harajuku.

Constantly mutating, Tokyo is a difficult animal to classify; a sense of artificiality and impermanence distinguishes it from all the other well-grounded, great cities of the world. Although Tokyo presents the visitor with glimpses of a mode of life that can seem both enigmatic and indecipherable, it need not be so.

Tokyo is a city that should be walked. Seen from a train window or the upper floors of an office block, what appears to be a bland mass from afar will, on close-up, afford endless stimulation in the form of surprising oddities and sudden transitions. In this ultra-modern mishmash, street and place names have survived intact from the ancient Edo era, sustaining history and nostalgia through their literary and narrative connections, long after their visible features on the cityscape have vanished. While Tokyo's streets, awash with the gizmos and gadgets of a portable, lightweight electronic culture, crackle with static and blink with neon, there is an older side to the city visible in quiet neighbourhoods of timeworn wooden houses and the leafy compounds of ancient temples and shrines.

Defying the Western stereotype.

Crowds on the streets of Harajuku.

TOKYOITES

Nearly 13.1 million people live within the boundaries of the modern metropolis that is Tokyo. To understand what makes them tick you need to look back to how the city developed, as well as where it's headed.

Today, nearly 150 years since Japan's capital changed its name to Tokyo, you may still hear elderly Tokyoites born and bred in the city referring to themselves as Edo-ko – children of Edo. It's a small, but telling, sign of the pride Tokyo natives take in their city's illustrious past: Edo was the capital's name for over 400 years during which time it became the most populous and one of the most sophisticated metropolises on the planet.

A respect for history and tradition in Tokyo often comes as a surprise to visitors who are only aware of the city as a thoroughly modern metropolis in the process of perpetual change. But Tokyo wouldn't be what it is today without the events of the past and its citizens are

> *Tokyo-to covers 2,187 sq km (844 sq miles). Besides the 23 central wards of the inner city, it also incorporates 26 smaller cities, five towns and eight villages.*

keenly aware of that fact and seek to preserve the city's unique spirit be it in the traditional craft shops, a *shitamachi* (Tokyo's 'low city') area such as Asakusa, or the daily rituals observed in thousands of Shinto shrines across the city.

A crowded city

One thing hasn't changed about Tokyo in centuries: it remains a densely packed urban environment. Within the central 23 wards (Adachi, Arakawa, Bunkyo, Chiyoda, Chuo, Edogawa, Itabashi, Katsushika, Kita, Koto, Meguro, Minato,

Children add to the squash at rush hour.

Nakano, Nerima, Ota, Setagaya, Shibuya, Shinagawa, Shinjuku, Suginami, Sumida, Taito and Toshima) live around 8.95 million people. As armies of commuters travel into work from the greater Tokyo area and suburbs in the nearby prefectures of Chiba, Kanagawa and Saitama, the daytime population of the city's core swells to over 11 million. You only have to try and get on a train during rush hour to experience this swell of humanity. Buildings are frequently built so close together there is barely any room for sunlight to penetrate windows. And in all the main city shopping areas, crowds predominate: one of Tokyo's most awe-inspiring experiences

Hygiene-conscious in Shibuya.

is when the traffic lights outside Shibuya station turn green and a sea of people flows in all directions across the 'scramble' crossing.

A culture of convenience

Having long lived under such pressure-cooker conditions Tokyoites have become masters of

GERM PHOBIC

The Japanese obsession with cleanliness has resulted in some interesting products on the market. Cosmetics maker Shiseido Company has isolated a substance called noneal as the source of body odour in older people. A line of shampoos, lotions and deodorants inhibits the breakdown of fatty acid in skin that creates noneal. Alongside the usual mints, convenience stores sell an array of liquid capsules and other products designed to blast garlic and beer breath, while Elizabeth Arden Japan's Lip Lip Hooray lip balm neutralises compounds that cause bad breath. All manner of surgical masks and antibacterial hand gels and wipes sell well year round, but especially so during flu season and (for masks) when spring brings with it uncomfortably high pollen counts.

urban survival. There may be a fair amount of pushing and shoving to get on and off crowded trains but, other than that, you'll find Tokyoites almost faultlessly polite and respectful with each other. Locals seem to have an amazing ability to screen out the perpetual cacophony of noise and visual pollution assaulting them on a daily basis on every major shopping street. While the area of land given over to parks and gardens per capita is low, greenery in the form of potted plants and bonsai outside shops and homes frequently helps soften the urban landscape.

It is highly uncommon to see instances of aggression in public, and crime figures remain amazingly low for a city of such a size and density. Tokyo is one of the few cities in the world where a salaried worker can pass out drunk on the street and wake up to find his wallet intact. Temples and shrines stay open day and night without incident or loss. Even the graffiti when it happens (which is rarely) looks artful.

To further ease living, Tokyo has also developed a culture of convenience that is impressive. By and large the city still operates as the collection of independent communities it once was, each insular and self-reliant. There is no need to cross Tokyo to make a purchase as facilities are generally just around the corner. In particular you are rarely more than a few hundred metres/yards from a vending machine or round-the-clock convenience store, or *konbini* as it's known, stocking everything from hot takeout meals, magazines, deodorants and stationery to socks and prophylactics.

Population growth and decline

After a post-war population boom from 3.5 million in 1945 to more than 10 million by the mid-sixties, the population of Tokyo has grown steadily from 11 million in the 1970s to 13 million today. Looking at those stats, you might forget that Japan now has a very low birth rate and the nation is actually experiencing popu-

> The Ogasawara islands are among the many distant islands falling under the control of the Tokyo Metropolitan Government. Over 1000km (620 miles) southeast of Tokyo, they are connected to the mainland only by a 25-hour ferry ride.

lation decline. Despite estimates that Tokyo's population may approach 14 million by 2020, even the great metropolis is expected to see numbers tail off soon after. If birth rates continue as they are, government figures predict a population of around 12 million by 2040 and less than 8 million by 2100.

One group that has seen a particular increase in numbers are non-Japanese residents. Despite a slight decrease post 3/11, the total population has increased from around 300,000 to 400,000 in the last ten years. These days, Tokyo certainly feels a much more international place than it did, say, a decade ago. Not only are more non-Japanese calling Tokyo home (and many raising multicultural families), more locals are travelling abroad (particularly the young) and feeding back into the city the fashions and styles they encounter. This fascination with foreign cultures also manifests itself in a superb array of restaurants offering every cuisine under the sun from Belarusian to Vietnamese.

Don't be fooled, though, into thinking that Tokyo is anything like London or New York in terms of multicultural diversity. Figures from 2012 show that Tokyo's expat community accounts for just 3 percent of the city's total population – the most common foreign nationalities being Chinese (164,199), Korean (105,552), Filipino (29,540), American (17,342), Indian (8,750), Nepalese (7.786), Thai (7,177), British (6,064), Myanmarese (5,328) and French (4,945). Even these numbers are misleading since many Chinese and Korean families have lived in the capital for generations (they just don't have Japanese passports) and to outsiders will appear fully assimilated.

A creative generation

Lack of ethnic diversity aside, you can find in Tokyo as vast range a range of personalities as in any other major metropolis. Japanese from more rural parts of the country and even other big cities, such as Osaka and Nagoya, are likely to label their cousins in the capital somewhat aloof and unfriendly, but in a city of Tokyo's size it's commonplace to find plenty of exceptions to this stereotype.

Fashionable teenagers in Harajuku.

Role-playing with light-sabres.

day – to see what a colourful, style-conscious place Edo was, with the geisha of Yoshiwara and the *kabuki* stars of Asakusa setting the tone and driving the fashions. Likewise, young Tokyoites today flick through mountains of glossy magazines and look towards Harajuku's girls and Shibuya's boys to find out what to wear and buy next.

The greying population

It is to Sugamo, though, that you should cast a glance to discern part of Tokyo's future. In this central northern area of the city is Jizo-dori, a street nicknamed *'obachan-no-Harajuku'* (old ladies Harajuku) because of the predominance of shops catering to pensioners. By 2040, about 40 percent of the population of greater Tokyo will be aged 65 or older – a doubling of the current figure – giving rise to concern as to how welfare services will manage in the future. The bright neon lights of Tokyo's youth hotspots are not about to go out, but the city will surely adapt to accommodate a greying population.

Tokyo's youth are always on the cutting edge of fashion.

If there's one characteristic that many of Tokyo's inhabitants do share it's an ability to think creatively out of the box and embrace the new. While the ancient capital of Kyoto can be viewed as Japan's wise and sophisticated pensioner, a repository of the nation's traditional cultural values and pursuits, Tokyo lives up to its image as an attention deficit-disordered teen, feverishly chasing the latest trend. The city's crackling energy is fuelled by the highly disposable incomes of young people, many of whom still live with their parents, refusing to start families of their own. Companies are constantly engaged in creating, developing and marketing new products and services to serve these insatiable consumers – at times it can seem as if the city's prime, if not only, hobby is shopping.

There's actually nothing new to this. At the height of the Edo era the city experienced a flourishing economy and artistic outpouring that was driven by the merchants and lower ranks living in the *shitamachi* (low city). You only need look at *ukiyo-e* prints from those times – the snapshots of their

In a few ways it already is. Tokyo may have failed in its bid for the 2016 Olympics but the 10-year plan put in place as part of that campaign remains current as part of Tokyo's bid for the 2020 games and one of its eight key goals is for the city to become 'an urban model for a super-ageing society'. The rebuilding of the Mitsubishi Ichigokan (see page 90) and the historic facade of Tokyo Station are also signs of a renewed respect for older elements of the capital and the need for preservation alongside regeneration.

Home sweet home

Land ownership rules in Tokyo, with coordinated town planning and green belt conservation very low on the list of priorities. As a result, small farms operate alongside factories; a neon-lit *pachinko* parlour may stand amid paddy fields. The result is a startling mish-mash of the good, the bad and the ugly, which, while never broadly pleasing to the eye, is full of interest and always immensely human.

A tiny apartment, be it in a private block or on a state-subsidised estate, is home to the average Tokyoite. As technology improves to cope with the very real prospects of a major earthquake in Tokyo, there continues to be an increase in the number of high-rise apartment complexes (known as mansions, or, if for the extra tall, tower mansions) sprouting across city. Around these, though, there are still many small concrete, brick and wooden houses.

While many people continue to rent homes, a growing number, especially in the inner and outer suburban areas, are buying property, grabbing the opportunity to secure loans while interest rates remain low and land prices in all but the most chic areas of Tokyo continue to decline. Victims of the recession and the decline in traditional Asian family networks of support, Tokyo's ranks of homeless people have also swelled in recent years. They are most noticeable in major rail stations (such as Shinjuku), along riverbanks and in parks like Ueno-koen where their homes made from cardboard boxes and blue tarpaulin tents are kept remarkably neat and tidy.

Ways of escape

Tokyoites are busy, active people – even those who are retired seem to have plenty of energy,

The official retirement age in Japan is 60 for women and up to 70 for men, but some work longer.

gathering for trips around the city to cultural institutions or for games of gateball (a kind of croquet) in a local park. The best time to observe, interact with and really get to know the locals, then, is to join them when they are relaxing. Top of the list of favourite pursuits is a boozy night in a bar or *izakaya*, often in the company of fellow workers. Under such alcohol-fuelled circumstances normally reticent, shy people will risk their fractured English to attempt conversation with overseas visitors.

When needing a bit more TLC, some men and occasionally women will head to hostess and host bars where – for a price – they can be sure of attractive, fawning company and having their fragile egos stroked. It has been said the hosts at such bars are no different from shrinks in other countries – professionals who are paid to listen to other people's problems.

Tokyoites drinking in a bar.

The ubiquitous pinball game of *pachinko*, another favourite pastime, can also be viewed as a psychological safety valve: the deliberately induced sensory overload in noisy, brightly lit *pachinko* halls is hypnotic and gridlocks players into a mindless world focused purely on gambling. Similarly, you'll often find Tokyoites young and old with heads buried in thick magazines of manga escaping into imaginary worlds.

Ironically, a fantasy made real is how visitors often feel about Tokyo's extraordinary environment. What keeps the city vibrant and alive is the way in which it so richly and confidently reinterprets its own age-old norms and practice as well as imported Western ones. Fads and fashions come and go, as do buildings, businesses and people. The city is a living organism, hungry for change and renewal, and eternally in a state of flux.

MEETING PEOPLE

Japanese people typically bow on meeting each other. It's polite to follow suit, but as a foreigner you are not expected to. Younger people are typically more comfortable with handshakes than their seniors – be gentle as the grip is seldom firm.

Exchanging business cards *(meishi)* is an essential ritual if you're at a business meeting. Since you are expected to give your card to everyone you are introduced to, be sure to bring a copious number with you. If you can, have your name printed in katakana script, so non-English speakers can pronounce it more easily. It is customary to place the cards you receive on the table in front of you, rather than stuffing them away in your pocket immediately. This will also help you remember people's names and positions. It is considered rude to jot notes or scribble on these cards.

Do not be surprised if you are asked many personal questions regarding age, education, family and work. Identity and 'proper' affiliation are very important in Japan. So is dressing appropriately – if you're at any kind of formal meeting wearing a suit and tie is important. The pecking order for seating matters, too. Wait for someone to indicate where your seat is before sitting down.

Manga and Anime

From *Hello Kitty* and the robots of *Neon Genesis Evangelion*, it's impossible to ignore the omnipresent images of *manga* and *anime* characters across Tokyo.

Manga refers to drawn cartoons, be they the kind of four-panel strips found in newspapers and magazines or the telephone directory-size weekly comic books and the spin-off collections of strips in book form (known as *tankobon*), which are the equivalent of graphic novels. *Anime* is any animation, Japanese or foreign, for the cinema or for TV; although to non-Japanese fans, who are legion, *anime* means only animation that's Japanese in style.

The city is the centre of a multi-billion yen industry derived from these hand- and computer-drawn ambassadors of Japanese cool, with areas associated with these creative arts – such as Akihabara (see page 197), Ikebukuro (see page 107) and Nakano (west of Shinjuku) – all attracting armies of Japanese and overseas fans.

The Japanese are brought up on steady diet of *manga* and *anime*. Practically every organisation, from the police down, sports a cuddly cartoon mascot, and it's common to see adults reading comic books on the subway and elsewhere. The top seller is *Weekly Shonen Jump*, a magazine aimed at young male readers, which sells around 2.83 million copies per edition.

Some of Japan's biggest grossing movies are those made by Studio Ghibli, the animation studio co-established by Hayao Miyazaki who won an Oscar for his film *Spirited Away*. Miyazaki was the driving force behind the creation of the **Ghibli Museum** in Mitaka (www.ghibli-museum.jp). This beautifully designed set of galleries and exhibitions on the art of animation, to which entry is limited to 2,400 people daily with advanced tickets only, is a must-visit attraction in Western Tokyo for all *anime* fans.

There are *manga* and *anime* aimed at all ages, and on all kinds of subjects. But both media have developed a reputation, not entirely justified, for focussing on sexually lurid and violent topics. The word *otaku* is mostly used in Japan as a derogatory term for people with pathologically obsessive interests in *anime* and *manga*. To some Japanese the term conjures up images of socially awkward losers whose *anime* and *manga* obsessions are so great that they take precedent over relationships and personal grooming and hygiene. However to overseas fans, *otaku* has been fondly adopted as a label to be worn proudly. *Many go to* events such as the **Tokyo International Anime Fair** (www.tokyoanime.jp) and **Comiket** (www.comiket.co.jp), the world's biggest *manga* convention dedicated to *dojinshi*, or self-published cartoon books.

A typical anime character.

Conscious of the economic benefits of *otaku* patronage, the Japanese government have also jumped on board. Characters such as the blue robot cat Doraemon and Astro Boy have been appointed international cultural ambassadors, and the cosplaying (see page 198) maids of scores of cafés in Akihabara are touted in tourism brochures like contemporary geisha.

DECISIVE DATES

Tokugawa with 16 samurai.

Pre-Edo Periods

AD 628
Senso-ji Temple is founded in the Asakusa district.

1180
First recorded use of the name Edo.

1457
Ota Dokan builds a fortified compound at Edo.

1590
Warlord Toyotomi Hideyoshi makes Edo his base.

1600
Tokugawa Ieyasu takes control after defeating rivals in Battle of Sekigahara.

Edo Period (1603–1868)

1603
Tokugawa makes Edo Japan's Capital.

1639
The system of national seclusion is introduced.

1657
The 'Furisode-no-kaji' (Long-Sleeves Fire) devastates Edo, lasting three days and killing a quarter of the city's population.

1688–1704
The cultural flowering of Edo under the influence of the Genroku era.

1703
The 47 ronin incident occurs.

1707
Mount Fuji erupts, covering Edo in a shroud of ash.

A painting of a Japanese tea garden.

Commodore Matthew Perry meeting the Imperial Commissioners in Yokohama.

1742
Floods kill about 4,000 people in Edo.

1780
Edo's population reaches 1.3 million; probably the largest city in world at the time.

1804–29
The Bunka-Bunsei period marks the zenith of Edo merchant culture.

1853
Commodore Perry arrives with US naval ships. Japan is forced to accept trade and diplomatic contact; the shogunate is weakened as a result.

1855
The Ansei Edo Earthquake kills over 7,000 in Edo. Floods and epidemics follow.

Meiji Period (1868–1912)

1868
Meiji Restoration returns emperor Mutsuhito to power. The last shogun Yoshinobu retires without resistance. The capital is renamed Tokyo.

1869
Yasukuni Shrine is established for Japan's war dead. Tokyo's first rickshaws appear on its streets.

Earthquake damage, 1923.

Emperor Meiji.

1872
Samurai class is abolished by imperial decree. The first train service runs from Shimbashi to Yokohama.

1874
Tokyo first adopts the use of gas lighting.

1882
Bank of Japan established in the Nihombashi district.

1883
The Rokumeikan, Tokyo's first Western-style building, is completed in Hibiya.

1889
The new constitution is promulgated.

1894
Marunouchi becomes the site of a European-style business quarter known as 'London Town'.

1895
Japan wins the First Sino-Japanese War.

1905
Japan wins the Russo-Japanese War.

1910
Japan annexes Korea.

Taisho Period (1912–26)

1912
Mutsuhito dies marking the end of the Meiji Period. He is succeeded by his mentally ill son Yoshihito.

1918
Japan is hit hard by economic chaos; rice riots occur.

1922
The Imperial Hotel, designed by Frank Lloyd Wright, opens in Hibiya.

1923
The Great Kanto Earthquake kills 140,000. Much of the city is destroyed.

1925
Completion of the Yamanote loop line.

Showa Period (1926–89)

1926
Taisho Emperor dies. Hirohito ascends the throne.

1927
Asia's first subway line opens in Tokyo, between Asakusa and Ueno.

1931
Japanese occupy Manchuria. Japan leaves League of Nations.

1936
Tokyo sees a bloody but unsuccessful military uprising, one of many in the 1930s.

1941
Japan attacks Pacific and Asian targets. Within a year, Japan occupies most of East Asia and the western Pacific.

1945
Tokyo is firebombed and atomic bombs are dropped on Hiroshima and Nagasaki. Japan

Atomic bombs devastated Hiroshima and Nagasaki.

surrenders. General MacArthur sets up HQ in Tokyo. Start of US Occupation.

1946
New constitution under Allied occupation forces.

1952
The San Francisco Peace Treaty settles all war-related issues; Japan is returned to sovereignty, except for some Pacific islands, including Okinawa. Japan regains its prewar industrial output.

1955
Socialist factions merge to form the Japan Socialist Party; Liberals and Democrats create the Liberal Democratic Party (LDP).

1958
The building of Tokyo Tower is completed.

1960
The first demonstrations against the renewal of the

Tokyo hosted the Summer Olympics in 1964.

US-Japan Security Treaty take place.

1964
The Summer Olympics are held in Tokyo and the bullet train begins service between Tokyo and Osaka.

1968–9
Tokyo becomes the focus of massive student unrest.

1980s
Japan's economy becomes the world's second most powerful. Banks extend loans to corporations and small companies based on over-inflated land values.

Heisei Period (1989–present)

1989
Hirohito dies; his son Akihito begins the Heisei Period.

1990
The 'economic bubble' starts to deflate, leading to Japan's worst post-war recession.

1991
Kenzo Tange-designed Tokyo Municipal Government Office (Tocho) opens.

1993
A series of bribery scandals sees the LDP lose election. The new coalition government lasts seven months. Another coalition takes over, led by socialists.

1995
The religious cult Aum Shinrikyo releases sarin nerve gas in the subway system, killing 12 people and sending Tokyo's citizens into a sheer panic.

1996
The LDP returns to power.

1999
Shintaro Ishihara, an outspoken nationalist, is elected as Tokyo Governor.

2001
Junichiro Koizumi, a self-proclaimed reformist, is elected as prime minister.

2002
The FIFA world cup final is played in Yokohama following Japan and South Korea's co-hosting of the soccer tournament.

2003
The opening of Roppongi Hills complex heralds the reinvention of the nightlife district into a chic shopping and arts hub.

2006
Shinzo Abe takes over as prime minister, and

Japanese fan at the 2002 FIFA World Cup.

almost immediately upsets Asian countries with revisionist comments about Japan's wartime activities.

2007
Shintaro Ishihara is re-elected as governor for a third consecutive term.

2008
The Fukutoshin line, the 13th on the city's metro, goes into operation.

2009
The LDP defeated in the general election and replaced by the Democratic Party of Japan (DPJ) with Yukio Hatoyama as prime minister.

2010
Naoto Kan of the DPJ becomes Japan's fifth prime minister in as many years.

2011
The Great East Japan earthquake and tsunami in March kills more than 15,000 people in northeast Japan and triggers the Fukushima nuclear disaster. Tokyo is rocked by aftershocks throughout the year. In September, after Kan resigns amid criticism of his handling of the disaster, Yoshihiko Noda of the DPJ becomes Japan's 62nd prime minister.

2012
Tokyo Skytree, the tallest structure in Japan at 643 metres (2,100ft), opens to the public.

2013
Shinzo Abe and the LDP are swept back into power in a landslide victory. Just like Abe's previous tenure as PM, he starts by upsetting Asian countries with revisionist comments about Japan's wartime activities.

Tokyo Skytree is Japan's tallest structure.

CREATING THE EASTERN CAPITAL

The rise of the great shogunates and their samurai warlords during the Edo Period has instilled in Japanese culture ways of thinking and behaviour that persist even in modern Tokyo.

Travelling across the marshy Musashino Plain, future location of Tokyo, Lady Sarashina apparently failed to notice both the imposing riverside temple and the squalid fishermen's huts and nets nearby. The year was 1020 and the 12-year-old girl, her nurse and entourage were on their way to Kyoto after four years in the eastern provinces where her father had served as assistant governor. The journey, however, was not an easy one. The noblewoman recorded in her now-famous diary that the reeds growing across the plain were so high that 'the tips of our horsemen's bows were invisible.'

Four centuries later, the Musashino Plain was still a wild and desolate place. It also held the largest expanse of arable land for the grazing and exercising of warrior steeds. These auspi-

Toyotomi Hideyoshi, the commoner who became general.

cious natural features were among the considerations that led a minor member of the Taira clan in the 12th century to build a house and fortified compound on the central of five ridges that descended to the bay. He then renamed his family Edo, which means 'Mouth of the River.' After his death, the lands were split up and divided among his sons.

> *People had lived on the Musashino Plain for over 2,000 years prior to the founding of what was to become Tokyo in 1457. From then on, while the emperor held court in Kyoto, Japan's true centre of power was based in Edo.*

Settlement of the plain

Little was heard of the area until Ota Dokan, a vassal of the Ashikaga shoguns, decided to build a castle above the Hibiya inlet in 1457. Dokan was taking advantage of a confused political climate in which two rival representatives of the shogun in Kyoto claimed dominion over the provinces. Dokan's creation of an efficient, well-drilled conscript army, his efforts to drain the marshes along the bay and create the area's first landfills, and his decision to charge levies on goods in transit at the mouth of the river aroused the suspicion and jealousy of his own lord, head of one of the branches of the Uesugi clan, who had his vassal murdered in 1486.

In the century that followed, the powerful Hojo family occupied the site, but they in turn lost control over it after trying to resist the overwhelming forces of the warlord and future shogun Toyotomi Hideyoshi and his powerful ally, Tokugawa Ieyasu. The latter was awarded the eight provinces of the east that included the strategic site of Edo. Despite the insalubrious marshlands that formed the coastal areas and a lack of natural spring water, Ieyasu grasped the potential of Edo. The area's position at the point where the Koshu Kaido (a road connecting Edo with the mountain province of Kai and the eastern route to Kyoto) promised a strategically positive placement.

The Shogun's fortress

Ieyasu made his formal entry into town as shogun in 1603 and wasted little time in constructing an impregnable castle on the site of Dokan's old fortifications and redesigning the city. To keep his lords militarily hobbled and in a constant shortage of funds, Ieyasu introduced the *sankin kotai* (alternate residence duty) system, whereby all lords – both Inner and Outer – were obliged to spend two years in Edo before returning to their provinces. Costly processions were also made compulsory for their exits and re-entrances. Financially bled, they were less likely to raise armies of resistance. The families of these lords were also expected to live permanently in Edo in a virtual state of hostage. The security-obsessed Ieyasu took the added precaution of setting up barriers along the trunk roads into Edo, where a strict 'no women out, no guns in' rule prevailed.

Although the castle was still unfinished, labourers, merchants and craftsmen trickled into the new settlement from the provinces,

> Englishman Richard Cocks, visiting Edo in 1616, was astonished by the scale of its fortress: 'We went rowndabout the Kyngs castell or fortress, which I do hould to be much more in compass than the city of Coventry.'

Statue of Tokugawa Ieyasu, founder of the shogun dynasty of the same name.

eventually forming the nucleus of Edo's townspeople. Conforming to the strictly enforced division of classes, the newcomers were accommodated on reclaimed land lying between the castle and the sea. The merchants clustered around the bridge named Nihombashi and the waterways flowing into the port, while the craftsmen inhabited Kanda and Kyobashi, areas to the north and south. The system required that each trade or craft should be identified with a specific quarter, plasterers in one area, dyers, smiths and carpenters in another. In practice, however, the system of strict zoning soon broke down as more people poured into the city.

The Long-Sleeves Fire

The final blow to the original plan for segregation came in 1657 with the 'Furisode-no-kaji' (Long-Sleeves Fire), a series of conflagrations that raged for three days. When the fires eventually abated, Edo's population of 400,000 inhabitants had been slashed by a quarter.

If the speed of destruction was astonishing, so too was the successive reconstruction.

Wood block print of fireworks on the Sumida River in the 18th century.

Firebreaks were created, and to relieve overcrowding, the city was enlarged and temples and shrines removed to less populous areas. More land was reclaimed from the sea, particularly in areas to the east of the Ginza, such as Fukagawa, Tsukiji and Honjo. A bridge, Ryogokubashi, was built to connect the new areas east of the Sumida River with the main city. Despite the improvements, fire – poetically called the 'Flowers of Edo' – remained a scourge. Between 1603 and 1868, no less than 97 major conflagrations broke out.

As the population grew, the good intentions of the town planners were soon disregarded. In the central districts of Kanda, Nihombashi and Kyobashi, open spaces disappeared as tenement

CREATING THE CITY

By the standards of the day, Edo Castle was massive, and when completed in 1636 it was the world's largest, with moats, a canal reaching into the salt flats along the bay and a conduit to transport potable water. Under Ieyasu's orders, earth was transported from the Kanda Hills to the north, and the Hibiya Inlet became the first of Edo's many landfills – a process of transformation that continues to this day.

Further landfills were made to the east, forming the *shitamachi*, or 'Low City', where the commoners, merchants, artisans, labourers, gardeners, and others who worked for the shogun and his entourage, lived. Ieyasu's trusted Dependent Lords – those who had supported him in his campaigns – were assigned villas between the outer and inner moats; the Outer Lords – those who had taken sides against Ieyasu at the decisive Battle of Sekigahara in 1600 – were consigned land beyond the outer moats in the vicinity of present-day Kasumigaseki and Hibiya. These estates were intended not only as living quarters but also as a first line of defence on the outer edge of the city.

The Sumida River formed Edo's eastern border and along it were sited the shogunate's official rice storage warehouses. At Edo's far northeast, beyond the city limits, lived the *eta* (outcasts), Edo's lowest caste of people who carried out unclean trades such as tanning and butchery.

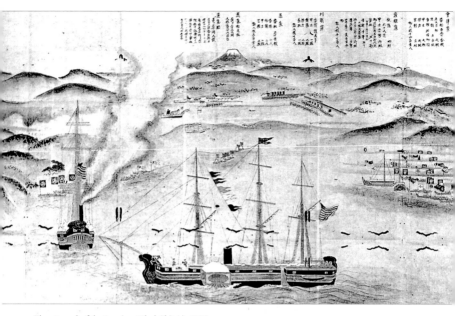

The approach of the American 'Black Ships' in 1853.

huts were set up. These dwellings, occupied by labourers, tinkers, litter-bearers, itinerant entertainers and clerks from the large dry-goods stores of Nihombashi, were one-storey back-street slums fronting onto alleys often less than a yard wide. Toilets and drinking water were communal.

Rise of the Edo-ko

While Edo continued its inexorable expansion, it was also beginning to create its own distinctive counterculture. A gritty, rambunctious affair, it was closer to entertainment and the life of the people than high art, although that would eventually follow.

Ryogoku Bridge was a good example of how ordinary people requisitioned space for their entertainment. Ryogoku Hirokoji, a broad fire-break leading to the bridge, was known for its outrageous concentration of freak shows, tricksters, erotic puppets, professional storytellers and models of Dutch galleons and giants, all packed into show tents or jammed behind tea stalls. This area was also the haunt of 'silver and golden cats', as the unlicensed prostitutes who staked out this area were known.

Adding to the visible pleasures of Edo were festivals; a love of potted plant fairs, cherry blossom viewing in the spring and great annual summer fireworks displays along the river. By the early 1720s, Edo had become the most populous city in the world. It had developed its

> The largest of Japan's three rice-growing plains, the Musashino Plain, site of present-day Tokyo, was blessed with an excellent river system and was the furthest removed from potential invasion from continental Asia.

own ethos and style, marked by a love of comic verse, ribald and satirical, of *haiku* (a Japanese verse form) and of the *kabuki* theatre. This increasingly mercantile society, fixated on the here and now, found in *ukiyo-e* – woodblock prints of the 'floating world'– the perfect art form to express the transience, the delectable beauty and sadness of existence.

Although the shogunate was generally hostile to Edo's cultural *laissez-faire*, and periodic crackdowns took place, the cultural life of the irrepressible Edo-ko (Edo residents) proved too resilient. When the flamboyant *kabuki* theatre was banished to Asakusa, a district already boasting the important Senso-ji (or Asakusa Kannon) Temple and the pleasure quarter of Yoshiwara a short distance away in the rice fields to the north, the area's position as the foremost pleasure district was assured.

The Black Ships

Powerful earthquakes in the Edo region in 1854 and 1855 killed thousands of people and were followed by torrential downpours that caused flooding to low-lying areas. There was also a cholera epidemic, famines and an unprecedented crime wave. These calamities were superstitiously blamed on the appearance of US Commodore Matthew Perry's so-called 'Black Ships.'

The coal-powered vessels *Mississippi*, *Plymouth*, *Saratoga* and *Susquehanna* had first dropped anchor in 1853 in Uraga harbour near Yokosuka at the southwestern end of Edo Bay. Perry

Ukiyo-e woodblock print.

demanded that Japan restore imperial rule and open its doors to international trade – for the previous 200 years only the Chinese and Dutch had been allowed to trade with the Japanese and then only under very strict conditions.

Six months later, Perry returned and the Kanagawa Treaty was signed, opening the ports of Shimoda and Hakodate to US trade and guaranteeing the safety of shipwrecked American sailors (previously such foreign sailors had either been imprisoned or killed). This, and another treaty in 1858 granting the US more trade concessions, effectively ended Japan's self-imposed isolation from the world.

The Meiji Restoration

The shogunate's inability to defend the country from the 'Southern Barbarians' shattered its credibility and accelerated its demise. In 1859, the first US consul, Townsend Harris, arrived and set up a mission at the temple of Zenpuku-ji in Azabu. The following year Ii Naosuke, the shogun's senior councillor and the man who had signed the treaties with the Americans, was assassinated outside Edo Castle by 17 young samurai loyal to the Emperor in Kyoto.

The shogun and his military government were so shocked by Ii's murder that they didn't formally announce his death until several months later. But it was too late for the shogun to restore his power. The feudal lords abandoned their residences in Edo and Japan moved towards civil war. The deaths of both shogun Iemochi and Emperor Komei in 1866 spurred on events and by 1868 a coalition of powerful families from the western and

WEALTHY MERCHANTS

Many merchants amassed great wealth during the Edo Period and built large, impressive homes made of thick, fire-resistant mud walls covered in tiles, then stucco finished in shiny black paint. At the same time, impoverished samurai were growing more and more dependent on the merchant class to provide them with loans.

Attempting to contain the merchants, the government introduced prohibitions that were cleverly evaded. Forbidden to wear quality fabrics, the merchants lined the inner sections of rough garments in the finest silk; prevented from building homes with more than two stories, they added extra interior levels to the existing structures.

The first American Legation at Zenpukuji, 1859.

southern provinces of Japan had seized control of the capital in the name of the 15-year-old Emperor Meiji.

The last Tokugawa shogun Yoshinobu had resigned the year earlier (he lived until 1913). At the end of 1868 a formal procession led the young Emperor into Edo from Kyoto, and the Meiji Restoration thus began. The city was renamed Tokyo, or the 'Eastern Capital', and the Meiji Period, which was to last till 1912, saw Japan rapidly industrialise and prosper.

Westernisation of Tokyo

In the flurry of excitement and activity at the creation of a new capital and the abolition of the old class system, many of the physical and mental trappings of the old feudal city were swept away. Among the curious foreigners who arrived to see what it was all about was Isabella Bird. The intrepid Victorian travel writer, observed that 'it would seem an incongruity to travel to Yedo [Edo] by railway, but quite proper when the destination is Tokiyo.'

The eastern bank of the Sumida River, the home of the poorer townspeople and impoverished samurai, was the first area of the city where factories and yards were built. Housing conditions along the river and further east were deplorable and exacerbated by flooding. The river could be expected to flood on average once every three years.

A faddish interest in everything Western, from food, clothing and hairstyles, to the new European-style brick buildings that were springing up, was accompanied by the introduction of telephones, beer halls, department stores and gas lighting. New roads were constructed, and tens of thousands of rickshaws, horse-drawn buses and bicycles crowded the streets. Many working people adopted Western clothing – a welcome convenience for the office, shop and factory workers. Men abandoned their top-knots, and women, in imitation of the newly enlightened empress, stopped the traditional blackening of their teeth.

Taisho Democracy

Japan's extraordinary Meiji era came to an end in 1912, with the death of the Meiji Emperor. In accordance with a tradition that stretched back

Emperor Meiji presides over the first meeting of Parliament, 1890.

over a millennium, the funeral was a Shinto rite. The hearse that passed through the hushed streets of Tokyo was drawn by five white oxen and escorted by an entourage of bowmen and banner-bearers. Sand was laid over the streets to muffle the sound of the wheels.

During the succeeding Taisho era (1912–1926), the authorities temporarily relaxed their hold on civil conduct, a reaction perhaps to the physically and morally corrupted state of its central symbol, the Emperor Yoshihito. Portrayed as a syphilitic lunatic, partial to bouts of drinking, womanising and eccentric behaviour; the new emperor was a poor successor to his father. The brief flowering of the so-called 'Taisho Democracy' saw innovation in

TODAI: A LIFELONG TROPHY

Britain has Oxford and Cambridge – the US Harvard and Yale. But none comes close to the near-divine status given by Japanese to the University of Tokyo, or Todai. Its graduates are virtually guaranteed excellent career opportunities in the civil service and in top Japanese corporations.

Because of the university's hallowed status – it dates back to 1877 – competition for entry to Todai and other top universities is very stiff; parents place relentless pressure on their children to study very early in life. The proliferation of *juku* (cram schools), which prepare students for compulsory school advancement tests, is testament to the extraordinary emphasis the nation places on education.

In 1992, then-prime minister Kiichi Miyazawa introduced measures to reduce Todai's over-representation in the civil service to less than half of all employees hired by government agencies. One of these measures prohibited graduates attending interviews from revealing their alma mater. Miyazawa's target was achieved in most ministries by 1996, and his efforts also resulted in a decision by several major companies not to consider the university background in hiring new graduates.

However, prejudices die hard, and today, students from the University of Tokyo, despite a reputation in some circles for having had any inventiveness and creativity drilled out of them, are still popularly portrayed as the brains behind the nation.

Ruins left by the Kanto Earthquake.

the arts, political dissidence and the advance of the women's movement, as well as the growth of unions.

The Great Kanto Earthquake

At precisely one minute before noon on 1 September 1923, as charcoal and wood fires and stoves were being lit for lunch, the Great Kanto Earthquake struck. The firestorm that engulfed and destroyed three-quarters of the city and the adjacent area of Yokohama claimed 140,000 lives out of a population of over two million. Aftershocks rocked the city for days and the fires raged on, creating a hellish, charred landscape. The Sumida River was dense with the corpses of victims who had tried to escape the flames by jumping into the river, only to find its waters boiling.

Once again, Tokyo began to reconstruct itself; parks and reinforced-concrete apartments were the most visible responses to the disaster. More people moved into the city, however, swelling its population and putting new demands on its transportation system. Buses and taxis began to appear, and in 1925,

After the Great East Japan Earthquake of March 2011, officials estimated that a 7.3-magnitude earthquake in Tokyo Bay, registering a maximum level 7 on the Japanese intensity scale, could destroy 390,000 buildings and claim 10,000 lives.

the Yamanote railway loop line was completed, enlarging the commuter belt and spurring the expansion of new urban subcentres like Shibuya and Shinjuku.

In the following year, the ailing Taisho Emperor passed away. With the military back at the helm and a highly acquiescent new emperor, Hirohito, generals and officers were the new arbiters of taste.

World War II

Japan's entry into the war made Tokyo the target of air raids whose intensity few could have imagined at the time. The sense of impending doom that hung over the city during the

Emperor Hirohito as a child.

closing days and months of World War II was captured by Robert Guillain, a correspondent for *Le Monde*. Sensing the atmosphere of despair and doom in the city at the time, Guillain wrote, 'The raids had still to begin, and yet, night after night, an obsession gripped the city plunged into darkness by the blackout, an obsession that debilitated and corroded it more than even the appearance overhead of the first enemy squadrons was able to do. Tokyo was a giant village of wooden boards, and it knew it.'

Many of the firebombs fell on the civilian populations of Sumida-ku and other wards to the east, during the 102 raids that were launched between January 1945 and Japan's surrender in August. Robert McNamara, then captain in the US Army Air Force – whose name would later be forever linked with the Vietnam War – took part in the planning of the raids, and he recalled later that 'in a single night we burnt to death 100,000 civilians … men, women, and children.' Tens of thousands of residents of Fukagawa also perished that night beneath the fuselages of over 300 B-29s, which dropped lethal incendiary cylinders that the locals nicknamed 'Molotov flower baskets.'

Economic recovery

Reconstruction and economic growth took centre stage in the post-war years, with the US military presence continuing until 1952. By the late 1950s the city was firmly back on its feet, thriving under stable political conditions and a booming economy. The great strides forward were made evident to the world during Tokyo's successful hosting of the Olympics in 1964. However, despite Japan's phenomenal economic progress since the war, there were growing undercurrents of social unrest that had first come to a head four years before the Olympics when hundreds of thousands of people took to the streets of Tokyo to protest the renewal of the Japan-US security treaty. Later that decade, in 1968 and 69, the city would see more unrest with waves of student protests.

The economy, however, remained the main focus. Fixed exchange rates were dropped in 1971 and, after the Plaza Agreement in 1985, which saw the creation of the Group of Five (G5)

Rooftop defenders in Tokyo.

Mount Fuji can be seen behind Tokyo's impressive skyline.

popular culture, and under three terms of governorship by the right-wing, yet popular Shintaro Ishihara, set about – yet again – reinventing its landscape.

The ever-present threat of earthquakes had long dissuaded Tokyo from creating Manhattan-like districts but improved technological know-how now saw developers keener to reach for the skies. The results, from the towers of Roppongi Hills and Tokyo Midtown to those of Shiodome and the refurbished Marunouchi and Ginza districts, stand out in what remains, beyond its very centre, a predominantly flat city.

In 2012 these were all trumped by the Tokyo Skytree, a new communications tower and associated complex rising on the hitherto neglected east bank of the Sumida River – at 643 metres (2,100ft) it is not only the tallest structure in Japan but one of the highest in the world. If the restless remodelling of the city seems to hint at a weak preservation ethic, one must remember that change itself *is* a tradition in Japan. And that renewal is second nature for Tokyo, where almost anything seems possible.

Tokyo's public transport system heaves under throngs of commuters.

countries (US, Japan, West Germany, UK and France) – a coordinated effort to make the US dollar fall in value – the rise of the yen seemed unstoppable. This led to artificially inflated asset values, speculation fuelling the so-called 'bubble economy', and a construction frenzy the likes of which the city had never seen. The inevitable collapse in land and stock values came in 1990, leaving Japanese banks with mountains of bad debts. The 1995 sarin gas attack on the Tokyo subway by members of the doomsday cult Aum Shinrikyo added to the sense of unease that characterised Japan's 'lost decade'.

Tokyo rising

The pendulum of fortune began an upwards trajectory for Tokyo in the new millennium as the economy again picked up and a reform-minded Prime Minister Junichiro Koizumi came to power. The city successfully co-hosted the FIFA World Cup in 2002, became the focus of global interest in the 'soft power' of Japanese

Today's Royal Family

The Japanese monarchy is the oldest existing continuous hereditary monarchy in the world, and its head, the emperor, is the symbol of the state.

Royal mania hit a high on 9 June 1993, when tens of thousands of well-wishers turned out for a glimpse of the royal couple, Princess Masako and the heir to Japan's 2,600-year-old Chrysanthemum Throne Crown Prince Naruhito. The bubbly princess had given up a promising diplomatic career to marry Crown Prince Naruhito. Hopes, however, that she would become a 'royal diplomat' who would give a human face in the manner of European princesses to the protocol-ridden Imperial Court were quickly dashed. The initial spontaneity was smartly squashed by the notoriously protocol-ridden Imperial Household Agency, and the princess was soon seen behaving in the self-effacing tradition of female royals.

In December 2001 Masako gave birth to a girl, Princess Aiko. As the practice of crowning a female as Empress was terminated under the 1889 Meiji Constitution, which now limited the throne to male descendants, the pressure on a woman now in her forties to produce a future Emperor has been intense. Although the Agency preferred to keep imperial family problems under wraps, it had not been able to muzzle the reasons for Masako's long absence from public view. Hospitalised first in December 2003 with shingles, a stress-induced viral infection, she was also said to have suffered from a stress-induced adjustment disorder.

Masako's problems were not the first of its kind in the modern history of the court. In 1963, after a miscarriage, Empress Michiko, then Crown Princess, went into a three-month-long retreat at the Imperial villa. The first commoner to marry into the monarchy, she had to deal with hostility for the miscarriage from both the Agency and other royals. In a series of nervous disorders characteristic of royal females, the Empress lost her voice for several months in 1993 due to 'strong feelings of distress'.

The discontent built up inside the Crown Prince Naruhito over the years finally exploded at a press conference on 10 May 2004 during which he made surprisingly blunt comments in defence of his wife and hinted that members of the Imperial Household Agency were involved in repressing his wife's personality and denying her talents.

In 2006 the succession crisis was resolved after Princess Kiko, the wife of the Crown Prince's younger brother Akishino,

Crown Prince Naruhito, Princess Aiko and Crown Princess Masako.

gave birth to a male heir, Prince Hisahito; he is third in line to the throne after his uncle and father. However, the pressure on the Crown Prince's family continues. Princess Masako remains a sickly, sad figure rarely seen in public, and in 2010 came reports that her daughter had suffered bullying at her elite elementary school.

Sake barrels at Meiji-jingu.

FESTIVALS

The Japanese sensitivity to the character and changes of the seasons is reflected in their festivals. Exuberant *mikoshi* (portable shrine) fights also indicate a willingness to embrace frivolity within the solemn.

Shinto priests at a ceremony at Meiji-jingu.

One of the great thrills of travelling in Japan – for first-time visitors, foreign residents and Japanese alike – is running across a local festival (*matsuri*). Almost every day of the year a festival or other celebration takes place in Japan. Seasonal differences are the basis for almost the whole system of festivals; exceptions are observances of historic events, foundings, birthdays and the like.

Yet even the way in which events are feted may take the nature of a seasonal observance, especially if the festival is an old one.

Portable shrines

One basic element in a typical Japanese religious festival is the *mikoshi*, or portable shrine. The god-presence embodied in the *mikoshi* is carried about the village or urban neighbourhood on the shoulders of the young men of the community, although women are increasingly permitted to join, with ritual purification beforehand and much drinking of *sake* – or whatever other alcohol might be on hand.

A common practice is to jounce the *mikoshi* to express the exuberance of the god. In communities where nearby shrines have festivals on the same day, *mikoshi* fights are a custom. Those carrying one *mikoshi* may try to jostle their way through and 'win' over other *mikoshi* on the same road.

Japanese festivals often bear strong sexual symbolism, whether implicit or explicit. The god of a number of shrines scattered about

SHINTO IN DAILY LIFE

Shinto, the indigenous anamist religion that forms the basis of many of Japan's festivals, also plays a role in the professional and daily lives of Tokyoites.

One of the most common rites is *oharai*, at which the priest waves a wand with strips of paper attached. With this a new car is blessed for accident-free driving and purification rites are held at a construction site or at the completed building. Amulets are popular purchases at shrines. *Omamori*, special talismans, are purchased to ensure good luck, or to ward off evil. Taxi drivers often have a 'traffic safety' talisman dangling from the rearview mirror of their vehicle.

Miniature lanterns on sale, Naka-mise.

the country is manifested as a huge phallus, which is carried about the streets at festival time – the most famous of these near Tokyo is Jibeta Matsuri held around Kanamara-jinja in Kawasaki, in April.

Oshogatsu and Obon

The two major observances of the year are Oshogatsu (New Year) and Obon, which is similar to 'All Souls' Day'. Occurring in mid-winter and mid-summer, respectively, both are celebratory occasions that bring the extended family together. Oshogatsu is a series of rituals and observances that lasts many days.

The ending of one year and the beginning of the next is a time of purification and an occasion to start afresh. Although a religious festival, the event is centred on the individual and the family, not the temple or shrine. The mood is calm, optimistic and joyful. It's a time when people catch up with friends and family, most obviously by sending out *nengajo* (New Year postcards) that always seem to be designed on Chinese zodiac motifs and on which people often print a family photo or montage of photos from the past year.

The New Year traditionally starts with a thorough cleaning of the house at the end of December – *shoji* screens are repapered and worn things replaced – and ends around 5 January. There are different things to do at set times during the festival – special decorations to put up and special food to prepare. The symbolism behind them hinges on the values of longevity, happiness and prosperity. As part of the latter, children receive *otoshidama* –small sums of money (usually not more than ¥5,000) given in decorated envelopes called *otoshidama-bukuro*.

January, February

New Year's Day: *Shogatsu* is a national holiday. People visit Buddhist temples and Shinto shrines to make wishes for the new year. *Osechi-ryori* is eaten during the first few days of the year.
Water Purification Rites: 10 to 12 January at the Kanda Shrine. Young people coming of age during the year use buckets to pour freezing water over themselves and undergo other cleansing rituals.
Coming-of-Age Day: Second Monday of January is Seijin-no-Hi. Women and men aged 20 put on their best kimono and suits for an 'adulthood' ceremony at a shrine, very often followed by a night of drinking.
Hatsubasho: the first sumo tournament of the year goes on for two weeks in January.
Setsubun: On 3 February, this bean-throwing ceremony is held to purify the home. Beans are thrown out the windows and doors to shouts of '*Oni wa soto*' (Devils, go out), followed by, '*Fuku wa uchi*' (Good luck, come in). Ceremonies are held at various temples and shrines.
Plum Viewing: The most famous spot for this mid-February event is the Yushima Tenjin shrine, with its floral displays and tea ceremonies.

March, April

Girls' Day: On 3 March is Hina Matsuri, when *hina* dolls representing imperial court figures are displayed at home and elsewhere.

Votive offerings.

Celebrating the arrival of cherry blossom.

Golden Dragon Dance: 18 March in the precincts of Asakusa's Senso-ji (or Asakusa Kannon). A lively event that is repeated at 11am, 2pm and 3pm.

Cherry Blossom Viewing: From early to mid-April is Ohanami, an important spring rite. Japanese picnic, drink and sing under the pink cherry blossoms. Some famous spots are Aoyama cemetery, Chidorigafuchi Park, Sumida Park, Ueno Park and Yasukuni-jinja.

Birthday of Buddha: On 8 April is Hana Matsuri with commemorative services at temples such as Senso-ji, Zojo-ji and Hommon-ji.

Azalea Festival: 10 April to 5 May at Nezu-jinja. Hundreds of the colourful bushes planted here are in dazzling bloom.

Horseback Archery Event: early-mid April is

Japanese carp banners.

when *yabusame*, mounted archers in samurai costumes, storm through Sumida Park.

Golden Week: 29 April marks the first day of the Golden Week holiday period.

Meiji Shrine Spring Festival: From 29 April to 3 May (main rituals 2 to 3 May), this colourful celebration features *yabusame* (horseback archery) and other traditional displays.

May

Children's Day: On 5 May is Kodomo-no-Hi. Though supposedly for all children, its focus is on little boys. Carp banners are flown from homes where boys reside and it is hoped they will grow up big and strong like the carp – a symbol of strength and manhood in Japan.

Summer sumo tournament: In mid-May, not summer despite the name, catch the 15-day Natsubasho at the Kokugikan in Ryogoku.

Sanja Matsuri: This important festival is one of Tokyo's 'Big Three' traditional events. On the third Saturday and Sunday, Tokyo honours the two brothers who found the image of the bodhisattva (enlightened being) Kannon in the Sumida River and were inspired to found Senso-ji. There are shrine processions, traditional dancing and music at Senso-ji Temple in Asakusa.

Kanda Matsuri: The second of Tokyo's 'Big Three' traditional *matsuri*. It takes place in mid-May, but only during odd-numbered years. Parades involving around 200 *mikoshi* alongside other floats and people in traditional garb start from the Kanda Myojin.

A local deity is paraded around a Tokyo temple.

June, July

Torigoe-jinja Taisai: This night-time festival based at Torigoe-jinja falls on the second Sunday in June, is when the biggest *mikoshi* is carried through the streets of Tokyo.

Tsukiji Shishi Festival: Held in the precincts of the fish market and the neighbouring Namiyoke Inari Shrine, this several-day event is wonderfully boisterous when it culminates on 10 June. Drum performances, portable shrines, sushi-cutting displays and more.

> On Valentine's Day (14 February), it is the custom for women to give men gifts of chocolate. The men get a chance to return the favour on White Day (14 March).

Sanno Matsuri: Held in even-numbered years in mid-June, the third of Tokyo's big festivals culminates after a week of smaller events with a day-long parade that starts at the Hie-jinja in Akasaka.

Iris Viewing: See the irises on the grounds of Meiji-jingu Shrine or at Kiyosumi Teien in full bloom during June.

Morning Glory Fair: 6 to 8 July is Asagao Ichi, when over 100 merchants set up stalls selling flowers at Iriya Kishimojin.

Tanabata Matsuri: 7 July is the only day in the year when two legendary lovers are able to cross the Milky Way to meet. People write wishes on coloured paper and hang them on bamboo branches before floating them down a river the next day.

Ground Cherry Fair: From 9 to 10 July, Hozuki Ichi takes place at Senso-ji from early morning to midnight.

Sumida River Fireworks: On the last Saturday in July is Sumidagawa Hanabi Taikai – the biggest fireworks display in Tokyo. The best spots are the Komagata Bridge and between the Kototoi and Shirahige bridges.

August, September

Obon: Mid-August is a time when people return to their hometowns to clean up ancestral graves and offer prayers to departed ancestors.

Koenji Awa-Odori: In this spin-off from the centuries-old Awa-Odori festival in Tokushima, 12,000 dancers take to the streets of Koenji in Tokyo over a weekend in late August for manic dancing that goes on well into the night.

Asakusa Samba Carnival: On the last Saturday in August teams of scantily costumed samba dancers parade through the streets of Asakusa.

Autumnal Equinox Day: Shubun-no-Hi is on 23 September, a national holiday.

October, November

Chrysanthemum Viewing: Mid-October to mid-November is the time to head for Shinjuku Imperial Garden, Meiji-jingu and Asakusa-jinja shrines and Yushima Tenjin and Daien-ji temples, which are some of the best viewing places.

Shichi-Go-San: On 15 November, this ceremony (literally, 'Seven-Five-Three') has five-year-old boys and three- and seven-year-old girls taken round to visit local shrines, commonly dressed in traditional attire.

December

Gishi Sai: On 14 Dec, a service at Sengaku-ji recalls the famous 47 *ronin* (masterless *samurai*) who, on this day in 1703, avenged the death of their master and later committed suicide. They are buried at Sengaku-ji.

Hagoita Ichi: A 'battledore' fair is held at Senso-ji 17 to 19 Dec.

Joya-no-Kane: At midnight on 31 December, every temple bell throughout the country begins to toll. The bells toll 108 times to represent the 108 evil human passions. The public is allowed to join in and strike the bells at two places in Tokyo: Zojo-ji in Shiba Park and Kan'ei-ji in Ueno.

FESTIVALS AND STREET PERFORMANCES

There is always something interesting to see on Tokyo's streets, be it an elaborate religious procession or an impromptu music performance.

Something extraordinary happens to the usually decorous Japanese when they attend festivals, as the customary *pro forma* manners and inhibitions vanish. *Matsuri* (festivals) have always been integral to the life of Tokyo, and hardly a week goes by without one. More often than not linked to Shinto religious beliefs and to the honouring of local gods, they can seem more like community street parties, with plenty of food and drink to confirm the impression. If their function is to give thanks, petition the gods for favours and protection, and promote the solidarity of the community, they are also about celebrating the sheer joy of life.

The range of festivals is staggering, from the tolling of bells (108 times as the New Year arrives to atone for the old year's sins) to a more earthy event celebrating how, with the intercession of an iron phallus, a young maiden was saved from the attentions of a razor-toothed demon. The synergetic Japanese have even made Christmas, stripped of any religious meaning, their own. No sooner than the autumn leaves have begun to fall, watch out for Santas in shop windows, fairy lights strung along main streets, and Muzak arrangements of *White Christmas* belting out from cafés. For details of festivals see page 44.

A girl in a 'cosplay' outfit in the Harajuku area.

Performer wearing the traditional mask of a fool performs an intentionally funny dance.

Medaman-medaman street performers eyeball the crowds during a performing arts festival in Yokohama, near Tokyo.

Attendants push a float during the Tokyo Jidai Matsuri, a festival held at Senso-ji Temple in Asakusa.

Geisha making a rare public appearance in a temple procession; they are known for their social skills and are adept at singing, dancing and playing music. In fact, the word 'geisha', means 'art person'.

LIFE ON THE STREETS

A performance of butoh in Yoyogi Park.

If a healthy street life means a healthy city, then Tokyo is brimming with vitality. The Japanese may not be exhibitionists, but they can be just as expressive as anyone else. Tokyo street life is a lively spectacle, with a varied repertoire of acrobats, magicians, parading brass bands, even fire-eaters. On weekends, Yoyogi Park (see page 140) hosts rock bands, stand-up comics and buskers singing their hearts out on everything from Elvis to J-Pop. You might even come across a performance of *butoh* (see photo above), a modern dance form that, depending on your point of view, is either art, or life reduced to tortured gestures and grimaces.

A major secular addition to the city's packed schedule of annual religious street celebrations is Roppongi Art Night (www.roppongiartnight.com). From dusk to dawn in late March the infamous nightlife district becomes the stage on which a spectacular series of street performances and public art exhibitions are held. The area's major galleries also stay open through the night.

Saxophonist at a Shibuya street corner.

CUISINE

Japanese cuisine is as much a sensation for the eyes as for the taste buds. Seasoning is minimal and chefs worship at the altar of freshness. The most sophisticated of meals are easy to handle as food is served in delicate portions.

Many Japanese dishes are fish based.

MEAL ETIQUETTE

Good table manners – Japanese-style – go a long way. It is bad manners to wave your chopsticks around, use them to point at someone, to spear food or to pull dishes forward. Do not pass food from your chopsticks to someone else's, let alone into their mouths.

Japanese soups and noodles in broth are sipped straight from the bowl. Vigorous slurping is acceptable when eating noodles. Pour soy sauce into the dipping saucer provided, not onto your food (especially rice). It is polite to say *'itadakimasu'* (lit. 'I accept') before starting to eat and *'gochisosama deshita'* (lit. 'it was a banquet') after every meal.

When it comes to number and variety of restaurants, Tokyo has no rival anywhere else on the planet – not even Paris, which, according to the hallowed Michelin Guide, it comfortably trumps in terms of outstanding places to eat. Even in simple eateries, the quality is remarkable; in the best places, it is exceptional. The degree of specialisation is impressive. A sushi shop serves only that. If you want *tempura*, go to a *tempura* restaurant. A place serving only *shabu-shabu* may sit next door to another devoted to grilled eel.

Tokyo claims many dishes as its own, from Edomae sushi to the clam-based pilaf known as Fukagawa *meshi*, but it is also a microcosm of the entire country. It is possible to sample the local specialities of any region of Japan, from Hokkaido to Okinawa, without straying past the confines of the Yamanote loop line.

Creative, cosmopolitan tastes

At the same time, Tokyo's sophisticated and cosmopolitan tastes encompass not only other Asian cuisines but also those of Europe, Africa and the Americas. Explore the traditional by all means, but sample the contemporary as well when you eat your way around Tokyo.

Eating out is not as expensive as one would expect it to be, especially with budget-priced lunch sets as low as ¥500 in places. Dinner is more expensive; budget at least ¥2,000 per head if you opt for something more than a simple *teishoku* restaurant or one dish meal. The top places are pricier and can easily go up to ¥10,000 per person or more depending on the

Seaweed is used extensively in Japanese cooking.

type of food and drink ordered; if there is no menu posted at the entrance, look elsewhere.

It is quite possible to eat well in Tokyo without resorting to the ubiquitous fast-food chains. Neighbourhood Japanese diners may have little ambience but prices are low. Noodle shops are found everywhere. Conveyor-belt sushi shops (*kaitenzushi*) are good value and *okonomiyaki* pancakes are fun dining. If all else fails, follow the example of local students and head for convenience stores. They offer good, ready-to-eat snacks and light meals, such as *bento* (lunch boxes) and instant noodles.

If Tokyo lacks anything, it is in choices for vegetarians. A small but increasing number of restaurants, however, are catering to those who cannot afford the vegetarian delights of *shojin ryori* (traditional but expensive temple cuisine). Beyond restaurants that are exclusively vegetarian, however, menus may not always match expectations. A 'vegetarian salad' may be green, but topped with diced ham. Essentially, there are no food taboos in Japan, only preferences. People with diet restrictions may have some difficulty. Tofu and bean dishes are usually a safe bet. Check the plastic samples in restaurant windows as they are generally accurate indicators of what you will be served.

Fresh, naked flavours

The foundations of a typical Japanese meal are rice, a bowl of savoury *miso* soup, a small plate of *tsukemono* (pickles) and a cup of green tea. The pickles add nutrition and texture, cleanse the palate and assist the digestive process. They can be made from a wide variety of produce including cucumber, turnip, cabbage, eggplant, burdock, lotus root and ginger. Even on their own, these basic elements are enough for a square meal. Usually, however, the staple grain is accompanied or preceded by side dishes.

Unlike Western cuisines, Japanese cooking tends to focus on accentuating the inherent flavours rather than enhancing them with sauces or seasonings. Meals are most commonly based on fish, vegetables, seaweed and tofu. Eggs, meat and fowl are used in lesser quantities, while dairy foods play no part in the traditional diet.

Ingredients traditionally reflect the seasons. Every self-respecting chef tailors his menu to what is at its peak of freshness. Seafood and produce are generally at their best in spring and autumn, while local gourmets look forward to hearty hotpots in winter and the aroma of broiled eel in midsummer.

Presentation is equally important. Plates, bowls and utensils are made of ceramic, glass, stone, wood or lacquer and are often beautifully

Seafood in Japanese cooking is fresh and not disguised by rich sauces.

Be experimental with Japanese food and you'll be rewarded.

decorated and designed. Like the ingredients, they are changed to fit the season for maximum rapport with the food.

The pleasures of *kaiseki*

This celebration of the seasons finds its ultimate expression in the formal cuisine known as *kaiseki ryori*. If time and budget permit, do not pass up an opportunity to sample the exquisite and refined pleasures of such a traditional multi-course banquet. The taste and visual appeal of the dishes are heightened in a setting created to ensure perfect harmony. At the most exclusive restaurants, the dining room is decorated with calligraphy, a seasonal flower arrangement and perhaps a view of a Zen garden with ancient rocks or a pool.

Kaiseki ryori is composed of numerous small courses, some little larger than a mouthful, and each prepared using a different cooking style. They follow a prescribed order. First, a selection of appetisers (*zensai*); next, some sashimi (*nama mono*) and a clear soup (*suimono*). Then follows dishes that have been grilled (*yakimono*); seasoned with a thick dressing (*aemono*); simmered (*nimono*); steamed (*mushimono*); deep-fried (*agemono*); and dressed with vinegar (*su-no-mono*).

Sake – a wine like drink made from fermented rice – is served alongside the dishes but never with the final course, which consists of rice, a bowl of *miso* soup and a few pickles. Hot green tea is served alongside, and dessert is usually a small portion of fresh fruit.

Sushi and sashimi

The Japanese love seafood and are enthusiastic about eating it as close as possible to its natural state – either as *sashimi*, served as raw slices with a dip of soy sauce, usually seasoned *wasabi* (Japanese horseradish) or on vinegared rice, as sushi.

There are various kinds of sushi, but the best known both in Japan and abroad is the Tokyo style, known as *nigiri-sushi*. The concept of eating small patties of rice topped with cuts of raw seafood originated in the days of Edo. This variety is still also called *Edomae sushi*, because the seafood was all caught in the waters of the bay right in front of the city. Some of the best *sushiya* (sushi shops) are found near the central fish market in Tsukiji.

There are two approaches at a *sushiya*: either sit at the counter and choose each serving from the seafood arrayed in front of you, or sit at a table and order a mixed selection of sushi (most places offer a variety of set courses).

> *Kaiseki ryori is derived from the formal banquets served as part of the tea ceremony. More than just pleasing the taste buds and filling the stomach, it is a total aesthetic experience.*

Whichever style you try, the sushi is best washed down with *sake* – be that chilled in summer or heated in winter.

Good sushi demands that ingredients are of good quality and absolutely fresh. That may mean a dauntingly expensive experience. The alternative is a *kaiten-sushi* shop, where small dishes of sushi pass by on a conveyor belt along the counter, often for as little as ¥100 per plate. These are easy to find all over Tokyo. The atmosphere may lack sophistication and the fish is not from a premium cut, but the outlay will not be excessive and the quality is still good.

Bottles of sake for sale.

Making noodles.

Warming winter dishes

One of the pleasures of visiting Japan in the cold season is the variety of hearty stews or hot-pots served throughout the winter. Known as *nabe-ryori* (casserole cuisine), every area has its own distinctive variations, many of which can be found in Tokyo's speciality restaurants.

Originating from Japan's northern island of Hokkaido is *ishikari-nabe*, based on salmon and vegetables. *Hootoo*, from Yamanashi Prefecture, includes handmade noodles very similar to *udon*. In Ibaraki Prefecture, the specialty is *anko-nabe*, made with angler fish. *Fugu chiri*, from Yamaguchi, in western Japan, features the white meat of the puffer fish. Tokyo's best-known home-grown *nabe* is *Yanagawa-nabe*, made with *dojo* (an eel-like loach) cooked in a savoury omelette.

A favourite among locals – and an acquired taste for visitors – is *oden*. Made with *daikon*, (a radish-like vegetable), potatoes, whole hard-boiled eggs, tofu and other ingredients, this hot-pot is one of the standard dishes served at *yatai* street stalls and is even available at convenience stores in the winter months.

Eel, chicken and *fugu*

The classic dish of summer is *unagi*, broiled eel served on a bed of rice. Since Edo times, this has enjoyed a reputation for imparting energy during the hot and humid days of summer. This belief has some nutritional basis since *unagi* contains more protein than beef.

Popular year round is *yakitori*, skewers of chicken, often grilled over charcoal, much like the *satay* of Thailand and Indonesia. Almost every part of the bird is eaten, from the breast to the gizzard and heart. Gourmet versions can be had in upscale restaurants but most people prefer the ambience of the smoky street stalls (check out those under the railway tracks near Yurakucho Station or at the eating and drinking alley Omoide Yokocho in Shinjuku).

If you like a frisson of fear with your food, you will enjoy the dangerous delicacy known as *fugu* (puffer fish). The flesh of the fish is safe for eating, but its internal organs are so poisonous that it can only be prepared by licensed fishmongers or skilled chefs at licensed restaurants. If ingested, the

The Japanese take pride in the presentation of dishes.

toxin paralyses the nervous system, eventually leading to heart failure. Once the chef has removed all the dangerous parts, along with the spiny skin, *fugu* is served as *sashimi*, sliced so thinly the pattern of the plate shows through the translucent slices. *Fugu-sashimi* is a great delicacy with a subtle flavour. The rest of the fish goes into a casserole that is served with a spicy dip.

Oodles of noodles

Noodles are the original Japanese fast food. Wholesome, filling, quick to prepare and even quicker to eat, they make a good light lunch or dinner. Just as often, they are eaten as a simple snack to keep energy levels up.

There are three main types: thin, greyish-brown *soba* noodles made with buckwheat flour; chunky *udon*, made from white wheat flour; and *ramen*, yellow noodles also made from wheat flour. *Ramen* is usually served with a hot savoury broth, while *soba* and *udon* are equally popular either hot or cold.

Noodle shops range from venerable establishments that have been in business for generations (Kanda Yabu Soba is the prime example) to cheap and cheerful stand-and-slurp counters on the platforms of railway stations.

A delicious noodle-based dish.

Soba noodles are sure to satisfy your hunger.

(shaved flakes of dried bonito), together with *wasabi* (Japanese horseradish) and thinly sliced scallions. Prepared like this, it is known as *zaru-soba*. The same noodles may also be served with lightly battered and fried *tempura*-style shrimp and grated *daikon*.

In colder weather, *soba* is more often eaten with a hot broth, topped with *tempura*, *sansai* herbs, *wakame* seaweed, deep-fried tofu (*kitsune*) or with a raw egg cracked into it (*tsukimi*). The classic dish, however, is *kamo-nanban*, in which the hot broth contains slices of rich duck meat and sliced leeks.

While *soba* is favoured more in northeast Japan, the central mountains and around Tokyo, the heartland for *udon* is Nagoya, Osaka and the western region. The wheat-flour noodles are a cold-weather favourite, served in a hot soy-based broth with scallions and a variety of toppings. A thinner *udon*, known as *hiyamugi*, is eaten chilled in summer.

The classic hot-weather noodle is the fine vermicelli known as *somen*, served chilled with strips of omelette, shrimp and green vegetables and a sesame-flavoured dip. It is a light, refreshing treat on a hot summer day.

Despite its Chinese roots, *ramen* has become an honorary part of the Japanese diet. It is served in a very hot, broth (that can be soy, *miso* or pork-bone based), typically with pickled bamboo, chopped scallion and slices of *cha-shu* (roast pork). The best *ramen* places attract hour-long queues for what amounts to little more than five minutes of noodle slurping.

The best *soba* is *te-uchi*, freshly prepared and chopped by hand to order. This typically has a buckwheat content of 80 percent, with just 20 percent wheat flour to add bulk (in cheaper, mass-produced noodles, the proportions are reversed). Buckwheat is not just a nutritious source of vitamins, but also contains plenty of dietary fibre. Top-quality *soba* needs little seasoning. It is cooked, chilled and served on a bamboo tray, accompanied by a dip made from soy sauce, *mirin* (sweet sake) and *katsuobushi*

GOOD SPOTS FOR FOOD HOUNDS

Whether you fancy Japanese, Chinese, French or Italian, there is never a shortage of eating options anywhere. Generally speaking, Ginza is for upscale eating; Shimbashi for raucous salarymen; Shibuya for young people; and Aoyama, Azabu and Roppongi for anyone who appreciates chic, contemporary cuisine. Akasaka has a good cross section of choices, while Shinjuku has it all, from designer bars to insalubrious dives.

Apart from noodle and *kaiten-zushi* shops, most restaurants close between lunch and dinner. English-language menus are not common, but many eateries, especially those in tourist areas, have plastic food displays in their windows or have picture menus. The restaurant floors of department stores usually offer a good selection of local and foreign fare.

In the evening, *izakaya* (restaurant-pubs) are a reliable source for reasonably priced local food and alcohol, and plenty of ambience. They sometimes identify themselves with a string of red lanterns hanging over the door. *Izakaya* don't do full-course meals and there is no pressure to eat quickly. Order beer, *sake* or *shochu* (a vodka-like spirit), and sample a few dishes such as *sashimi*, grilled fish, *yakitori* or tofu. If you want to splurge, luxury hotels like the Mandarin, Park Hyatt, Ritz Carlton and the like, all have highly rated restaurants and English-speaking staff.

Socialising in an izakaya bar.

TOKYO AFTER DARK

Evenings are when the neon-clad capital comes alive.
There is much to see, hear and do, whether your taste
tends towards the traditional or the new.
You can catch a rousing *kabuki* play or dance the
night away at an ultramodern club.

Tokyo's neon-spangled streets, as night descends, are an irresistible invitation to come out and play. While the older generation are enjoying a *kabuki* performance, the city's youth may be catching the latest hit movie or gyrating at a Shibuya hip-hop club. The variety of entertainment can be bewildering – what follows is a brief introduction. For more information check out Time Out Tokyo (www.timeout.jp), which has listings for all current events.

Traditional and modern music

Gagaku: Literally meaning 'elegant music', *gagaku*, is the same today as it was at least 1,500 years ago. Orchestral pieces are played on wind instruments such as the *shakuhachi* (bamboo flute), string instruments, and gongs and drums; when singing and dancing are added

> Commercial sex in Tokyo spells big bucks and many 'pink' businesses trade openly; however, the spread of Aids has led many establishments to close their doors to non-Japanese patrons.

it becomes known as *bugaku*. Most *gagaku* is based on music imported centuries ago from Korea, India, China and Southeast Asia. There are occasional outdoor performances at some shrines, or at the National Theatre.

Hogaku: This refers to Japanese music in its entirety, from *minyo* (folk songs) accompanied on the *shamisen* (a banjo-like instrument) to

Bugaku combines gagaku music with action.

contemporary *enka* (ballads) and J-pop – exuberant and youthful Japanese pop music. While concerts of the latter two musical forms are common, it is rare to come across more traditional music performances; one place where you can listen to live *shamisen* music is the Asakusa restaurant Waentei-Kikko (www.waentei-kikko.com).

Japanese theatre and dance

Noh: This minimalist theatre form has its origins in religion. Aristocratic patronage led to the development of its characteristic form from earlier temple plays. The aristocrats demanded

Checking the programme for samurai drama.

esoteric poetry, sophisticated language and a refined simplicity of movement, precisely what you see now six centuries later. It is difficult to describe *noh* – words like ethereal, inaccessible and subtle spring to mind. Fortunately, English translations are available. Catch *noh* performances at the National Noh Theatre and the Cerulean Tower Noh Theatre.

Kyogen: Many people much prefer *kyogen*, comic interludes designed to provide light relief between *noh* performances. Some last only 10 minutes and present amusing situations based on folk tales and Buddhist parables. Universal human foibles are represented, much like in Shakespeare.

Bunraku: This traditional art form can be traced back to the 7th century, when itinerant Chinese and Korean performers presented semi-religious puppet plays. *Bunraku* is adult theatre and deals with themes such as revenge and sacrifice, love and rejection, reincarnation and futility. Each major puppet is manipulated by three operators, a logistic marvel in itself. The idea is that the audience ignores the shuffling around of these silent professionals, concentrating instead on the puppets themselves, which are roughly one-third human size. The

real tour de force, though, is perhaps the narrators, the *gidayu* performers, who speak, gesture and weep from a kneeling position at stage left. The National Theatre is the best venue for *bunraku*.

Kabuki: Japan's most splendid theatre form is *kabuki*. Difficult to categorise, *kabuki* includes elements that are similar to opera and ballet. The word *kabuki*, which translates as 'song-dance skill', with no mention of theatre, in the early 16th century, also came to mean 'avant-garde' and referred to all-female performances, often of a licentious nature. The Tokugawa shogunate took exception to this and, in 1629, banned female performers. This started the all-male tradition that continues today, actresses being allowed only for certain special events.

Kabuki developed into its present form during the 17th and 18th centuries when it

A geisha tea ceremony in progress.

was theatre for the Edo masses. The main *kabuki* theatres are the National Theatre, the Shimbashi Embujo and the newly rebuilt Kabuki-za theatre in Higashi-Ginza. Full programmes can span 10 hours, with generous intervals for tea drinking and socialising; it's usually possible to buy tickets for just one act of around an hour.

Butoh: This avant-garde dance form, conceived by Tatsumi Hijikata and Kazuo Ohno in the early 1960s, is more popular abroad than it is in Japan. Its basic message stresses inhumanity, desperation and nihilism – a devotion not to physical beauty and harmony but ugliness and discord. The best places for viewing *butoh* are the Setagaya Public Theatre and the *butoh* company Dairakudakan's Studio Kochuten in Kichijoji.

Western influences

Western theatre and comedy: Translations of foreign plays and hit musicals imported from London or New York are very popular. Most are performed in Japanese by Japanese dancers and singers. Lyrics, however, are often sung in English. A handful of drama and comedy groups performing in English call Tokyo their home, the longest running being the Tokyo International Players. The Tokyo Comedy Store has regular performances at the 'live house' Crocodile.

Classical concerts: Fine concert halls include Suntory Hall, Casals Hall and Orchard Hall at the Bunkamura complex in Shibuya. Next to the concert hall, Tokyo Opera City – a mammoth skyscraper and arts complex near Shinjuku – is the New National Theatre. Smaller adjoining theatres offer ballet and drama.

Pop and rock: Tokyo has long had a fevered pop and rock music scene where the stars of J-Pop, such as Hikaru Utada and Ayumi Hamazaki, can be heard alongside top international acts. Concerts take place most nights at venues ranging from the enormous Tokyo Dome and the Budokan to more intimate 'live houses' such as Club Quattro and Liquid Room, which sprinkle Tokyo's trendy youth districts.

Jazz: There are hundreds of small jazz clubs and coffee shops featuring all styles from swing to free jazz. Many performers have had great success abroad, notably saxophonist Sadao Watanabe and trumpeter Terumasa Hino. Likewise, many American jazz greats visit Japan regularly, performing at nightclubs such as the

A street restaurant in Shinjuku.

Tokyo's largest clusters of love hotels – where rooms are rented for a few hours (called a 'rest' stay) or overnight – are in Kabuki-cho (Shinjuku), Maruyama-cho (Shibuya) and next to Uguisudani Station near Ueno.

A DVD shop in the Kabukicho district.

world-class Blue Note Tokyo, the Pit Inn and B-Flat. Another highlight is the annual Tokyo Jazz Festival (www.tokyo-jazz.com) usually held at the beginning of September.

Karaoke: In the 1970s, Japan gave karaoke to the world. Even if not all the world is thankful, singing along to music videos is here to stay. Karaoke, meaning 'empty orchestra', is either masochistic or sadistic, depending on your tolerance level and on which side of the microphone you are. It is a popular stress reliever and a bonding platform for co-workers or friends. There are karaoke bars in Roppongi and other central locations offering thousands of songs in English (and other languages) targeted at English-speaking foreigners and Japanese who wish to bone up on their English.

Bars and clubs

With its liberal alcohol laws and tolerance of public drunkenness, Japan is a barfly's paradise. Innocents entering the wilds of nightlife hubs Roppongi and Shinjuku will be dazzled by the dizzying array of watering holes. The city's constantly morphing mass of bars and clubs range from the tiniest hole-in-the-wall bar to flashy see-and-be-seen mega discos. Since the 1990s dance culture explosion, Tokyo has incubated a sophisticated club culture on par with New York and London.

Japan's answer to the corner pub is the *izakaya*, the small roll-up-your shirtsleeves restaurant-bars where Japan's army of salarymen go to unwind after work. You can always find *izakaya* near train stations, ranging from mom-and-pop affairs to chains such as Tsubohachi and Watami.

Over the last decade there has been a surge in English-Irish pubs, such as the chains The Dubliners and The Hub, with the Japanese broadening their drinking tastes from the home grown lagers of Sapporo, Kirin and Asahi to British-style beers. These establishments allow homesick tourists to quaff a pint of Bass or Guinness. For a better quality brew, there are also a steadily growing number of bars specialising in craft beers made in Japan and overseas, such as Baird Brewery's Taprooms in Harujuku and Meguro, Goodbeer Faucets in Shibuya, and Beer Club Popeye in Ryogoku.

THE ART OF THE GEISHA

Geisha are female performers who sing, dance, play silly games and serve *sake* with finesse. In Tokyo there are very few true geisha left, and that's why one has to pay a lot – cash, no credit cards – for their company. Usually they perform in exclusive private restaurants (*ryotei*), in Tokyo's *roku kagai* (six flower districts) of Akasaka, Asakusa, Kagurazaka, Mukojima, Shimbashi and Yoshicho (Nihombashi), for expense-account businessmen and politicians. There are, however, occasional chances for lesser mortals to see the geisha in their finery: at parades, such as the Sanja Matsuri in May, and at special performances of Japanese dancing, or *buyo*, at theatres including the Shimbashi Embujo.

A DJ mixes tunes at a nightclub.

Dozens of miniature DJ bars devoted to rock, reggae, hip-hop, techno, house, garage and other styles provide Tokyo's spin-masters the chance to hone their technique, and patrons a venue for that most ancient of youthful preoccupations – dating and mating. Tokyo's clubs are similar in nature to its DJ bars with one difference – size. Bigger venues such as Womb and Air in Shibuya, and Ageha in Shin-Kiba play host to top touring DJs spinning the latest sounds from Europe and the US. For hard-core clubbers, there are after-hours parties that often stretch past noon on weekends. Check out Time Out Tokyo (www.timeout.jp) to find out about events.

Individual nightlife spots are listed in the Travel Tips section (see page 255).

ALL SINGING AND DANCING TAKARAZUKA

The most accessible and unique forms of modern Japanese theatre are the plays, musicals and revues performed by the all-female theatre troupe Takarazuka. This seven-hundred strong company's first performance was back in 1914 when it was the brainchild of department store and railway mogul Ichizo Kobayashi. He had the idea that Japanese audiences might like Western-style operas and musicals, but he wanted to give his productions a local twist, so he adopted the glitz and glamour of *kabuki* as well as its single sex rule – only this time it would be women performing both male and female roles.

Kobayashi's vision has proved an enormous and enduring success. Thousands of young girls apply to join the Hyogo Prefecture-based troupe each year and the company's established performers are treated like superstars by armies of adoring and predominantly female fans – in fact, it's estimated that more than 90 percent of each Takarazuka audience is female. Particularly popular are the male impersonators *(otoko-yaku)* who embody an idealised, highly camp form of manly traits. The invariably over-the-top shows – anything from *West Side Story* to *The Rose of Versailles*, which is adapted from a classic *manga* about Marie Antoinette and has become Takarazuka's most famous production – are performed at the Takarazuka Theatre in Hibiya.

FASHION AND DESIGN

The ceaseless innovations in fashion and product design coming out of Tokyo reflect the chaotic diversity of the city, and the world's attention has been caught by their potent mix of simplicity, asymmetry and irreverence.

Walk down Takeshita Street in Harajuku to see the latest fashions.

The easy co-existence of the traditional and the contemporary in Tokyo is one of the city's most refreshing features. The Japanese have long demonstrated a rare syncretic genius in borrowing and adapting from their own culture and elsewhere, and then retooling and recodifying these materials into something uniquely Japanese.

The willingness to accommodate any number of seemingly conflicting ideas, beliefs and styles – drawing strength, in fact, from polarities – partly explains why it is so easy for Japanese consumers to move on to a new development in fashion and design so quickly, without apparent regret or sentimental attachment to older models. A willing collusion exists between consumer and designer, with both sides understanding that new models are only provisional and soon to be superseded. Durability is not the virtue being marketed: of-the-moment perfection is.

Deconstruction in fashion

It is no accident that the concept of deconstruction in fashion – the idea of effecting asymmetry while maintaining balance – was born in Japan. Haute couture examples are seen in a coat with no armholes; sleeves of different lengths sewn tightly to the body; dresses with

> For a study in Tokyo's very latest (and invariably colourful) teen fashions, take a stroll along Takeshita-dori in Harajuku or explore the Shibuya 109 building. New designs come and go here in a heartbeat.

sewn-in humps. These attempts to transcend the logic of symmetry are echoed in other art forms: *ikebana* (floral arrangement), which rejects symmetry as unnatural, and *shodo* (calligraphy), in which the young are taught to pay attention to the empty spaces of a page just as readily as the inked ones.

When Rei Kawakubo's controversial catwalk creations debuted in front of an entrenched and sceptical European fashion establishment nearly 30 years ago, it marked

A model at the Kimono Fashion Show.

Tokyo's grassroots designers, like those of any other fashion capital, are firmly grounded in the chaotic diversity of the metropolis. Young and streetwise brands like Undercover, Fur Fur, mercibeaucoup, Mintdesigns, Miharayasuhiro, Factotum, Yoshio Kubo and N.Hoolywood are all on the radar of the city's top fashionistas.

Tokyo as fashion centre

Japan's post-war generation approached fashion from a position of cultural insecurity. For them, 'Made in Japan' labels at the time bore the stigma of poor quality and lack of style and status, while the opposite was true of American and European products. Today's fashion conscious are more knowing and multifaceted. At one end of the spectrum are Tokyoites who think nothing of blowing an entire month's salary on high-end designer goods and international labels. Among these imports, brands such as Louis Vuitton, Prada, Gucci, Fendi and Paul Smith reign supreme. At the other end of the scale, are young people who identify strongly with various fashion tribes defined by distinct looks and influences, such as the 'Gothloli' (standing for 'gothic Lolita') style mixing dark menace with an antique innocence, or the Shibuya girls who slavishly follow the bleached blonde, suntanned style of J-Pop star Ayumi Hamasaki.

Regardless of which subculture they subscribe to, Japan's young consumers are becoming ever more discerning about quality, and this is helped by relatively high disposable incomes and extensive media coverage. Twice a year, Tokyo plays host to the fashion world during

more than the birth of a new star. Faced with her success, the Western fashion scene was forced to accept the unusual beauty of distortion in shape and cut, and the world grudgingly began to admire this new concept of beauty. Asymmetry as a viable fashion movement was born, and Tokyo gained the reputation of an innovative fashion trailblazer.

Who's who in Tokyo fashion

Ask the general public about Japanese fashion today and they will likely throw out the names of long-established Japanese couture pioneers: Yohji Yamamoto, Issey Miyake and Kawakubo whose best known brand is Comme des Garçons. Those more *au fait* with Japan's current fashion scene will also know about Tsumori Chisato, Kosuke Tsumura, Takahashi Jun, Arakawa Shinichiro and Maruyama Keita – designers who have also captured the attention of the fashion capitals of Paris, Milan, London and New York. Outside this new fashion establishment, more daring and ever-younger designers, shops and labels are springing up.

THE KIMONO

The kimono as we know it today originated in the Edo Period (1600–1868), although descriptions of various versions of the garment can be found in classical Japanese literature that dates back more than 1,000 years. Sewn from a single piece of material, high-end kimonos are made of silk, although they also come in cotton, wool and linen fabrics. The one-size-fits-all kimono is relatively easy to make and is simply adjusted to fit a customer's measurements.

A woman cannot put on a formal kimono without assistance and must enlist the help of a professional dresser or a knowledgeable member of the family.

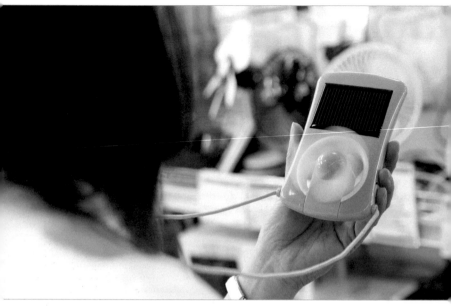

A woman tries out a solar power mobile fan in a Tokyo department store.

the spring/summer and autumn/winter collections unveiled during Japan Fashion Week (http://tokyo-mbfashionweek.com). As domestic and international fashion cognoscenti turn out to see some of the biggest names in design, these shows, organised by the Council of Fashion Designers (CFD), provide an opportunity for fashion's movers and shakers to showcase their newest creations.

Viewings are not easy for the general public to gain access to, and strong connections are required for those who want to peek at Tokyo's fashion czars. Standing room is available at certain shows, which are worth attending for their glamorous atmosphere as well as the designs themselves. The collections are shown all over the city and locations are decided just before each season. Those who enjoy the trappings

MECHANICAL FRIENDS

Gimmicks, gadgets and gizmos, objects that are both innovative and fun have been around for a long time in Japan. Whereas Westerners tend to anthropomorphise animals, the Japanese have the habit of personalising objects, superimposing human qualities on them that promote a comfortable, almost intimate co-existence in both the workplace and at home. This fondness is evident in Japan's early spring-operated dolls.

Karakuri ningyo (mechanical dolls), first appeared in the 18th century, and were made for both pleasure and amusement as well as a design spectacle. Testifying to the excellence of Japan's mechanical technology in the 17th century was the intricate *chahakobi ningyo*, a tea-serving doll. Besides its novelty value, the fact that it was required to carry a bowl of green tea without spilling a drop, hints at the exacting mechanics involved in the doll's conception.

A happy symbiosis with tools, machines and gadgets has made the transition from dolls to life-like robots a relatively small conceptual step. The basic ideas, aesthetics and skills required to develop today's humanoid robots – creations that embody bipedal ambulation technologies unrivalled in the world – were already in place long before Honda developed its Asimo 'mechanical assistant', or Sony their popular Aibo robot.

of the fashion world – streets teeming with models, cafés catering to sophisticated purveyors of style and a nightlife brimming with attractive, well-groomed people – will not be disappointed.

Hi-tech, hi-culture designs

Tokyo is unquestionably Japan's design mecca. At the end of every October (or early November) is Tokyo Design Week (www.tdwa.com) when innovative local as well as international product designs are showcased at shows, exhibitions and stylish parties all over the city. The week, which is broadly split into the 100 Percent Design main show and the fringe show Design Tide, not only allows interior and industrial designers exposure to local and international talent, but is also carnival time for admirers of good design.

At other times of the year it's simple enough to encounter great local product design by trawling trendy shopping complexes such as Omotesando Hills (designed by Tadao Ando) or Tokyo Midtown's floor of contemporary interior design stores. A preview of the latest concepts in electronic goods is available at the showcases for Sony in Ginza and Panasonic in Odaiba. Also not to be missed is Tokyu Hands, a department store with branches across Tokyo (the best two in are Shinjuku and Shibuya) that specialises in providing the raw materials for a million and one design projects – anything from making your own clothes to your own house!

Insatiable quest for the new

The average Tokyo home stocks a continuous series of replaceable products. 'Big Garbage' day, a pre-arranged time for the disposal of furniture and appliances, provides a veritable treasure trove of functioning electronics and interior goods as households chuck out the old to make room for the new.

Industrial design in Tokyo can be shoeboxed into four categories: miniaturisation, the element of fun, disposability and minimalism. Miniaturisation is most evident in the world of technology. Japan has long been praised for its ability to make Western ideas better, faster and ever smaller. One glance around Tokyo's bustling streets will reveal countless mobile phones, electronic organisers and portable video games, many of which can be hidden in one's palm.

Fun with product design can be seen in items such as shocking pink vacuum cleaners or ironing boards encrusted with plastic jewels and glitter; mundane household products transformed by urban fantasy.

Minimalism versus clutter

Perhaps one of the biggest paradoxes in Japanese design is its association, in the Western mind, with minimalism. The austere sparseness of the *tatami* room is increasingly confined to temples, traditional *ryokan*, *minshuku* hotels and the imaginations of tourists. In their daily lives, most Japanese cannot afford the luxury of empty space.

In Tokyo, where rent is often astronomical, small homes are filled to bursting with clothes, toys and collections of *mono* (objects) that reflect a hectic and fast-paced city life. In his highly recommended photo book, *Tokyo Style*, Kyoichi Tsuzuki brilliantly demonstrates the character of the modern Tokyo dwelling.

One often gets the feeling that whether stripped down to the elemental beauty of its ancient aesthetics or dressed up in the gaudy glow of its crowded entertainment districts, Japan's capital city is searching and finding, then searching again, for the design ideal.

Imported brand Louis Vuitton.

ARCHITECTURE

Tokyo's skyline is like a drawing on an immense whiteboard that can suddenly be erased and replaced by something completely different. The city's astonishing penchant for rebuilding is reflected by its mishmash of architectural styles.

Contrasting architectural styles in Tokyo.

If Tokyo ever possessed a blueprint showing everything in its ordained place, it has vanished without a trace in the face of countless natural disasters that have been visited upon the city with an almost Old Testament wrath.

There are historical antecedents, though, to suggest that the erasing of the past is not altogether involuntary. Long before Nara, Kamakura, Kyoto and, finally, Tokyo became permanent seats of power, it was the custom to demolish entire capitals with the enthronement of a new emperor. Today, economic imperatives rather than ritual purity are the catalysts for pulling down buildings. Japanese architecture has always – and to a far greater extent than elsewhere in the world – been linked to the fluctuations of the economy and the progress of technology. This has led to intense periods of creative activity followed by the abrupt shelving, in some cases, of entire projects.

An urban laboratory

Tokyo is a permanently unfinished cityscape driven as much by pragmatism as human needs. Deprived of the cosy illusion that anything could ever be permanent, Tokyoites have voiced little objection to seeing their city transformed into the world's foremost urban laboratory. With Tokyo's sights firmly set on 'the now and the next', there is little compulsion to dwell on the past: a condition ideal for aspiring architects eager to make their mark.

The problem of how futuristic buildings can be adapted to an existing, older urban landscape is resolved by simply ignoring altogether the aesthetics of coordination. New structures are inserted into the body of the city as if they were random but coincidentally harmonious pieces in a giant jigsaw puzzle, the result being a constantly surprising patchwork.

The organic labyrinth

The city's original 17th-century master plan comprised a series of concentric rings radiating from Edo castle, which combined the interests and needs of defence, commerce and geomancy. Only the faintest traces of this grid remain under the modern mire of spontaneous urban expansion.

Watanabe Hitoshi's 1932 Wako Building.

Organic growth has replaced the civic model in a city where plots of land generally take precedence over streets. Any transport infrastructure linking these sites had to be superimposed on the existing mass, in the form of elevated or buried expressways, train and subway lines. The result is a layered complexity that seems to obey organic rather than structural codes.

Japanese architects

Tokyo's early Meiji- and Taisho-period architects were strongly influenced by Western models and by the European architects and teachers such as Josiah Conder – he designed Nikolai Cathedral and the rebuilt Mitsubishi Ichigokan – and Conder's student Tatsuno

Kingo, responsible for the grand redbrick Tokyo Station, which was renovated in 2012. The Showa Period saw more experimentation: Watanabe Hitoshi's 1932 Wako Building on one corner of Ginza Crossing is a good example. Architect Ito Chuta turned to Asian culture for the inspiration for his Tsukiji Hongan-ji in Tsukiji, and to ancient Shinto forms for Meiji-jingu in Harajuku. Contemporary architects, such as the world-famous master Tadao Ando, have their own unfettered vision. Ando's Collezione building in Omotesando is a prime example.

Beyond their obvious functional purposes, the more experimental of Tokyo's buildings are design catalysts that can also be read as discourses on aesthetics and the role of modern architecture. The Aoyama Technical College in Shibuya, designed by Makoto Sei Watanabe, is, for example, a bizarre yet compelling construction of a sci-fi-like montage of poles, lightning rods, water tanks and posts that creep almost organically over the building's surfaces. Other Shibuya constructions, such as the Bunkamura, Shibuya Beam and the Humax Pavilion – not to mention the latest addition, the 2012-built 34-story Hikarie Building next to Shibuya Station – seem tame by comparison.

One of Kenzo Tange's final additions to the Tokyo skyline is the headquarters for the

Monorail tracks in Tokyo.

Fuji-Sankei Communications Group, better known as Fuji TV Building, in Odaiba. Its 'corridors in the sky' – connecting walkways that link the two main towers – and a titanium-panelled silver sphere positioned in between, give the impression of a building resembling a widescreen TV. This is no coincidence, as the building houses both Nippon Broadcasting and Fuji Television.

Foreign architects

Flexible building regulations and the vision of developers combined with deep financial pockets have encouraged many foreign architects to work in Japan. Rafael Vinoly's majestic Tokyo International Forum, for example, is a premier culture convention centre in Yurakucho. Comprising four graduated cubes, encased in granite, abutting a high, tapering trajectory of glass and steel, it is aptly named 'Glass Hall'.

The striking Prada fashion boutique in Aoyama also generates a new architectural experience. Origami-like surfaces and vertical planes form an exoskeleton where there is no separation between the structure itself, its surface and

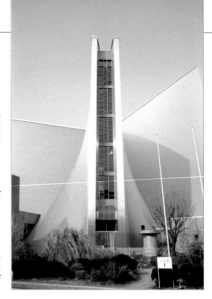

Kenzo Tange's Yoyogi National Stadium.

the interior space. The drama of the building is most evident at night, when the glass skin, latticed frame and interior lighting turn the whole building transparent.

Philippe Starck's distinctive design touch is evident at Super Dry Hall in Asakusa, with its giant rooftop sculpture, officially called Flamme d'Or, but which looks like a giant golden blob of toothpaste, or worse – some locals refer to the structure as 'unchi biru' (turd building). In contrast, Sir Norman Foster found inspiration in the design of the *torii* (shrine gate) for his Century Tower near Ochanomizu

Kenzo Tange's Fuji TV Building in Odaiba.

NEW MILLENNIUM DESIGNS

Tokyo embraced the new millennium and its architectural possibilities without so much as a moment's hesitation. Highlights from the first decade of the century include **National Art Centre**, Kisho Kurokawa's glass facade inspired by cliffs and seashores; **Prada Aoyama**, which dazzles like a greenish yellow spacecraft at night; **Mikimoto Ginza 2**, Toyo Ito's design inspired by jewel boxes, which glitters through randomly positioned, cell-like windows; and Tadao Ando's **21_21 Design Sight**, whose plunging triangular rooftops look like wing tips balanced on sheets of glass; and most obvious of all, the towering **Tokyo Skytree**, which soars 634 meters (2,080ft) above Tokyo's east end.

– *ten torii* appear to be piled on top of each other on the building's facade.

Some foreign architects have become so enamoured of Tokyo and its design possibilities that they have relocated here, including British architect Benjamin Warner whose glass Audi Forum looks like a giant iceberg that just happened to float down Meiji-dori. Fellow Brit Mark Dytham, and Astrid Klein from Germany are also longtime Tokyo transplants whose practice Klein Dytham created Uniqlo's flagship store in Ginza.

A sci-fi city

Contrasting with Tokyo's techno-aided verticality is a counter-tendency to burrow deeper into the earth's surface. Tokyo already has a considerable underground life. In addition to the world's largest subway system, which is still vigorously expanding, miles of subterranean corridors connect train lines and concourses with countless underground shopping malls. Tokyo Electric Co. has operated a power station under a Buddhist temple for almost two decades now; and an Asahi television studio, built 20 metres (66ft) below ground in Roppongi, operates a simulated downpour behind the announcers when it rains above ground.

In William Gibson's sci-fi novel, *Idoru*, skyscrapers in Shinjuku are hatched from an organic building substance that seems 'to ripple, to crawl slightly... a movement like osmosis or the sequential contraction of some sea creature's palps.' This is not as far-fetched as it sounds. Tokyo, with its natural propensity to

shed old skins, has become ideal place to test new building materials and concepts. Witness Chanel's store in Ginza, its entire facade composed of hundreds of thousands of computer controlled LEDs; the Uniqlo flagship building whose facade is also made up of a matrix of one thousand illuminated cells, whose luminosity can be individually controlled to produce different patterns; and Shibuya's QFront building which incorporates a giant electronic billboard.

Perpetual change

Japanese contractors, particularly the big five – Kajima, Takenaka, Taisei, Obayashi and Shimizu – have played a key role in transforming Tokyo's appearance. The design and construction management within these companies work closely with their own cutting-edge research laboratories. With their immense financial resources, these companies have been called 'the richest powerhouses of advanced technology in the world.'

Where building values are only one-tenth the asset value of the land, it is hardly surprising that the urban building stock undergoes constant change. The downside, of course, is a city with no memory, or at best, an inaccuracy-prone collective memory.

As with the structures in Italo Calvino's novel, *Invisible Cities* – a spider-web of 'ropes and chains and catwalks suspended in the air' – Tokyo knows that its edifices are not built to last. As a highly corporeal, perpetually embryonic city, it is ideally suited, however, to a transition in which, from its monuments to its lean-to shacks, the mortality of its structures is keenly sensed.

KENZO TANGE'S VISION

No other architect has left his mark on Tokyo more than Kenzo Tange (1913–2005). His style is writ large across the city, not only in his signature Yoyogi National Stadium, where the 1964 Olympic Games were held, or the controversial Tocho building in Shinjuku, but also in such projects as St Mary's Cathedral in Mejirodai, the Aoyama's United Nations University and the 1996 Fuji TV Building in Odaiba. Tange's ambitious 1960 proposal to impose a vast grid system on Tokyo was never implemented, however.

The company he founded is responsible for one of the most striking additions to Tokyo's skyline: Mode Gakuen Cocoon Tower, a 50-story college building in Shinjuku.

21_21 Design Sight near Tokyo Midtown.

THE ART OF LANDSCAPING

Compact, organised and highly introspective: words which stereotypically describe the Japanese might just as well be applied to their gardens.

As a fully developed art, gardening in Japan can be traced to its introduction from China and Korea during the 6th century. The balance between nature and man-made beauty, with water and mountain as prototypical images, are the principles that form the basis for the traditional Japanese garden.

Artfully blended with ponds, gurgling brooks, banks of irises and moss-covered rocks, carefully contrived Japanese gardens are objects of quiet contemplation. 'In order to comprehend the beauty of a Japanese garden,' the 19th-century writer Lafcadio Hearn wrote, 'it is necessary to understand – or at least to learn to understand – the beauty of stones.' This is especially true of Japanese Zen gardens. Essentially, there are three types: stroll, pond and so-called flat gardens. The dry-landscape garden, the *karesansui*, is the best example of the latter Zen-style garden.

The idea of confined space combined with the Zen idea of discovering limitless dimensions in the infinitely small saw the creation of the *kansho-niwa*, or 'contemplation garden', created as both tools for meditation and works of art. Carefully framed like a scroll, they are intended to be appreciated like a painting that changes with the seasons and the quality of light.

Originally used to light the way to temples and shrines, stone lanterns are now a popular and characteristic feature of Japanese gardens.

Vermilion-painted arched bridges are a traditional feature of Japanese gardens and suggest a link between heaven and earth. One of the most famous red bridges is Nikko's Shin-kyo.

Traditional Japanese gardens often feature serene ponds containing koi fish.

BLUE-BLOODED BLOOMS

In Japan, the cultivation of exhibition chrysanthemums is considered an art form. *Kiku* (chrysanthemums) were first introduced from China in the late 7th century, though legend has it that the first flowers materialised from the necklace of Izan-agi, the legendary father of the gods. Heian courtiers were known to drink *sake* tinted with the flower petals in the 9th century.

A chrysanthemum bloom.

In the 13th century, the 16-petal chrysanthemum was adopted as a symbol of the Imperial household, and used as design motifs for clothing, on sword blades, banners and on official documents.

Blooming late in the year, the flower is a symbol of longevity. In November, many of Tokyo's gardens and temple grounds become venues for the Kiku Matsuri (Chrysanthemum Festival). *Kiku-ningyo*, life-size dolls representing court ladies and historical figures, are fashioned out of the chrysanthemums. Connoisseurs of the flower look for uniformity, enhanced by subtle differences; colours should be lively but not vulgar.

Tidal waters fill the three ponds at Hamarikyu Gardens beside Tokyo Bay. A wisteria-covered trellis, a teahouse, peony and cosmos fields, and a plum tree grove are other features of the garden.

A carved stone basin filled with water is used by tea ceremony guests to cleanse themselves before entering through the garden to the teahouse.

Raked stones at the Raikyu-ji Zen Garden.

The 54th-floor observation deck at Mori Tower in Roppongi.

Tokyo's skyline at sunrise.

Neon-lit Shinjuku.

INTRODUCTION

A detailed guide to Tokyo and its surroundings
with principal sites numbered and clearly
cross-referenced to maps.

For all its modernity, Tokyo is a city steeped in the past. In its backstreets and in the crevices between its post-modernist architecture and elevated expressways lie hundreds of temples, shrines, stone steles, Buddha images and statues. Parts of Tokyo – its formal gardens, remnants of old Edo-Period estates, teahouses, restaurants and craft shops run by generations of the same family, and schools dedicated to the traditional arts – are easily sought-out time capsules. At first glance, the world's largest city resembles a formless, over-sized suburb. Closer examination, however, reveals concentrated patterns and order to the chaos.

For administration purposes, the centre of the city is made up of 23 special wards, or *ku*, which are segmented into districts that are sub-divided into numbered sections called *chome*. Individual buildings, blocks and mini-zones that fall within their parameters are numbered separately (see page 260). Combining with the 23 *ku* to form *Tokyo-to* (Tokyo Metropolis) are another 39 municipalities west of the centre and two island chains to the south.

The sprawling, lit-up city of Tokyo by night.

Good maps are an essential part of Tokyo life. Only important streets, the city's main thoroughfares, have names. Addresses are seldom written in English. Adding to the confusion is the fact that buildings are usually assigned numbers according to when they are built. Numbers are therefore often unsequenced. Every neighbourhood has a local police box *(koban)*, which is invaluable if you are lost or in doubt about an address. Police officers have detailed maps of the area and are usually very helpful.

Prayer cards at Gokoku-ji Temple.

Tokyo has an extensive bus network, but its routes are often convoluted or plagued by traffic congestion. By far the easiest way around the city is to use the underground Tokyo subway (made up of Tokyo Metro and Toei Subway-run lines) and the overground Japan Railways (JR) trains such as the Chuo, Keihin Tohoku, Sobu and Yamanote lines. This last route takes roughly an hour to complete a full loop around the inner city, with almost all the main sights, as well as Tokyo's major hotels and nightlife spots, located inside or near one of its 29 stops. Tokyo's 13 subway lines intersect at all but a few of the stations on the Yamanote Line. Helpful maps can be found inside stations or at their exits.

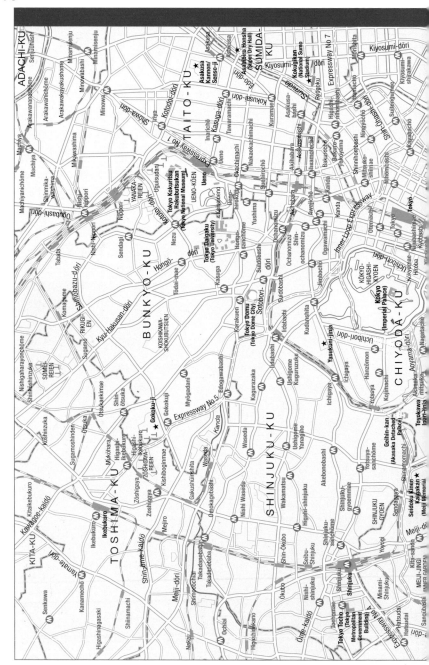

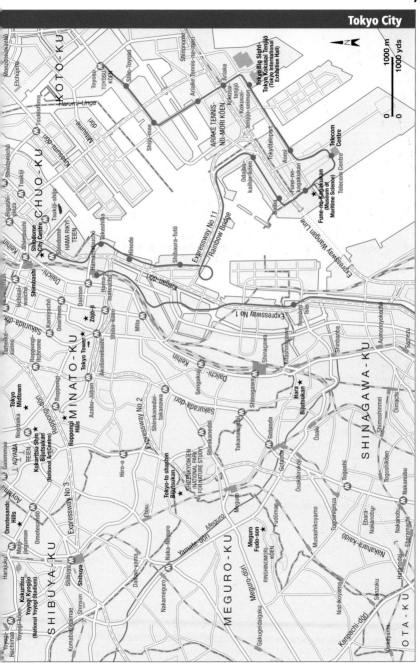

The elegant Niju stone bridge at the Imperial Palace.

IMPERIAL PALACE, MARUNOUCHI AND NIHOMBASHI

Little is left of the once formidable imperial compound, but its grounds offer leisurely exploration in the heart of Tokyo. Here too are the city's main business districts of Marunouchi and Nihombashi, interspersed with fine museums and glitzy shops.

At the historic and topographic core of a city struggling to accommodate over 13 million people, lies, quite unexpectedly, a sublimely empty space – the grounds of the Imperial Palace, home to the Japanese Emperor and his family, the world's longest unbroken line of monarchs. This once impregnable compound occupies a 110-hectare (280-acre) expanse of green – its innermost folds the habitat of rabbits and pheasants, its outer ring of moats and bridges the home of turtles, carp and gliding swans.

This idyll of meticulously controlled ecology is deceptive. The palace, sitting at the centre of a district that also includes the National Diet Building (see page 88), a number of key ministries, the Supreme Court and the Metropolitan Police Quarters, remains a fortified citadel at the core of establishment Japan, nourishing as it has always done the centres of power. Very little remains of Ieyasu's fortress. However you can get a very good impression of the medina-like ground plan for his castle and the city that grew around it by exploring the concourse of moats, interconnecting canals and defensive gates that still exist.

Policemen in the palace grounds.

THE IMPERIAL PALACE AND SURROUNDINGS

There are several entrances to the outer grounds of the palace which are open throughout the year: a popular approach is to head directly west from Tokyo Station along broad Gyoko-dori towards the east section of the inner defensive canal known as the Babasaki Moat (Babasaki-bori).

Wadakura Fountain Park ❶

Address: Kyokyo-Gaien, Chiyoda-ku
Entrance Fee: free

Main Attractions
Niju Bridge
Imperial Palace East Garden
National Museum of Modern Art
Science Museum
Yasukuni Shrine
Hibiya Park
Tokyo Station
Kite Museum
Bridgestone Museum of Fine Art
National Film Centre

Maps and Listings
Map, page 82
Shopping, page 92
Restaurants, page 95
Accommodation, page 245

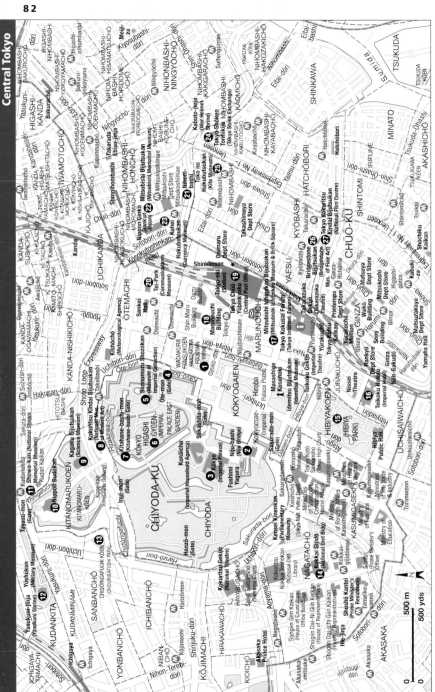

Central Tokyo

- Yasukuni-jinja (Yasukuni Shrine) ⑫
- Yūshūkan (Military Museum)
- Nippon Budōkan ⑩
- Kōgeikan (Crafts Gallery)
- Shōwa-kan (National Museum)
- Kagaku Hakubutsukan (Science Museum) ⑨
- Kokuritsu Kindai Bijutsukan (National Mus. of Modern Art) ⑧
- Kōkyo Higashi Gyoen
- Sainomaru Shozōkan (Museum of Imperial Collection) ④
- Kitahane-bashi-mon (Gate) ⑤
- Ōte-mon (Gate)
- Sekacho-mon (Gate) ⑥
- Kitanomaru-kōen
- Inui-mon (Gate)
- Chidorigafuchi Kōen
- Tayasu-mon (Gate)
- Hanzō-mon (Gate)
- Niju-bashi (Niju bridge) ⑦
- Kōkyo (Imperial Palace) ③
- Fushimi Yagura
- Kunaicho (Imperial Household Agency)
- Sakurada-mon (Gate)
- Kensei Kinenkan (Parliamentary Museum)
- Tokyo Met. Police Dept
- Kokuritsu Gekijō (National Theatre)
- Kokkai Gijidō (National Diet Bldg) ⑭
- Kokuritsu Toshokan (National Diet Library)
- Ministries
- Shushō Kantei (Prime Minister's Residence)
- Sōrifu (Prime Minister's Office)
- Hie-Jinja
- Akasaka Prince Hotel
- Sengaku Gim Kaikan (House of Councillors Office Building)
- Shūgiin Dai-ni Gim Kaikan
- Shūgiin Dai-ichi Gim Kaikan (House of Representatives)
- Saikō Saibansho (Supreme Court)

- Tokyo Chūō Yūbinkyoku (Central Post Office) ⑲
- Tokyo-eki (Station) ⑲
- Tei-Park (Communications Museum) ⑳
- Sankei Hall
- Marunouchi Building ⑱
- Tokyo Kokusai Forum (Tokyo International Forum) ⑰
- Mitsubishi Ichigokan Bijutsukan (Mitsubishi Ichigokan Museum & Brick Square)
- Idemitsu Bijutsukan (Idemitsu Museum)
- Masashige Kusunoki
- Takarazuka Gekijō (Imperial Theatre) ②
- Teikoku Gekijō (Imperial Theatre)
- Nissei Theatre
- Teikoku Hotel ⑯
- Hibiya Public Hall
- Tokyo Kōto Saibansho (Tokyo High Court)

- Nihon-bashi ㉑
- Kabuto-jinja (War Helmet Shrine)
- Tokyo Shōken Torihikijo (Tokyo Stock Exchange)
- Mitsukoshi Dept Store
- Tako no Hakubutsukan (Kite Museum) ㉕
- Nippon Ginkō (Bank of Japan) ㉓
- Kahei Hakubutsukan (Currency Museum) ㉒
- Mitsubishi Bijutsukan (Mitsubishi Memorial Museum)
- Takarada Ebisu-jinja
- Shinnihombashi
- Daimaru Dept Store ㉔
- Takashimaya Dept Store
- Tokyo Kokuritsu Kindai Bijutsukan (National Film Centre) ㉖
- Bridgestone Bijutsukan (Bridgestone Mus. of Fine Art)
- Takaya Dept Store
- Matsuya Dept Store
- Mitsukoshi Dept Store
- Matsuzakaya Dept Store
- Kabuki-za
- Shōchiku Kaikan
- Printemps Dept Store
- Wako Building
- Sony Building
- Hankyū Dept Store
- Seibu Dept Store
- Mullion
- Yamaha Hall

- Chūō-ku
- Chiyoda-ku

500 m
500 yds

Transport: Tokyo or Otemachi

Crossing the Babasaki Moat, you'll pass the pretty **Wadakura Fountain Park** (Wadakura Funsui Koen), built to celebrate the royal wedding of the Emperor and Empress in 1961and refurbished on the occasion of their son's marriage in 1995; inside is a restaurant/café that's often used for weddings.

Further on are the gravel paths of the broad **Imperial Palace Plaza** (Kokyo-mae Hiroba) planted with some 2,000 Japanese black pine trees and lawns in 1899, and split from the inner palace grounds by another ring of moats. Across the water in the plaza's southwest corner leaps the **Niju Bridge** (Niju-bashi) ❷, a two-tiered construction referred to as the 'Double Bridge'. Framed by willow trees, and the water that flows beneath it, stocked with orange carp and gliding swans, this is one of the most photographed of Tokyo's sights. The image is completed by massive

stone ramparts and the graceful outline of the 17th-century **Fushimi Tower** (Fushimi Yagura), one of the few remaining original buildings in the complex.

The only times the general public are allowed beyond the bridge, further into the palace's inner grounds, are on 23 December (the emperor's birthday) and 2 January, when the Emperor and other key members of the Imperial family, standing on a balcony in front of the main palace building, wave to thousands of well-wishers. Tourists, however, can sign up for a free place on one of the two official daily tours into the inner sanctum – see www.kunaicho.go.jp for details.

On the tour you see that the current **Imperial Palace** (Kokyo) ❸ is a 1968 ferro-concrete structure that embodies several traditional Japanese design elements – the exterior is all you will get to see of this state reception building that replaced older buildings

A protective moat surrounds the grounds of the Imperial Palace.

The grounds of the Imperial Palace.

TIP

The Imperial Palace jogging route is one of the most popular for runners in Tokyo. Start and finish a loop around the palace grounds at Sakurada-mon for a 5km run uninterrupted by traffic lights or crossings.

damaged by fire in 1945. Separate from it are the offices of the **Imperial Household Agency** (Kunaicho), a body which exercises a very strict (some might say sinister) hand over everything to do with the royal family, from their personal appearances and conduct to press releases.

Ote Gate ❹

In its heyday, the Ote Gate (Ote-mon) was the main entrance to Edo Castle. The present gate is an impressive 1967 replica of the original, which was destroyed by a bomb towards the end of World War II. Just inside the Ote-mon is the **Museum of the Imperial Collections** (Sannomaru Shozokan; Tue–Thu, Sat–Sun 9am–4pm; free) ❺, which displays a tiny fraction of the collection of 6,000 pieces of Japanese art owned by the Imperial family.

Imperial Palace East Garden ❻

Ote Gate is one of three entrances to the **Imperial Palace East Garden** (Kokyo Higashi Gyoen; Tue–Thu, Sat–Sun 9am–4pm; free), an immaculately kept ornamental Japanese garden

Manicured grounds of the Imperial Palace East Garden.

replete with a pond, stone lanterns, a miniature waterfall, bridges and an authentic tea pavilion. The garden was the site of Edo's original five-tiered keep, which burnt down in 1657. Only the keep's sturdy stone base survives but it's worth climbing to get a view of the surroundings including the mosaic-decorated **Peach Blossom Music Hall** (Toka Gagudo), built in celebration of the Empress Kojun's 60th birthday in 1963. One original feature of the old fortress is the **Shiomizaka** (or 'Tide-Viewing Slope') that once offered views of Tokyo Bay and Mount Fuji. Today's main prospect looks onto the business districts of Nihombashi and Otemachi.

Kitahane-bashi Gate (Kitahane-bashi-mon) ❼, the northern passageway out of the Imperial Palace East Garden, leads into a central, stone-walled square and yet another gate, wickedly angled to ensnare any assailant who might be foolish enough to approach the castle.

National Museum of Modern Art ❽

Address: 3-1 Kitanomaru Koen, Chiyoda-ku

Tel: 03-5777 8600
Website: www.momat.go.jp
Opening Hours: Tue–Sun
10am–5pm, Fri until 8pm
Entrance Fee: charge
Transport: Takebashi

The lush and extensive grounds of **Kitanomaru Park** (Kitanomaru Koen; daily 24 hours; free), with trails through dense woodland, is home to several important cultural institutions including, on its southern edge the **National Museum of Modern Art** (Kokuritsu Kindai Bijutsukan), which displays contemporary Japanese art from the Meiji Period to the present day. The 3,000 or more pieces in the collection, which also includes work by Western artists, are exhibited in rotation. Look for works by key Japanese artists here including Kishida Ryusei, Fujita Tsuguhara and Yoshihara Jiro. Outside is Gate, a sculpture by Noguchi Isamu made for the museum in 1969.

A little further west, the museum's superb annexe, the **Crafts Gallery** (Kogeikan; tel: 03-5777 8600; Tue–Sun 10.30am–5pm; charge), is housed in a 1910 government-listed building,

one of only a handful of Meiji-era brick structures left in Tokyo. The gallery exhibits a fine collection of lacquerware, bamboo, ceramics and textiles, and has occasional demonstrations by craftsmen.

The Kogeikan (Crafts Gallery) annexe of the National Museum of Modern Art.

Science Museum ❾

Address: 2-1 Kitanomaru Koen, Chiyoda-ku
Tel: 03-3212 8544

PALACE HISTORY

The palace grounds mark the spot where Ota Dokan built a fortified mansion in 1457 on a bluff rising from an inlet overlooking present-day Tokyo Bay. Edo's elevation to the world's largest city began when Ieyasu Tokugawa, the future shogun, chose the site as his new headquarters in 1590. Ieyasu's purpose was to create an unassailable stronghold, a military capital that would also reflect his own position as Japan's de facto ruler.

In the construction of Edo Castle, which took half a century, nothing was left to chance. The first line of defence involved the construction of a complex system of moats and canals integrating existing bodies of water to form a web that would entrap, or at least delay, the enemy. The water spirals were spanned by bridges guarded by fortified gates. By the time the castle was completed in 1640, it was the largest fort in the world comprising an astonishing 110 entry gates, 30 bridges, 21 watchtowers and 28 armouries. Following the rules

of Chinese geomancy, temples were also built in Ueno and Shiba to provide additional spiritual protection.

Fires, euphemistically referred to by the townspeople as 'the flowers of Edo', were a far greater problem to the city than armed rebellion. One of the most devastating, the infamous so-called 'Long-Sleeves Fire', occurred in 1657. The intensity of the heat not only destroyed most of the castle buildings, but also melted the shogun's gold reserves.

The Imperial Palace Plaza has also been witness to some fairly momentous scenes of recent history. Survivors of the Great Kanto Earthquake gathered here in 1923 and, in August 1945, several members of Japan's officer corps committed *seppuku* (ritual suicide) here, in order, it is said, to atone for their failure in World War II. In the 1950s and 1960s, student radicals and workers rallied at the plaza to take part in sometimes violent political demonstrations.

Volcanic rocks from quarries on the Izu Peninsula were used to build the Imperial Palace walls. So precise was the work of the stonemasons that, it was said, not even a knife blade could be inserted between the blocks.

Votive tablets on display at Yasukuni Shrine.

Website: www.jsf.or.jp
Opening Hours: daily 9.30am–4.50pm
Entrance Fee: charge
Transport: Takebashi

A short walk north from the National Art Museum, under a section of the Shoto Expressway, sticking to the paths of Kitanomaru Park (Kitanamaru koen), leads you to the **Science Museum** (Kagaku Gijutsukan). Despite its unpromisingly austere exterior, the museum is both instructive and fun, especially for children. Its four floors include space-age exhibits, working models, interactive displays and even a robot that gives lectures on electricity.

The octagonal **Nippon Budokan** ❿ (tel: 03-3216 5100; www.nippon-budokan.or.jp), which lies just northwest of the Science Museum along the same main pathway, was built in 1964 to stage the Olympic judo events. Designed by Rokkaku Kijo, the roof of the building is designed to suggest overlapping mountains as seen in traditional screen paintings. Until the Tokyo Dome was built in 1986, the Nippon Budokan

was the city's main rock venue. The Beatles performed at the Budokan in 1966 to scenes of mass hysteria. It is still used for concerts, exhibitions and tournaments of Japanese martial arts.

National Showa Memorial Museum ⓫

Address: 1-6-1 Kudan-minami, Chiyoda-ku
Tel: 03-3222 2577
Website: www.showakan.go.jp
Opening Hours: Tue–Sun 10am–5.30pm
Entrance Fee: charge
Transport: Kudanshita

Exiting Kitanomaru Park by the **Tayasu Gate** (Tayasu-mon), one of the castle's finest gates, turn right and follow Yasukuni-dori towards the **National Showa Memorial Museum** (Showa-kan) which houses exhibitions relating to Japan during World War II and the subsequent occupation. It's the first national museum to tackle Japan's war legacy and takes a predictably sanitised approach. Next door is the **Kudan Kaikan**, once a hall for soldiers but

now an events hall and hotel that hosts one of Tokyo's best roof top beer gardens every summer from May to September.

Yasukuni Shrine ⑫

Address: 3-1-1 Kudankita, Chiyoda-ku
Tel: 03-3261 8326
Website: www.yasukuni.or.jp
Opening Hours: daily sunrise–sunset
Entrance Fee: free (museum charged)
Transport: Kudanshita or Ichigaya

Taking a left out of the **Tayasu Gate** (Tayasu-mon), then crossing Yasukuni-dori (Yasukuni Street) will lead you to the **Yasukuni Shrine** (Yasukuni-jinja). Originally built in 1869 to commemorate the Imperial soldiers who had died in the civil war with the Togukawa's forces that engulfed Japan before the Meiji Restoration (see page 35), this controversial Shine shrine has since become the place where all of Japan's war dead are worshiped – including the 2 million who died in World War II. The original gate was requisitioned in 1943 as part of the war effort, and then melted to make armaments. To the shrine's rear you'll find a pretty

ornamental garden with a teahouse and an adjacent sumo ring where bouts are held during the shrine's spring festival.

Yasukuni's fascinating museum **Yushukan** (tel: 03-3261 0998; www.yasukuni.or.jp; daily Apr–Sept daily 9am–5pm; Oct–Mar 9am–4.30p; charge) displays torn uniforms, fading photos and letters from soldiers,

Admiring cherry blossoms from a row boat in Chidorigafuchi Park.

JAPAN'S WAR DEAD

Before an important battle, soldiers would sometimes exchange the words, 'Let us meet at Yasukuni', meaning the place where their spirits would be honoured. There are currently nearly 2.5 million souls enshrined at Yasukuni, including those of women and students who fought in the name of the Emperor in 13 different conflicts. This total also includes some Koreans and Taiwanese (Japan had occupied both countries before World War II).

The most controversial enshrinement was in 1978 when 14 convicted or suspected Class-A war criminals were added to Yasukuni's register, outraging Japan's neighbours who had suffered under Japan's colonial occupation. Emperor Hirohito was also not amused and refused to visit the shrine from that time until his death in 1998. Shrine officials have proved resistant, however, to calls to remove the war criminals from enshrinement, stating that all the soldiers' souls are combined at Yasukuni making individual removal impossible.

Every 15 August – the anniversary of Japan's defeat in World War II – the controversy erupts anew when a special ceremony is held at Yasukuni to mark the conflict's end. Japan's very vocal and heavily financed (yet minority) ultranationalist groups descend on the shrine en masse along with groups in opposition to them. What usually results is a highly charged, and at times bloody, day of confrontation. Japan's post-war constitution renounces both militarism and state-sponsored religion, so cabinet members who attend are asked whether they are there as private individuals or public figures. Prime Minister Koizumi Junichiro's public visit to the shrine in 2002 caused a diplomatic rift between China and Japan. Current Prime Minister Shinzo Abe reignited the issue when he visited Yasukuni in an official capacity as leader of the then opposition Liberal Democratic Party in October 2012, shortly after taking over as the party's leader. Should Abe decide to do the same as Prime Minister, you can expect already frayed Japan-China relations to become even more tense for a few weeks.

Marunouchi district by night.

National Diet Building ⑭

Address: 1-7-1 Nagatacho Chiyoda-ku
Tel: 03-5521 7445
Website: www.sangiin.go.jp
Opening Hours: Mon–Fri 8am–5pm
Entrance Fee: free
Transport: Nagatacho

Two blocks south of the National Theatre, past the Supreme Court and National Diet Library, is the Japanese parliament's **National Diet Building** (Kokkai Gijido) in the area known as Nagatacho. A plaza with fountains and gardens stands in front of the main edifice, which dates from 1937 and is split into the House of Councillors and House of Representatives. Free hour-long tours of the former are available when parliament isn't in session. The Diet is surrounded by an assortment of government offices including, to the south, a handsome modern construction that is the **Prime Minister's Residence** (Shusho Kantei).

Modern architecture along Naka-dori, Marunouchi.

as well as a Zero fighter plane used in World War II. There's a deliberate absence of data on the horrors perpetrated by the Japanese military in Asia, resulting in the museum conveying a disturbingly one-sided impression of the war.

Chidorigafuchi Park ⑬

Leaving the shrine and returning to the Imperial Palace grounds you'll find **Chidorigafuchi Park** (Chidorigafuchi Koen; daily 9am–5pm; free) between the eastern part of Uchibori-dori and the moat. The boathouse rents out rowing-boats which are an ideal way to view the many cherry trees that blossom along here during *hanami* season.

Further south along Uchibori-dori is the **National Theatre** (Kokuritsu Gekijo; tel: 03-3265 7411; www.ntl.jac.go.jp/english/access/facilities_01.html), a centre for traditional Japanese performing arts. The larger of its two auditoriums stages *kabuki* plays and *gagaku* recitals. Performances of *bunraku* puppet dramas and *kyogen* farces take place in the smaller hall.

FACT

There are hundreds of cherry trees in Yasukuni's grounds, making this a prime spot for *hanami*, cherry-blossom viewing, in spring. Festivals to entertain the spirits of the dead are also held in the shrine grounds at the end of April and in mid-October.

Hibiya Park ⑮

Continuing along Uchibori-dori, past **Sakurada Gate** (Sakurada-mon) – another gate leading to the Imperial Plaza – turn right into **Hibiya Park** (Hibiya Koen; open 24 hours; free). This 16-hectare (41-acre) former parade ground was restyled as Japan's first Western-style park in 1903. It remains a curious mixture of Meiji-Period Japanese and European landscaping, with its original wisteria trellis, crane fountain and a Japanese garden, tucked into the southwest corner, complete with stone lanterns and a pond. At weekends events are often held here, including charity fun runs for Tokyo English Lifeline in May and Run for the Cure in late November.

Imperial Hotel ⑯

Across from the park on the corner of Hibiya-dori and Miyuki-dori stands the Imperial Hotel (Teikoku Hoteru; see page 245). The present building was completed in 1970, but there's been a Western-style hotel here since 1890. Its most famous incarnation is the Mayan-style building designed by Frank Lloyd Wright. It opened in 1923, on the day the Great Kanto earthquake struck Tokyo, yet managed to survive that tremor and the devastation of World War II. After Wright's decaying building was torn down in 1968, the front section was rebuilt in Meiji-Mura architectural park near Nagoya; the only part of the present Imperial to bear Wright's design is the Old Imperial Bar (see page 95).

MARUNOUCHI AND SURROUNDINGS

Meaning 'Within the Castle Walls' Marunouchi – an area extending from the Imperial Plaza, down to Yurakucho (see page 97) and over to the old western facade of Tokyo Station where it meets the neighbouring business district of Otemachi – has long been identified with power and prestige. This was where Tokugawa Ieyasu instructed his senior retainers to build their mansions in the early 1600s. Concealed from view behind steep walls of their own, the defining features of the area's sprawling feudal villas were their gates, plain or ostentatious according to wealth and

FACT

Naka-dori is lined with luxury Japanese and overseas brands, including Armani Collezioni, Comme des Garcons and Bottega Veneta. For a full directory see www.marunouchi.com.

Artists at work outside Tokyo Station.

FACT

Aside from being one of the main gateways into the city centre, Tokyo Station also has the dubious distinction of being the place where two prime ministers were assassinated in the 20th century.

rank. With the fall of the shogunate in 1868, the walls and gates were torn down and, with the land eventually sold off, Marunouchi became the site of Japan's first Western-style office buildings.

Naka-dori

Over the decades Marunouchi's office buildings have gone through several incarnations. The last of the original red-brick buildings designed by Josiah Conder was torn down in 1968. In the late 1990s, Mitsubishi Estates commenced an ambitious plan to revive the area's aging stock of office buildings, at the same time adding high-end consumer shopping and entertainment facilities to rival nearby Ginza. Particularly benefiting from Marunouchi's revival has been **Naka-dori**, a chic thoroughfare dotted with public art that has been dubbed Tokyo's 'Rodeo Drive' for its abundance of luxury boutiques.

Mitsubishi Ichigokan Museum ⓱

Address: 2-6-2 Marunouchi, Chiyoda-ku

Tel: 03-5777 8600
Website: www.mimt.jp
Opening Hours: Tue, Wed, Sun 10am–6pm, Thu–Sat until 8pm
Entrance Fee: charge
Transport: Tokyo

An unexpected bonus has been the meticulous recreation of Conder's original office building which, with its brick facade and copper roof detailing, forms an elegant corner of the **Brick Square** commercial development. Inside, the **Mitsubishi Ichigokan Museum** (Mitsubishi Ichigokan Bijutsukan) has changing exhibitions focusing on 18th- and 19th-century Japanese and European art as well as a café-bar (Café 1894) in the lofty space that was once a banking hall. Behind the museum is charming courtyard garden that is an oasis for the area's office workers.

Mitsubishi Estates

Among the buildings that Mitsubishi Estates has reconstructed and expanded is the **Marunouchi Building** ⓲ (ww.marunouchi.com/marubiru). Commonly known as the 'Maru-biru'

BIRTH OF A BUSINESS DISTRICT

In 1890, the Japanese government, needing to drum up funds to feed its growing military machine, persuaded the Iwasaki clan (founders of the giant trading firm Mitsubishi) to purchase 267,300 sq metres (319,688 sq ft) of land near the palace grounds for commercial development. The price for this land, plus sections of Yurakucho and Kanda, was ¥1.28 million to be paid in eight instalments.

Mitsubishi hired the English architect Josiah Conder to realise their vision of a Western-style business complex. Conder was one of the many 'foreign experts' the Japanese government had employed to introduce modern technology into their formerly feudal society. Doubts about earthquakes and Tokyo's sub-tropical summers were put aside as Conder's blueprint for Marunouchi materialised with the block of three-storey, red-brick neoclassical buildings known as Iccho Rondon, (One Block London), and the Mitsubishi Ichigokan. Conder went on to design several other key buildings in the city including Nikolai Cathedral in Ochanomizu and Rokumeikan recep-

tion hall in Hibiya (which was destroyed in 1940).

Although the European architecture eventually overcame the problems of its transplant, Paul Waley in his collection of narratives *Tokyo: City of Stories* said that it revealed 'a pronounced sense of unease. The buildings need carriages and trolleys and the bustle of late-Victorian and Edwardian London. Instead, all they have to look out on is a few rickshaws and the occasional disoriented passer-by.'

Most of Conder's buildings were replaced in the 1930s by larger, more modern structures and the last of the original Mitsubishi blocks was demolished in the late 1960s. As Japan's economy matured, Mitsubishi Estate, still the majority landowner in the immediate area, began to look to the past as a way of moving forward the development of the area, and in 2009 the meticulous resurrection of the original Mitsubishi Ichigokan was completed. It is now a museum and a monument to the birth of Japan's first modern office district.

this 36-storey office complex also has superb gourmet food stores, a shopping zone and all manner of restaurants. The upper levels offer sweeping views of the Imperial Palace grounds and beyond – ignoring the one-time ban on buildings over eight floors high in Marunouchi in deference to the privacy of the royal family.

Across the street on the same side, the **Shin Maru Building** (www. marunouchi.com/shinmaru) a 38-storey structure designed by the British architect Sir Michael Hopkins, offers a similar mix of shopping, dining and offices. Its opening in 2007 capped the first 10-year phase of Mitsubishi Estate's redevelopment plans for the area.

Tokyo Station ⑲

An outstanding survivor of Marunouchi's early 20th century glory days is the **Tokyo Station** (Tokyoeki). With the extension of the railway from Shimbashi into the centre of the city and the completion of Tokyo Station in 1914, Marunouchi's future was assured. The station's red-brick, Queen Anne-style design, based on the Amsterdam Central Station, was the work of Tatsuno Kingo, a former student of Josiah Conder. Along with the redevelopment of Marunouchi, the station, which handles 4000 train arrivals daily, has undergone a massive reconstruction. Modern facilities and buildings on the eastern Yaesu side of the station have been completed, and the old red-brick entrance on the Marunouchi side has been restored to its original splendour, reopening in winter 2012 with a great deal of hype. The new facilities include the very plush Tokyo Station Hotel (see page 245).

Communications Museum ⑳

Address: 2-3-1 Otemachi, Chiyoda-ku
Tel: 03-3244 6811

Website: www.teipark.jp
Opening Hours: Tue–Sun 9am–4pm
Entrance Fee: charge
Transport: Otemachi

Opposite the station, Tokyo's Central Post Office is another of the heritage buildings that is being refashioned as part of Marunouchi's upgrade. Stamp enthusiasts can, however, get their fix at the four-floor **Communications Museum** (Tei-Park), two blocks northwest of Tokyo Station. Along with a collection of 290,000 stamps, the museum traces the history, present operations and future of communications networks.

NIHOMBASHI ㉑

Heading over to Tokyo Station's east side via Eitai-dori, you'll soon hit **Nihombashi**, an area named after the bridge of the same name. Meaning 'Bridge of Japan' Togukawa Ieyasu had the original wooden, arched Nihombashi built here as a starting point and distance post for the five main roads that led out of the city. These included the Tokaido, the great 'Eastern Road' connecting Edo and Kyoto. The present bridge, a solid,

TIP

The Tokyo rush hour is not confined to a single hour in the morning and evening. On subway lines and routes like the Yamanote Line, which has one of the highest passenger capacities of any urban railway in the world, the evening crush can easily last from 5pm until 8 or 9pm.

Mitsukoshi department store's well-known label.

The Kite Museum brings colour to a business district.

serve as a distance post for the city's national highways.

Mitsui Memorial Museum ㉒

Address: 2-1-1 Nihonbashi-Muromachi, Chuo-ku
Tel: 03-5777 8600
Website: www.mitsui-museum.jp
Opening Hours: Tue–Sun 10am–5pm
Entrance Fee: charge
Transport: Mitsukoshimae

Walking north along Chuo-dori, past the original branch of department store **Mitsukoshi** is the **Mitsui Honkan Building** on the seventh floor of which is the **Mitsui Memorial Museum** (Mitsui Bijutsukan). Here are featured beautiful items from the collection of the Mitsui family – exhibitions change five times a year but there's always a section showcasing tea ceremony utensils including a replica of the fine teahouse Jo'an.

elegant structure made of stone and metal, was completed in 1911; unfortunately it is overshadowed by the raised Shuto Expressway. A bronze marker called the **Zero Kilometre Marker** (Tokyo-to Dorogenpyo) in the middle of the bridge continues to

SHOPPING

Maruzen
1-6-4 Marunouchi, Chiyoda-ku
Tel: 03-5288 8881
www.maruzen.co.jp
p278, C2
Located in the Oazo building next to Tokyo Station, this has one of Tokyo's largest selections of foreign books and a reasonably good range of imported magazines.

Department Stores

Daimaru
1-9-1 Marunouchi, Chiyoda-ku
Tel: 03-3212 8011
www.daimaru.co.jp
p278, C2
Very handy if you need to pick up anything while at Tokyo Station. Its food section offers a great selection for picnics on train journeys.

Mitsukoshi
1-4-1 Nihombashi-Muromachi, Chuo-ku
Tel: 03-3241 3311
www.mitsukoshi.co.jp
p278, C3
A giant statue of the Buddhist Goddess of Sincerity greets customers at this famous store which started trading in 1673 and became the first Tokyo shop to display goods in glass cabinets, employ women sales assistants, sell imported wares and install an escalator.

Takashimaya
2-4-1 Nihombashi, Chuo-ku
Tel: 03-3211 4111
www.takashimaya.co.jp
p278, D2
Open since 1933, this venerable department store sports a beautiful interior, a fine kimono department, a gallery and a roof garden and café. The basement level cake shops and deli counters are worthy of a visit in their own right.

Lacquerware

Kuroeya
2F, 1-2-6 Nihombashi, Chuo-ku
Tel: 03-3272 0948
www.kuroeya.com
p278, D2
Dealing in high-quality *makie* since 1689, this is the place to pick up a beautiful piece of Japanese lacquerware.

Tea

Yamamoto Yama
2-5-2 Nihombashi, Chuo-ku
Tel: 03-3281 0010
p278, D2
Purveyor of an astonishing range of quality green teas from both Japan and China – many are only available in season. You can sample before you buy in their in-store café.

Currency Museum ㉓

Address: 1-3-1 Nihonbashi-Hongokucho, Chuo-ku
Tel: 03-3277 3037
Website: www.imes.boj.or.jp/cm
Opening Hours: Tue–Sun 9.30am–4.30pm
Entrance Fee: free
Transport: Mitsukoshimae

A block northwest of Mitsukoshi along Nichigin-dori, and directly behind Mitsui Honkan Building is the imposing **Bank of Japan** (Nippon Ginko; www.boj.or.jp). Built in 1898 on the former site of the shogun's gold, silver and copper mints, the bank represents the city's first Western-style construction designed by a Japanese architect and is said to be modelled after the Bank of England in London. An annexe houses the **Currency Museum** (Kahei Hakubutsukan), displaying coinage from the Roman Period to the introduction of Chinese currency during the late Heian Period, as well as all the Japanese coins ever put into circulation.

Tokyo Stock Exchange ㉔

Address: 2-1 Nihombashi Kabutocho, Chuo-ku
Tel: 03-3665 1881
Website: www.tse.or.jp
Opening Hours: Mon–Fri 9am–4.30pm
Entrance Fee: free
Transport: Kayabacho or Nihombashi

Facing the Nihombashi River (Nihombashi-gawa), the enormous **Tokyo Stock Exchange** (Tokyo Shoken Torihikijo) is located a few minutes' walk north of Kayabacho Station on the Tozai Line. When the exchange opened in Kabutocho in 1878, trading hours were determined by burning a length of rope. Business was conducted in a kneeling position above *tatami* mats, and messages were relayed by young boys positioned at street corners. When the rope burned down, the day's trading came to an end. In this computer age, such charming practices are long gone. If you want to learn how the exchange's business is conducted today make an advance

Creating masterpieces at the Kite Museum.

A film poster at the National Film Centre showing a heavily tattooed woman.

The Bridgestone Museum boasts an excellent collection.

reservation for one of the 20-minute guided tours in English held Monday to Friday at 1.30pm, or try one of the trading simulation games held weekdays from 2.30pm.

Kite Museum ㉕

Address: 5F Taimeiken, 1-12-10 Nihombashi, Chuo-ku
Tel: 03-3271 2465
Website: www.tako.gr.jp
Opening Hours: Mon–Sat 11am–5pm
Entrance Fee: free
Transport: Nihombashi

West of the stock exchange, just out from the A4 Exit of Nihombashi station – on the fifth floor above the restaurant Taimeiken – the **Kite Museum** (Tako-no-Hakubutsukan) is a splash of colour in this business district. Kite flying has a long tradition in Japan among children and adults, who stage jousting contests. The museum's collection exceeds 3,000 kites from around the world. Among the Japanese displays are kites shaped to resemble birds, squid and Mount Fuji. Others are like canvases, with paintings of samurai warriors, manga characters and ukiyo-e style woodblock images.

Bridgestone Museum of Fine Art ㉖

Address: 1-10-1 Kyobashi, Chuo-ku
Tel: 03-3563 0241
Website: www.bridgestone-museum. gr.jp
Opening Hours: Tue–Sun 10am–6pm, Fri until 8pm
Entrance Fee: charge
Transport: Nihombashi

Returning to Chuo-dori and heading south past the department store Takashimaya, on the corner of Yaesu-dori is the Bridgestone Building, with the **Bridgestone Museum of Fine Art** (Bridgestone Bijutsukan) on its second floor. Its excellent collection comprises mainly the works of the Impressionists, but there are some works of early 20th-century painters and post-Meiji-period Japanese artists, as well as Greek and modern sculptures. Check the schedule before visiting as the museum closes for two weeks between each major exhibition.

National Film Centre ㉗

Address: 3-7-6 Kyobashi, Chuo-ku
Tel: 03-3561 0823
Website: www.momat.go.jp
Opening Hours: Tue–Sat 11am–6pm
Entrance Fee: charge
Transport: Takaracho or Kyobashi

Continue south along Chuo-dori then turn east at the next major intersection (above Kyobashi subway station) to reach the **National Film Centre** (Tokyo Kokuritsu Kindai Bijutsukan) set up to research and preserve Japanese archival footage and foreign films. There are almost 20,000 films in its collection. Two cinemas hold screenings throughout the year. Film buffs can enjoy its gallery of photos and posters and film-related design, as well as its library.

BEST RESTAURANTS, BARS AND CAFÉS

Restaurants

Australian

Salt

Shin-Marunouchi Building, 5F, 1-5-1, Marunouchi, Chiyoda-ku. Tel: 03-5288 7828. www.pjgroup.jp/salt Open: L & D daily. ¥¥¥¥ ❶ p278, C2

Aussie celebrity-chef Lujk Mangan's first overseas venture offers superb modern fusion cuisine. The menu offers lots of great seafood matched with an excellent selection of wines from Down Under.

French

Signature

Mandarin Oriental, 34F, 2-1-1 Nihombashi-Muromachi, Chuo-ku. Tel: 03-3270 8800. www.mandarinoriental.com/tokyo Open: L & D daily. ¥¥¥¥ ❷ p278, D1

Chef Olivier Rodriguez's Mediterranean-inspired cuisine lives up to its Michelin star billing and comes with views over Tokyo to match.

Italian

Locanda Elio

2-5-2 Kojimachi, Chiyoda-ku. Tel: 03-3239 6771. www.elio.co.jp Open: L & D Mon–Sat. ¥¥¥ ❸ p278, A2

Elio Orsara is a European restaurateur of the old school. He serves great focaccia, freshly rolled pasta, Calabrian country-style soups and some of the best southern Italian food in Tokyo.

Japanese

Breeze of Tokyo

Marunouchi Building, 36F, 2-4-1 Marunouchi, Chiyoda-ku. Tel: 03-5220 5551. www.breezeoftokyo.com Open: L & D daily. ¥¥¥¥ ❹ p278, C2

A skilful blend of Japanese and French cuisine in a setting with sweeping views of the Imperial Palace grounds. There are over 30 types of champagne, sparkling wines and cocktails. Very refined ambience.

Kizushi

2-7-13 Nihombashi-Ningyocho, Chuo-ku. Tel: 03-3666 1682. Open: L & D Mon–Sat. ¥¥¥¥ ❺ p278, D1

Blending perfectly into an old neighbourhood, Kizushi strives to be individualistic in the competitive world of sushi, offering some of the best *nigiri* sushi to be found in Tokyo.

Kurosawa

2-7-9 Nagatacho, Chiyoda-ku. Tel: 03-3580 9638. Open: L & D Mon–Sat. ¥¥¥ ❻ p278, A3

A great place for fans of the filmmaker Akira Kurosawa (*The Seven Samurai*). The top-quality *soba* (buckwheat noodles), *shabu shabu* pork and other dishes are those favoured by the late director; the building is modelled on sets used in his films.

Muromachi Sunaba

4-1-13 Nihombashi-Muromachi, Chiyoda-ku. Tel: 03-3241 4038. Open: L & D Mon–Sat. ¥ ❼ p278, D1

Sunaba is more of a pit stop for office workers on a tight budget. The *tenzaru soba* (cold soba with shrimp *tempura* dipping sauce) is the most popular dish, but the sticks of *yakitori* (charcoal-grilled chicken) are good value.

Ten-mo

4-1-13 Nihombashi-Honcho, Chuo-ku. Tel: 03-3241 7035. www.tenmo.jp Open: L & D Mon–Sat. ¥¥¥ ❽ p278, D1

This tiny old-style tempura shop is a gem. Ten-mo's third-generation owner prepares the morsels of seafood and vegetables in the traditional Edo way, using rich sesame oil. Only half a dozen seats at the counter, so reservations are essential.

Yukari

3-2-14 Nihombashi, Chuo-ku. Tel: 03-3271 3436. www.nihonbashi-yukari.com Open: L & D Mon–Sat. ¥¥¥¥ ❾ p278, D2

Superb fish dishes with all the seasonal ingredients and garnishings, and beautifully presented. Specialities include snapper, conger eel sashimi and *sanpoukan* (Japanese citrus stuffed with crab, shrimp, ginger and milt). No children allowed.

Bars and Cafés

100% Chocolate Café

2-4-16 Kyobashi, Chuo-ku Tel: 03-237 3184 www.meiji.co.jp/sweets/choco-cafe ❶ p278, C2

Chocoholics rejoice. Local chocolate maker Meiji offers chocoholic heaven at this café specialising in drinks and confections made from the cocoa bean.

Marunouchi-House

1-5-1 Marunouchi, Chiyoda-ku www.marunouchi.com/shinmaru ❷ p278, C2

On Shin-Maru's seventh floor is this appealing collection of cafés, bars and casual restaurants – all with access to a broad terrace.

Old Imperial Bar

1-1-1, Uchisaiwai-cho, Hibiya, Chiyoda-ku Tel: 03-3539 8088 ❸ p278, C3

A legendary (and expensive) bar in the Imperial Hotel that preserves the original Frank Lloyd Wright design. Take a seat at the main counter so you can watch the bartenders conjuring up their famed cocktails.

Towers

2-8-10 Yaesu, Chuo-ku Tel: 03-3272 8488 ❹ p278, C3

This small standing bar near Kyobashi Station is a good place to sample Japanese craft beers and strike up a conversation with fellow customers.

YURAKUCHO, GINZA AND SHIODOME

Both elegance and exclusivity mark Ginza as a world-famous shopping destination. But there are also theatres, a traditional bathhouse, stunning contemporary architecture and lots of tiny art galleries.

During the Edo Period there was little to suggest the sartorial elegance and good taste the name Ginza now conjures up. Contiguous with the southern ribbon of the teeming, plebeian quarters of the townspeople, it occupied a rather undefined area between the feudal mansions of the Outer Lords and the newly reclaimed land of Tsukiji.

History of the area

Tokugawa Ieyasu (see page 32), established a silver mint (*gin-za*) here in 1612. The mint moved on to nearby Nihombashi in 1800, but the name stuck. Fire and steam rather than coinage were the two main elements in Ginza's rise. In 1872, Ginza and Tsukiji suffered the second of two almost consecutive fires. Nearly 3,000 homes were destroyed and the area virtually reduced to cinder. The governor of Tokyo decided to build a European-style quarter in Ginza, consisting of hundreds of fireproof red-brick buildings, arcades and tree-lined avenues.

The plan coincided nicely with the opening the same year of a train line from Yokohama to Shimbashi, a district adjacent to Ginza. The rail terminus at Shimbashi brought new life to Ginza, which suddenly found itself in the enviable position of being the main gateway into Tokyo.

The remodelling of Ginza took 10 years. By the time it was completed, its streets could boast a horse-drawn tram (soon replaced by an electric tram system), shops selling Western goods, theatres, European-style cafés, bakeries, beer halls, tearooms and the offices of several newspaper companies. By 1894, the district's most famous landmark, the Hattori Clock Tower was already in place. The city's

An advertisement for a Jackie Chan movie in Ginza.

keen instinct for merchandising had found a new home. Many of the best-known businesses and shops that line Ginza today date from this time.

Despite its new reinforced buildings, Ginza was not immune to disaster – its brick buildings were laid to waste in the Great Kanto Earthquake of 1923. Undeterred, larger, more fortified buildings sprang up in the 1930s. Most, however, suffered a similar fate during the air raids of 1945. The Wako Building at Ginza Crossing, dating from 1932, is virtually all that remains of an older Ginza, with the exception of a few smaller prewar structures in some of the backstreets.

Facing stiff competition from trendy new retail complexes in Roppongi and Aoyama, not to mention from nearby Marunouchi, Ginza has had to up its game in recent years in order to maintain its position as the city's most exclusive shopping district. It has succeeded with a mixture of architectural upgrading of older establishments such as Mikimoto, Shiseido and Chanel

– mainstays of its core clientele of well-heeled older women – as well as providing a platform for brand names such as Abercrombie and Fitch, Apple and Uniqlo that appeal to a younger crowd.

YURAKUCHO

Idemitsu Museum of Arts ❶

Address: 9F Teigeki Building, 3-1-1 Marunouchi, Chiyoda-ku
Tel: 03-3213 9402
Website: www.idemitsu.com/museum
Opening Hours: Tue–Thu, Sat–Sun 10am–5pm, Fri until 7pm
Entrance Fee: charge
Transport: Yurakucho or Hibiya

There are several possible starting points from which to explore Ginza and its environs. One of the easiest is from the JR Yurakucho Station or the Yurakucho Line subway. This area is named after a *daimyo* (powerful land-owning lord) who established his estate here in the 17th century. On the west side of the station, and across Naka-dori, your

The plush Matsuya department store in Ginza.

first port of call should be the outstanding **Idemitsu Museum of Arts** (Idemitsu Bijutsukan), on the ninth floor of the Teigeiki Building. Its collection, one of the finest showcases for Asian art in the city, reflects the eclectic but discerning tastes of its wealthy founder, petroleum industrialist Idemitsu Sazo.

Its main room features an impressive collection of Chinese ceramics. There are fine Japanese pieces here too, including examples of Kakiemon, Imari, Kutani and Seto wares. Ancient pottery shards from all over the world crowd the showcases of a room with a magnificent view of the Imperial Palace. There are also gold-painted screens, Zen calligraphy and *ukiyo-e* prints.

An excellent place to sample different brands of sake and learn about the brewing process is the Sake Plaza. Located at Nishi-Shimbashi (tel: 03-3519 2091), it is open from Mon to Fri 10am–6pm.

Tokyo International Forum ❷

Address: 3-5-1 Marunouchi, Chiyoda-ku
Tel: 03-5221 9000
Website: www.t-i-forum.co.jp
Opening Hours: daily 7am–11pm
Entrance Fee: free
Transport: Yurakucho

Two blocks east of the Idemitsu Museum of Arts, pressed against the tracks of the Yamanote Line, an architectural vision unlike any other you are likely to have seen rises in the spectacular form of the **Tokyo International Forum** (Tokyo Kokusai Forum). In a tough international competition, New York-based architect Rafael Vinoly won the contract to design this exhibition space divided into two enormous, interconnecting buildings. The right side contours of the east building, the forum's Glass Hall, follow the curving tracks of the elevated JR train lines.

Completed in 1996, this postmodernist masterpiece includes a conference, concert, dance and theatre space. The visual highlight of the complex is its futuristic 60-metre (196ft) -high glass atrium, with its

Yurakucho, Ginza and Shiodome

sweeping skywalks, curved walls and immense roof. For the best experience of the space take the lift up to the seventh floor and then descend by the stairs. The open-air plaza in the middle of the forum is the venue for the Oedo Antique Market (see page 102), while in the basement is an excellently presented **museum to poet and calligrapher Mitsuo Aida** (www.mitsuo.co.jp/museum; Tue–Sun 10am–5.30pm; charge).

Tokyo Kotsu Kaikan ❸

Heading south from the Tokyo International Forum and walking back under the railway tracks brings you to the **Tokyo Kotsu Kaikan**, a building in which you will not only find the Tokyo HQ of the Japan National Tourism Organisation on the 10th floor (see page 267), but also several shops that specialise in products from different prefectures in Japan. For example, there's one that sells goods made in Hokkaido. Nearby, fronting Harumi-dori, is the 14-storey **Yurakucho Center Building** (Yurakucho Mullion), a cinema and theatre complex that

Ginza by night.

also includes the department store **Hankyu**.

GINZA

Sony Building ❹

Address: 5-3-1 Ginza, Chuo-ku
Tel: 03-3573 2371
Website: www.sonybuilding.jp
Opening Hours: daily 11am–7pm
Entrance Fee: free
Transport: Ginza

Harumi-dori heads east into the heart of Ginza. At the main intersection with Sotobori-dori is one of the area's landmarks: the **Sony Building**, its several floors crammed with the newest gadgetry and plenty of hands-on and interactive equipment to play with. There's a free internet space in the foyer, souvenir shops and even restaurants (open until 9pm) here.

Next to the Sony Building is **Maison Hermes** (5-4-1 Ginza, Chuo-ku; tel: 03-3289 6811; daily 11am–7pm). The Japan HQ of the French luxury fashion group occupies a five-storey block built from

Wako Building is a landmark feature at the Ginza 4-chome intersection.

days as an experiment in continental shopping and leisure.

Modern architecture

Heading north along Chuo-dori you'll come to **Chanel** (3-5-3 Ginza, Chuo-ku; tel: 03-3779 4001; www. chanel-ginza.com) **⑥**. The entire facade of the 10-storey tower is a giant LED screen that looks its best at night. Inside, apart from clothes, is an exhibition hall and Beige, one of the several Tokyo operations of star French chef Alain Ducasse. Next down the street from the Chanel building is the striking golden-brown flagship store of Cartier, and directly across Chuo-dori are the Matsuya department store (www.matsuya.com) and major branches of **Bvlgari** and **Louis Vuitton**.

Turn the corner at Chanel to view a couple more striking pieces of contemporary architecture along Marronnier-dori. The first is the gracefully curvy **De Beers Ginza ⑦** (2-5-11 Ginza, Chuo-ku; tel: 03-5524 6055; Mon–Sat 11am–8pm, Sun until 7pm), a steel-clad showroom for the diamond merchant. Further along is

glass bricks, designed by Renzo Piano. There's a rooftop garden, a private cinema and a gallery – one of the many small art spaces you'll find tucked away in Ginza.

Ginza 4-chome crossing ❺

Two of the area's best-known retail landmarks stand on the corner of the **Ginza 4-chome crossing** (often just called 'Ginza Crossing') where Harumi-dori meets Chuo-dori – Wako and Mitsukoshi department stores. A little further on the left after Wako Building, is the famous jewellery shop **Mikimoto**. Chuo-dori from 1-chome to 8-chome is closed to traffic on Saturday 2pm to 6pm and Sunday, noon to 5pm, when it becomes a pleasant pedestrian zone, with café tables and umbrellas placed along its stretch, where you can enjoy a traditional *Gin-bura* (Ginza stroll), a tradition that goes back to the district's early

KABUKI THEATRES

The *kabuki* theatre Kabuki-za on the corner of Harumi-dori and Showa-dori was one of Ginza's, if not Tokyo's, most famous and photographed structures, until it closed in April 2010. A modern *kabuki* venue opened on this site in April 2013.

Highly stylised *kabuki* melodramas (see page 58) combine art and high jinks in a programme of dance, sword fighting, romantic episodes and tragedy. Matinée and evening performances are staged twice a day, and at Kabuki-za English-language audio guides are available to help you make sense of proceedings. If a whole play seems too daunting, buy tickets for a single act. The nearby Shimbashi Embujo theatre (see page 254) also stages *kabuki*.

the 10-storey **Mikimoto Ginza 2 ❽** (2-4-12 Ginza, Chuo-ku; tel: 03-3562 3130; daily 11am–7pm), designed by the renowned architect Toyo Ito. Its jewel-box-inspired architecture features a pinkish facade perforated by irregular-shaped windows. Besides pearls, the store sells cosmetics and high-quality sweets.

Yamaha Ginza ❾

Address: 7-9-14 Ginza, Chuo-ku
Tel: 03-3572 3139
Website: www.yamaha.co.jp/yamahaginza
Opening Hours: Mon–Sat 10.30am–8pm, Sun 10.45am–7pm
Entrance Fee: free
Transport: Shimbashi

Walking in the opposite direction along Chuo-dori from the Ginza 4-chome crossing will take you past the small, but sleek car showrooms of the **Nissan Gallery** on the left and flagship store of fast fashion retailer **Uniqlo** on the right. Further down the street, past the department store **Matsuzakaya**, are a couple more of Ginza's best modern structures. **Yamaha Ginza** (7-9-14 Ginza, Chuo-ku; www.yamaha.co.jp/yamaha ginza) also occupies a dazzling building, which is home to a professional concert hall, as well as a showroom rammed with keyboards, guitars and other instruments. Next door is the equally impressive **Nicolas G. Hayek Center** (7-9-14 Ginza, Chuo-ku; www. swatchgroup.jp; Mon–Sat 11am–8pm, Sun until 7pm), designed by Shigeru Ban. It's home to seven boutiques of the watchmaker Swatch.

Shiseido Gallery ❿

Address: B1F, 8-8-3 Ginza, Chuo-ku
Tel: 03-3572 3901
Website: www.shiseido.co.jp/e/gallery
Opening Hours: Tue–Sat 11am–7pm, Sun until 6pm
Entrance Fee: free
Transport: Shimbashi

Opposite Yamaha Ginza is the **Shiseido Gallery**, located in the basement of Shiseido, the famous cosmetics boutique. The gallery which is one of Ginza's longest running, (it opened in 1919), features experimental art by mainly young Japanese and foreign artists.

Other notable galleries in the area include **Ginza Graphic Gallery** (7-7-2 Ginza, Chuo-ku; tel: 03-3571 5206; www.dnp.co.jp/gallery; Mon–Sat 11am–7pm, Sat until 6pm; free), Tokyo's only space specialising in graphic art; and **Tokyo Gallery + BTAP** (7F, 8-10-5 Ginza; tel: 03-3571 1808; www.tokyo-gallery.com; Tue–Sat 11am–7pm, Sat until 6pm; free) specialising in Japanese, Chinese and Korean contemporary art.

Konparu-yu ⓫

Address: 8-7-5 Ginza, Chuo-ku
Tel: 03-3571 5469
Opening Hours: Mon–Sat 2–10pm
Entrance Fee: charge
Transport: Shimbashi

The traditional communal bathhouse **Konparu-yu** has been located on the small street behind Shiseido since 1863. Most Tokyo neighbourhoods had *sento* (public baths) until

TIP

For full listings of the many small commercial art galleries in Ginza and other areas of Tokyo check the website of Tokyo Art Beat (www. tokyoartbeat.com). Note most galleries are closed on Monday.

Pearls are a girl's best friend at Mikimoto's newest store in Ginza.

SHOPPING

Antiques

Antique Mall Ginza
1-13-1 Ginza, Chuo-ku. Tel: 03-3535 2115.
www.antiques-jp.com p278, C3
Located in the Davinci Building, with 300 shops this is one of the biggest antique stores in Japan.

Oedo Antique Market
3-5-1 Marunouchi, Chiyoda-ku. Tel: 03-6407 6011. www.antique-market.jp p278, C2
One of Tokyo's best antique fairs and flea markets held at the Tokyo International Forum from 9am to 4pm on the first and third Sunday of the month.

Chopsticks

Natsuno
6-7-4 Ginza, Chuo-ku. Tel: 03-3569 0952.
www.e-ohashi.com p278, C3
Thousands upon thousands of chopsticks (*hashi*) for all budgets, from cheap souvenirs to jaw-droppingly expensive handcrafted utensils. In the backstreets of the same block as Printemps store.

Clothing and Homewares

Hayashi Kimono
International Arcade, 2-1-1 Yurakucho, Chiyoda-ku. Tel: 03-3501 4012. p278, C3
New, used and antique kimonos and *yukata* (lighter cotton robes) are sold here with English-speaking staff under the railway tracks.

Muji
3-8-3 Marunouchi, Chiyoda-ku. Tel: 03-5208 8241. www.mujiyurakucho.com p278, C2
The flagship store of the trendy homewares, fashion and lifestyle store where you can buy practically anything for your house or body, from snack foods to a new bed.

Uniqlo
5-7-7 Ginza, Chuo-ku. Tel: 03-3569 6781.
www.uniqlo.com/jp p278, C3
The main Tokyo branch of this colourful, inexpensive unisex fashion store has great fashion basics and a changing range of fun T-shirts.

Cosmetics

Shiseido
8-8-3 Ginza, Chuo-ku. Tel: 03-3571 7735.
http://stg.shiseido.co.jp p278, C3
The scarlet building of this Japanese cosmetics giant also contains cafés and an art gallery.

Department Stores

Matsuya
3-6-1 Ginza, Chuo-ku. Tel: 03-3567 1211.
www.matsuya.com p278, C3
A good selection of Japanese souvenirs on the seventh floor and a clothing department with items by renowned designers. Nine decent restaurants on the eighth floor.

Matsuzakaya
6-10-1 Ginza, Chuo-ku. Tel: 03-3572 1111.
www.matsuzakaya.co.jp p278, C3
As well as several floors dedicated to high-end fashion, there's a branch of the Laox electronics store on the sixth floor and a large branch of Muji in the basement.

Mitsukoshi
4-6-16 Ginza, Chuo-ku. Tel: 03-3562 1111.
www.mitsukoshi.co.jp p278, C3
A 12-storey branch of the Nihombashi store with an interesting roof garden with a small Shinto shrine. Fantastic basement level deli counters and bento shops.

Wako
4-5-11 Ginza, Chuo-ku. Tel: 03-3562-2111.
www.wako.co.jp p278, C3
To enter Wako, said to attract shoppers from Tokyo's older, well-connected families, is to pass into a world of refined taste with prices to match.

Electronics

Bic Camera
1-11-1 Yurakucho, Chiyoda-ku. Tel: 03-5221 1111. www.biccamera.co.jp p278, C3
All kinds of electronic goods are sold at a discount at this massive emporium taking up an entire block.

Jewellery

Mikimoto
4-5-5 Ginza, Chuo-ku. Tel: 03-3535 4611.
p278, C3
The famous pearl jewellers' first Ginza showroom opened in 1899 here. The shop's founder, Mikimoto Kokichi, discovered that by inserting an irritant into the shell of the oyster, it was possible to create a cultured pearl.

Sake

Sake Plaza
1-1-21 Nishi-Shimbashi, Minato-ku. Tel: 03-3519 2091. p278, C3
An excellent place to try a vast range of sake from across the country before buying and learn about the brewing process.

Stationery and Incense

Ito-ya
2-7-15 Ginza, Chuo-ku. Tel: 03-3561 8311.
www.ito-ya.co.jp p278, C3
Dating back to 1904, the main branch of this stationery shop, sells beautiful handcrafted paper and art and calligraphy items.

Kyukyudo
5-7-4 Ginza, Chuo-ku. Tel: 03-3571 4429.
www.kyukyodo.co.jp p278, C3
This 300-year-old stationery store near Ginza Crossing sells traditional paper goods, tea ceremony utensils and beautiful, crafted lacquer letter boxes.

Toys

Hakuhinkan
8-8-11 Ginza, Chuo-ku. Tel: 03-3571 8008.
www.hakuhinkan.co.jp p278, C3
Tokyo's top toy store calls itself a 'toy park' and gives kids a chance to play with some of the goods before their parents buy.

the 1970s, but these institutions (no longer necessary as most families have private baths) are sadly fast disappearing. A Shinto altar sits in the rafters above the men's and women's sections, which have two baths apiece – one marked 'tepid', the other 'very hot'. For ¥450 you can soak in both until prune-like.

SHIODOME

Railway History Exhibition Hall ⑫

Address: 1-5-3 Higashi-Shimbashi, Minato-ku
Tel: 03-3572 1872
Website: www.ejrcf.or.jp/shinbashi
Opening Hours: Tue–Sun
11am–6pm
Entrance Fee: free
Transport: Shimbashi

The raised Tokyo Expressway separates Ginza from Shimbashi and the Shiodome City Centre complex, both to the south. Shiodome's clutch of shiny new skyscrapers stand where the original Shimbashi Station was located in 1872. A copy of that stone building now houses

the **Railway History Exhibition Hall**. Inside you can see foundations of the original building and get an idea of what Shimbashi looked like back in its late nineteenth century heyday as the birthplace of Japan's railway system.

ADMT Advertising Museum Tokyo ⑬

Caretta Shiodome, 1-8-2 Higashi-Shimbashi, Minato-ku,
Tel: 03-6218 2500
Website: www.admt.jp
Opening Hours: Tue–Fri
11am–6.30pm, Sat–Sun until
4.30pm
Entrance Fee: free
Transport: Shiodome

Among the many big corporations that have their HQs in Shiodome is advertising giant Dentsu, who occupy much of the Caretta Shiodome building. In the basement you'll find the **ADMT Advertising Museum Tokyo**, which provides wonderful glimpses into Japanese commercial art. Starting with woodblock flyers from the Edo Period, moving to Art Deco, Meiji- and Taisho-period creations, the exhibits bring you right up to date with the best of TV advertising.

JAPANESE BATHHOUSES

In the 8th century, some of the larger temples in Nara had baths built for monks and local residents. The connection between cleanliness and godliness may explain why many traditional public baths resemble temples. Edo's first public bath was built in 1591. A modest entrance fee of one *sen* was charged; public baths were henceforth called *sento*, meaning 'money water'. Mixed bathing was common and baths were not only centres for social intercourse but also sexual license. Although the number of public baths left in the Tokyo area is dwindling you'll still find one in many neighbourhoods, particularly in the old *shitamachi* districts to the north and east of the city such as Asakusa, Ueno and Yanaka.

TIP

Bathhouse etiquette dictates that everyone should thoroughly soap and rinse themselves before entering the shared bath, which is for soaking only.

BEST RESTAURANTS, BARS AND CAFÉS

Restaurants

Chinese

Hei Fung Terrace
The Peninsula Tokyo
1-8-1 Yurakucho, Chiyoda-ku
Tel: 03-6270 2888
Open: L & D daily
¥¥¥ ⑩ p278, C3
Enjoy a feast at this excellent restaurant specialising in Cantonese cuisine located in this luxury hotel also famed for its lavish afternoon teas.

French

Aux Amis des Vins
2-5-6 Ginza, Chuo-ku
Tel: 03-3567 4120
www.auxamis.com/desvins

Tasty yakatori (skewers).

Open: D Mon–Fri, L & D Sat
¥¥¥ ⑪ p278, C3
Standing rib roast is the speciality of the house. The meat comes from *Yoshida-buta*, a species of pig raised in the Kawagoe area in Saitama. Also tasty fish-of-the-day dishes. As the name suggests, this restaurant is renowned for its wine list: several hundred to choose from.

Gordon Ramsay at the Conrad
37F, Conrad Hotel, 1-9-1 Higashi-Shimbashi, Chuo-ku
Tel: 03-3688 8745
http://gordonramsay.jp
Open: D Tue–Sat
¥¥¥¥ ⑫ p278, C4
The view over Hamarikyu Gardens and Tokyo Bay is one of the appeals of celebrity chef Gordon Ramsay's first Tokyo venture (his second, Cerise, is also at the Conrad), but it's Ramsay's creative French cuisine that steals the show.

Fusion

Cardenas Ginza
Ginza Kanematsu Building
7F, 6-9-9 Ginza, Chuo-ku
Tel: 03-5537 5011
www.cardenas.co.jp

Open: L & D daily
¥¥¥ ⑬ p278, C3
Creative California fusion cuisine with a large selection of West Coast wines. Special house dishes include grilled chops with Thai sauce, linguine with prawns and tomato cream sauce, and sea bream carpaccio.

Indian

Dhaba India
2-7-9 Yaesu, Chuo-ku
Tel: 03-3272 7160
www.dhabaindia.com/dhaba
Open: L & D Mon–Sat
¥¥ ⑭ p278, C2
The best South Indian cuisine in the city is here. Fragrant, coconut-milk-rich curries, generous *thali* meals and superb *masala dhosas*, prepared by chefs from the Kerala and Tamil. Finish with a cup of fragrant chai tea, which is served up with theatrical aplomb. There are plenty of choices for vegetarians too.

Japanese

Ajioka
7-7-12 Ginza, Chuo-ku
Tel: 03-3574 8844.
Open: D Mon–Sat
¥¥¥¥ ⑮ p278, C3
The potentially lethal (if prepared incorrectly) blowfish (*fugu*) is the specialty at this refined restaurant, and it comes in all forms: fried, raw, in hotpots, and more. All the *fugu* is shipped in from Shimonoseki, Japan's premier *fugu* fishing region.

Bird Land
Tsukamoto Sozan Building, B1F, 4-2-15 Ginza, Chuo-ku
Tel: 03-5250 1081
http://ginza-birdland.sakura.ne.jp
Open: D Tue–Sat
¥¥¥¥ ⑯ p278, C3
Yakitori (grilled skewers of chicken) is basically blue-collar fare, but Bird Land presents it in upmarket form, using free-range chicken carefully prepared over premium charcoal. The set meals (¥6,000 or ¥8,000)

include chicken liver pâté and the delectable *sansai-yaki* (chicken breast grilled with Japanese pepper). Wash it down with Belgian beer, Chablis or Champagne.

Little Okinawa
8-7-10 Ginza, Chuo-ku
Tel: 03-3572 2930
Open: L & D Mon–Fri, D Sat–Sun
¥¥ **17** p278, C3

The exotic cuisine of Japan's southernmost prefecture is strong on pork (from the ears to the trotters), stir-fries featuring bitter gourd (*goya*), and Chinese-style noodles, to be washed down with *awamori*, Okinawa's extra-potent take on the rice-based liquor *shochu*.

Ohmatsuya
7F, 5-6-13 Ginza, Chuo-ku
Tel: 03-3571 7053
Open: D Mon–Sat
¥¥¥¥ **18** p278, C3

Gourmet fare from the mountains and fishing villages of far-off Yamagata, by the Sea of Japan. Ancient farmhouse setting with wooden beams and smoky charcoal grills where fresh seafood and mountain herbs are cooked right in front of you. Also known for its excellent *sake*.

Rangetsu
3-5-8 Ginza, Chuo-ku
Tel: 03-3567 1021
www.ginza-rangetsu.com
Open: daily 11.30am–8pm
¥¥¥¥ **19** p278, C3

This long-established restaurant offers refined Japanese cuisine based around shabu-shabu (hotpot) and sukiyaki (one-pot meal), cooked at your table for you by kimono-clad waitresses. Only the finest cuts of beef from premium Wagyu steer are used. A range of seafood dishes, with the speciality being crab, is also served.

Robata
1-3-8 Yurakucho, Chiyoda-ku
Tel: 03-3591 1905
Open: D Mon–Sat
¥¥¥ **20** p278, C3

The down-home interior of this old-style restaurant evokes a rustic farmhouse, but the menu blends Western dishes with Japanese country fare. Choose from the large platters of cooked food arrayed on the wooden counter, or order simple grilled foods and salads from the kitchen out back.

Sakyo Higashiyama
Oak Ginza, B1F, 3-7-2 Ginza, Chuo-ku
Tel: 03-3535 3577
www.r.gnavi.co.jp/g508406/lang/en
Open: L & D Mon–Sat
¥¥¥¥ **21** p278, C3

A chance to sample Kyoto cuisine – the most sophisticated in Japan. Fish and meat dishes are prepared with charcoal using a traditional sand pot. All ingredients are from Kyoto, including organic vegetables from Ohara and water from the city's Higashiyama district, said to have a soft taste.

Shin Hinomoto (aka 'Andy's')
2-4-4 Yurakucho, Chiyoda-ku
Tel: 03-3214 8021
www.andyfish.com/shin-hinomoto
Open: Mon–Sat 5pm–midnight
¥¥ **22** p278, C3

Noisy, friendly no-nonsense *izakaya* (tavern) built under the railway tracks, serving good fresh seafood at very reasonable prices. English-speaking and foreign visitors welcomed: after all, the owner is a Brit. The aromas drift out to the street luring customers with the promise of hearty *yakitori* (grilled skewers of chicken), fish and ice-cold draught lager and Japanese craft ales.

Ten-Ichi Deux
4-1 Ginza, Chuo-ku
Tel: 03-3566 4188
Open: L & D daily
¥¥ **23** p278, C3

Budget offshoot of a well-known *tempura* house serving simple meals of deep-fried battered seafood and vegetables in a stylish café ambience. While the *tempura* sets are delectable, simpler lunchtime fare is available in the form of tendon: tempura prawns on rice served with *miso* (fermented soybean) soup.

Tonton Honten
2-1-10 Yurakucho, Chuo-ku
Tel: 03-3508 9454
Open: L & D daily
¥¥ **24** p278, C3

Noisy and full of life, this casual *yakitori* chicken place is not for the squeamish. Located in the east-west tunnel section, bullet trains rumble overhead every few minutes, though some tables outside on the pavement can be pleasant with good company and ice-cold beer.

Yukun Sakagura
1-16-4 Shinbashi, Minato-ku
Tel: 03-3508 9296
www.shinbashi-yukun.com
Open: L & D Mon–Fri, D Sat
¥¥ **25** p278, B3

The boisterous atmosphere in this eatery, which specialises in dishes from the island of Kyushu, replicates the supposed feisty character of the good folk there. The dishes are displayed on a 10-metre (33ft) -long counter. *Mutsu-goro*, a grilled fish from Ariake Bay, is a popular choice.

Thai

Aronya Tabeta
3-7-11 Marunouchi, Chiyoda-ku
Tel: 03-5219 6099
Open: 11am–11pm daily
¥ **26** p278, C2

Spicy, fragrant Thai food is served up at budget prices at this eatery under the rail tracks near Yurakucho Station.

Bars and Cafés

Lion Beer Hall
7-9-20 Ginza, Chuo-ku
Tel: 3571-2590
www.ginzalion.jp
5 p278, C3

Worth dropping by, if only to marvel at the ground floor beer hall's vaulted ceiling and mosaic-lined decor. German-style sausages and the like accompany brewery Sapporo's beers.

The Lobby
The Peninsula Tokyo, 1-8-1 Yurakucho, Chiyoda-ku
Tel: 03-6270 2888
6 p278, C3

The Peninsula Hotel's tearoom is a refined setting for a classic afternoon tea: a triple-tiered plate of finger sandwiches, dainty cakes, and scones topped with clotted cream and strawberry jam.

Creative advertising near Ikebukuro Station.

IKEBUKURO

Sightseeing options of a more eclectic nature can be found in these northern districts of Tokyo, including two giant department stores, a famous cemetery, several beautiful gardens and a Catholic cathedral.

One of the premier shopping and entertainment centres along the Yamanote Line, Ikebukuro was a relative latecomer to the Tokyo scene. While other sub-cities such as Shinjuku and Shibuya were rapidly developing in the latter part of the 19th century, Ikebukuro, literally meaning 'pond bag', was an unfashionable neighbourhood favoured by struggling writers and artists. But the coming of the railway in 1903 started to change all that.

The final phase in Ikebukuro's transformation from agricultural hamlet to one of Tokyo's main sub-cities, came about through the sibling rivalry of two half-brothers, Yasujiro Tsutsumi and Kaichiro Nezu, respective heads of the Seibu and Tobu commercial groups. Their first incisions into the area, the Seibu and Tobu train lines, were crowned with two opulent department stores of the same name. Seibu now dominates the east side, with a building that runs like a firewall along the edge of the station, while Tobu defends its interests along the western portion of the tracks.

NISHI-IKEBUKURO

Exit on the west side of Ikebukuro Station – the Tobu side. Navigate south to the well-signposted Metropolitan Plaza building to get your bearings.

Tokyo Metropolitan Theatre ❶

Address: 1-8-1 Nishi-Ikebukuro, Toshima-ku
Tel: 03-5391 2111
Website: wwsw.geigeki.jp
Opening Hours: daily 9am–10pm
Transport: Ikebukuro

Two blocks west of Metropolitan Plaza, Tokyo Metropolitan Theatre (Tokyo Geijutsu Gekijo) is a concert,

Main Attractions
Ikebukuro Bosaikan
Sunshine City
Ancient Orient Museum
Zoshigaya Cemetery
Gokoku-ji
St Mary's Cathedral
Rikugien Garden
Kyu Furukawa Garden
Koishkawa Botanical Gardens

Maps and Listings
Map, page 108
Shopping, page 111
Restaurants, page 113
Accommodation, page 246

Statues at Gokoku-ji temple.

theatre and exhibition venue. The main attraction of the building is its giant escalator, which carries visitors beneath a 28-metre (90ft) glass atrium up to hallway with a colourful domed ceiling painted by Koji Kinutani.

Ikebukuro Bosaikan ②

Address: 2-37-8 Nishi-Ikebukuro, Toshima-ku
Tel: 03-3590 6565
Website: www.tfd.metro.tokyo.jp/hp-ikbskan/
Opening Hours: Wed–Mon 9am–5pm
Entrance Fee: free
Transport: Ikebukuro

From Tokyo Metropolitan Theatre follow Gekijo-dori south to the corner where you'll see the Ikebukuro Fire Station. Inside you'll find the **Ikebukuro Bosaikan**, an earthquake simulation centre. It is not the most obvious sight that springs to mind on a trip, but in a city like Tokyo,

earthquakes are an ever-present possibility. The experience of being in a room during an earthquake of magnitude six is decidedly weird, as is escaping from the smoke maze that simulates fleeing a burning building. You can also play with fire extinguishers.

Jiyu Gakuen Myonichilkan ③

Address: 2-31-3 Nishi-Ikebukuro, Toshima-ku
Tel: 03-3971 7535
Website: www.jiyu.jp
Opening Hours: Tue–Sun 10am–4pm
Entrance Fee: charge
Transport: Ikebukuro

Follow signs on the residential streets behind the Bosaikan to discover the only Frank Lloyd Wright-designed building still standing in Tokyo. Myonichilkan means 'House of Tomorrow' and the American architect was assisted by Endo Arata on

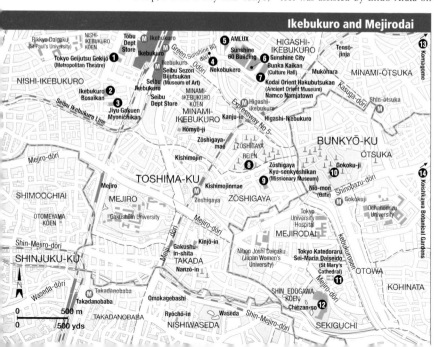

the project, which originally housed the Jiyu Gakuen (meaning 'School of Freedom') and opened in 1921. Appreciate the low-slung building's interior while sipping tea in its central hall. Weddings are often held here and at the chapel across the road on weekends.

HIGASHI-IKEBUKURO

Returning to the main road, turn right and head for the tunnel beneath the railway tracks, emerging on Meiji-dori. You're now in Higashi-Ikebukuro (East Ikebukuro). The broad avenue Green Odori runs east from the main exit of Ikebukuro Station. Branch off along the mainly pedestrian shopping street Sunshine 60-dori leading past several cinemas and a large branch of the handicrafts store Tokyu Hands (see page 111).

Nekobukero ❹

Address: 1-28-10 Higashi-Ikebukuro, Toshima-ku
Tel: 03-3980 6111
Website: www.petfirst.jp/shop/shop90_nkbtop
Opening Hours: daily 10am–8.30pm
Entrance Fee: charge
Transport: Ikebukuro

On the eighth floor of Tokyu Hands you'll find one of the latest crazes in Tokyo – a cat café! Actually at **Nekobukero**, unlike at other cat cafés around the city, they don't serve any food or drink but you can spend time petting several dozen pedigree kitties.

AMLUX ❺

Address: 3-3-5 Higashi-Ikebukuro, Toshima-ku
Tel: 03-5391 5900
Website: www.amlux.jp
Opening Hours: Tue–Sun 11am–7pm
Entrance Fee: free
Transport: Ikebukuro

Just beyond the raised expressway is **AMLUX**, a high-tech Toyota car showroom, where besides being

able to check out the 70 or so cars on display you have a chance to try computer games featuring the company's racing cars. Around here you won't fail to notice a rash of shops selling anime and *manga* products. There's no official sign, but the area has been dubbed **Otome Road** (Maiden Road) after the legions of female fans who gather here to shop for products that feature their favourite cartoon characters. On a much smaller scale, it's the girls' equivalent of male *otaku* paradise, Akihabara (see page 197).

Sunshine City ❻

Opposite AMLUX is Sunshine City (www.sunshinecity.co.jp), a complex of four buildings. Built in 1978, this self-styled 'city within a city' looks dated in comparison with newer developments such as Roppongi Hills and Tokyo Midtown. Nevertheless, its attractions could easily fill up a day's sightseeing.

The first building in the set is Sunshine 60. One of the world's fastest elevators will carry you up to the 60th floor of the tower where there is

TIP

Ikebukuro Station is a veritable labyrinth with five overhead train tracks and subway lines feeding into it. To add to the confusion, there are over 40 exits. Find the first exit at hand, and then use the department stores and other cardinal buildings to orient yourself.

Inside Sunshine City.

FACT

Car buffs will be thrilled by the displays at the AMLUX Toyoto Auto Salon, some of which are prototype models not seen elsewhere.

an observation gallery (charge) with a sweeping view of Tokyo: suburbs vanishing into infinity, the neon towers of Shinjuku and, on a clear day, the distant outline of Mount Fuji.

The Sunshine City Prince Hotel (see page 246) occupies the second building, and the World Import Mart, the third. On the 10th floor of the latter are a large planetarium (daily 11am–8pm; charge) and an aquarium (daily Apr–Oct 10am–8pm, Nov–Mar 10am–6pm; charge).

Ancient Orient Museum ❼

Address: 7F Bunka Kaikan, Sunshine City, 3-1-4 Higashi-Ikebukuro, Toshima-ku
Tel: 03-3989 3331
Opening Hours: daily 10am–5pm
Entrance Fee: charge
Transport: Ikebukuro

On the seventh floor of Sunshine City's Bunka Kaikan section, the Ancient **Orient Museum** (Kodai Orient Hakubutsukan) is an archaeological museum with a fine collection of artefacts from the Indian subcontinent and the Middle East. These include objects excavated and retrieved by Japanese teams before a dam was built on the Euphrates River in the 1970s.

If you have kids to entertain, or are looking for bizarre pop cultural and culinary distractions, you might also want to visit **Namco Namjatown**

Gokoku-ji Temple.

(tel: 5950 0765; www.namja.jp; daily 10am–10pm; charge) a noisy, inventively decorated indoor theme park notable mainly for its **Ikebukuro Gyoza Stadium** offering dumplings from chefs around Japan.

Zoshigaya Cemetery ❽

Exit Sunshine City at its southeastern corner and continue south for about five minutes through the side streets towards the raised expressway and Higashi-Ikebukuro subway station, also a stop on the Toden Arakawa tram line. You can hop on the tram here for one stop to Zoshigaya-mae or continue walking for another two minutes to reach **Zoshigaya Cemetery** (Zoshigaya Reien).

The cemetery's tree-lined paths and avenues of cherry trees lead you to the resting grounds of several well-known literary figures, including the novelists Natsume Soseki and Lafcadio Hearn and one of Tokyo's finest chroniclers, Nagai Kafu. The inscription on the headstone of this self-effacing novelist modestly reads: 'The Grave of Kafu the Scribbler.' Pick up a map (in Japanese) from the Funeral Hall to locate their graves.

Zoshigaya Missionary Museum ❾

Address: 1-25-5 Zoshigaya, Toshima-ku
Tel: 03-3985 4081
Opening Hours: Tue–Sun 10am–4.30pm
Entrance Fee: free
Transport: Higashi-Ikebukuro

A short walk south of the cemetery in a quiet residential street is the little-visited but charming **Zoshigaya Missionary Museum** (Zoshigaya Kyu-Senkyoshikan), a lovingly preserved American colonial-style house built in 1907 by an American missionary, John Moody McCaleb. The interior has been kept pretty much as it was during the 50 years he spent living in Japan.

Gokoku-ji ⑩

Walking east from the cemetery, under the raised expressway, will bring you to a gate opening into another cemetery in the grounds of this well-preserved temple complex (tel: 03-3941 0764; www.gokokuji.or.jp). Established by the fifth Shogun Tokugawa Tsunayoshi in 1681, it has been designated an Important Cultural Property. The Emperor Meiji (1852–1912) is buried here, as are several of his children. Exit the temple by its magnificent Nio-mon Gate housing two fierce-looking statues placed at either side to ward off evil spirits. The entrance to Gokoku-ji subway station is also here.

MEJIRODAI

St Mary's Cathedral ⑪

Address: 3-15-16 Sekiguchi, Bunkyo-ku
Tel: 03-3943 2301
Website: www.tokyo.catholic.jp
Opening Hours: daily 9am–5pm

Entrance Fee: free
Transport: Edogawabashi

About 10 minutes south on foot from Gokoku-ji, through the prosperous residential back streets of Mejirodai, is **St Mary's Cathedral** (Tokyo Katedoraru Sei Maria Daiseido) with its towering steel-clad bell tower. Designed by Kenzo Tange in 1964, the seat of Tokyo's Roman Catholic church – like the architect's Olympic stadium in Yoyogi (see page 140) – still appears utterly modern. The interior is dominated by a giant pipe organ, the largest of its kind in Japan, on which concerts are occasionally given.

Chinzan-so ⑫

Opposite the cathedral, a wedding hall and the Hotel Chinzan-so (see page 246) share the view across these lovely gardens (www.chinzanso.com; daily 9am–8pm; free), whose name means 'House of Camellias'. Designed in the late 19th century, the 66,000 sq metres/yds of gardens

Feline friend at Namco Namjatown theme park in Sunshine City.

SHOPPING

This area has branches of major retailers including Parco and Tokyu Hands. In the Sunshine 60 building you'll find pretty much every type of retail outlet.

Anime and Manga

Animate
1-20-7 Higashi-Ikebukuro, Toshima-ku
Tel: 03-3988 1351
www.animate-group.info
Located at the start of Otome Road, this is the main branch of the largest retailer of *anime*, games and *manga* in Japan. The products here are aimed at a largely female clientele.

Mandarake
Lions Mansion Ikebukuro B1F, 3-15-2 Higashi-Ikebukuro, Toshima-ku
www.mandarake.co.jp/en/shop/bkr.html
The Ikebukuro branch of this used

anime/manga goods store specializes in *dojinshi* (self-published comics) by and for girls.

Department Stores

Seibu
1-28-1 Minami-Ikebukuro, Toshima-ku
Tel: 03-3981 0111
www2.seibu.co.jp/ikebukuro
Constructed on the site of a postwar black market that existed up to the early 1960s, Seibu is known for its innovative clothing and designs. Its basement food halls offer a vast selection of Japanese and imported food.

Tobu
1-1-25 Nishi-Ikebukuro, Toshima-ku
Tel: 03-3981 2211
www.tobu-dept.jp/ikebukuro
Tobu sells everything from haute couture to hardware and tradi-

tional Japanese products. It has a gigantic food basement and six floors of restaurants.

Tokyu Hands
1-28-10 Higashi-Ikebukuro, Toshima-ku
Tel: 03-3981 6111
www.tokyu-hands.co.jp
The local branch of the handcrafts and DIY superstore with an astonishing array of stock.

Home Electronics Stores

Bic Camera
1-41-5 Higashi-Ikebukuro, Toshima-ku
Tel: 03-5396 1111
www.biccamera.co.jp/shoplist/honten
This major branch of one of Japan's biggest home electronics retailers has nine floors crammed with everything from the latest cameras and audio gear to mobile phones and even cosmetics.

Cherry blossoms in Zoshigaya Cemetery.

St Mary's Cathedral (Katedoraru Sei Maria Daiseido) is located in the Sekiguchi district.

include a 1,000-year-old pagoda that originally hails from a temple in Hiroshima prefecture, ancient stone lanterns and monuments, and several fine traditional restaurants including **Mucha-an** and **Kinsui** (see page 113).

KOMAGOME AND AROUND

East of Ikebukuro, the Yamanote Line takes you to **Komagome** ⑬ which has two excellent gardens. **Rikugien** (6-16-3 Hon-komagome, Bunkyo-ku; www.teien.tokyo-park.or.jp/en/rikugien; daily 9am–5pm; charge), the closest to the station, was created in 1702 by feudal lord Yoshiyasu Yanagisawa and is a prime example of an Edo-era stroll garden with the landscaping of hills and ponds inspired by the verses of Waka poetry. The garden is especially attractive in autumn and when the cherry blossoms briefly bloom in early spring.

The other sight of note is **Kyu Furukawa Garden** (Kyu Furukawa Teien; 1-27-39 Nishigahara, Kita-ku; www.tokyo-park.or.jp/en/kyu-furu-kawa; daily 9am–5pm; charge), a 10-minute walk north of the station. The garden and its main building, a charcoal-grey stone residence resembling a Scottish manor house and completed in 1917, are the work

of British architect Josiah Conder. There's a teahouse in the garden where you can sip *matcha* (powdered green tea). The garden is known for its display of azaleas in April.

Koishkawa Botanical Gardens ⑭

Address: 3-7-1 Hakusan, Bunkyo-ku
Tel: 03-3814 0139
Website: www.bg.s.u-tokyo.ac.jp/koishikawa
Opening Hours: Tue–Sun 9am–4.30pm
Entrance Fee: charge
Transport: Hakusan

Nature lovers and botanists will also want to check out these leafy gardens belonging to Tokyo University's Graduate School of Science. This 161,588-sq-metre (193,258-sq-yd) compound, home to 4,000 different living species, is Japan's oldest botanical garden, originally having been established as a medicinal herb garden in 1684 by the Tokugawa Shogunate. While strolling the grounds look for 'Newton no Ringo' – an apple tree grown from a cutting from the very same one Isaac Newton sat under when the apocryphal apple fell.

THE CHIN CHIN DENSHA

Less than a century ago Tokyo was crisscrossed by tramlines. Practically all of them have long since been ripped up to be built or paved over. The sole remaining central service is the Toden Arakawa Line, running between Waseda and Minowa-bashi. It's affectionately known as the *chin chin densha*, meaning 'ding, ding train' after the bell that the driver sounds on leaving each station.

Tickets cost ¥160 regardless of how far you travel on the line: the stretch between Higashi-Ikebukuro and Shin-Koshinzuka Station, next to Nishi-Sugamo station on the Toei Mita line will give you a taste of what public transport in Tokyo was once like.

BEST RESTAURANTS, BARS AND CAFÉS

PRICE CATEGORIES

Prices for a three-course dinner per person without drinks and taxes:
¥ = under ¥2,000
¥¥ = ¥2,000–¥3,000
¥¥¥ = ¥3,000–¥5,000
¥¥¥¥ = over ¥5,000

Restaurants

Chinese

Chion Shokudo
Miyakawa Building, B1F, 1-24-1 Ikebukuro, Toshima-ku. Tel: 03-5951 8288.
Open: Mon–Tue 5pm–3am, Wed–Sun 11am–3am. ¥ Off map
Sichuan cuisine as spicy and authentic as you'll find anywhere in China. Most of the customers are from the Mainland too. The *mabo-dofu* (ground pork and tofu) is recommended, and so are the fiery Sichuan hotpots. Situated two blocks north of Tobu department store.

Japanese

Akiyoshi
3-30-4 Nishi-Ikebukuro, Toshima-ku. Tel: 03-3982 0644. Open: D daily. ¥¥ Off map
Tasty *yakitori* restaurant that is visible from the street with its long counter and the flames that spit appetisingly over the grills. The basic skewered chicken dishes on offer here are popular with after-hour office workers and locals. Just north of Nishi-Ikebukuro Koen.

Chinzan-so
2-10-8 Sekiguchi, Bunkyo-ku. Tel: 03-3943 1111. Open: daily 11am–8pm . ¥¥¥¥ **27** p269, D2
Located in Chinzan-so, this traditional restaurant overlooking a lush garden is the ideal location for immaculately presented and sublimely flavoured *kaiseki* cuisine.

Goemon
1-1-26 Hon-Komagome, Toshima-ku.
Tel: 03-3811 2015. Open: L & D daily. ¥¥ Off map
The healthful properties of tofu need little introduction these days. Goemon serves multicourse meals featuring tofu in numerous guises, in a traditional setting overlooking a quiet garden. It also has a couple of rustic bowers outside that are popular in warm weather.

Ikebukuro Gyoza Stadium
Sunshine City, 2F, 3 Higashi-Ikebukuro, Toshima-ku. Tel: 03-5950 0765.
Open: daily 10am–10pm. ¥ Off map
After sating yourself on fried and boiled dumplings stuffed with prawns, beef, pork, and even *kimchee* and cheese, head upstairs to Ice Cream City for an amazing range of flavours.

Mucha-an
Chinzan-so, 2-10-8 Sekiguchi, Bunkyo-ku. Tel: 03-3943 1111. Open: L & D daily.
¥ **28** p269, D2
Slurp hot or cold soba noodles – the duck *(kami)* soup ones are delicious – at this small restaurant tucked behind a bamboo grove.

Mutekiya
1-17-1 Minami-Ikebukuro, Toshima-ku. Tel: 03-3982 7656. Open: daily 10.30am–4am. ¥ Off map
This tiny *ramen* joint, on a corner 100 metres/yds south along Meijidori from the east exit, serves up eight varieties of great tonkotsu-based *ramen* noodles. You might have to wait in line to get a seat, but it'll be worth it.

300B ONE
3-30-11 Nishi-Ikebukuro, Toshima-ku. Tel: 03-3986 6612. Open: daily 4pm–midnight. ¥¥ Off map
Its name pronounced 'Sambyaku B One', this is a lively *izakaya*- (tavern) style restaurant with an eclectic choice of dishes ranging from grilled fish to skewered meats. The all-you-can-drink deals (from ¥2,500 for two hours) are hugely popular. Situated one block west from exit 1a of Ikebukuro Station.

Southeast Asian

Malaychan
3-22-6 Nishi-Ikebukuro, Toshima-ku. Tel: 03-5391 7638. Open: L & D daily.
¥¥ Off map
This restaurant serves Chinese and Malay dishes mainly, with a few Thai treats thrown in. It's a bit eclectic but fun. Chinese shark's fin soup, Thai green curries, Malay *nasi lemak* (rice cooked with coconut milk and spicy toppings) and grilled fish are some offerings that go well with Tiger beer or a Singapore Sling.

Saigon
Torikoma Dai-ichi Building, 3F, 1-7-10 Higashi-Ikebukuro, Toshima-ku. Tel: 03-3989 0255. Open: L & D daily.
¥¥ Off map
This is a down-to-earth and moderately priced Vietnamese eatery. Hot pancakes in spicy sauce, beef noodle soup and spring rolls are the order of the day, while mouth-watering desserts made from fresh fruits, taro flour and jelly are worth sampling. Located one block behind Bic Camera on Ikebukuro's east side.

Bars and Cafés

Bobby's Bar
3F, 1-18-10 Ikebukuro, Toshima-ku. Tel: 03-3980 8875. Off map
A well-known bar in the area, patronised by a mix of expats, travellers and Japanese customers. Moderately priced and friendly atmosphere. Located one-minute north from exit 9 of Ikebukuro Station.

Café Pause
2-14-12 Minami-Ikebukuro, Toshima-ku. Tel: 03-5950 6117. **7** p272, C1
Contemporary pop culture permeates this laid-back café and gallery that hosts interesting art exhibitions and events, including monthly get-togethers for local designers and artists to meet and discuss their work.

SHINJUKU

Over 3.5 million people pass through Shinjuku each day. This unrivalled density makes it a microcosm of all that is Tokyo: soaring high-rises, massive malls, tiny shops, classy boutiques and a maze of entertainment venues.

With no castle, river or temple to found itself on, Shinjuku came into existence because of its position at the junction of two key arteries leading into the city from the west. It even had to invent its own name. Shinjuku simply means 'New Lodgings', a reference to the post station that was built on the more important of the two routes, the Koshu Kaido, to allow weary horses and travellers to rest overnight before completing the last leg of their journey in Edo.

The facility, proposed by five brothel owners from Edo's thriving pleasure quarters, was little more than a pretence to tap the captive market of travellers. Inns and stores soon lined the streets of Naito Shinjuku, as it was called. Its main attractions were the teahouses employing dozens of 'rice-serving girls', whose function was more carnal than culinary. The district was closed down after an incident at one teahouse involving a relative of the shogun, but reopened in 1772. Within a decade, over 50 inns and teahouses had sprung up.

Freight trains started to roll into Shinjuku Station in 1885, followed by passenger trains and a tram system. The major factor in Shinjuku's rise to urban pre-eminence, however, occurred with the Great Kanto Earthquake of 1923. While most of the old city centre was laid to waste, Shinjuku largely emerged unscathed. Huge numbers of residents moved in and, soon, department stores like Mitsukoshi and Isetan opened new branches here, followed by theatres, cafés and artists' studios. By the early 1930s, with writers, painters and students *in situ*, Shinjuku had become Tokyo's bohemian quarter.

The area's commercial importance and high civilian population made

The bright lights of lively Shinjuku.

it an inevitable target for American bombing missions, the most terrifying of which occurred on 25 May 1945, when air raids levelled the entire district, leaving only one building standing, the Isetan department store. The area quickly resurrected itself, however. The first skyscraper to go up in this part of Tokyo was the Keio Plaza Hotel in 1971 (see page 246). Since then many have followed, the latest being the dazzling Mode Gakuen Cocoon Tower. Multiple railway lines and subways make Shinjuku Station the busiest in the world.

Shinjuku today likes to style itself as 'the city of the future'. Like so many other self-designations in Tokyo, this is only half-true, applicable in this case to just one side of the mini-city – its western interface, Nishi-Shinjuku, where the Keio and Odakyu department stores face the locus of skyscrapers that define this area.

NISHI-SHINJUKU

Tokyo Metropolitan Government Office ❶
Address: 2-8-1 Nishi-Shinjuku

Tel: 03-5321 1111
Website: www.metro.tokyo.jp
Opening Hours: daily 9.30am–10.30pm
Entrance Fee: free
Transport: Tochomae

Nishi-Shinjuku's most conspicuous structure is the capital's City Hall (Tocho). Its twin 48-storey towers are the work of Kenzo Tange, who designed the original metropolitan offices in Yurakucho in 1957. The observation galleries (daily 9.30am–10.30pm; free) on the 45th floors of

Tokyo Metropolitan Government Office building, or Tocho.

The commercial side of Shinjuku has a thriving nightlife.

Vending machines are a ubiquitous feature of Tokyo life. They sell everything from food and beverages to flowers and film tickets. There are an estimated 5 million nationwide. The first machines appeared at Tokyo and Ueno stations in 1926 and have remained a fixture since then.

both towers afford superlative views across the city and, on fine days, even Mount Fuji.

South of the Tocho, along Tocho-dori, the highlight of the 30-storey **NS Building ②** (www.shinjuku-ns. co.jp) is its hollowed-out interior and a roof made from 6,000 pieces of glass. With a glass elevator to match, the views as you ascend the exterior of the building are spectacular. An observatory on the 29th floor, and restaurants there, afford more good views.

Shinjuku Central Park ③

West Shinjuku has tended to develop vertically, leaving plenty of intermittent space between tower blocks in which to stroll. Adding to that sense of space is **Shinjuku Central Park** (Shinjuku Chuo Koen; daily 24 hours; free), with its pleasant pathways, trees and hillocks – it has also been adopted by some of the area's homeless as a place to live.

Tucked into the northwest corner of the park is **Kumano-jinja**, a small shrine founded in the 15th century. The shrine, which once stood at the centre of a geisha district, seems cowed by the wall of skyscrapers that rise on its eastern flank.

Bunka Gakuen Costume Museum ④

Address: 3-22-7 Yoyogi, Shibuya-ku
Tel: 03-3299 2387
Website: www.bunka.ac.jp/museum/hakubutsu.htm

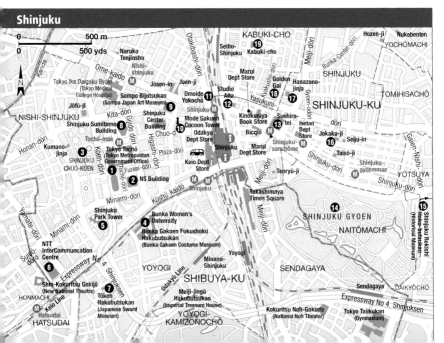

Opening Hours: Mon–Sat
10am–4pm
Entrance Fee: charge
Transport: Shinjuku

Walking southeast and crossing the broad avenue Koshu Kaido that brought Shinjuku into existence brings you to the **Bunka Women's University**, with its prestigious fashion school, and the **Bunka Gakuen Costume Museum** (Bunka Gakuen Fukushoku Hakubutsukan). The complete collection is too large to show at one time, but its partial displays are always interesting, particularly its Edo-Period clothing. Exhibits range from *kosade* dresses and *noh* drama costumes to tribal wear from overseas and the cream of modern design.

Shinjuku Park Tower ❺

A little west of the museum, back on the other side of Koshu Kaido, the hand of Kenzo Tange surfaces again in the 52-storey **Shinjuku Park Tower** (www.shinjukupark tower.com). Six floors are set aside for the shops and showrooms of the **Living Design Centre Ozone**

(tel: 03-5322 6500; www.ozone.co.jp; Mon, Tue and Thu 10.30am–7pm, Fri–Sun 10.30am–7.30pm; free), which has exhibitions relating to modern interior design, much of it eco-conscious.

Occupying the top 14 floors is the luxury **Park Hyatt Tokyu** (see page 246). The bamboo garden on the 41st floor that forms the centrepiece of Peak Lounge, with its superb views, is one of the most sophisticated spots in the city to take high tea. Park Hyatt Tokyo was where Sofia Coppola's award-winning film *Lost in Translation* was set: the 52nd-floor New York Bar was an on-screen watering hole of Bill Murray's character.

NTT InterCommunication Center ❻

Address: 4F Tokyo Opera City Tower, 3-20-2 Nishi-Shinjuku, Shinjuku-ku
Tel: 0120 144 199
Website: www.ntticc.or.jp
Opening Hours: Tue–Sun 10am–6pm
Entrance Fee: charge

Kumano-jinga shrine in Shinjuku Central Park.

TIP

The epicentre of Tokyo's gay scene is Shinjuku ni-chome, near Shinjuku Sanchome Station. There's not much going on during the day but come sundown around 300 gay bars, clubs and restaurants open for business; for some recommendations see page 256.

Transport: Hatsudai

Southwest of Shinjuku Park Tower, **Tokyo Opera City** (www.operacity.jp/en) is a 54-floor complex of shops, offices and restaurants. There's an art gallery (tel: 03-5353 0756; Tue–Sun 11am–7pm; charge) here with a focus on emerging Japanese artists, and a concert hall, but you're likely to find the most interesting part of the complex to be the **NTT InterCommunication Center** on the fourth floor. This interactive high-tech exhibition space also has an electronic library and internet café. Also part of the complex is the **New National Theatre** (Shin Kokuritsu Gekijo).

Japanese Sword Museum ❼

Address: 4-25-10 Yoyogi, Shibuya-ku
Tel: 03-3379 1386
Website: www.touken.or.jp
Opening Hours: Mon–Fri 9.30am–5pm
Entrance Fee: charge
Transport: Hatsudai

In the backstreets on the other side of the Koshu Kaido from NTT, the **Japanese Sword Museum (Token Hakubutsukan)** is a must-see for history buffs. The museum displays *katana* (samuri swords) produced by legendary sword smiths such as Nobuyoshi and Kuniyuki, in addition to sword fittings, armour and other related exhibits dating from the Heian to Edo eras (782 to 1807).

Shinjuku Sumitomo Building ❽

Back on Chuo-dori – the street that runs from Shinjuku's west exit to the Tokyo Metropolitan Government Office – is a cluster of older buildings, many of them with observation floors that allow free entry and/or restaurants that provide panoramic views. A good example is the six-sided 52-storey **Shinjuku Sumitomo Building** constructed around an open well. Light floods down to the lobby through a massive glass roof.

In the basement of the nearby **Shinjuku Center Building** you'll find **Pentax Forum** (tel: 03-3348 2945; www.pentax.jp/english/forum/index.html; Mon–Fri 10.30am–8pm, Sat–Sun until 6.30pm; free) a showroom for the photographic equipment manufacturer's products.

Sompo Japan Museum of Art ❾

Address: 42F Sompo Japan Building, 1-26-1 Nishi-Shinjuku
Tel: 03-5405 8686
Website: www.sompo-japan.co.jp/museum/english
Opening Hours: Tue–Sun 10am–5.30pm
Entrance Fee: charge
Transport: Shinjuku

Behind the Center Building is the **Sompo Japan Building** where, on the 42nd floor, you'll find the **Sompo Japan Museum of Art** (Sompo Bijutsukan) displaying works by several Japanese artists. The core of the exhibition is the collection of works by Seiji Togo (1897–1978), a skilful

Bustling Chuo-dori.

Exploring Shinjuku at night.

painter who specialised in portraits of young women. The highlight of the museum, however, is Van Gogh's *Sunflowers*, which was bought for a whopping ¥6 billion (US$40 million) during the free-spending bubble economy years. There is also one work apiece by Cezanne, Gauguin and Renoir.

TOKYO'S 'KOREATOWN'

The narrow roads or alleys that run north from Kabuki-cho lead to lively Okubo-dori. From here up to and around the overland train stations Shin Okubo and Okubo, the prevalence of Korean script on hotel, shop and restaurant signs is noticeable. This is Tokyo's Koreatown, a place where locals flock when they want to sample the most authentic and spicy Korean cuisine as well as buy CDs of the latest music from Korean pop singers (K-Pop) or a DVD of one of the hugely popular South Korean TV soap operas. There are around 100,000 Koreans living in Tokyo, but the area has become popular with other Asian immigrants, too, so you'll also find several good Thai, Filipino and Chinese restaurants here.

Mode Gakuen Cocoon Tower ⑩

The most recent addition to Nishi-Shinjuku's collection of skyscrapers is the ultra-contemporary crosshatched **Mode Gakuen Cocoon Tower**. Designed by Tange Associates, and occupied by a fashion and computer studies school, this 50-story glass stunner has a large bookstore **Book 1st** (www.book1st.net) in its basement including the Tokyo Magazine Centre with some 5,000 titles from around the world.

Omoide Yokocho ⑪

Hard up against the thick band of tracks heading north out of Shinjuku Station you'll find a remnant of the old Shinjuku before giant neon-clad

Shinjuku Gyoen is worth visiting in any season but it's particularly beautiful in April when acres of cherry blossom trees are in full bloom, or in late October when the autumn leaves are the attraction. Displays of chrysanthemums, the imperial flowers, are held during the first two weeks of November.

A typical eatery in the Shinjuku area.

buildings became the norm. This cramped, run-down, four-block neighbourhood is officially called **Omoide Yokocho** (www.shinjuku-omoide.com). However it's also popularly known as Shomben Yokocho (Piss Alley) a reference to the time when there were no toilets here and patrons would urinate in the alley (there are toilets these days). Hung with red lanterns and packed with more than 60 friendly hole-in-the-wall restaurants and bars, it's a great place to return in the evening for inexpensive *yakitori* (grilled chicken), *ramen*, *yakiniku* (Korean barbecue), and beers. On the southwest corner of you'll find the appealing **Tajimaya Coffee House** (see page 125).

HIGASHI-SHINJUKU

The east exit of the station, incorporating the fashion shopping complex called **My City**, comes out onto a small plaza in front of the landmark **Studio Alta** ⑫, several floors of youthful designer clothing with a huge, signature video screen, one of Tokyo's best-known rendezvous points. The Alta sits at the head of

Shinjuku-dori, the area's main commercial thoroughfare along which you'll find department stores such as Marui and the venerable **Isetan** ⑬, as well as **Bicqlo**, a joint venture megastore launched in 2012 combining goods from home electronics giant Bic Camera and budget fashion retailer Uniqlo.

Two small blocks east of Isetan, north of the main road, look out for the rows of coloured lanterns that decorate the outside of **Suehiro-tei** (3-6-12 Shinjuku, Shinjuku-ku; tel: 03-3351 2974; www.suehirotei.com;) a small wooden theatre. It's one of the few stages left in Tokyo dedicated to *rakugo*, a form of traditional storytelling in which the narrator addresses the audience in a seated position, as well as *manzai*; comic performances by a pair of actors.

Shinjuku Gyoen ⑭

Address: Naito-machi, Shinjuku-ku
Tel: 03-3350 0151
Website: www.env.go.jp/garden/shinjukugyoen/english
Opening Hours: Tue–Sun 9am–4.30pm

Shinjuku Gyoen.

Entrance Fee: charge
Transport: Shinjuku-Gyoen-Mae

From Shinjuku-dori head back towards Koshu Kaido to find the main entrance of **Shinjuku Gyoen**. The lovely 60-hectare (150-acre) grounds, once part of the estate of the *daimyo* (feudal lord) Naito during the Edo Period, were opened to the public in 1949.

The park is divided into three sections: a northern section containing a garden in the formal French manner; a landscaped English garden at the centre; and a traditional Japanese garden, with winding paths, arched bridges, stone lanterns and artificial hills, in the southern section. Look out for the **Taiwankaku Pavilion**, a Chinese-style gazebo built to commemorate the wedding of the Emperor Hirohito in 1927. The park's old botanical greenhouse contains some splendid subtropical plants.

Shinjuku Historical Museum ⑮

Address: 22 Saneicho, Shinjuku-ku
Tel: 03-3359 2131
Opening Hours: Tue–Sun 9am–5pm
Entrance Fee: charge
Transport: Yotsuya-Sanchome

A fair distance northeast of the garden, signposted from Yotsuya-Sanchome Station, is the small but stimulating Shinjuku Historical Museum (Shinjuku Rekishi Hakubutsukan), which provides insights into what the district must have looked like in its days as a post town.

Jokaku-ji ⑯

A little north of Shinjuku Garden, next to **Shinjuku Ni-chome**, the enclave of gay and lesbian bars is this easily passed, unexceptional looking temple. Closer scrutiny reveals a tombstone, placed here in 1860 by innkeepers from the brothel district,

The steamier side of things in Kabukicho district.

marking the spot of a communal grave where prostitutes who died were unceremoniously disposed of without the usual burial rites. The place is a sober reminder of the unglamorous existence of Shinjuku's 'rice serving girls.'

Hanazono-jinja ⑰

Address: 5-17-3 Shinjuku, Shinjuku-ku
Tel: 03-3209 5265
Website: www.hanazono-jinja.or.jp
Opening Hours: daily sunrise–sunset
Entrance Fee: free
Transport: Shinjuku-Sanchome station

Retrace your steps to Isetan, walk along its eastern flank down Meiji-dori, until you reach the wide boulevard called Yasukuni-dori. Cross it and turn left. Immediately on your right you will see the narrow entrance to the **Hanazono-jinja**, an oasis of calm at the edge of one

of Tokyo's raunchiest entertainment and red-light areas. The shrine dates back to the 6th century, but the current concrete and granite structure is more recent. One of the ubiquitous Inari fox shrines (Inari being a major fox deity and also messenger to Ebisu, the god of business and commerce), Hanazono is popular with local shop-keepers who come here to pray for success in business. The vermillion and gold interior of the main hall is impressive. Stone lamps and spot-lights come on at night, creating an enchanting atmosphere. A lively flea market is held in the shrine grounds every Sunday.

Golden Gai ⑱

Shinjuku has a relationship with alcohol not unlike like that of Venice with water: it's built on it. Right next door to the shrine, forming a warren of narrow alleys with a grid of tiny, two-storey bars, is **Golden Gai** (www.goldengai.net) an endearing retro crevice of Tokyo saved, for the time being, from the clutches of the speculator. Each of the some 200 bars in this area has a different clientele – some attract just writers, others mostly photographers, and so on – and most have a cover charge, to dissuade non-regulars, of anything from ¥1,000 to ¥4,000; it's one of the most atmospheric nightlife areas of Tokyo and worth looking at even if you're not planning to drink.

Kabuki-cho ⑲

Follow Shiki-no-michi (Four Seasons Pathway), the attractive pedestrian route that skirts the east side of Golden Gai, to emerge just a few steps to the right of Kuyakusho-dori, and the heart of **Kabuki-cho**. Relatively tame-looking by day, Kabuki-cho undergoes a transformation at twilight, when the area's seedy host-ess bars, strip joints, porno fleapits, peepshows and brothels (innocu-ously named 'Soaplands') spark into neon-lit action. All these red-light establishments share the streets with numerous reputable bars, restaurants and small music venues.

Kabuki-cho is so called because, after World War II, it was proposed that a *kabuki* theatre be built here. That plan never came to pass but this raunchy area of Shinjuku kept the classier-sounding name. The area's former lynchpin, the Koma Theatre and neighbouring Toho Kaikan building, closed at the end of 2008 to undergo major (and still ongoing) redevelopment signalling a possible change of direction for the entertainment area. For now though you can still enjoy the lively atmosphere before heading back a few blocks south across Yasakuni-dori to Shinjuku station, or you could head north to the neighbouring **Hyakunincho** area, where you'll find a collection of Southeast Asian restaurants, and on to Shinjuku's **Koreatown**.

SHOPPING

Books

Kinokuniya
5-24-2 Sendagaya, Shibuya-ku
Tel: 03-5361 3301
www.kinokuniya.co.jp.
p276, B1
Find a wide selection of English books and magazines at the main branch of this store, which is connected to Takashimaya Times Square. There's another branch in Sinjuku, a couple of hundred metres along Shinjuku-dori from Alta building.

Electronics

Yodobashi Camera
1-11-1 Nishi-Shinjuku, Shinjuku-ku
Tel: 03-3346 1010
www.yodobashi.com
p276, B1
This eight-storey branch of one of Japan's biggest home electronics chains is a great place to check out the latest audio gear, cameras, and more. They also have a huge store in Akihabara (see page 196).

Department Stores

Isetan
3-14-1 Shinjuku, Shinjuku-ku
Tel: 03-3352 1111
www.isetan.co.jp
p276, C2
One of Japan's top department stores is divided into two sections:

the old store, the only pre-war building in the area, and a newer section to the rear.

Takashimaya Times Square
5-24-2 Sendagaya,
Shibuya-ku
Tel: 03-5361 1111
www.takashimaya.co.jp/shinjuku
p276, B1
This huge shopping complex on the southeast side of Shinjuku Station also includes many restaurants and a big branch of the handicrafts store Tokyu Hands.

Fashion

Bicqlo
3-29-1 Shinjuku, Shinjuku-ku
Tel: 03-5363 5741
p276, B2
Opened in late 2012 on the site of the former Mitsukoshi department store, this megastore combines goods from budget fashion retailer Uniqlo and home electronics giant Bic Camera.

Journal Standard
4-1-7 Shinjuku, Shinjuku-ku
Tel: 03-5367 0175
p276, B1
Youthful boutique for boys and girls with a great American-style burger and hot-dog diner on its roof. It's on the east side of Takashimaya Times Square and shares a street with branches of Uniqlo and Zara.

Souvenirs and Novelties

Don Quixote
1-16-5 Kabuki-cho, Shinjuku-ku
Tel: 03-5291 9211
www.donki.com
p272, C4
Bargain hunters flock to this novelty and discount goods shop. It's open 24 hours and packed to the rafters with everything from fancy dress costumes to sex toys.

Sporting Goods

L-Breat
4-1-11 Shinjuku, Shinjuku-ku
Tel: 03-3354 8951
www.victoria.co.jp
p276, B1
One of the best outdoor goods shops in Tokyo, this 10-floor place on Takashimaya Times Square's east side has everything from bags and clothing to oxygen.

Victoria Golf
4-1-10 Shinjuku, Shinjuku-ku.
Tel: 03-3352 5281
www.victoria.co.jp
p276, B1
This store next to L-Breath (and run by the same company) has nine floors crammed with every piece of golf gear imaginable. You will find cheaper elsewhere by shopping for used goods (in great condition) in and around Kanda, amongst other places, but the selection of new gear here is exceptional.

BEST RESTAURANTS, BARS AND CAFÉS

Restaurants

American

New York Grill
Park Hyatt Hotel, 52F, 3-7-1 Nishi-Shinjuku, Shinjuku-ku
Tel: 03-5322 1234
Open: L & D daily
¥¥¥¥ 29 p276, A1
Power dining with North American bravado in a spectacular sky-view setting in the glass-fronted apex of Shinjuku's Park Hyatt Hotel. The steaks here are sumptuous and the wine list vast: the restaurant's walk-in cellar holds 1,600 bottles.

Chinese

Din Tai Fung
12F Takashimaya Times Square, 5-24-2 Sendagaya, Shibuya-ku
Tel: 03-5361 1381
www.rt-c.co.jp

Shinjuku is packed with bars and nightclubs.

Open: L & D daily
¥¥ 30 p276, B1
This branch of a famous Taiwanese dumpling shop has scored a big hit on Takashimaya's restaurant floor with a long line usually waiting for a seat – the food is worth it.

Rouben Gyoza-kan
3F, 1-18-1 Nishi-Shinjuku, Shinjuku
Tel: 03-3348 5810
www.rouben.co.jp
Open: L & D daily
¥¥ 31 p276, B1
Excellent pan-fried gyoza and other steamed dumplings are a highlight of this good value restaurant serving lots of other Chinese favourites.

French

Le Coupe Chou
1-15-7 Nishi-Shinjuku, Shinjuku-ku
Tel: 03-3348 1610
Open: L & D daily (closed 3rd Mon of the month)
¥¥¥ 32 p276, B1
In the unlikely heart of Shinjuku's discount camera and electronic district, Le Coupe Chou has a ¥1,575 four-course lunch that is one of the best French deals in

town. Go early as the small dining room fills up quickly with the local office crowd. Dinner courses range from ¥4,000 to ¥7,000.

Japanese

Hayashi
2-22-5 Kabuki-cho, Shinjuku-ku
Tel: 03-3209 5672
Open: D Mon–Sat
¥¥¥ 33 p272, C4
Here you sit around the sand hearth, nibbling on meat, fish tidbits and seasonal vegetables grilled over charcoal in a traditional rustic setting that seems light years away from Kabuki-cho's carefully cultivated image as sin city. To make ordering easier, opt for one of the three course options (¥4,000 to ¥7,000).

Kurumaya
2-37-1 Kabuki-cho, Shinjuku-ku
Tel: 03-3232 0301
www.kuruma-ya.co.jp/honten
Open: L & D daily
¥¥¥ 34 p272, B4
This restaurant represents good value in smart surroundings. The steak and seafood sets are tasty and plentiful. A popular choice for Japanese customers is the *ise ebi* (Japanese lobster), a succulent monster that is served straight or slightly garnished.

Shion
3-25 Kabuki-cho, Shinjuku-ku
Tel: 03-3356 1319
Open: daily 11.30am–11pm
¥ 35 p272, B4
Located just below street level around the corner from Studio Alta, this is one of Shinjuku's cheapest conveyor-belt sushi operations (with plates from ¥105) – which explains why there's often a queue for a place to sit.

Suzuya
1-23-15 Kabuki-cho, Shinjuku-ku
Tel: 03-3209 4480
www.toncya-suzuya.co.jp
Open: daily 11am–11pm
¥ 36 p272, B4

This Kabuki-cho restaurant has been serving its unusual take on *tonkatsu* (deep-fried breaded pork cutlet) since 1953. As with usual tonkatsu meals, the cutlet comes with a bowl of rice, shredded cabbage, miso soup and pickles, but here's the odd bit: it's also drenched in green tea.

Tenkaippin

1-14-3 Kabuki-cho, Shinjuku-ku
Tel: 03-3232 7454
http://tenkaippin.co.jp
Open: daily 11am–4am (until 8am Fri–Sat, 2am Sun)
¥ **37** p272, B4

Calorie-rich ramen noodles served in the thickest broth you'll find anywhere. Look out for the red lanterns and red-and-white decor. *Kotteri* is the thick soup; *assari* is the thin one, but they are both dense and savoury. Popular with clubbers and night owls.

Tsunahachi

3-31-8 Shinjuku, Shinjuku-ku
Tel: 03-3352 1012
www.tunahachi.co.jp
Open: daily 11am–11pm
¥¥¥ **38** p272, B4

Serving big portions of satisfying no-frills tempura (deep-fried battered seafood and vegetables) in a lively downtown atmosphere. There's another Shinjuku branch in Keio department store.

Yusoshi

6F Lumine 1, Nishi-Shinjuku 1-1-5, Shinjuku-ku
Tel: 03- 5321 7233
Open: daily 11am–11pm
¥ **39** p276, B1

Department store Lumine has brought together a good collection of distinctive operations on its restaurant floors, including this contemporary Japanese-themed place that's very affordable.

Korean

Shinjuku Pojanmacha

1-2-3 Hyakunincho, Shinjuku-ku
Tel: 03-3200 8683
www.s-pocha.com
Open: L & D daily
¥¥¥ **40** p272, B3/B4

Great *yakiniku* (Korean barbecue) is the order of the day here, but

there are also other Korean dishes on the menu, as well as cloudy *makgeolli* rice wine. Opens until early morning on weekends.

Tokaien

1-6-3 Kabuki-cho, Shinjuku-ku
Tel: 03-3200 2934
Open: daily 11–2am (Mon until 11.30pm).
¥¥¥ **41** p272, B4

For *yakiniku* (Korean beef or pork barbecue) lovers, this is the final portal. For those who can manage it Tokaien offers all-you-can-eat blow-outs on the sixth floor, as well as courses that include all-you-can-drink from ¥4,900.

Southeast Asian

Angkor Wat

1-38-13 Yoyogi, Shibuya-ku
Tel: 03-3370 3019
Open: L & D daily
¥¥ **42** p276, B2

Cheap, crowded and as consistently authentic – right down to the spices – as any Cambodian street market stall. Perky Cambodian waitresses serve chicken and green mango salads, rice and pork dishes, plus fiery side dishes in a dining room full of ambience.

Ban-Thai

1-23-14 Kabuki-cho, Shinjuku-ku
Tel: 03-3207 0068
www.ban-thai.jp
Open: L & D daily
¥¥¥ **43** p272, B4

Well situated just at the entrance to Kabuki-cho, this long-running Thai restaurant serves curries and soups that are first rate, which explains why it always draws plenty of Thai customers.

Hyakunincho Yataimura

2-20-25 Hyakunin-cho, Shinjuku-ku
Tel: 03-5386 3320
Open: L & D daily
¥¥ **44** p272, B3

Street food from half a dozen Asian countries under one very low-budget roof is the nearest thing Tokyo has to a Malaysian-style indoor hawker centre. Wander from stall to stall, making up a combination meal from the Indonesian, Thai, Korean and other cuisines represented here. It's also open to the wee hours.

Bars and Cafés

Albatross G

2F 5th Ave, 1-1 Kabuki-cho, Shinjuku-ku
Tel: 03-3203 3699
www.alba-s.co
8 p272, C4

There's only a ¥300 cover charge at this welcoming Golden Gai bar that's the sister operation of a slightly larger Albatross in Omoide Yokocho.

Donjaca

3-6-12 Shinjuku, Shinjuku-ku
Tel: 03-3357 8090
9 p276, C1

This cheerful, sometimes boisterous specialist *sake* pub stocks numerous brews from around the country, with many rarely found in Tokyo. There's a selection of tasty tavern fare, including good sashimi and grilled fish. Has other branches around the city.

La Jetee

1-1-8, Kabuki-cho, Shinjuku-ku
Tel: 03-3208 9645
10 p272, C4

Cosy Golden Gai bar patronised by film buffs, including visiting luminaries like Jim Jarmusch, Quentin Tarantino and Francis Ford Coppola. Incidentally the second language here, spoken fluently by the master of the establishment, is French.

New York Bar

3-7-1 Nishi-Shinjuku, Shinjuku-ku
Tel: 03-5323 3458
11 p276, A/B2

Located on the 52nd floor of the luxurious Park Hyatt Hotel this is a popular spot because of its sophisticated atmosphere and night views over Tokyo. There's a cover charge for the nightly jazz shows (¥2,200 after 8pm).

Tajimaya Coffee House

Omoide Yokocho, Shinjuku-eki Nishi-guchi, Shinjuku-ku
Tel: 03-3342 0881
www.tajimaya-coffeeten.com
12 p272, B4

Retreat from the crowds swarming Shinjuku Station at this warm and welcoming, wood-furnished establishment on the corner of the first set of alleys here. They serve a first-rate brew and nice cakes.

Dior store on Omotesando Street.

AOYAMA AND OMOTESANDO

Fashionistas should make a beeline to Aoyama and, in particular, the luxury shopping boulevard Omotesando, lined with zelkova trees and an amazing collection of modern architecture.

oyama is centred on the main axes of Aoyama-dori and Omotesando-dori. Tokyoites like to think of gently sloping **Omotesando-dori** as the capital's Champs Elysées, a boulevard whose chic designer label establishments carry a hallmark of quality. However, the boulevard was originally created as the frontal approach to the important shrine Meiji-jingu (see page 129). More recently it has also become known for its impressive stash of contemporary-designed buildings. This chapter covers the sights along and around Omotesando up to Meiji-dori; sights further west of here are covered in the chapter Harajuku and Shibuya (see page 137).

AOYAMA

Although there is little to remind you of Tokyo's past in Aoyama, where designer quarters, cosmopolitan tastes and sophistication reign today, the area was once home to lush rice paddies, hunting grounds and sprawling feudal estates. A close advisor of the shogun Tokugawa Ieyasu, Aoyama Tadanari, was given land here in 1590, the year Edo became the nation's martial capital.

Aoyama Cemetery ❶

In the years after the Meiji Restoration, these estates were turned into military parade grounds and cemeteries. **Aoyama Cemetery** (Aoyama Reien) was one of Tokyo's four largest burial grounds, created by the government after it had abandoned a rather quirky scheme to plant the area with mulberry trees in the hope of cultivating raw silk to export in exchange for foreign currency.

The area's arboreal dreams resurfaced, however, when hundreds of

The busy shopping area of Omotesando.

attractive cherry trees were planted later. The plaintive setting of the cemetery is perfect for the evanescence the cherry blossoms symbolise. Well over 100,000 people are buried here, including many of Tokyo's eminent political and military leaders, writers, a few notable foreigners and the ever-faithful dog Hachiko (see page 140). The cemetery can be approached from several directions but one of the easiest is to alight at the subway at Gaienmae station from where it's just a few minutes' walk south.

Baiso-in ❷

Address: 2-24-8 Minami-Aoyama, Minato-ku
Tel: 03-3404 8447
Opening Hours: 9am–5pm
Entrance Fee: free
Transport: Gaienmae
Many people choose to have a Buddhist funeral in Japan so it's common to find temples clustered around cemeteries. From Aoyama-dori, a corridor of lofty bamboo plants leads to Baiso-in, founded in 1643 as a family temple of the Aoyama clan. It is the 24th point on the Great 33 Kannon pilgrimage of temples in Tokyo and is also known for its Gujo-odori dance festival, which is held every June.

What is most unusual about the temple is its thoroughly modern main building, designed by Kengo Kuma, a famous local architect who is responsible for several other projects in the area. The coolly beautiful structure features plenty of glass shaded by steel louvres.

Meiji Memorial Picture Gallery ❸

Meiji Period
Address: 1-1 Kasumigaokamachi, Shinjuku-ku
Tel: 03-3401 5179
Website: www.meijijingugaien.jp/ english/seitoku-gallery.html
Opening Hours: daily 9am–5pm

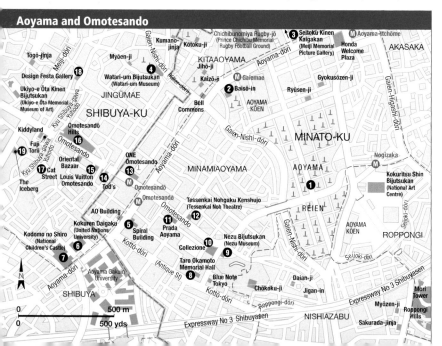

Aoyama and Omotesando

Aoyama Cemetery.

Entrance Fee: charge
Transport: Kokuritsu-Kyogijo

Heading northeast from Baison-in along Aoyama-dori, Icho-Namiki, better known as **Gingko Tree Avenue**, is on the left, equidistant between Gaienmae and Aoyama-Itchome metro stations. The trees are at their best in October when their leaves turn gold and yellow.

The avenue leads straight to the **Meiji Shrine Outer Gardens** (Meiji-Jingu Gaien), home to several sporting stadia, tennis courts, and baseball and golf practice ranges. The highlight, however, is the **Meiji Memorial Picture Gallery** (Seitoku Kinen Kaigakan), built in 1926 to commemorate the life and achievements of the Meiji Emperor. Solemn looking on the outside, its interior is more impressive, with a domed ceiling and an imposing stairwell made of marble from Gifu Prefecture. Its 80 Japanese- and Western-style works have detailed explanations in English. The gallery can also be approached

from the north from either the overground station Sendagaya or the subway station Kokuritsu-Kyogijo, in which case you'll pass both the **Tokyo Gymnasium** and **National Stadium** on the way.

Watari-um Museum ❹

Address: 3-7-6 Jingumae, Shibuya-ku
Tel: 03-3402 3001
Website: www.watarium.co.jp
Opening Hours: Tue–Sun 11am–7pm, Wed until 9pm
Entrance Fee: charge
Transport: Gaienmae

Heading back west in the direction of Gaienmae station, where Aoyama-dori crosses Gaien-Nishi-dori, turn right.

On the left side is the exposed concrete and black granite striped **Watari-um Museum** (Watari-um Bijutsukan), an ultra modern art space designed by Swiss architect Mario Botta in 1990. It features the work of some of today's best Japanese and international avant-garde artists.

FACT

The leaf of the gingko is the symbol of Tokyo. At the Meiji Shrine Outer Gardens, gingko trees were planted to commemorate the lives of the Meiji Emperor and the Empress Dowager Shoken.

Modern design on Minami-Aoyama.

and its centrepiece is a spiral ramp, a structure that floats and curves upwards to the next floor around the exhibition space below.

Of late, Spiral Hall has been given some competition in the architectural showstopper stakes by the **AO Building** (www.ao-aoyama. com), designed by Sakura Associates, which stands on the opposite side of the street. The glass tower, which looks spectacular when lit up at night, houses many top fashion boutiques, restaurants and, in the basement, the supermarket Kinokuniya whose original building once stood on this spot.

United Nations University ⑥

Just along from the AO Building is the **United Nations University** (Kokuren Daigaku; www.unu.edu), a development and coordination centre for the world peace organisation. Kenzo Tange, who won the Pritzker prize in 1987 – the equivalent of the Oscar in the architectural world – designed this UN facility. It's a symmetrical building with a solid main axis, said to represent well-intended authority. Every weekend one of Tokyo's best farmer's markets is held here.

National Children's Castle ⑦

Address: 5-53-1 Jingumae Shibuya-ku
Tel: 03-3797 5666
Website: www.kodomono-shiro.or.jp/english
Opening Hours: Tue–Fri 12.30–5.30pm, Sat–Sun 10am–5.30pm
Entrance Fee: charge
Transport: Omotesando

Built to commemorate the UN Year of the Child in 1979, the **National Children's Castle** (Kodomo-no-Shiro), next to the university, strikes a fun note. Several floors here are set aside for music and computer

Also in the building is a chilled out café and the excellent art bookshop **On Sundays.** Watch out when crossing Gaien Nishi-dori – it's also rather disconcertingly known as 'Killer-dori' on account of the huge number of traffic accidents that have occurred along it.

Spiral Building ⑤

Address: 5-6-23 Minami-Aoyama, Shibuya-ku
Tel: 03-3498 1171
Website: www.spiral.co.jp
Opening Hours: daily 8am–11pm
Entrance Fee: free
Transport: Omotesando

Return south to Aoyama-dori and continue west (take a right turn at the Bell Commons mall), past Omotesando, to discover the contemporary lines of the striking **Spiral Building**. Owned by the lingerie company Wacoal, the building incorporates a gallery, theatre, gift shop and café. The building is the work of leading architect Fumihiko Maki

TIP

Every weekend (Sat–Sun 10am–4pm) there is a farmers' market at the United Nation's University, where organic farmers and specialist food makers sell to the public. On the third Saturday of every month there is also a night market (www.farmersmarkets.jp).

rooms, an art space where kids can decorate the walls, jungle gyms and a rooftop playground. Everything here is beginning to show its age a little, but that doesn't stop the Castle from being a great place to let smaller kids go wild for an afternoon. Outside is the colourful, strange sculpture *Tree of Children* by Taro Okamoto, one of Japan's most prolific and zaniest artists.

Taro Okamoto Memorial Hall ❽

Address: 6-1-19 Minami-Aoyama, Minato-ku
Tel: 03-3406 0801
Website: www.taro-okamoto.or.jp
Opening Hours: Wed–Mon 10am–6pm
Entrance Fee: charge
Transport: Omotesando

More works by Okamoto can be seen at the **Tara Okamoto Memorial Hall** (Okamoto Taro Kinenkan), a small museum created out of an old studio, a short walk back towards Omotesando. To find it hang a right on **Kotto-dori**, also known as 'Antique Street', for its proliferation of antiques shops and art dealers, then duck into the backstreets near where you see the famous jazz club Blue Note Tokyo.

Nezu Museum ❾

Address: 6-5-1 Minami-Aoyama, Minato-ku
Tel: 03-3400 2536
Website: www.nezu-muse.or.jp
Opening Hours: Tue–Sun 10am–5pm
Entrance Fee: charge
Transport: Omotesando

Further along the street, down the same side street as Blue Note Tokyo, is the excellent **Nezu Museum** (Nezu Bijutsukan). In a beautiful new building designed by Kengo Kuma and opened in 2009, it houses the collection of Meiji-era politician and railway tycoon Kaichiro Nezu.

The museum's collection exceeds 7,000 pieces and among the permanent displays are fine examples of Chinese bronzes, ceramic and lacquerware, calligraphy, textiles and Chinese and Japanese paintings. Several exceedingly rare objects are registered as National Treasures. Among these is a screen painting by Ogata Korin called *Irises*, which is

Delicate screen painting of purple irises by Ogata Korin (1658-1716) – on display at the Nezu Museum.

Omotesando Hills has had a mixed reception.

TARO OKAMOTO

Taro Okamoto (1911–96) is remembered for the saying 'art is an explosion'. The Japanese avant-garde artist, who studied at Panthéon-Sorbonne in the 1930s, came to international attention in 1970 when his sculpture *Tower of the Sun* was the symbol of the World Expo held in Osaka.

In Aoyama, Okamoto's home and studio is now a museum while his *Tree of Children* sculpture stands in front of the National Children's Castle. A corridor in Shibuya Station houses his monumental mural *Myth of Tomorrow*. Further afield is the Taro Okamoto Museum of Art (www.taromuseum.jp), in the artist's birthplace of Kawasaki, between Tokyo and Yokohama.

SHOPPING

Antiques, Arts and Crafts

Fuji-Torii
6-1-10 Jingumae, Shibuya-ku. Tel: 03-3400 2777. www.fuji-torii.com p276, C3
Specialises in traditional screens and *Imari* porcelain. Has helpful English-speaking staff who can assist with international shipping.

Kawano Gallery
102 Flats-Omotesando, 4-4-9 Jingumae, Shibuya-ku. Tel: 03-3470 3305. p276, C3
Stocks a wide range of colourful used and vintage kimonos, *yukata* and *obi*.

Oriental Bazaar
5-9-13 Jingumae, Shibuya-ku. Tel: 03-3400 3933. www.orientalbazaar.co.jp p276, C3/C4
A nice place to pick up traditional toys, *washi* paper, pottery and kimonos. It also stocks some reasonably priced antiques.

Books

On Sundays
Watari-um Museum, 3-7-6 Jingumae, Shibuya-ku. Tel: 03-3470 1424. www.watarium.co.jp/onsundays p276, C3
A museum store with art, photography and architecture books, and a great selection of postcards.

Fashion

Bape Exclusive
5-5-8 Minami-Aoyama, Minato-ku. Tel: 03-3407 2145. www.bape.com p276, C4
Once one of Tokyo's fashion underground, A Bathing Ape is now an established brand.

Comme des Garçons
5-2-1 Minami Aoyama, Minato-ku. Tel: 03-3406 3951. p276, C4
Matt-black chic and other brighter tones from legendary designer Rei Kawakubo are offered here.

Hysteric Glamour
5-5-3 Minami Aoyama, Minato-ku. Tel: 03-6419 3899. www.hystericglamour.jp p276, C4
Americana with a youthful Japa-nese twist or two. There are other branches around Tokyo, including in Roppongi Hills and Shibuya.

Issey Miyake
3-18-11 Minami Aoyama, Minato-ku. Tel: 03-3423 1407. www.isseymikaye.co.jp p276, C4
Miyake continues his experimentation with fabrics and curious shapes and forms. The window displays are often startling. Across the road from Prada Aoyama.

Loveless
3-17-11 Minami-Aoyama, Minato-ku. Tel: 03-3401 2301. www.loveless-shop.jp p276, C4
Hyper-hip basement boutique showcasing a range of up-and-coming Japanese designers.

Prada Aoyama
5-2-6 Minami-Aoyama, Minato-ku. Tel: 03-6418 0400. p276, C4
Stock up on the clothes and accessories of Miuccia Prada as well as admiring the dazzling architecture by Herzog & de Meuron.

Sou Sou
5-3-10 Minami Aoyama, Minato-ku. Tel: 03-3407 7877. www.sousou.co.jp p276, C4
Affordable and contemporary takes on traditional clothing and footwear; Sou Sou offers styles unique even by Aoyama standards.

Tsumori Chisato
4-21-25 Minami-Aoyama, Minato-ku. Tel: 03-3423 5170. www.tsumorichisato.com p276, C4
The ever-youthful Paris-based Ms. Tsumori's vibrant colours and designs cater to a wide age range.

Yohji Yamamoto
5-3-6 Minami-Aoyama, Minato-ku. Tel: 03-3409 6006. www.yohjiyamamoto.co.jp p276, C4
Flagship store of the respected designer stocking his trademark designs in flattering dark hues.

Food

Kinokuniya
3-11-7 Minami-Aoyama, Minato-ku. Tel: 03-3409 1231. http://super-kinokuniya.jp p276, C4
This high-class delicatessen and wine shop is great for imported food items like cheeses, processed meats and sausages.

Homewares and Interior Design

Cibone
B1F Aoyama Bell Commons, 2-14-6 Kita-Aoyama, Minato-ku. Tel: 03-3475 8017 www.cibone.com p276, C3
Check out pieces by local designers. Also sells books and CDs.

Jewellery

Niwaka
313 Minami Aoyama Building, 3-13-18 Minami-Aoyama, Minato-ku. Tel: 03-3796 0803. www.niwaka.com Off map
The elegant boutique of a Kyoto-based bauble manufacturer.

Shopping Mall

Omotesando Hills
4-12-10 Jingumae, Shibuya-ku. Tel: 03-3497 0310. www.omotesandohills.com p276, C3
Premium shopping destination where you can get everything from quality *sake* to the hippest *Harajuku*-style threads.

Stationery

Winged Wheel
4-5-4 Jingumae, Shibuya-ku. Tel: 03-5785 0719. www.winged-wheel.co.jp p276, C3
Have your name cards and letter paper embossed with beautiful designs, traditional and modern.

Toys

Kiddyland
6-1-9 Jingumae, Shibuya-ku. Tel: 03-3409 3431. www.kiddyland.co.jp p276, B3
One of Tokyo's best toy stores; four floors of character goods, games and the latest gadgets.

displayed for a month each year at the end of April when the museum is very busy.

As much as the art, the highlight of the museum is its lovely garden in a densely wooded and hilly landscape with a small iris pond and a number of traditional teahouses. None of these are open to the public, but in his renovation of the property, Kuma added a modern café that provides a wonderful view of the gardens and is a lovely spot for lunch or tea.

OMOTESANDO

From the Nezu Museum, turn left into the start of Aoyama's principal shopping destination: Omotesando.

Architectural statements

On the left is the striking mass of concrete, glass and aluminium panels that make up **Collezione** ⓾, a 1989 work by well-known architect Tadao Ando. Completely self-taught, the Osaka-born Ando was a boxer before turning to creating buildings. The inspiration for this 'strata architecture', as Ando calls it, came from a visit to an Indian well where, descending to the water's edge, 'the eyes perceive gradations of light and the skin experiences a reduction in temperature.'

Even more arresting is **Prada Aoyama** ⓫ completed in 2004 and just further along on the same side. A diamond-shaped, steel latticework wraps around the building, creating the effect of a three-sided column of bubble wrap. The design is the work of Swiss architecture firm Herzog & de Meuron, who are reported to have said, 'We could only do this building here in Japan.' Across the street from Prada, and nowhere near as impressive on the eye on the outside, is the **Tessenkai Noh Theatre** ⓬ (www.tessen.org). Inside, however, the theatre's stark wooden stage, which is accented by ornately painted backdrops, is a thing of beauty.

Heading across Aoyama-dori, into the heart of Omotesando, the roll call of modern architectural masters reaches fever pitch. First on the right is **ONE Omotesando** ⓭ where Kengo Kuma's trademark steel louvres are again in evidence on a building that houses several boutiques.

On the opposite side of the zelkova-lined avenue, the branches of the trees are the clear inspiration for the bands of concrete and angled panes of glass wrapping the facade of shoe boutique **Tod's** ⓮, the work of architect Toyo Ito. Next door is **Louis Vuitton Omotesando** ⓯, the flagship store of the luxury brand. It was designed by Jun Aoki to resemble a series of stacked ornamental boxes, and looks as if a giant has left his Vuitton luggage piled up on the sidewalk.

Omotesando Hills ⓰

From the exterior, **Omotesando Hills** – another Tadao Ando design – appears a relatively modest, low-key structure. But this is deceptive since the luxury shopping mall and

Funky Cat Street in Omotesando offers more affordable shopping options.

Shoppers outside the Hermes store.

Brightly painted signs direct visitors towards an exhibition at the Design Festa Gallery.

apartment complex is best viewed from inside where the space opens up to reveal a 12-storey building with a huge atrium, half of which is buried underground. Ando's complex replaced the ivy-covered Dojunkai Apartments dating from 1927 which were much loved and missed: the architect paid homage to them by recreating a small section of the apartments and incorporating it into his design (at the far south end of the complex).

Opposite Omotesando Hills are several other shops you'll most likely want to check out including the antiques and souvenir shops **Oriental Bazaar** and **Fuji Torii**, and the toy-shop **Kiddyland** (see page 132).

Cat Street ⑰

Kiddyland is on corner of the junction with Kyu Shibuya-gawa, a sinewy retail promenade that follows the path of the cemented-over Shibuya River. It's more popularly known as Cat Street and provides a funkier, more youthful and affordable counterpoint to the high gloss,

luxury brand shopping experience of Omotesando. Heading south the street shadows Meiji-dori, which it eventually joins to bring you to Shibuya Station.

Design Festa Gallery ⑱

Address: 3-20-2 Jingumae, Shibuya-ku
Tel: 03-3479 1442
Website: www.designfestagallery.com
Opening Hours: daily 11am–8pm
Entrance Fee: free
Transport: Meiji-Jingumae

Follow Cat Street northeast from Omotesando to the point where there's a fork in the road, then take the left-hand lane to reach one of the entrances to the **Design Festa Gallery**, an anarchic explosion of contemporary art galleries that have taken over several old houses and an apartment block. The art here reaches beyond the exhibition spaces to engulf every part of the complex, from the paint-bombed toilets and graffiti-covered trash cans to the friendly café-bar and *okonomi-yaki* restaurant Sakuratei (see page 135). It's great fun to explore this ever-interesting complex, which has grown out of a twice-yearly design event of the same name that takes place at Tokyo Big Sight on Odaiba (see page 220).

The Iceberg ⑲

There's one more contemporary structure worth seeing before moving on from this area. From the junction of Omotesando and Meiji-dori, head south until you reach, on the left, the Audi Forum (www.audi.co.jp/jp/brand/aft). This showroom for the German car manufacturer is housed in a building known, for obvious reasons, as The Iceberg. Designed by British-born, Tokyo-based architect Benjamin Warner, this multifaceted glass tower looks as if it has floated to Tokyo from the Antarctic.

BEST RESTAURANTS, BARS AND CAFÉS

PRICE CATEGORIES

Prices for a three-course dinner per person without drinks and taxes:

¥ = under ¥2,000
¥¥ = ¥2,000–¥3,000
¥¥¥ = ¥3,000–¥5,000
¥¥¥¥ = over ¥5,000

Restaurants

French

Benoit
La Port Aoyama, 10F, 5-51-8 Jingumae, Shibuya-ku. Tel: 03-6419 4181. www.benoit-tokyo.com Open: L & D daily. ¥¥¥ **45** p276, C4
Compared with Beige in Ginza, the other restaurant opened by Michelin-starred chef Alain Ducasse, Benoit is more informal and affordable, and focuses on Mediterranean flavours. Dinner courses range from ¥3,600 to ¥8,300.

Indian

Nataraj
Sanwa-Aoyama Building, B1F, 2-22-19 Minami-Aoyama, Minato-ku. Tel: 03-5474 0510. www.nataraj.co.jp Open: L & D daily. ¥¥ **46** p276, D3
Tokyo's foremost Indian vegetarian restaurant serves a range of curries and grills from the tandoor oven. Spice levels are generally mild but can be toned up on request. Also has a branch in Ginza.

Japanese

Heirokuzushi
5-8-5 Jingumae, Shibuya-ku. Tel: 03-3498 3968. Open: daily 11am–9.30pm. ¥¥¥¥ **47** p276, C4
Popular and affordable *kaiten-zushi* restaurant handily located amid the high-end opulence of Omotesando. Plates start from ¥130.

Maisen
4-8-5 Jingumae, Shibuya-ku. Tel: 0120-428 485. Open: daily 11am–10pm. ¥¥ **48** p276, C3
The main branch of a large chain serving reliable *tonkatsu* (deep-

fried breaded pork cutlets). Besides pork, the menu also includes deep-fried chicken and oysters.

Sakuratei
3-20-1 Jingumae, Shibuya-ku. Tel: 03-3479 0039. www.sakuratei.co.jp Open: daily 11.30am–11pm. ¥ **49** p276, C4
Tucked away in a courtyard in the Design Festa complex is this fun, inexpensive place where you can try your hand at cooking *okonomiyaki* (savoury batter pancake), or *yakisoba* (fried noodles).

Ume no Hana
2-27-18 Minami-Aoyama, Minato-ku. Tel: 03-5412 0855. www.umenohana.co.jp Open: L & D daily. ¥¥¥ **50** p276, C3/D3
Tofu and *yuba* (tofu curd) served in traditional surrounds. The tofu is prepared in many ways: in hotpots, steamed, with crabmeat, with *fugu* (blowfish), chilled with delicate toppings, and more. You can go à la carte, but it's easier (and more fun) opting for one of the courses.

Korean

Jap Cho Ok
Alteka Belte Plaza, B1F, 4-1-15 Minami-Aoyama, Minato-ku. Tel: 03-5410 3408. Open: D daily. ¥¥¥ **51** p276, D4
This spot near Aoyama Cemetery proves that there's much more to Korean cuisine than just barbecue beef and *kimchee* (pickled vegetables). The menu includes seafood dishes and even Zen Buddhist vegetarian temple cooking. Reservations are recommended.

Scandinavian

Aquavit
2-5-8 Kita-Aoyama, Minato-ku. Tel: 03-5413 3300. www.aquavit-japan.com Open: L & D daily. ¥¥¥¥ **52** p276, D3
Chef Marcus Samuelsson brings New York style to his elegant Tokyo outpost, offering a contemporary take on Scandinavian cuisine.

Vegetarian

Hiroba
3-8-15 Kita-Aoyama, Minato-ku. Tel:

03-3406 6409. Open: L & D daily. ¥¥ **53** p276, C4
The basement of children's bookstore Crayon House features this organic (but not entirely vegetarian) restaurant with a nicely priced buffet lunch.

Pure Café
5-5-21 Minami-Aoyama, Minato-ku. Tel: 03-5466 2611. www.pure-cafe.com Open: daily 8.30am–10.30pm. ¥ **54** p276, C4
Housed inside the Aveda beauty salon, this self-service café serves vegan and additive-free breakfasts and light meals.

Bars and Cafés

Anniversaire Cafe
3-5-30 Kita-Aoyama, Minato-ku. Tel: 03-5411 5988. www.anniversaire.co.jp **13** p276, C4
Chic Parisian-style café, with terrace tables facing onto Omotesando for prime people watching. Anniversaire's staff tend to be young actors, so you might be getting served by a future star.

Helmsdale
Minami-Aoyama Mori Building, 2F, 7-13-12 Minami-Aoyama, Minato-ku. www.helmsdale-fc.com Tel: 03-3486 4220 **14** p276, D4
Alongside a good range of ales, this Scottish pub-restaurant boasts a remarkable whisky list, with over 300 single-malts. The menu includes Scotch eggs and haggis.

Montoak
6-1-9 Jingumae, Shibuya-ku. Tel: 03-5468 5928. www.montoak.com **15** p276, C3
Three-storey hipster bar and café with contemporary interiors and a very laid-back vibe. Good light lunches and dinner, and DJs playing on most evenings.

Yoku Moku
5-3-3 Minami-Aoyama, Minato-ku. Tel: 03-5485 3330. **16** p276, C4
Famous for its crisp, wafer-thin biscuits, this blue-tiled café, with lovely outdoor patio, is an elegant place to pause for refreshments.

HARAJUKU AND SHIBUYA

While Harajuku, home of the stately Meiji Shrine, has a few time-honoured reminders of the past, Shibuya is firmly wedged in the present, partying (and shopping) with youthful vigour.

Harajuku has become well known beyond Tokyo as a byword for youthful style. On any day of the week you need only linger around the station – take your pick from either the Takeshita-dori end or by the top of Omotesando – to see many a prime example of the so-called 'Harajuku Girls': women whose fearless fashion sense results in looks ranging from *kawaii* (super cute) Victorian doll meets punk rock princess to the edgier Goth-loli (standing for Gothic Lolita) glamazon.

Back in the 11th century, Harajuku was a post station on the Kamakura Kaido, the road to the wild northern provinces. Hara, in fact, means 'field', juku, a 'place of lodging'. Beyond the area's multitude of cafés there are hardly any places for travellers to rest these days but even so, among Harajuku's swirl of boutiques and fashion houses and other contemporary implants are reminders of an older city in the roadside shrines and cultural museums.

Ukiyo-e Ota Memorial Museum of Art ❶

Address: 1-10-10 Jingumae, Shibuya-ku
Tel: 03-3403 0880

Website: www.ukiyoe-ota-muse.jp
Opening Hours: Tue–Sun 10.30am–5.30pm
Entrance Fee: charge
Transport: Harajuku

A short stroll from the intersection of Meiji-dori and Omotesando-dori, just behind the boutique complex Laforet is the **Ukiyo-e Ota Memorial Museum of Art** (Ukiyo-e Ota Kinen Bijutsukan) with what is arguably the city's finest collection of Edo-Period *ukiyo-e* woodblock prints, over 12,000 works in all, including

Fancy dress shop in Harajuku.

Eye-catching sign on Takeshita-dori.

extremely rare prints by artists such as Utamaru, Sharaku and Hiroshige. Visitors have to remove their shoes before entering the museum.

Takeshita-dori ②

A short walk northeast from the museum the atmosphere couldn't be more different on **Takeshita-dori**, a pedestrian street that runs between Meiji-dori and Harajuku Station. Cheap fashion, accessories, cuddly toys, 'idol goods' and fast food restaurants lure teenagers for a taste of distilled subcultural kitsch. It can get very busy along this shopping strip, particularly at weekends when the street is as packed as a Tokyo train at rush hour.

Togo-jinja ③

Address: 1-5-3 Jingumae, Shibuya-ku
Tel: 03-3403 3591
Opening Hours: daily 8am–5pm
Entrance Fee: free
Transport: Harajuku

Behind Takeshita-dori, but light years away in spirit are the peaceful grounds of the **Togo-jinja**, a shrine dedicated to Admiral Heihachiro Togo, whose ships defeated the Russian fleet in the Tsushima Straits during the 1904–5 Russo-Japanese

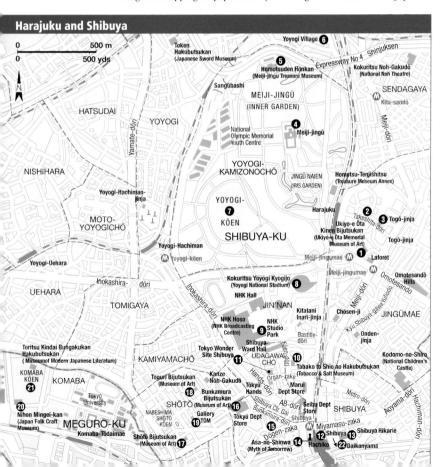

War. The original building was destroyed in a World War II air raid, but was rebuilt along with the Togo Memorial Hall and a treasury.

Meiji-jingu and gardens ❹

Exiting west out of Takeshita-dori, the mock-Tudor facade of **Harajuku Station** (Harajuku-eki) comes into view as you climb the hill. Designed in 1924, it is one of the few Tokyo stations to have survived intact from that era. The station abuts one of Tokyo's major sights, the Imperial shrine **Meiji-jingu.** To reach the main entrance to the shrine, you have to pass across an open plaza above the railway tracks, a popular spot on weekends for cosplay-dressed kids, buskers and other street performers, and then through the **Ichi-no-torii**, a massive gate made from 1,700-year-old cypress trees taken from Mount Alishan in Taiwan.

The shrine, opened in 1920 and dedicated to the memory of the Meiji Emperor and his wife, Empress Shoken, is tucked in the centre of **Meiji Shrine Inner Gardens** (Meiji-Jingu Gyoen), an expanse of dense forest of over 125,000 trees and shrubs brought from all over Japan. The park's famous **Iris Garden** (Jingu Naien; daily Mar–Oct 9am–4.30pm, Nov–Feb 9am–4pm; charge), where over 100 varieties come into bloom in mid-June, was designed by the Meiji Emperor for his wife. The benches by the garden's carp-filled pond are some of the most peaceful places in central Tokyo.

The shrine itself, about 1km (.5 mile) from the entrance, is a sublimely beautiful example of Shinto architecture, with its plain cypress pillars, sweeping copper roof and a white gravel forecourt. The original buildings burnt down in an air raid; what you see today is a perfect 1958 reconstruction. The compound, with its shrine maidens in white kimonos and orange tunics, plays host to lively events including formal Japanese weddings.

Wooden votive tablets outside Meiji-jingu in Harajuku.

Meiji-jingu Treasure Museum ❺

Address: 1-1 Yoyogi-Kamizonocho, Shibuya-ku
Tel: 03-3261 8326
Website: www.meijijungu.or.jp
Opening Hours: daily Mar–Oct 9am–4.30pm, Nov–Feb 9am–4pm
Entrance Fee: charge
Transport: Kita-sando

Located in the northern section of the park, the **Treasure** Museum (Homotsuden Honkan), in a building dating from 1921, displays a rather modest collection of sacred objects, garments and personal effects of the Imperial family. There's also a modern annex (Homotsu-Tenjishitsu) with a further display hall in a modern building near the main entrance to the shrine.

Detail of Meiji-jingu.

Yoyogi Village ❻

Address: 1-28-9 Yoyogi, Shibuya-ku
Tel: 03-5302 2073

Rockabilly fans in Yoyogi Park.

Website: www.yoyogi-village.jp
Opening Hours: daily 10am – 7pm (cafés and bar open much later)
Entrance Fee: free
Transport: Yoyogi

A five-minute walk northeast of the Treasure Museum is this very hip eco-friendly 'village' of stores in Yoyogi. Opened in 2011, the two-storey complex was put together by the producer of Japanese pop-rock band Mr. Children in collaboration with trend-conscious company Kurkku, who run an organic café and shop in Omotesando. As well as half a dozen or so stores, the Village is home to a chilled out café, an organic Italian restaurant, a spa, and very trendy bar that attracts a good line-up of local DJs.

Yoyogi Park ❼

Fringing the southwestern borders of the Meiji-jingu Inner Gardens is another generous swathe of green, **Yoyogi Park** (Yoyogi Koen). American military personnel and their families were billeted here for several years after the war when the area was known as Washington Heights. The land was handed back to the Japanese government and turned into a village for athletes attending the Tokyo Olympics in 1964.

Ever since then the park has been a favourite gathering place for Tokyo's rockabilly devotees particularly on weekends and holidays when quiff-haired, leather-jacket boys and hoop skirted and bobby sock-clad girls can be found twisting to Elvis and the music of other rock legends. There's often free entertainment at weekends in the centre of the park from musicians, mime artists and other street performers. **Earthday Market** (www.earthdaymarket.com) selling organic food and drink and other eco-friendly products, is also held here one Sunday each month.

Opposite Harajuku station and the main entrance to Yoyogi Park is **Yoyogi National Stadium** (Kokuritsu Yoyogi Kyogijo) ❽. Used for the 1964 Olympic Game's swimming and diving events Kenzo Tange's highly original design looks remarkably contemporary even today. The smaller No. 2 Gymnasium, also part of the complex, houses a basket-ball court. Despite being born out of the Olympics, there are concerns that the Olympics could eventually

---

HACHIKO THE FAITHFUL

A popular rendezvous spot for the youths who throng Shibuya is a small bronze statue of a dog named Hachiko, which stands in front of the Hachiko exit at Shibuya Station. Hachiko accompanied his owner Ueda Eisaburo, a university professor, to the station each day and waited for his return in the evening, a pattern that continued until a spring day in 1925, when his master died while teaching a class. Undaunted, Hachiko returned each day to the same spot to wait, even after the professor's relatives had moved the dog to Asakusa, a distance away. In order to shorten the tireless dog's daily treks to the station, a new home was found for him in nearby Yoyogi.

Commuters grew fond of the dog and, after the newspaper *Asahi Shimbun* ran the story in 1932, Hachiko's fame as a symbol of almost samurai-like loyalty was assured. A bronze statue was unveiled in 1935, and a special ceremony is held every year on 8 April to honour Hachiko's memory. When Hachiko died at age 13, the responsibility for his immortalisation passed into the hands of taxidermists. The very life-like Hachiko can be seen encased in Tokyo's National Science Museum (see page 175).

Outside the Tobacco and Salt Museum.

sound Yoyogi Park's death knell. If Tokyo's bid for the 2020 Summer Games is a success, the park and the current sport venues will be expected to make way for new facilities – that's one of the reasons many Tokyoites are decidedly lukewarm on the idea of Tokyo 2020. There is also the feeling that the campaign money and redevelopment costs could be better used to speed the post-3/11 earthquake recovery in Tohoku.

SHIBUYA

During the late Edo Period, Shibuya sat on the western outskirts of the city, marking the transition from urban to rural. It is difficult to imagine that, only a century ago, this stridently trendy district, with its love hotels and consumer implants, was a place of tea plantations and rice mills.

NHK Studio Park ❾

Address: 2-2-1 Jinnan, Shibuya-ku
Tel: 03-3485 8034
Website: www.nhk.or.jp/studiopark
Opening Hours: daily 10am–6pm.
Entrance Fee: charge
Transport: Shibuya

Next to the sports stadia is the **NHK Broadcasting Centre**, the national television and radio headquarters, which has its main entrance on Inokashira-dori. Tours (only in Japanese) of its **Studio Park** complex, with its entrance near Koen-dori, offer the chance to see programmes as they are filmed, play around with broadcasting technology and become acquainted with NHK's big mouthed mascot Domo-kun.

Tobacco and Salt Museum ❿

Address: 1-16-8 Jinnan, Shibuya-ku
Website: www.jti.co.jp/Culture/museum
Tel: 03-3476 2041
Opening Hours: Tue–Sun 10am–6pm
Entrance Fee: charge
Transport: Shibuya

A five-minute walk directly south of the NHK complex, along Koen-dori, is the **Tobacco and Salt Museum** (Tabako to Shio no Hakubutsukan). The museum is less of an abnormality than you might think, in a country where tobacco consumption is distressingly high. Salt and tobacco were a government monopoly until the early 20th century. Even after sales were liberalised, it remained under strict state control until 1985.

The museum, built from the lucrative profits of Japan Tobacco Inc. (formerly the Japan Tobacco and Salt Public Corporation), traces the history of salt and tobacco production in Japan and overseas through fascinating displays that include smoking implements and salt sculptures. The highlight is the fourth-floor special exhibition of *ukiyo-e* woodblock prints of courtesans and other Edo-Period figures in relaxed poses as they prepare their pipes.

Tokyo Wonder Site Shibuya ⓫

Address: 1-19-8 Jin'nan, Shibuya-ku
Tel: 03-3463 0603

An interactive display at the TEPCO Electric Energy Museum.

Tokyo's Love Hotels

In a city where space is at a premium, it's no wonder that the love hotel business rakes in trillions of yen each year.

While you'll find clusters of so-called 'love hotels' in all of Tokyo's major entertainment centres, it is Shibuya's Dogenzaka area that is best known for these establishments that rent rooms by the hour. Given that many couples share homes with their families or just don't want to bring their partner back to a cramped apartment that is likely to be miles from work in the centre of town, love hotels provide a valuable service for many. And not just love-struck youth; they are also commonly used by prostitutes and cheating spouses: one study found that on average 2 percent of Japan's population (2.6 million people) visit a love hotel every day.

There's a long history of such establishments in Japan, dating back to the 'tea-

A love hotel in the Shibuya district.

houses' of feudal times where travellers could find prostitutes. In the post-war period the term *tsurekome yado* (bring along inn) was adopted and there's even a move today by some places to label themselves as 'fashion' or 'couples' hotels. Euphemistic, romantic or curious hotel names such as Casanova, Hotel Chez Moi, Dixy Inn and P&A Plaza abound. There's only a small chance of you stumbling into one by mistake, though, since they all have quite distinctive and common features.

First up you'll always see a sign outside that advertises rates for either a 'rest' or 'stay': the rest period can vary from one to three hours (with day-time discounts sometimes available) while the stay period usually runs from after 10 or 11pm to 10am. There's also a trend to build love hotels in various wacky kitsch styles and themes – there's a famous one in Meguro resembling a fairytale castle.

The entrance to the hotel is almost always hidden behind a wall to protect users' privacy, a level of discretion that continues inside with dim lighting and minimal contact between customers and staff. Quite often there's no receptionist at all, but instead a push button panel displaying illuminated pictures of each of the rooms available and their rates. Pay attention to this as many love hotels offer themed rooms with all manner of special features beyond the usual mirrored ceilings, waterbeds and Jacuzzi bathtubs. You may find karaoke and video game machines, all manner of sex toys and other dressing-up paraphernalia. Windows are rare – it's not the view from the hotel that you're paying for!

Knowing that it's often the woman who chooses the love hotel, some places offer luxurious boutique-hotel style rooms, making them a great place to indulge the sybarite in you whether you plan to have fun with a partner or not. Rates range from around ¥8,000 for a three hour stay to ¥16,000 for an overnight stay and as with anything you get what you pay for. To find out more see *Love Hotels* by Ed Jacob, while the site www.lovehomap.com details in Japanese many popular Tokyo establishments.

Website: www.tokyo-ws.org/English
Opening Hours: Tue–Sun
11am–7pm
Entrance Fee: free
Transport: Shibuya

One block southwest of the Tobacco and Salt Museum along Koen-dori, on the ground floor of the Shibuya Workers Welfare Hall, is a gallery that's part of the **Tokyo Wonder Site**. It's always worth taking a look at what's going on at this project dedicated to the generation and promotion of contemporary art and culture in Tokyo.

Across the road there are a couple more gallery spaces within the fashion department store Parco Part 1: **Parco Museum** (tel: 03-3477 5873; www.parco-art.com; daily 10am–9pm; charge) on the third floor and Logos **Gallery** Parco Factory (tel: 03-3496 1287; www.parco-art.com; daily 10am–9pm; free) in the basement. The exhibitions focus on accessible pop-cultural themes and art, thus are well matched to the store's youthful consumers.

Shibuya Station ⑫

Both Meiji-dori and Koen-dori lead south down towards the human congestion of Shibuya Station (Shibuya-eki). Along with the exodus of people who moved into the western suburbs after the 1923 Kanto Earthquake, Shibuya-eki played a significant role in the growth of the area. What really put the district on the map were the choice of Shibuya as the site for the terminals for the Inokashira and Toyoko lines, and the incorporation of the Ginza and Hanzomon subway lines.

More recently they have been joined by the Fukutoshin subway line in an underground terminal designed by Tadao Ando – the plan is for this to eventually link up with the Tokyu Toyoko Line that runs to Yokohama (see page 229). Above ground to the east of the station, **Shibuya Hikarie**, a

Young shoppers in the Shibuya district.

34-storey tower containing shops, restaurants, offices and cultural facilities including a 2,000-seat theatre, modernised the area even further when it opened in 2012.

The plaza in front of the station's northwest exit – better known as the Hachiko exit (see page 140) – is the site of one of the city's most otherworldly concentrations of neon advertisements, giant video screens and illuminated glass.

Shibuya Hikarie ⑬

Address: 2-21-1 Shibuya, Shibuya-ku
Tel: 03-5468 5892
Website: www.hikarie.jp
Opening Hours: daily 10am–9pm
(restaurants until 11pm)
Entrance Fee: free
Transport: Shibuya

The newest landmark on the block, opened in 2012, is the 34-storey **Shibuya Hikarie** commercial complex connected to the east side of

SHOPPING

Both Harajuku and Shibuya are great places to catch the latest Japanese street fashions and gadgets.

Aoi Art
4-22-11 Yoyogi, Shibuya-ku. Tel: 03-3375 5553. www.aoi-art.com p276, B4
Shop for authentic antique pieces, sold by a long-established dealer in Japanese swords and armour.

Crafts and DIY

Tokyu Hands
12-18 Udagawa-cho, Shibuya-ku. Tel: 03-5489 5111. www.tokyu-hands.co.jp p276, B4
A fascinating hardware and craft-making store stocking things you'd be hard pressed to find elsewhere in Tokyo, as well as many novelty goods that make wonderful souvenirs.

Shibuya Crossing.

Department Stores

Loft
21-1 Udagawa-cho, Shibuya-ku. Tel: 03-3462 3807. www.loft.co.jp p276, B4
Part of the Seibu empire in Shibuya this store specialises mainly in fun interior decoration and other accessories.

ShinQs
2-21-1 Shibuya, Shibuya-ku. Tel: 03-5468 5892. www.hikarie.jp p276, B4/C4
Combining food, beauty, fashion and lifestyle goods, all presented in uber-modern surroundings. ShinQs occupies eight floors above and below ground in Shibuya Hikarie.

Tokyu Honten
2-24-1 Dogenzaka, Shibuya-ku. Tel: 03-3477 3111. www.tokyu-dept.co.jp/honten p276, B4
Start by browsing designer fashions and high-end home goods, then head down to the basement where there's a delicious range of foods to sample.

DVDs and Music

Recofan
4F Shibuya BEAM, 31-2 Udagawacho, Shibuya-ku. Tel: 03-3463 0090. www.recofan.co.jp p276, B4
This chain store is a good place to hunt for second-hand CDs and also used vinyl.

Tower Records
1-22-14 Jinnan, Shibuya-ku. Tel: 03-3496 3661. http://tower.jp p276, B4
Shibuya is well known for its record stores – this is one of the biggest. The seventh floor also has a wide selection of English books and magazines.

Fashion

109 Building
2-29-1 Dogenzaka, Shibuya-ku. Tel: 03-3477 5111. www.shibuya109.jp p276, B4
Even if you don't fit into the targeted teenage demographic, just walking through the countless boutiques filled with young fashionistas and echoing with loud dance music is quite the adventure.

Hysteric Glamour
6-23-2 Jingumae, Shibuya-ku. Tel: 03-3797 5910. www.hystericglamour.jp p276, B4
This highly distinctive store sells a famous line of graphic T-shirts and other hippy-chic clothes.

Laforet
1-11-6 Jingumae, Shibuya-ku. Tel: 03-3475 0411. www.laforet.ne.jp p276, B4
A Harajuku landmark full of small and innovative boutiques, as well as a branch of Topshop.

Parco
15-1 Udagawa-cho, Shibuya-ku. Tel: 03-3464 5111. www.parco-shipuya.com p276, B4
Split into three main parts (Part 1, Zero Gate, and Part 3), this fashion boutique offers a wide range of local and international designers at pretty affordable prices.

Shopping Malls

Daikanyama Address Dixsept
17 Daikanyamacho, Shibuya-ku. Tel: 03-3461 6492. www.17dixsept.jp
Off map
A small but stylish retail complex that attracts those who monitor the Tokyo fashion scene. Besides two floors of boutiques there are also several nice cafés and restaurants.

La Fuente
11-1 Sarugakucho, Shibuya-ku. Tel: 03-3462 8401. www.lafuente-daikanyama.com Off map
Another winning Daikanyama retail complex located right near Daikanyama. La Fuente has a Tsumori Chisato boutique and a branch of Sedona, a groovy mix of new and old clothes, in addition to a half dozen or so good cafés, bars and restaurants to choose from.

Shibuya Station – the area's answer to developments like Roppongi Hills and Tokyo Midtown. From the basement up to the fifth floor Hikarie is home to the ultra-fashionable **ShinQs department store**, which combines deli and food floors, fashion, cosmetics, and lifestyle goods. Above that are restaurant floors and a **five-floor theatre**, as well as a hipster-attracting 'creative space' on the eighth floor that brings together a café, museum, gallery and travel store. The rest of the glistening complex is comprised of offices.

Myth of Tomorrow ⓮

Look up from the Hachiko statue and you'll see a pedestrian corridor bridging across from the Tokyu Toyoko department store to the terminus for the Keio-Inokashira Line (which you can hop on later to visit the Japan Folk Crafts Museum, see page 147). In this corridor is the giant 14-panel painting **Myth of Tomorrow** (Asu no Shinwa) by Okamoto Taro (1911–1996), a powerful Guernica-like mural of the atomic bomb explosion. Originally created

SHIMO–KITAZAWA

Four stops west of Shibuya, where the Keio Inokashira Line crosses the Odakyu Line from Shinjuku, is the counter-cultural hub of Shimo-Kitazawa. The word that best describes this shabby but vibrant district is eclectic. Its carefully cultivated collegiate ambience, the assorted bric-a-brac and clothing shops, used record stores and offbeat bookstores, not to mention its lively mix of restaurants and bars, suggest a kind of Ivy League junk shop. The area grew off the back of a black market that existed after World War II and also happens to be packed with tiny live music houses and theatres. Plans to create a major new road means locals fear some of the area's chaotic charm will be destroyed. For details see www.shimokitazawa.org.

in the late 1960s for a luxury hotel in Mexico, the monumental work was rediscovered in 2003 and took five years to be restored and find its new home in the station. For more about Okamoto see page 131.

Dogenzaka ⓯

Immediately west of Shibuya Station's Hachiko exit, the **109 Building** – a striking silver capsule resembling a silo and housing a fashion emporium that embodies the trends and culture of the teenage girls who play a leading role in Japanese consumer culture – forms a wedge between Bunkamura-dori and Dogenzaka-dori, the slope that splits off to the left. The hilly area of **Dogenzaka** gets its name from a 13th-century highwayman, Owada Dogen, who attacked travellers here as they passed up the slope towards the mountains.

The narrow backstreets that snake around the slope, offering short-stay rooms in dozens of whimsically designed buildings, have given rise to its nickname: 'Love Hotel Hill' (see page 142). Dogenzaka's nightlife does not revolve exclusively around discreet carnality. This tiny but enthralling area, with cosy restaurants – some offering dishes regarded as sexually fortifying, such as grilled eel – old coffee shops and corner shrines, has a lively music night scene with rock venues like O-East and its counterpart O-West, and nightclubs such as Womb and Club Asia (see page 256).

Bunkamura Museum of Art ⓰

Address: 2-24-1Dogenzaka, Shibuya-ku
Tel: 03-3477 9111
Website: www.bunkamura.co.jp
Opening Hours: Mon–Thu 10am–7pm, Fri–Sun until 9pm
Entrance Fee: charge
Transport: Shibuya

This bronze statue of Hachiko near Shibuya Station makes for a popular meeting place.

Find all manner of toys along Takeshita-dori.

Bunkamura sign in Shibuya.

Entrance Fee: charge
Transport: Shinsen

The Bunkamura is located on the edge of an expensive residential district called Shoto, the site of tea plantations in the 19th century. A pleasant stroll at any time of the year, this leafy district has a number of interesting small museums and Galleries. The **Shoto Museum of Art** (Shoto Bijutsukan) – a short walk from the Shinsen Station on the Inokashira Line – features local artists in a cosy setting with a tearoom where pictures can be viewed from the comfort of armchairs.

Toguri Museum of Art ⑱

Address: 1-11-3 Shoto,Shibuya-ku
Tel: 03-3465 0070
Website: www.toguri-museum.or.jp
Opening Hours: Tue–Sun
9.30am–6pm
Entrance Fee: charge
Transport: Shinsen

Anyone with even a passing interest in ceramics will appreciate the exquisite collection at **Toguri Museum of Art** (Toguri Bijutsukan), a short walk north of the Shoto Museum. Housed in a yellow brick building, only a small selection from the Toguri's 3,000-strong collection is shown at any one time. Its Imari, Nabeshima and Hagi ceramic pieces, captioned in both Japanese and English, are outstanding. On the third Thursday of each month is a fascinating hour-long tour of the museum conducted in English, starting at 2pm (no additional fee; reservations required).

Gallery TOM ⑲

Address: 2-11-1 Shoto, Shibuya-ku
Tel: 03-3467 8102
Website: www.gallerytom.co.jp
Opening Hours: Tue–Sun
10.30am–6pm
Entrance Fee: charge
Transport: Shinsen

The nearby **Gallery TOM** provides a very different experience. Owned

To the north of Dogenzaka, at the end of Bunkamura-dori is the main branch of department store **Tokyu** and the attached Bunkamura culture centre – its 2,150-seat Orchard Hall is home to the Tokyo Philharmonic. The name of this multi-complex art centre means 'Culture Village' in Japanese and it houses galleries, shops, boutiques, a cinema and the **Bunkamura Museum of** Art (Bunkamura Bijutsukan), well regarded for its displays of modern art by Japanese and foreign artists. In the **Bunkamura Gallery** (free) to the left of the main lobby, exhibitions of photography, painting and contemporary art installations are regularly held.

Shoto Museum of Art ⑰

Address: 2-14-14 Shoto, Shibuya-ku
Tel: 03-3465 9421
Website: www.shoto-museum.jp
Opening Hours: Tue–Sun 9am–5pm

by a constructivist sculptor, the concept gallery (the acronym stands for 'Touch Our Museum') is designed for the blind. Broad stairs and handrails lead you to sculptures, which are set at waist level. Visitors are encouraged to touch the forms and let their hands lead them around.

AROUND SHIBUYA

Japan Folk Crafts Museum ⑳

Address: 4-3-33 Komaba, Meguro-ku
Tel: 03-3467 4527
Website: www.mingeikan.or.jp
Opening Hours: Tue–Sun 10am–5pm
Entrance Fee: charge
Transport: Komaba Todaimae

Return to Shibuya Station and go two stops on the Inokashira Line to Komaba Todaimae, where a few minutes' walk west of the station you'll find the excellent Japan **Folk Crafts Museum** (Mingei-kan). Considered to be one of the best among Tokyo's several hundred museums, the lovely old wood and stone building, once owned by master potter Soetsu Yanagi, is a shrine to *mingei*, Japan's folk craft movement. A variety of ceramics, furniture and textiles are exhibited here and the museum's gift shop is a great place to buy unusual souvenirs.

Komaba Park ㉑

Address: 4-3-55 Komaba, Meguro-ku
Tel: 03-3460 6725
Opening Hours: Tue–Sun 9am–4.30pm
Entrance Fee: free
Transport: Komaba Todaimae

Nearby the Folk Crafts Museum is **Komaba Park** (Komaba Koen) formerly the estate of the Maeda family. The last daimyo (lord) of the Maeda clan died during World War II and the estate was requisitioned by the Occupation. Komaba Park includes the **Former Maeda Residence**, a 1929 Tudor-style structure with a separate Japanese-style building used for receiving guests. The estate interiors give a good idea of the life of a member of the Japanese nobility in the early half of the 20th century. Behind the house, in a structure dating from the 1960s, is the **Museum of Modern Japanese Literature** (Toritsu Kindai Bungakukan; www.bungakukan.or.jp).

Daikanyama ㉒

One final destination that can be easily accessed from Shibuya Station is the fashionable residential and shopping quarter of **Daikanyama**, one stop southwest on the Tokyu Toyoko Line. Many interesting boutiques are dotted around the station, and again as you climb up the hill towards the shopping complexes Daikanyama Address and La Fuente. Daikanyama is also the location of Hillside Terrace, an architectural ensemble that took Pritzker Prize-winning architect Fumihiko Maki 23 years to complete, and which is seen as something of a model urban development.

Official residence, Daikanyama.

BEST RESTAURANTS, BARS AND CAFÉS

PRICE CATEGORIES

Prices for a three-course dinner per person without drinks and taxes:

¥ = under ¥2,000
¥¥ = ¥2,000–¥3,000
¥¥¥ = ¥3,000–¥5,000
¥¥¥¥ = over ¥5,000

Restaurants

British

The Aldgate
Shiniwasaki Building, 3F, 30-4 Udagawa-cho, Shibuya-ku
Tel: 03-3462 2983
www.the-aldgate.com
Open: Mon–Fri 6pm–2am, Sat–Sun 5pm–2am
¥¥ 55 p276, B4
A home-away-from-home for expats and Anglophiles. Besides a great line-up of ales from the UK and Japan (21 in all), the usual fish 'n' chips, sausages, pasties, shepherd's pie and other solid, no-frills pub food, the Aldgate also has surprisingly good vegetarian dishes. Another big plus – it's entirely non-smoking.

American

Beacon
1-2-5 Shibuya, Shibuya-ku
Tel: 03-6418 0077
www.tyharborbrewing.co.jp/en/beacon
Open: L & D daily
¥¥¥¥ 56 p276, C4
This sleek, upmarket 'urban chop house' serves some of the best steaks in the city, grilled to perfection over charcoal. There's also good seafood and free-range chicken, plus a huge cellar of Californian wines and a selection of locally made craft beers.

French

L'Artemis
2-31-7 Jingumae, Shibuya-ku
Tel: 03-5786 0220
www.artemisjp.com/artemis-eng/sub5.html

Open: L & D Thu–Tue (closed 2nd Tue of the month)
¥¥¥ 57 p276, C3
Excellent and affordable French cuisine worthy of far grander surroundings. Chef Nakada has studied with some of the best in France, and his all-you-can-eat-and-drink course for ¥5,500 is a steal by Tokyo standards. When the kitchen closes at 9pm, the restaurant turns into a late-night wine bar.

Chez Matsuo
1-23-15 Shoto, Shibuya-ku
Tel: 03-3485 0566
www.chez-matsuo.co.jp
Open: L & D daily
¥¥¥¥ 58 p276, B4
Top-end cooking in one of the most elite residential areas of Tokyo. Soak up the atmosphere of privilege in an exclusive 1920s ivy-covered villa with leafy garden views. A daunting wine list to go with the rich sauces and classic French dishes.

Japanese

Gonpachi
E.Space Tower, 14F, 3-6 Maruyamacho, Shibuya-ku
Tel: 03-5784 2011
www.gonpachi.jp
Open: L & D daily
¥¥¥ 59 p276, B4
The main Gonpachi (in Nishi-Azabu) may be grander and more atmospheric, but it cannot match this branch in terms of location. The main dining room serves a range of Japanese dishes, including *yakitori* (grilled skewers of chicken) and *soba* (buckwheat noodles), which you could wash down with Dom Perignon if you fancy a break from *sake*. The separate sushi shop offers a spectacular panoramic view.

Kaikaya
23-7 Maruyamacho, Shibuya-ku
Tel: 03-3770 0878
www.kaikaya.com

Open: L & D daily
¥¥¥ Off map
This fantastic, lively *izakaya* near Gonpachi specializes in fish dishes (the owners are fishmongers with a shop next door), but also has some decent vegetarian dishes and a good selection of *sake*. English menu available.

Kanetanaka-so
Cerulean Tower, Tokyu Hotel, 2F, 26-1 Sakuragaoka-cho, Shibuya-ku
Tel: 03-3476 3420
www.cerulean tower-hotel.com/en/restaurant/kanetanaka-so
Open: L & D daily
¥¥¥¥ Off map
Kaiseki ryori, Japan's traditional haute cuisine, can be hard to approach, but here it is presented in a modern dining room with chairs (not tatami mats). The exquisite multi-course banquets follow the traditional format, but with stylish, contemporary arrangements.

Sora-no-Niwa
4-17 Sakuragaoka-cho, Shibuya-ku
Tel: 03-5728 5191
Open: daily 5–11.30pm
¥¥ Off map
Tofu cuisine doesn't have to be stuffy, formal and expensive. This casual diner close to the JR railway tracks south of Shibuya is affordable and approachable. Highlights include tofu *shumai* dumplings and *yuba* (soymilk 'skin') prepared at the table. English menu available.

Sushi Ouchi
2-8-4 Shibuya, Shibuya-ku
Tel: 03-3407 3543
Open: L & D Mon–Sat
¥¥¥ 60 p276, C4
Maverick sushi chef Ouchi does everything a bit differently, from the restful, dark-wood decor and classical music on the sound system to his insistence on all-natural ingredients. That means no artificially reared fish and absolutely no MSG or other chemicals.

Tenmatsu
1-6-1 Dogenzaka, Shibuya-ku
Tel: 03-3462 2815
Open: L & D Mon–Fri
¥¥¥¥ ⑥ p276, B4

Great tempura without having to pay (relatively speaking) through the roof. Part of the fun of this restaurant is sitting at the wooden counter watching the chef cook right in front of you. Courses start from ¥5,250.

Korean

Tokyo Sundub
3-6-19 Shibuya, Shibuya-ku
Tel: 03-5778 3901
www.tokyo-sundubu.net
Open: L & D daily
¥¥ ⑥ p276, C4

A huge range of spicy tofu stews in a wide variety of styles is the deal at this chain with central branches also in Aoyama and Shinjuku. Great on a chilly night when you can have them crank up the spiciness. They also have some 'non-spicy' alternatives available.

Mexican

Fonda de la Madrugada
Villa Bianca, B1F, 2-33-12 Jingumae, Shibuya-ku
Tel: 03-5410 6288
www.fonda-m.com
Open: daily 5.30pm–5am
¥¥¥ ⑥ p276, C3

Located in an interior courtyard reminiscent of a village plaza, two floors below street level and complete with wandering mariachi musicians. As well as the usual burritos, enchiladas and other Mexican favourites, there are high-quality fish dishes and steaks. Drinks-wise, they serve a mean margarita.

Turkish

Ankara
Social Dogenzaka, B1F, 1-14-9 Dogenzaka, Shibuya-ku
Tel: 03-3780 1366
www.ankara.jp
Open: Mon–Sat 5–11.15pm, Sun 5–10pm
¥¥¥ Off map

This popular restaurant can be hard to find, up the hill behind the

Mark City mall, but it's worth the effort. The cooking is excellent, especially the selection of meze, the juicy kebabs, and the *pide* (Turkish pizza). Friendly and casual, and there's an English menu.

Vegetarian

Mominoki House
2-18-5 Jingumae, Shibuya-ku
Tel: 03-3405 9144
www.omotesando.mominokihouse.net
Open: daily noon–10.30pm
¥¥¥ ⑥ p276, C3

Vegetarians can be assured of eating well at this long-running macrobiotic restaurant, which has been in business since 1976. There's a laid-back atmosphere and sometimes live jazz performances at night. Owner Yamada-san also does macrobiotic cooking courses in English (see website).

Bars and Cafés

Cozmo's
1-6-3 Shibuya, Shibuya-ku
Tel: 03-3407 5166
www.cozmoscafe.com
⑰ p276, C4

In this sleek bar with very plush furnishings, extremely friendly staff serve gin and vermouth, Bass Pale Ale, and a curious line of coffee cocktails like Tiramisu Martini; a mix of Illy coffee, whiskey and steamed milk.

Harajuku Taproom
2F, No-surrender Building, 1-20-13 Jingumae, Shibuya-ku
Tel: 03-6438 0450
http://bairdbeer.com
⑱ p276, C3

The Taproom is one of two great pubs run by craft brewer Baird Brewing (the other is in Meguro). The 15 taps and two hand pumps here deliver all of Baird's year-round brews, which range from the heady Suruga Bay IPA to refreshing Wheat King Ale, as well as the company's innovative seasonal brews.

Insomnia Lounge
26-5 Udagawa-cho, Shibuya-ku
Tel: 03-3476 2735
⑲ p276, B4

This basement lounge bar is decorated from floor to ceiling in screaming crimson fabric; a great late-night spot for a date, but make sure you wear good socks – shoes have to be left at the door.

Sasagin
1-32-15 Uehara, Shibuya-ku
Tel: 03-5454 3715
⑳ p276, A3

Roughly 80 brands of premium *sake* are available at this *izakaya* along with an interesting but hit-and-miss selection of modern Japanese cuisine. Simple decor; moderate prices.

TWS Arts Cafe: Kurage
1-19-8 Jinnan, Shibuya-ku
Tel: 03-3463 3323
www.tokyo-ws.org/English
Open: daily 10am–11.30pm
㉑ p276, B4

Tokyo Wonder Site houses this trendy café, with internet access and offering a great-value lunch and interesting desserts such as *warabi mochi* (a sweet jelly coated in a brown sugar sauce). The open-air window seats make a great spot for people watching.

Fresh vegetarian sushi.

ROPPONGI

The nightlife districts of Roppongi and Akasaka have both had major makeovers with big art and shopping complexes adding to their daytime attractions, which include sights such as Tokyo Tower and several important shrines.

In the lower middle of the oval defined by the Yamanote Line, just to the southwest of the Imperial Palace, is **Minato-ku**, an area favoured by Tokyo's expatriate community. The ward is peppered with embassies and high-priced expat housing, and liberally spiced with nightclubs, bars, live music houses and restaurants. The development of mixed residential and commercial complexes such as Roppongi Hills in 2003 and Tokyo Midtown in 2007, both with their own art gallery components, is drawing a more diverse crowd to the area.

Up on a hill, and served by the Hibiya and Oedo subway lines, Roppongi, meaning 'six trees', was once a garrison town for the Meiji government, and later, after World War II, the Americans established barracks here. It is today the heart of Minato-ku's nightlife. Most people begin exploring Roppongi and adjacent Akasaka at the Roppongi Crossing, the intersection between Gaien-Higashi-dori and Roppongi-dori, situated underneath a raised expressway.

ROPPONGI

Ark Hills ❶

Following this stretch of raised motorway northeast leads to **Ark Hills** (www.arkhills.com) Japan's first large scale private redevelopment project by the construction company Mori, and a forerunner for more recent Mori projects such as Roppongi Hills and Omotesando Hills (see page 133). The **Suntory Hall** concert venue and the **ANA InterContinental Tokyo** are all within the complex (see page 247).

Entrance to the Mori Art Museum and Tokyo City View at Roppongi Hills.

Okura Shukokan Museum of Fine Arts ❷

Address: 2-10-3 Toranomon, Minato-ku
Tel: 03-3583 0781
Website: www.shukokan.org
Opening Hours: Tue–Sun 10am–4.30pm
Entrance Fee: charge
Transport: Roppongi-Itchome

Behind Ark Hills, nestled amid a number of embassies and exclusive residential backstreets, just beyond the American Embassy, the **Okura Museum of Art** (Okura Shukokan Bijutsukan) is found in front of the Hotel Okura (see page 247). Set up by Baron Okura Tsuruhiko in 1917, and housed in a Chinese-style building, the museum displays a small but intriguing collection of Asian antiquities and Buddhist sculptures.

Musée Tomo ❸

Address: 4-1-35 Toranomon, Minato-ku
Tel: 03-5733 5311
Website: www.musee-tomo.or.jp
Opening Hours: Tue–Sun 11am–6pm
Entrance Fee: charge
Transport: Kamiyacho

A few steps away, behind the Hotel Okura, is the extraordinary **Musée Tomo**. With a broad collection of the very best ceramics, from Imari vases to Raku tea bowls, the gallery also features the work of modern pottery masters.

Tokyo Tower ❹

Address: 4-2-8 Shiba Koen, Minato-ku
Tel: 03-3433 5111
Website: www.tokyotower.co.jp/english
Opening Hours: daily 9am–10pm
Entrance Fee: charge
Transport: Onarimon or Kamiyacho

Heading downhill from the museum towards Sakurada-dori and Kamiyacho subway station, the next sight makes itself very apparent. **Tokyo Tower**, a red-and-white copy

Tokyo is spectacular when lit up at night.

of the Eiffel Tower, dominates the skyline here. The 333-metre (1,090ft) structure, completed in 1958, was designed as a transmitting tower. Compensating for the lacklustre aquarium and wax museum at the base is its Special Observatory with exceptional views of the city, and on a clear day, of Mount Fuji.

Zojo-ji ❺

Address: 4-7-35 Shiba Koen, Minato-ku
Tel: 03-3432 1431
Website: www.zojoji.or.jp
Opening Hours: daily 6am–5.30pm
Entrance Fee: free
Transport: Daimon or Shiba-koen

Just behind the tower, in the spacious grounds of **Shiba Park** (Shiba Koen), stands one of Tokyo's grandest temples, **Zojo-ji**. Founded in 1393, the site was chosen by the Tokugawa clan in the late 1600s as their ancestral temple, as part of a scheme to protect Edo from evil spirits. Close to the bay

FACT

The much-maligned Tokyo Tower sheds its shabby daytime image at night, when it is illuminated to startling effect – a sight to silence its most vocal critics.

and the Tokaido Road, it also served as a post station for travellers and pilgrims. Most of the temple buildings, once numbering over 100, were destroyed by fires and air raids, but its main entrance, the 1612 red-lacquered **Sangedatsumon Gate**, an Important Cultural Treasure, is original.

Pass through the gate, with its large bell made from melted down hairpins donated by the ladies of the shogun's court, to the **Main Hall** (Daiden). It contains many important sacred objects, including ancient sutras and statuary. The new leaders of the Meiji government showed

their contempt for the outgoing Tokugawa by confiscating the temple, turning the grounds into a park and removing six of the mummified shogun to a less prestigious resting place at the rear of the Main Hall, near a row of cheerful Jizo statues, each with a windmill in its hand.

Roppongi Hills ❻

Returning to Roppongi Crossing and heading west along Roppongi-dori will bring you to **Roppongi Hills**. The 16-hectare (40-acre) site is impressive; its towering office blocks, luxe Grand Hyatt Tokyo (see page 247),

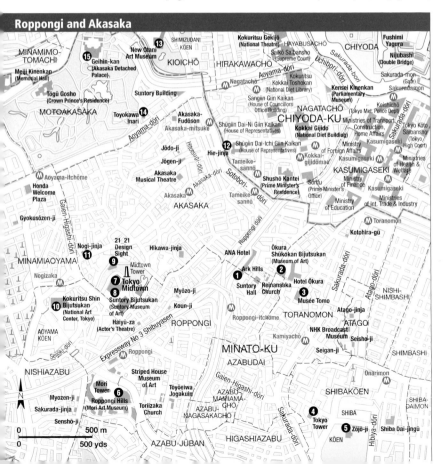

Roppongi and Akasaka

multiplex cinema, apartments, hundreds of shops and interconnecting walkways make up one of the largest developments in Japan. There's a pretty garden next to the TV Asahi building, and on the 54th floor of **Mori Tower** a first-rate contemporary gallery, the **Mori Art Museum** (6-10-1 Roppongi, Minato-ku; tel: 03-5777 8600; www.mori.art.museum; Tue 10am–5pm; Wed–Mon until 10pm; charge) as well as **Tokyo City View** (www. tokyocityview.com; Sun–Thu 10am–11pm, Fri–Sat until 1am; charge) an indoor observation deck with a heart-stopping 360-degree view of the city as well as access to the building's roof.

Tokyo Midtown ❼

Address: Tokyo Midtown, 9-7-4 Akasaka, Minato-ku
Tel: 03-3475 3100
Website: www.tokyo-midtown.com
Opening Hours: daily 10am–9pm (restaurants until midnight)
Entrance Fee: free
Transport: Roppongi

If you go northwest along Gaien-Higashi-dori from Roppongi Crossing you'll come to the area's second major development, which opened in 2007, **Tokyo Midtown**. The anchor property here is Midtown Tower, Tokyo's tallest building atwith its top floors occupied by the Ritz Carlton (see page 248). Like the nearby Roppongi Hills, Midtown's several buildings are home to hundreds of stores, restaurants and offices. And just as Roppongi Hills has the Mori Art Museum, so too Midtown has its own first-rate art venues, with the **Suntory Museum of Art** and **21_21 Design Sight**, as well as numerous artworks and installations scattered around the complex.

Suntory Museum of Art ❽

Address: Tokyo Midtown, 9-7-4 Akasaka, Minato-ku
Tel: 03-3479 8600
Website: www.suntory.co.jp/sma
Opening Hours: Mon, Wed, Thu, Sun 10am–6pm, Fri–Sat until 8pm
Entrance Fee: charge
Transport: Roppongi

Within Tokyo Midtown's shopping complex is the **Suntory Museum of Art** Suntory Bijutsukan). Its classy collection of lacquerware, ceramics and paintings from the 17th century to the present is housed in a very sleek and light-filled design by Kengo Kuma featuring high ceilings and louvred windows.

21_21 Design Sight ❾

Address: 9-7-6 Akasaka, Minato-ku
Tel: 03-3475 2121
Website: www.2121designsight.jp
Opening Hours: Wed–Mon 11am–8pm
Entrance Fee: charge
Transport: Roppongi

Greenery surrounds Tokyo Midtown. Across the 10-hectare (25-acre) site are many contemporary sculptures and, in one corner, the **21_21 Design Sight**. This Tadao Ando-designed space, which has fashion leader Issey Miyake among its directors, stages progressive theme-based design exhibitions in a subterranean gallery.

TIP

The National Art Center Tokyo, Suntory Museum of Art and Mori Art Museum form the three corners of the Art Triangle Roppongi. Keep your ticket stub after visiting any of these three museums and it will entitle you to reduced entry at each of the others. A map is also available at each museum showing other galleries in the area, or online at www.mori.art. museum/eng/atro.

Sanmon, the main entrance to Zojo-ji Temple in Shiba Park.

Every year in June, Hie-jinja is the stage for a great Tokyo festival, the Sanno Matsuri. Hundreds of participants in period costumes take part in an impressive parade, which includes the carrying of heavy *mikoshi* (portable shrines) on the shoulders of local residents.

National Art Center Tokyo ⑩

Address: 7-22-2 Roppongi, Minato-ku
Tel: 03-5777 8600
Website: www.nact.jp
Opening Hours: Wed–Mon 10am–6pm, Fri until 8pm
Entrance Fee: charge
Transport: Roppongi or Nogizaka

Two minutes' walk southwest of Tokyo Midtown is the **National Art Center Tokyo**. Designed by Kisho Kurokawa, this vast building is Japan's largest such gallery staging everything from blockbuster exhibitions of major artists to small-scale shows for local art groups. The atrium foyer, studded with three storey-tall conical pods, is worth a look on its own. There's also a good French restaurant, **Brasserie Paul Bocuse Le Musse**, on the third floor.

AKASAKA

Nogi-jinja ⑪

Address: 8-11-27 Akasaka, Minato-ku
Tel: 03-3478 3001
Website: www.nogijinja.or.jp
Opening Hours: daily 8.30am–5pm
Entrance Fee: free
Transport: Nogizaka

A five-minute walk north of Tokyo Midtown, along Gaien-Higashi-dori, and next to Nogizaka subway station is **Nogi-jinja,** a shrine named after General Nogi Maresuke, a hero of the Russo-Japanese War of 1904 who is buried, with his wife, in nearby Aoyama cemetery. Such was Nogi's loyalty to the Meiji Emperor, he and his wife killed themselves upon the Emperor's death in 1912. On the second Sunday of every month, an antique flea market is held in the shrine's grounds.

SHOPPING

As well as the modern malls of Roppongi Hills and Tokyo Midtown the *shotengai* (shopping street) of Azabu-Juban is worth a visit.

Books

Tsutaya
6-11-1 Roppongi, Minato-ku
Tel: 03-5775 1515
p276, E4
This book, CD and DVD shop has become a popular hang-out for the expat community mainly thanks to its great selection and an in-store Starbucks café.

Confectionary

Toraya
4-9-22 Akasaka, Minato-ku
Tel: 03-3408 4121
www.toraya-group.co.jp
p276, E2
This is the main branch of a maker of traditional Japanese sweets *(wagashi)* that is patronised by the Imperial family. Different products

are offered according to the season and there's a café downstairs where you can sample them along with drinks. There's also an outlet in the basement of Tokyo Midtown.

Crafts

Blue and White
2-9-2 Azabu-Juban, Minato-ku
Tel: 03-3451 0537
Off map
As the name of the shop implies, the majority of the attractive crafts on display here – including pottery, handmade paper, clothing and accessories – are coloured blue and white.

Shopping Malls

Roppongi Hills
6-10, Roppongi, Minato-ku
Tel 03-6406 6000
www.roppongihills.com
p276, D4/E4
You'll find over 200 outlets scattered across this huge complex.

Tenants include many international luxury labels such as Louis Vuitton, Giorgio Armani and Loro Piana (all along Keyakizaka-dori) as well as local companies such as United Arrows and Hysteric Glamour. The Mori Arts Center Gallery gift shop is also a great place to pick up unusual, stylish souvenirs. The observation deck offers spectacular views of Tokyo.

Tokyo Midtown
9-7 Akasaka, Minato-ku
www.tokyo-midtown.com
p278, A3
A worthy competitor to Roppongi Hills, the shopping experience at this luxury mall is more organised with floors devoted to clothing and interior goods and design. The Cover Nippon (www.thecover nippon.jp) on the third floor is one of the best places to look for a wide range of Japanese-made goods, while in the basement there's a branch of the chic-yet-utilitarian fashion and homewares store, Muji (www.muji.net).

Hie-jinja ⑫

Address: 2-10-5 Nagatacho,
Chiyoda-ku
Tel: 03-3581 2471
Website: www.hiejinja.net
Opening Hours: daily Apr–Sept
5am–6pm, Oct–Mar 6am–5pm
Entrance Fee: free
Transport: Tameike-Sanno

Heading due east from Nogi-jinja
soon brings you to Sotobori-dori
and **Hie-jinja**, one of Tokyo's major
shrines. Transplanted here in the 17th
century in the belief that it would
help to deflect evil from Edo Castle, a
massive stone *torii* (gate) leads uphill
through an avenue of smaller, red-lacquered gates to the current buildings,
put up in 1967. The shrine's role as
protector is still evident today; look
carefully at a carving to the left of
the main shrine and you will see a
monkey cradling its baby. Pregnant
women come here to pay wishful
homage to the image.

New Otani Art Museum ⑬

Address: 4-1 Kioicho, Chiyoda-ku
Tel: 03-3221 4111
Website: www.newotani.co.jp/en/group/
museum
Opening Hours: Tue–Sun
10am–6pm
Entrance Fee: charge
Transport: Akasaka-Mitsuke

North from the shrine, across the
Benkei Bridge (Benkei-bashi) spanning what was once Edo castle's outer
moat, lies the extensive buildings and
grounds of the **Hotel New Otani**
(see page 247). On the sixth-floor of
the Garden Court wing is the **New
Otani Art Museum** displaying a
small but notable collection of works
by Japanese and European painters,
including Modigliani and Chagall.
While here, take the opportunity to
stroll through the hotel's beautiful
traditional gardens (free) designed
over 400 years ago for the feudal lord
Kato Kiyomasa.

Cutting-edge art at 21_21 Design Sight.

Toyokawa Inari ⑭

Retracing your steps across the
Benkei Bridge, turn west to walk up
Aoyama-dori to the **Toyokawa** Inari
also called Myogon-ji. This combined
temple and shrine has a chaotic and
colourful clutter of images lining
the approach to the main sanctuary:
orange banners and lanterns, statues
of the goddess Kannon and the child-
protector deity Jizo, and figures of
red-bibbed foxes.

Akasaka Detached Palace ⑮

Toyokawa Inari is next to the extensive grounds of the Akasaka Detached
Palace (Geihin-kan, www8.cao.go.jp/
geihinkan). Completed in 1909, the
palace – which is reminiscent of
Buckingham Palace – is the only
neo-Baroque building in Tokyo and
serves as the State Guest House. It's
occasionally open in summer for public visits. The palace's front gates are
closest to Yotsuya Station on both the
JR and Metro lines.

BEST RESTAURANTS, BARS AND CAFÉS

Restaurants

Chinese

Chinese Café Eight
Court Annex, 2F, 3-2-13 Nishi-Azabu, Minato-ku.
Tel: 03-5414 5708
www.cceight.com
Open: 24 hours daily
¥¥ ⑥⑤ p276, D4
It's remarkable to find Chinese food at these budget prices so close to Roppongi Hills, and even more amazing that this place stays open around the clock. Peking duck (for three to four people) is a bargain by Tokyo standards at ¥3,680; the *gyoza* dumplings are three for just ¥105. It's always crowded and the staff tend to be brusque. Branches also in Akasaka, Ebisu and Shinjuku.

French

L'Atelier de Joël Robuchon
Roppongi Hills Hillside, 2F, 6-10-1 Roppongi, Minato-ku
Tel: 03-5772 7500
www.robuchon.jp/latelier
Open: L & D daily
¥¥¥¥ ⑥⑥ p276, D4/E4
Master chef Robuchon presents his impeccable cuisine in tapas style in a sophisticated but informal setting, less complex than his top-end restaurants. Diners sit not at tables but at the counter running along the open kitchen. Reservations are taken only for the first sitting at lunchtime; otherwise it's first come first served.
Brasserie Paul Bocuse Le Musée
National Art Center Tokyo, 7-22-2 Roppongi, Minato-ku

Tel: 03-5770 8161.
www.hiramatsu.co.jp
Open: L & D Wed–Mon
¥¥¥ ⑥⑦ p276, D4
Bookings aren't taken here, so come early or late if you want to avoid queuing up for lunch at this classy French operation. It is notable for its location, atop one of the giant concrete cones in the NACT lobby.
The French Kitchen
Grand Hyatt Tokyo, 2F, 6-10-3 Roppongi, Minato-ku
Tel: 03-4333 8781
Open: daily 7am–10pm
¥¥¥¥ ⑥⑧ p276, D4
The Grand Hyatt's main restaurant is a large, upmarket brasserie and bar serving superior regional French cuisine, backed up with an outstanding wine cellar. Sit inside in view of the busy open kitchen, or outside on the terrace.

Fusion

Roy's
West Walk Roppongi Hills, 5F, 6-10-1 Roppongi, Minato-ku
Tel: 03-5474 8181
Open: L & D daily
¥¥¥¥ ⑥⑨ p276, D4
Roy Yamaguchi, one of Hawaii's top chefs, creates delicious Asian-American fusion cuisine that's as impressive on the eyes as on the palate. The setting is stunning too, especially at night, with a panoramic view of Tokyo Tower on the horizon.

Japanese

Fukuzushi
5-7-8 Roppongi, Minato-ku
Tel: 03-3402 4116
www.roppongifukuzushi.com
Open: L & D Mon–Sat
¥¥¥¥ ⑦⓪ p278, A4
Upmarket, but there is none of the snooty attitude found at many of the traditional sushi shops. The English menu helps you to negotiate the familiar tastes of tuna, mackerel and cod, as well as the

unfamiliar delights of conger eel, shad and grouper.
Goshiki
6-1-6 Roppongi, Minato-ku
Tel: 03-3405 4480
Open: Mon–Sat 6pm–4am, Sun until midnight
¥¥¥ ⑦① p276, E4
This modern *izakaya* has some dishes you won't see on typical *izakaya* menus, such as deep-fried gnocchi with melted cheese and fish and chips, along with good quality pasta and pizzas. Just as good is the fine range of beers from local microbrewer Coedo.
Hassan
Denki Building, B1, 6-1-20 Roppongi, Minato-ku
Tel: 03-3403 8333
Open: L & D daily
¥¥¥¥ ⑦② p278, A4
The main attraction here is the ¥5,300 all-you-can-eat menu of *shabu-shabu* (thin slices of Japanese Wagyu beef dipped in broth) with side dishes of other Japanese favourites in a lovely traditional setting. Lunch is a bargain, with courses from ¥1,050 to ¥4,900.
Inakaya East
5-3-4 Roppongi, Minato-ku
Tel: 03-3408 5040
www.roppongiinakaya.jp
Open: D daily
¥¥¥ ⑦③ p278, A4
Together with its nearby sister restaurant, Inakaya West, this is a longtime favourite in Roppongi. Chefs in traditional *happi* coats grill fish, meat and vegetables to order, and then pass them on long wooden paddles across to where you're sitting. It's theatrical and fun.
Ninja
Akasaka Tokyu Plaza, 1F, 2-14-3 Nagatacho, Chiyoda-ku
Tel: 03-5157 3936
Open: Mon–Sat 5.30pm–2am, Sun 5–11pm
¥¥¥ ⑦④ p278, A2
In a rambling space designed to resemble the basement of a feudal castle, black-clad waiters dressed

like ninjas show you to your private room, then entertain you as you nibble on simple Japanese food.

Nobu Tokyo
4-1-28 Toranomon, Minato-ku
Tel: 03-5733 0070
Open: L & D Mon–Fri, D Sat–Sun
¥¥¥¥  75 p278, A3/A4
Famed chef Matsushima Nobu, who has award-winning restaurants in the US and Europe, combines classic Japanese cuisine with contemporary creativity.

Nodaiwa
1-5-4 Higashi-Azabu, Minato-ku
Tel: 03-3583 7852
www.nodaiwa.co.jp
Open: L & D Mon–Sat
¥¥¥ 76 p278, A4
The speciality here is *unagi* – fillets of wild eel carefully grilled over charcoal, daubed with a savoury sauce and served with rice. The restaurant also boasts a refined and unique setting in an old storehouse building relocated from the mountains.

Pintokona
Roppongi Hills Metrohat, B2F, 6-4-1 Roppongi, Minato-ku
Tel: 03-5771 1133
Open: 11am–11pm daily
¥¥ 77 p276, D4
Unlike most conveyor-belt sushi restaurants, this stylish eatery emphasises quality, not quantity. You can also order from a menu, which includes some light *izakaya*- (tavern) style dishes, rather than choosing from whatever passes in front of you.

Tofuya Ukai
4-4-13 Shiba Koen, Minato-ku
Tel: 03-3436 1028
www.ukai.co.jp
Open: daily 11am–10pm
¥¥¥¥ 78 p278, B4
Sitting in the shadow of Tokyo Tower, this remarkable restaurant boasts traditional architecture and a beautiful rambling garden complete with carp ponds. The refined multicourse meals, served in private rooms, revolve around numerous variations of tofu.

Tokyo Curry Lab
2F Tokyo Tower, 4-2-8 Shiba-Koen, Minato-ku
Tel: 03-5425 2900
Open: daily 11am–9pm
¥ 79 p278, B4
Tokyo's Tower's dining options are far from chic, but design fans will enjoy the clean lines and concept of this simple eatery celebrating Japan's unique take on curry and rice.

Korean
Grace
1-7-2 Azabu-Juban, Minato-ku
Tel: 03-3475 6972
Open: L & D daily (closed 3rd Sun of month)
¥¥ Off map
This simple restaurant serves a good range of Korean dishes but is particularly known for *samgyetan* – a chicken and gingseng herbal stew.

Singaporean
Hainan Jeefan Shokudo
6-11-16 Roppongi, Minato-ku
Tel: 03-5474 3200
www.route9g.com
Open: L & D daily (closed 3rd Mon of month)
¥¥ Off map
Tasty Singaporean street food, such as chicken rice and spicy noodles, are served up at this cute, relaxed place close by Roppongi Hills.

Vegetarian
Daigo
Forest Tower, 2F, 2-3-1 Atago, Minato-ku
Tel: 03-3431 0811
www.atago-daigo.com
Open: L & D daily
¥¥¥¥ 80 p278, B4
Buddhist temple cooking elevated to the finest level of *kaiseki* cuisine. Vegetarian banquets with 10 to 15 courses of amazing delicacy and complexity, all served in private rooms. Budget plenty of time (and expense). Reservations essential.

Bars and Cafés

Agave
B1F Clover Building, 7-15-10 Roppongi, Minato-ku.
Tel: 03-3497 0229
www.agave.jp
22 p278, A4

This atmospheric basement bar offers a Latin-American ambience in which to enjoy 400 varieties of tequila or puff on a Cuban cigar.

Ant 'n' Bee
5-1-5 Roppongi, Minato-ku
Tel: 03-3478 1250
23 p276, E4
A wide, albeit expensive selection of local and world craft beers (around 20) make this the best place for a decent beer in Roppongi, especially so if you like a pint around breakfast time. It opens daily until 7am.

Eat More Greens
2-2-5 Azabu-Juban, Minato-ku.
Tel: 03-3798 3191
www.eatmoregreens.jp
Off map
Near Azabu-Juban Station (a short walk south from Tsutaya near Roppongi Hills), this laid-back café serves up really good organic and vegetarian café fare.

The Pink Cow
Roi Building B1, 5-5-1 Roppongi, Minato-ku.
Tel: 03-3406 5597
www.thepinkcow.com
24 p278, A4
Beloved of the art, fashion and media crowd, this café-bar, which relocated here from Shibuya in 2012, is the brainchild of US expat artist-sculptor Traci Consoli. It offers a good range of food, wine, beers and cocktails, and events from poetry readings to jazz recitals, book launches and exhibitions.

Beef tataki.

SHINAGAWA

You can visit the burial grounds of the legendary 47 samurai, picnic among trees that were around when Edo was a fishing village, or drop by a massive, beautifully decorated wedding hall.

A key checkpoint and post station at the start of the great Tokaido (East Sea Road) that connected Edo with Kyoto, Shinagawa once stood on a stretch of dismal tidal flats at the edge of the city. Founded on fishing and the cultivation of seaweed, the area's main trade soon gave way to services catering to travellers, and inns and teahouses flourished. Along with these arose the inevitable facilities catering for pleasures of the flesh.

When the feudal system collapsed with the advent of the Meiji era however, railways and industry moved in. Shinagawa and its much sought after residential districts of Higashi-Gotanda, Takanawa and Shirokanedai have come up in the world since then. Shinagawa has also benefited from becoming a station on the main Shinkansen line heading south to Kyoto, Osaka and beyond. To the east of the station is a cluster of modern office buildings and residences.

SHINAGAWA

Takanawa Prince Hotels Garden ❶

Close to Shinagawa Station's west exit amid a cluster of Prince hotels (the Takanawa Prince Hotel, Takanawa Prince Hotel Sakura Tower and New Takanawa Prince Hotel) is a lovely traditional garden. The whole site was once occupied by three Imperial palaces and the gardens were created for Prince Takeda whose French-style mansion still stands next to the Takanawa Prince Hotel (it's now a restaurant and used for private functions). Within the gardens is the small

A Buddhist monk at Shinagawa's Sengaku-ji temple.

Kannon-do, a 13th-century temple relocated here in 1954.

Hara Museum of Contemporary Art ❷

Address: 4-7-25 Kita-Shinagawa, Shinagawa-ku
Tel: 03-3445 0651
Website: www.haramuseum.or.jp
Opening Hours: Tue–Sun 11am–5pm, Wed until 8pm
Entrance Fee: charge
Transport: Kita-Shinagawa

A fifteen-minute walk south of Shinagawa Station to the west of Dai-ichi Keihin, a broad road running beside the railway tracks, modern art finds an interesting home in the **Hara Museum of Contemporary Art** (Hara Bijutsukan). Five rooms with connecting corridors are used to display the museum's changing exhibitions, which have included works by international artists such as Christo and Andy Warhol. The grandfather of the museum's founder, Hara Toshio, had the Bauhaus-style home built in 1938 and it was then transformed into today's museum in 1979. One of Japan's leading architects, Isozaki Arata, was brought in more recently to add an annexe, the **Café d'Art**.

Shinagawa Aquarium ❸

Address: 3-2-1 Katsushima, Shinagawa-ku
Tel: 03-3762 3431
Website: www.aquarium.gr.jp
Opening Hours: Wed–Mon 10am–5pm
Entrance Fee: charge
Transport: Omori Kaigan

Hop on the Keihin Kyuko Line at Shinagawa Station and ride a few stops south to Omori Kaigan for the Shinagawa Aquarium where you can see dolphin and sea lion shows as well as a host of other aquatic life from sharks to stingrays displayed in giant tanks, one of which you can walk under.

Sengaku-ji ❹

Address: 2-11-1 Takanawa, Minato-ku
Tel: 03-3441 5560
Website: www.sengakuji.or.jp
Opening Hours: daily Oct–Mar 7am–5pm, Apr–Sept daily 7am–6pm

The garden of the Grand Prince Hotel, Takanawa.

Entrance Fee: free
Transport: Sengakuji

North of Shinagawa Station and a short walk west of the Sengakuji Station is the **Sengaku-ji**. This temple was the setting for part of one of Edo's best-known true stories (see page 164). Incense is placed every day on the graves of the 47 retainers and their Lord Asano, who are buried together here. Visitors often leave gifts for them, too, such as *sake*, snacks and small bunches flowers. The temple was rebuilt after the war, but its entrance gate, a beautifully carved and decorated work with a dragon motif dating from 1836, remains intact. A small side building, the **Gishiken** (Hall of Loyal Retainers), contains some of the personal effects of the 47 *ronin*.

Tozen-ji ❺

Directly south of Sengaku-ji is a small Zen temple with an air of purity and simplicity that is worth a short detour. **Tozen-ji** was the site of the British Legation between 1859 and 1873, its distance from the centre of Edo being considered appropriate for the Western 'barbarians'. The temple was not quite the shelter the British had envisaged. When retainers from the influential Mito clan burst in one day in 1861, Britain's first representative, Sir Rutherford Alcock, barely managed to escape death by hiding in the temple's bathtub. The minister's crime? He was spotted defiling sacred Mount Fuji by climbing to its summit. Sword marks and bullet holes from that skirmish are still visible on the pillars in the temple's entrance hall.

Hatakeyama Memorial Museum of Fine Art ❻

Address: 2-20-12 Shirokanedai, Minato-ku
Tel: 03-3447 5787
Website: www.ebara.co.jp/csr/hatakeyama

Keeping the flame alight for pilgrims to Sengaku-ji Temple.

Shinagawa, Meguro and Ebisu

Opening Hours: Oct–Mar Tue–Sun 10am–4.30pm, Apr–Sept Tue–Sun until 10pm
Entrance Fee: charge
Transport: Takanawadai

From the temple follow the Katsura-zaka west to Sakurada-dori; follow this major road south to Takanawadai Station from where you'll head a few blocks west for the **Hatakeyama Memorial Museum of Fine Art** (Hatakeyama Kinen Bijutsukan) located on a wooded hill at the heart of an estate once owned by the Lord of Satsuma in Kyushu. A section of the old garden still remains and is overlooked by a *kaiseki-ryori* restaurant. The museum reflects the interests of its founder, the industrialist and tea ceremony master, Hatakeyama Issei. Galleries display tea utensils and bowls, hand scrolls and other tea ceremony objects, but also lacquerware and *noh* costumes. There are three tea ceremony rooms as well.

Capsule hotels are an ingenious solution to limited space. A pigeonhole sleeping chamber includes bedding, a TV and an alarm clock.

Happo-en ❼

Address: 1-1-1 Shirokanedai, Minato-ku
Tel: 03-3443 3111
Website: www.happo-en.com
Opening Hours: daily 10am–5pm
Entrance Fee: free
Transport: Shirokanedai

A ten-minute walk north of the art museum will bring you to one of Tokyo's most beautiful stroll gardens. **Happo-en,** once part of an estate owned by retainers of Tokugawa shogun, now forms the backdrop to many a Tokyoite's wedding or special celebration. The 50,000 sq metres of gardens, arranged around an ornamental pond, sport a collection of bonsai, some over 200 years old. As with any classical Japanese garden, Happo-en is designed to reflect each season to its fullest, and it's especially successful at that during the cherry blossom season in early spring. It's also possible to have green tea served in Muan, a historic teahouse reconstructed here, or dine on fine *kaiseki* at Happo-en's restaurant.

National Park for Nature Study ❽

Address: 5-21-5 Shiroganedai, Minato-ku
Tel: 03-3441 7176
Website: www.ins.kahaku.go.jp
Opening Hours: Sept–Apr Tue–Sun 9am–4.30pm, May–Aug until 5pm
Entrance Fee: charge
Transport: Shiroganedai

From Happo-en follow Meguro-dori west to the entrance to the **National Park for Nature Study** (Shizenkyoikuen). This 20-hectare (49-acre) park is a valiant effort to preserve in its original form a section of the Musashino Plain that once covered much of the area Edo was built on. Among the 8,000 or more trees (160 species in all) in the park, stand moss-covered ones that were here when Edo was a mere fishing village.

TIP

One of the best points about Tokyo's National Park for Nature Study is that entrance is limited to only 300 people at a time (you will be issued with a returnable ribbon as you enter), making this one of the least crowded parks in the city.

Encounters with 'Janglish'

Be it bizarre product names or inadvertently obscene T-shirts, the Japanese flair for mangling the English language is one of the country's most endearing features.

While riding on a bus, a visitor once spotted a restaurant sign with the name 'Cheese Doll'. What an odd name for an eatery, he thought. Not long afterwards, the bus passed a second establishment with the same appellation, and at this point, he noted that both of them had been housed in matte yellow buildings. Then suddenly it all made sense: the owner had tried to emulate the name 'Chez d'Or', but unaware that it meant 'house of gold' in French, and unable to find either of these words in his English dictionary, settled for the closest equivalents he could find. The Japanese chop up the English language and reassemble it in imaginative ways that resemble the linguistic equivalent of abstract art.

Janglish manifests itself everywhere.

When English is packaged solely for domestic consumption, Japanese seem indifferent to the rules of correct usage; and when informed of this fact, they seldom care. English exists, not as a medium of international communication, but rather as decorative icing on the cake of commercialism.

In addition to names of businesses, this fractured English, known as 'Janglish' and 'Japlish', can be encountered in building signs, on T-shirts and shopping bags, in advertising slogans, menus, subway posters, product names and publications of all sorts. The internet has vastly multiplied the opportunities to disseminate this strange mutant of English around the globe, while less than perfect computer translation programmes have increased its prevalence in Japan.

Accurate rendering of mispronunciations are part of the problem. For example 'r' and 'l' often get confused by locals because there is no equivalent of the 'l' sound in Japanese and so 'r' is often used as a substitute – hence you may hear a flight attendant say 'We hope you enjoy your fright'. A similar mix-up happens between 'b' and 'v' (Sign in a hotel: 'Tooth Brush Bending Machine'.)

Japanese themselves refer to this linguistic phenomenon as *Wasei Eigo* (Made-in-Japan English). Indeed, rather than adopt English words as they are, they have been known to create their own unique forms. A car's windscreen is 'front glass'. A rear-view mirror is a 'back mirror'. The steering wheel is a 'handle', a hubcap is a 'wheel cover', and so on.

Some of the greatest mirth is created when these spill over into oddball product names, such as 'Creap' for a powdered coffee creamer, 'Flavour My Drip' for individual pre-mixed coffee servings and 'Pocket Wetty' for pre-moistened hand wipes.

Word borrowings seem most likely to be adopted when the subject is negative. When the 3 percent consumption tax was introduced in 1989, government posters identified it as *nyuu takusu*. Another highly unpopular subject, *risutora* – restructuring – generally implies laying off workers. And although a perfectly good Japanese word exists for sexual harassment (*seiteki iyagarase*) the media invariably refers to this as *seku-hara*.

In a city deprived of greenery, this reserve provides an invaluable space to breathe in, not only for humans but also the aquatic flora that flourish in its ponds and wetlands, and the large variety of birds that stop by.

MEGURO

Kume Museum of Art ❾

Address: 2-25-5 Kami-Osaki, Shinagawa-ku,
Tel: 03-3491 1510
Website: www.kume-museum.com
Opening Hours: Tue–Sun 10am–5pm
Entrance Fee: charge
Transport: Meguro

Just opposite Meguro Station's west exit on the left corner, the small **Kume Museum of Art** (Kume Bijutsukan) houses a collection of paintings by Kume Kuchiro, one of the first Japanese painters to practice Impressionism.

Daien-ji ❿

A five-minute walk southwest of the station, down a rather steep slope, **Daien-ji** is home to 500 lifelike *rakan* (Buddha disciple) images. Made as an offering to the spirits of those who died in a disastrous fire that destroyed the original temple in 1772, the stone figures stand row upon row against one of the temple's walls. Highly individualised, each pose and face is different.

Meguro Gajoen ⓫

Address: 1-8-1 Meguro, Meguro-ku
Tel: 03-5434 3837
Website: www.megurogajoen.co.jp
Opening Hours: daily 9am–10pm
Entrance Fee: free
Transport: Meguro

Immediately downhill from the temple is Meguro **Gajoen**, one of Tokyo's most extravagant wedding halls. Not much is left of the original building, which dates back to 1931, save for the *hyakudan kaidan* (one-hundred-step stairway), off of which are a several ornately decorated rooms that contain lovely traditional works of art. This section of the complex – which also contains a luxury hotel and several restaurants – is only open for short periods during the year when there is an entry charge. It's well worth taking

Janglish on T-shirts.

Relaxing in the National Park for Nature Study.

a look inside the rest of the hall, which has other beautifully decorated function halls and corridors.

Across Meguro-gawa from Meguro Gajoen is a fairy-tale castle that looks better suited to Disneyland. This is the **Meguro Emperor** (tel: 03-3494 1211) one of Tokyo's most famous love hotels a kitsch relic dating back to 1973. The interior once sported racy rooms with all manner of decor and beds, including one shaped like

a gondola; today though it is pretty much like any business hotel.

Meguro Parasitological Museum ⑫

Address: 4-1-1, Shimo-Meguro, Meguro-ku
Tel: 03-3716 1264
Website: www.kiseichu.org/english.aspx
Opening Hours: Tue–Sun 10am–5pm
Entrance Fee: free
Transport: Meguro

Head west along Meguro-dori and cross Shimbashi Bridge to find one of the city's strangest institutions, the **Meguro Parasitological Museum** (Meguro Kiseichukan). There's a morbid fascination to peering at the 45,000 parasites collected by the museum, including the remains of an 8.8-metre (29ft) tapeworm removed from the body of a 40-year-old man, but otherwise it's not one of Tokyo's must-see museums. If you want to pick up a unique souvenir, the museum's shop does a range of tapeworm T-shirts you are unlikely to find anywhere else.

Meguro Fudo ⑬

Address: 3-20-26 Shimo-Meguro, Meguro-ku
Tel: 03-3712 7549
Opening Hours: daily 9am–5pm
Entrance Fee: free
Transport: Meguro

Head south from the Parasitological Museum, following the long, straight backstreet shooting off of Meguro-dori, and in five minutes you'll be at the first of a cluster of temples. **Meguro Fudo** (also known as Ryusen-ji) is the largest temple in the area, and is said to have been founded in the 9th century by the monk Ennin. Its main feature is a pond that stands near the main hall, into which water flows from the mouths of two bronze dragons – a feel of these waters (or for the very hardy, a few minutes standing under them in midwinter) is supposed to bring religious purification.

THE 47 RONIN

The tragic fate of 47 *ronin* (masterless samurai) is a true-life event reproduced countless times in *kabuki* and *bunraku* plays. The story, often called *Chu-shin-gura* (The Story of the Loyal Retainers) is much admired by Japanese as a morality tale demonstrating the code of duty and self-sacrifice that was the highest samurai ideal. Hollywood seems to have been impressed by the story, too: a film about the 47 *ronin* starring Keanu Reeves is set to be released in December 2013.

The story goes like this: Lord Asano, scorned by his teacher Lord Kira, caused grave offence by drawing his sword in anger. Because the offence occurred within the castle grounds, Asano was obliged to perform *seppuku* (ritual suicide). Almost two years later on 14 December 1702, Asano's 47 retainers, in a carefully planned act of revenge, decapitated Kira in his mansion on the banks of the Sumida River and carried the head through the streets of Edo to their lord's grave at Sengaku-ji. Honour restored, the 47 *ronin* immediately turned themselves in to the authorities who, on 4 February 1703, ordered them to commit *seppuku* on 4 February 1703. One month later, they dutifully obliged.

Just to the northeast of Meguro Fudo is **Gohyaku Rakan-ji,** which like Daien-ji is known for its *rakan* (Buddha disciple) images. Some 300 of the temple's original 536 disciples, all carved by a monk called Shoun, survive today. One street southeast of Meguro Fudo is the less interesting **Joju-in,** another temple connected to Ennin and one that has become associated with Yakushi, the Buddhist deity of healing.

Meguro Museum of Art Tokyo ⓮

Address: 2-4-36 Meguro, Meguro-ku
Tel: 03-3714 1201
Website: www.mmat.jp
Opening Hours: Tue–Sun 10am–6pm
Entrance Fee: charge
Transport: Meguro

Returning to where Meguro-dori crosses the Meguro-gawa head north along the riverbank to the **Meguro Museum of Art Tokyo** (Meguro Bijutsukan) a spacious gallery in pleasant surroundings, housing a collection of craft and fine-artworks by modern and contemporary Japanese artists as well as pieces from overseas artists.

Naka-Meguro ⓯

Keep following the Meguro-gawa northwards and you will soon hit Naka-Meguro, a station on the overland Tokyu Toyoko Line to Shibuya as well as the underground Hibiya Line. Around here are many relaxed boutiques and cafés that are great places to check out the latest trends. Cherry trees line both sides of the river making this one of the most pleasant places in the city to celebrate *hanami* season (see page 172). The running water also has a cooling effect in summer.

EBISU

One stop up the JR Line from Meguro Station, or along the Hibiya Line from Naka-Meguro, is **Ebisu,** a district that takes its name from the beer Yebisu (an older spelling of Ebisu; Japanese no longer uses 'ye'), which was first brewed here back in 1887. The beer itself is named after one of the seven Shinto gods of good fortune. The train station here was originally a freight depot to transport beer from factories and breweries lining the Meguro and Shibuya rivers.

Yebisu Garden Place

Redesigned in the late 1990s, the south side of Ebisu Station has a long horizontal escalator that takes visitors to the **Yebisu Garden Place** (www.gardenplace.jp) a massive shopping, hotel, office and entertainment complex. Built on the site of the old Yebisu brewery, the name is a misnomer though as there is minimal greenery here. Around the plaza are shops and boutiques, bars, cafés, a concert hall, the Westin Hotel and French restaurant Taillevent Robuchon, housed in a florid Disneyesque French chateau.

Museum of Yebisu Beer ⓰

Address: 4-20-1 Yebisu Garden Place, Meguro-ku

Yebisu Garden Place.

Museum of Yebisu Beer.

A couple in traditional Japanese wedding apparel.

Tel: 03-5423 7255
Website: www.sapporoholdings.jp/english/guide/yebisu
Opening Hours: Tue–Sun 11am–7pm
Entrance Fee: free
Transport: Ebisu

Within the complex and celebrating the history of the beverage that the area's name and fortunes are founded on is the small **Museum of Yebisu Beer** (Ebisu Mugishu Kinenkan). You can wander around freely or take a 40-minute tour (in Japanese) with a 'brand communicator' (charge). At the end of the tour there are samples of Sapporo's beers on offer (charge) in the tasting salon.

Tokyo Metropolitan Photography Museum ⓱

Address: 1-13-3 Mita, Meguro-ku
Tel: 03-3280 0099
Website: www.syabi.com
Opening Hours: Tue, Wed, Sat–Sun 10am–6pm, Thu–Fri until 10pm
Entrance Fee: charge
Transport: Ebisu

On the eastern side of Yebisu Garden Place is the superb **Tokyo Metropolitan Photography Museum** (Tokyo-to Shashin Bijutsukan), the premier exhibition space for notable photography and video art. Major Japanese and Western photographers are featured here.

Yamatane Museum of Art ⓲

Address: 3-12-6 Hiroo, Shibuya-ku
Tel: 03-5777 8600
Website: www.yamatane-museum.or.jp
Opening Hours: Tue–Sun 10am–5pm
Entrance Fee: charge
Transport: Ebisu

Returning to Ebisu Station and walking about 10 minutes to the northeast along the main road will bring you to the interesting **Yamatane Museum of Art** (Yamatane Bijutsukan). The museum, founded in 1966 and based around a collection of 105 works by Hayami Gyoshu, focuses on kindai nihonga, Japanese paintings from the Meiji era onward. There are around six or seven differently themed exhibitions every year featuring these delicate artworks.

JAPANESE WEDDINGS

Meguro Gajoen (see page 163) and Happo-en (see page 161) are two of Tokyo's most famous wedding halls where the huge parties that accompany the happy event are held. Shinto, Buddhist, Christian or non-religious ceremonies are available, but the choice may not match whatever religious affiliation the couple has; the trappings of a traditional Christian wedding, with Western-style white dresses and priests (usually just a play-acting foreigner), have become particularly popular. Back in the 'Bubble era', when money came easy, it wasn't unheard of for some couples to also hire foreign actors to be guests to make it look as if they were cosmopolitan enough to have foreign friends.

Traditional Japanese weddings, however, are held at shrines and performed to Shinto rites – a good place to see these is Meiji-jingu (see page 129). The bride wears a white *shiromuku* kimono while the groom has on *montsuki* (black formal kimono), *haori* (jacket), and *hakama* (pants). The wedding reception parties *(kekkon hiroen)* can be lavish affairs where the happy couple are expected to change outfits several times. Guests are obliged to bring a substantial cash gift, which must be enclosed in a special envelope called a *shugi bukuro*. In exchange they will leave the celebration with a gift from the couple.

BEST RESTAURANTS, BARS AND CAFÉS

PRICE CATEGORIES

Prices for a three-course dinner per person without drinks and taxes:

¥ = under ¥2,000
¥¥ = ¥2,000–¥3,000
¥¥¥ = ¥3,000–¥5,000
¥¥¥¥ = over ¥5,000

Restaurants

American

MLB Café Tokyo

4-19-19 Ebisu, Shibuya-ku. Tel: 03-3448 8900. www.mlbcafe.jp Open: L Mon–Fri, D daily. ¥¥¥ Off map

As you'd expect at a restaurant themed around baseball the food mostly consists of burgers, steaks and hot-dogs – but are top-class renditions. On the ground floor is the casual Field Café 66, upstairs is the Diamond Club Restaurant where the dining floor is encircled by huge screens showing baseball games from around the world.

Fusion

Fummy's Grill

2-1-5 Ebisu, Shibuya-ku. Tel: 03-3473 9629. www.cardenas.co.jp/fummys Open: L & D daily. ¥¥¥ Off map

Fumihiro Nakamura was the first to serve Californian-inspired cuisine in Tokyo at affordable bistro prices, a brilliant formula that ensures he's always busy with a varied crowd of local business people, artsy types and the foreign community.

Stellato

3F, 4-19-17 Shiroganedai, Minato-ku. Tel: 03-3442 5588. www.stellato.jp Open: daily 5.30–11pm. ¥¥¥¥ Off map

Theatrical decor – chandeliers, log fire, Moroccan architecture – but serious contemporary cuisine with creative Asian flourishes. The rooftop lounge has views of Tokyo Tower. English menu.

Japanese

Chibo

Yebisu Garden Place Tower, 38F, 4-20-3 Ebisu, Shibuya-ku. Tel: 03-5424 1011. www.chibo.com Open: L & D daily. ¥¥ Off map

The speciality here is *okonomiyaki* – savoury pancake-like creations. Unlike at most *okonomiyaki-ya*, where you cook your own on a hot-plate set into the table, the *okonomiyaki* here are made for you and then set onto your hotplate when ready. It's fun and affordable anywhere, but here you also get a great view from the top of the high-rise Yebisu Garden Place mall.

Ebisu Imaiya

1-7-11 Ebisu-Nishi, Shibuya-ku. Tel: 03-5456 0255. Open: Sat–Thu 5pm–1am, Fri until 3am. ¥¥¥ Off map

This cosy diner specialises in delectable free-range Hinai chickens, which are served either as *yakitori* skewers, grilled over charcoal, or in warming *nabe* hotpots, cooked at the table.

Enju

1-1-1 Shirokanedai, Minato-ku. Tel: 03-3443 3125. Open: L & D daily. ¥¥¥¥ Off map

Exquisite *kaiseki-ryori* in traditional surrounds and accompanied by views over Happo-en's lovely garden. You'll have to be in the mood for a splurge: courses range from ¥8,400 to ¥12,600, without drinks.

Ippudo

1-3-13 Hiroo, Shibuya-ku. Tel: 03-5420 2225. Open: Mon–Thu 11–3am, Fri–Sat 11–4am, Sun 11–2am. ¥ Off map

This hole-in-the-wall ramen noodle shop is one of Tokyo's best. You specify how well cooked you want your noodles, and what kind of broth (red or white, both pork based). Add seasonings to taste (garlic, sesame seeds or spicy bean sprouts). Then just slurp it down. Cash only.

Tonki

1-1-2 Shimo-Meguro, Meguro-ku. Tel: 03-3491 9928. Open: Wed–Sun 4–10.45pm. ¥¥ Off map

This family-run restaurant specialises in classic *tonkatsu* (deep-fried crumbed pork cutlets). Dishes are served with a slightly spicy brown sauce, rice and shredded cabbage. For many of Tokyo's foodies, this is the city's best *tonkatsu*: be prepared to queue.

Bars and Cafés

Buri

1-14-1 Ebisu-Nishi, Shibuya-ku. Tel: 03-3496 7744. www.buri-group.com Off map

Casual and (usually) low cost, *tachinomi-ya* (standing-only bars) seem to be going through a bit of a renaissance in in Tokyo. Buri is a good one, in part thanks to a great list of *sake* from around the country. The food is tasty and affordable too. Open late.

Café d'Art

4-7-25 Kitashinagawa, Shinagawa-ku. Tel: 03-5423 1609. Off map

Enjoy drinks while overlooking a sculpture garden inside the Hara Museum of Contemporary Art.

Kissa Ginza

1-3-9 Ebisu-Minami, Shibuya-ku. Tel: 03-3710 7320. Off map

Not in Ginza but a short walk west from Ebisu Station is this deliciously retro café that morphs into a trendsters' DJ bar after 7pm.

TY Harbor Brewery

2-1-3 Higashi-Shinagawa, Shingawa-ku. Tel: 03-5479 4555. www.tyharborbrewing. co.jp Off map

A refreshing range of microbrewed ales and a peaceful canalside location on Tennoz Isle. Stand and nurse your drink at the high-tech bar, or sit in the restaurant next door, which serves steaks, burgers and pizzas. English menu.

What the Dickens!

1-13-3 Ebisu-Nishi, Shingawa-ku. Tel: 03-3780 2099. www.whatthedickens.jp Off map

This British pub near Ebisu Station is a popular expat hangout thanks to its decent selection of ales and whiskey, not to mention the almost-nightly comedy and live music nights. Closed Mondays.

Celebrating the bloom of cherry blossoms at Ueno Park.

UENO, YANESEN AND HONGO

Ameyoko's old black market alleys and Yanaka's atmospheric cemetery, temples and craft shops sandwich the rich cultural attractions of Ueno Park, including the Tokyo National Museum.

North of Tokyo Station, eight minutes on the Yamanote train, is Ueno Station (Ueno-eki). It is a subtle impression, but the area around the station seems more down to earth, if not grittier, than other parts of Tokyo. This was once the commoner's part of town, the *shitamachi*. In the post-war years, many of Tokyo's orphaned children lived in the park, and it still hosts many homeless people who live amid the trees under blue tarpaulin tents and in cardboard boxes.

Ameya Yokocho ❶

Accessed from Ueno station to the north and either Ueno Okachimachi or Okachimachi stations to the south, running parallel with Ueno's main street of Chuo-dori is **Ameya Yokocho** (daily 10am–8pm), one of Tokyo's liveliest street markets. **Ameyoko**, the commonly shortened name of the market, is a composite of *ame* (sweets) and *yoko* (alley). 'Confectioner's Alley' did a roaring trade in sweets, mostly made from sweet potato and beans, in the immediate post-war years. During the Korean War, it was a thriving black market for American goods. Here, under the railway tracks,

Dried fruits and nuts on sale at Ameya Yokocho market.

among the cheap clothes, fried noodle vendors and dried fish stalls, where young men hack blocks of ice and bellow the latest prices for strips of black seaweed, kelp and octopus, the working-class spirit of *shitamachi* lives on.

UENO PARK

Saigo Takamori statue ❷

The centrepiece of Ueno, a meeting place for the capital's old merchant culture, is **Ueno Park** (Ueno-koen;

www.kensetsu.metro.tokyo.jp/toubuk/ueno), a fine place for people watching, especially on weekends. In spring, the park is cherished among Japanese for its cherry blossom trees (see page 172).

If you enter the park at the south end, near **Keisei-Ueno Station** (Keisei-Ueno-eki), it is a short walk up a slight incline to the modest 1892 **statue of Saigo Takamori** (1827–73). Although he was a key architect of the Meiji Restoration, Takamori led an unsuccessful rebellion against the country's new leaders and eventually committed ritual suicide. The statue shows him

walking his dog, wearing a summer kimono, his sword safely sheathed.

To the left is the **Shogitai Tomb**, the resting place of loyal Tokugawa samurai who refused to accept the shogunate's collapse in 1868 and retreated to Ueno.

Kiyomizu Kannon Hall ❸

Ahead to the left, on the edge of a small bluff, is **Kiyomizu Kannon Hall** (Kiyomizu Kannon-do). Built in 1631 and moved to its present site in 1698, it is a dwarfish imitation of Kiyomizu-dera, the far grander temple in Kyoto. The main image

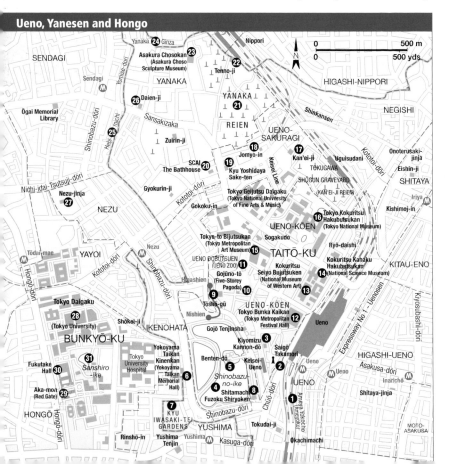

Ueno, Yanesen and Hongo

of worship is the Senju Kannon (Thousand-Armed Goddess of Mercy), but another image, the Kosodate Kannon, believed to answer the prayers of childless women, is more popular. Those who subsequently give birth return and leave a small doll as an offering of their gratitude.

Shinobazu Pond ❹

The temple's location was partly chosen for its fine view of the **Shinobazu Pond** (Shinobazu-no-ike) and its tiny island, home to the **Benten Hall ❺** (Benten-do), built in 1958 although its history dates back to the early 17th century. The abbot Tenkai dedicated the temple to Benten, patron of the arts and goddess of beauty. Now a freshwater pond, Shinobazu was once a salty inlet of Tokyo Bay. It is at its best in July and August when lotus plants bloom each morning. It is also a sanctuary for many species of birds and waterfowl, including egrets, grebes and cormorants. At weekends you will find quite a few food stalls, selling *yakitori* and the like, set up around Shinobazu.

Statue of Saigo Takamori.

Yokoyama Taikan Memorial Hall ❻

Address: 1-4-24 Ikenohata. Taito-ku
Tel: 03-3821 1017
Website: www.tctv.ne.jp/taikan
Opening Hours: Thu–Sun 10am–4pm
Entrance Fee: charge
Transport: Yushima

Two interesting diversions lay just to the west of the pond, across Shinobazu-dori. The **Yokoyama Taikan Memorial Hall** (Yokoyama Taikan Kinenkan) displays *nihonga* (traditional Japanese painting in a modern vein) by Yokoyama Taikan (1868–1958), one of the foremost practitioners of this style of art. Born Sakai Hidemaro (like many Japanese artists he adopted a pen name) Yokoyama lived in this house, which also has beautifully designed gardens.

Kyu Iwasaki-tei House and Gardens ❼

Address: 1-3-45 Ikenohata, Taito-ku
Tel: 03-3823 8340

The Benten temple overlooks the picturesque Shinobazu Pond.

Kiyomizu Kannon Hall.

Cherry Blossoms:
An Excuse to Party

The identification between the Japanese and the evanescent beauty of the cherry blossom, the national flower, is keen but intangible.

The springtime appreciation of the cherry blossom expresses the Buddhist notion of impermanence and transience. Japan's samurai warriors felt a special nostalgia for the cherry blossom, seeing in its brief and vivid spell a parallel with their own lives, which might end abruptly at any moment. Few nations have extracted so much pleasure and sadness from the contemplation of a single flower.

The notion of the cherry blossom's ephemerality is celebrated in countless poems. A haiku by the Japanese writer Ryota sums up the genre:

> This is the way of the world –
> three days pass,
> you look up –
> the blossom's out, or fallen.

Cherry blossoms in Ueno Park.

Far more than just a springtime rite, in many respects the blossoms mark the beginning of the Japanese year. It is also the start of the academic year, and the time new recruits enter companies. It is a season for renewal.

A national event

The progress of the flower is a national event all over Japan. The moment the first cherry blossoms, or *sakura*, bloom in Okinawa and Kyushu at the southern tip of the country in early March, television and newspaper reports follow. Until the last blossoms are blown off from the trees in the northern island of Hokkaido in early May, the media monitors the progress of the *sakura zensen*, or 'cherry blossom front', as it advances up the map.

In Tokyo, newspapers report that the flower is *sanbu zaki* (30 percent open) or *gobu zaki* (50 percent open). The most exquisite moment is when the flower is at *shichibu zaki* (70 percent open), which is considered the ideal time for a *hanami* (cherry-viewing party).

Ueno Park, one of the best-known venues in Tokyo for *hanami*, has over 1,000 trees and attracts as many as a quarter million celebrants a day at its busiest. This is when the Japanese are at their most exuberant mood. Blue tarpaulins are laid on the open spaces of the park, gargantuan quantities of food are consumed, women in kimonos dance, cameras pop, and portable karaoke sets appear from nowhere, producing a deafening beer- and *sake*-lubricated rowdiness. Despite the towering heaps of garbage, the sludge of discarded meat skewers, cornhusks and half-eaten fruit, no one dreams of picking a sprig of blossom, much less climbing a tree.

Purists insist the blossoms are at their best for no longer than three days. Connoisseurs seek out Tokyo's rarer species of tree, such as the wild cherries in the Hama Rikyu Garden (see page 216), or the twin-blossom cherries in the Shinjuku Gyoen (see page 120). The perfect end to a *hanami* occurs when a breeze releases a *hanafubuki* (petal storm), dusting the ground with pink and white flowers.

Website: http://.teien.tokyo-park.or.jp/en/
Opening Hours: daily 9am–5pm
Entrance Fee: charge
Transport: Yushima

A couple of minutes south, the **Kyu Iwasaki-tei House and Gardens** is another quiet Meiji-era retreat, though on a grander scale. The mansion, once the residence of the industrialist Hisaya Iwasaki (son of the founder of the trading company Mistubishi), was designed by the English architect Josiah Conder. Built in 1896, the house and estate, fine examples of *fin-de-siècle* Tokyo elegance and privilege, stand in immaculately kept landscaped gardens which you can observe while sipping green tea.

Shitamachi Museum ❽

Address: 2-1 Ueno-Koen, Taito-ku
Tel: 03-3823 7451
Website: www.taitocity.net/taito/shitamachi
Opening Hours: daily 9.30am–4.30pm
Entrance Fee: charge
Transport: Ueno

Return to Shinobazu-dori, which runs parallel to the southern end of the pond and leads to the park entrance for the **Shitamachi Museum** (Shitamachi Fuzoku Shiryokan), one of Tokyo's most insightful museums. A transplanted tenement block and merchant house display everyday objects such as kitchenware and children's toys, many donated by people living in the area. Demonstrations of handicraft skills are regularly staged, along with videos and photo displays depicting the area up to the 1940s.

Tosho-gu ❾

Back on the higher ground of Ueno Park, a stone *torii* leads to **Tosho-gu** (meaning 'Illuminator of the East'), a shrine established in 1627 (the present buildings date from a 1651 renovation) by a warlord wishing to honour the first Tokugawa shogun, Tokugawa Ieyasu. The walkway to the shrine is lined with dozens of large symbolic stone or copper freestanding lanterns – the tallest is 6 metres (20ft) – donated by warlords to cultivate merit with the shogun.

The main shrine building (closed for renovations until around December 2013) is a magnificent structure; its outer hall features murals by the famous Edo artist, Kano Tanyu. Also interesting is the Chinese-style **Kara-mon**, a gate decorated with dragons that are meant to be ascending to heaven. According to local folklore, the dragons slither over to nearby Shinobazu Pond under cover of night to drink. The good news for any thirsty dragons is that come nightfall they will find several cheap and cheerful *yatai* (food and drink stalls) around the pond where they can quench their thirst.

The 36-metre (120ft) high **Five-Storey Pagoda** (Gojuno-to) ❿, clearly visible from the grounds of the shrine, was originally a part of the Kan'ei-ji complex, much of which was burned down. You have to be

Penguins at Ueno Zoo.

Elaborately carved doors at the Tosho-gu Shrine.

Dinosaur displays at the National Science Museum.

within the precincts of the Ueno Zoo for a close-up look.

Ueno Zoo ⓫

Address: 9-83 Ueno Koen, Taito-ku
Tel: 03-3828 5157
Website: www.tokyo-zoo.net/english/ueno
Opening Hours: Tue–Sun 9.30am–5pm
Entrance Fee: charge
Transport: Ueno

Not one of the most attractive or best maintained of its kind, the **Ueno Zoo** (Ueno Dobutsuen), north of the Five-Storey Pagoda, has over 450 species of wildlife with some 2,600 animals on view, including a 'monkey mountain', where dozens of simians roam in semi-freedom. The star attraction for locals, however, is the pair of pandas, Li Li and Shin Shin. Children will especially like the enclosure where they can pet small animals like goats, sheep and ducks.

Tokyo Metropolitan Festival Hall ⓬

Address: 5-45 Ueno-Koen, Taito-ku
Website: www.t-bunka.jp/en
Tel: 03-3828 2111
Opening Hours: (library) Tue–Sat 1pm–8pm, Sun 1pm–5pm
Entrance Fee: free
Transport: Ueno

Moving across to the east side of Ueno Park, the first in a row of institutional-style buildings you'll approach is the **Tokyo Metropolitan Festival Hall** (Tokyo Bunka Kaikan). Designed in 1961 by the celebrated modernist architect Kunio Maekawa in commemoration of Tokyo's 500th birthday, its main attraction is a classical music concert hall that has a wonderful modern interior design and excellent acoustics. The hall also includes a music library with a collection of classical, ethnic and Japanese music.

TIP

Volunteers conduct free 90-minute walking tours of the Ueno, in English, on Wed, Fri and Sun at 10.30am and 1.30pm. They depart from in front of the tourist information booth next to the National Museum of Western Art on the east side of the park.

National Museum of Western Art ⑬

Address: 7-7 Ueno-koen, Taito-ku
Tel: 03-5777 8600
Website: www.nmwa.go.jp/en
Opening Hours: Tue–Thu, Sat, Sun 9.30am–5pm, Fri until 8pm
Entrance Fee: charge
Transport: Ueno

Ahead to the right is the **National Museum of Western Art** (Kokuritsu Seiyo Bijutsukan), consisting of two quite different buildings. The original, completed in 1959, is the work of Le Corbusier, while the new wing housing temporary exhibitions and completed in 1979 was designed by Kunio Maekawa. The permanent collection includes many works by French Impressionists such as Renoir, Degas, Monet, Tintoretto and Rubens, as well as more contemporary artists like Miro, Ernst, Picasso and Jackson Pollock. The outside courtyard has a display of 57 sculptures by Rodin.

National Science Museum ⑭

Address: 7-20 Ueno Park, Taito-ku
Tel: 03-3822 0111
Website: www.kahaku.go.jp
Opening Hours: Tue–Thu, Sat, Sun 9am–5pm, Fri until 8pm
Entrance Fee: charge
Transport: Ueno

Behind the art museum, on the right, the **National Science Museum** (Kokuritsu Kagaku Hakubutsukan) is devoted to science and technology, engineering, natural history and aerospace research. You won't be able to miss the building because it has a life-size sculpture of a blue whale in front of it. The museum's dinosaur displays and exhibits on oceanography and botany are popular with children. Two newer halls have interactive displays and simulated videos.

Tokyo Metropolitan Art Museum ⑮

Address: 8-36 Ueno Koen, Taito-ku
Tel: 03-3823 6921
Website: www.tobikan.jp
Opening Hours: daily 9.30am–5.30pm
Entrance Fee: charge
Transport: Ueno

On the left side of the park, the 1975 redbrick **Tokyo Metropolitan Art Museum** (Tokyo-to Bijutsukan), which underwent a major renovation in 2012, completes the set of Kunio Maekawa designs in Ueno Park. Over half the building is sunken to prevent the structure from intruding on the park surroundings.

The museum's three floors are set aside for its own collection of Japanese artists, temporary exhibitions, studio space and an art school. Exhibitions range from works by established painters and calligraphers to those of promising new artists. If you need a break from exploring Ueno, there are a couple of restaurants and cafés in the museum.

Tokyo Metropolitan Art Museum.

Kannon statue at Yanaka's Daien-ji temple.

A wide variety of rice crackers on sale.

Tokyo National Museum ⑯

Address: 13-9 Ueno Park, Taito-ku
Tel: 03-3822 1111
Website: www.tnm.go.jp
Opening Hours: Tue–Sun 9.30am–5pm, (Mar–Dec Sat–Sun until 6pm)
Entrance Fee: charge
Transport: Ueno

All the previous museums are but overtures to Ueno Park's centrepiece, the colossal **Tokyo National Museum** (Tokyo Kokuritsu Hakubutsukan). To tour this marvellous museum properly you will need to allow at least half a day.

Said to house the world's largest collection of Japanese art and archaeology, with in excess of 100,000 artefacts, the complex is divided into four main galleries. A permanent collection of paintings, textiles, calligraphy, ceramics and lacquerware are housed in the main **Honkan Gallery**. Archaeological relics from the Jomon Period right to the early 19th century can be found in the **Heisei-kan Gallery**, while the **Toyokan Gallery** has an eclectic mix of Chinese, Central Asian and Korean art treasures. The **Gallery of Horyu-ji Treasures** houses masks, scrolls, sculpture and treasures from the Horyu-ji Temple in Nara.

Kan'ei-ji ⑰

Northwest of Tokyo National Museum, running parallel to a small cemetery, the modest **Kan'ei-ji** is all that remains of an extensive complex established in 1625 as the Tokugawa family temple. Ueno was at the northeast entrance to the shogun's city; northeast being a less than auspicious compass point, a temple was needed to metaphysically guard this approach. At its peak the complex had 68 buildings and contained an enormous image of Buddha destroyed in the Great Kanto Earthquake of 1923.

YANESEN

Exiting Kan'ei-ji onto Kototoi-dori will bring you into **Yanaka,** one of the best-preserved older quarters of Tokyo, a veritable time capsule of old wooden houses, private galleries, traditional shops, temples, bathhouses and back alleys crowded with potted plants and trellises – all easily explored on foot.

FAMOUS GRAVES

Once part of a Buddhist temple, Yanaka Cemetery (Yanaka Reien) contains some 7,000 graves. At the graveyard offices (daily 8.30am–5.15pm) attendants provide a map of the graveyard (in Japanese) and direct you to some of the most famous graves in the cemetery. These include the burial places of talented composer and *koto* player Miyagi Michio, botanist Dr Makino Tomitaro, artist Yokoyama Taikan, and the notorious female mass-murderer Takahashi Oden. Japan's last shogun, Tokugawa Yoshinobu (1837–1913), is buried here too, alongside the ignominious and destitute, whose bodies were once requisitioned by the university as teaching aids for the medical faculty.

Together with the neighbouring areas of Nezu and Sendagi, quiet, low-rise Yanaka is one of the few old quarters of Tokyo to have come through both the Great Kanto Earthquake and the fire bombing of 1945 relatively unscathed. The three districts have become known by an amalgam of their names: **Yanesen.** Close to both the cultural institutions of Ueno Park and the campus of Tokyo University this has long been the living district of choice for artists, writers, professors and intellectuals. It also sports the city's highest concentration of temples, many of which date back to the mid-17th century.

Jomyo-in 18

On Kototoi-dori is the entrance to **Jomyo-in**, a temple best known for its 20,000 strong army of tiny Jizo figures. A minor incarnation of the Buddha, Jizo is revered in Japan as a deity, the god of health and healing as well as protector of children. He is recognisable all over the country from his red and white bib and, in the case of the Jomyo-in, sponge gourds held in the left hand. Jizo statues are continually donated to the temple in the hope that one day they will reach their target of 84,000.

Kyu Yoshidaya Sake-ten 19

Address: 6-10-2 Yanaka, Taito-ku
Tel: 03-3823 4408
Website: www.taitocity.net/taito/
shitamachi/sitamachi_annex/sitamachi_
annex.html
Opening Hours: Tue–Sun
9.30am–4.30pm
Entrance Fee: free
Transport: Nezu

Downhill from the temple along Kototoi-dori is the Kyu Yoshidaya Sake-ten, an annex of the Shitamachi Museum (see page 173) and another evocative remnant of Tokyo's past. This merchant's shop, made from wood and dating from 1910, has been preserved as a museum just like it was in its heyday, with nostalgic posters and giant glass flasks and wood barrels.

SCAI The Bathhouse 20

Address: Kashiwayu-Ato, 6-1-23
Yanaka, Taito-ku
Tel: 03-3821 1144
Website: www.scaithebathhouse.com
Opening Hours: Tue–Sat noon–6pm
Entrance Fee: free
Transport: Nezu

Around the corner is the wonderfully cutting-edge art gallery **SCAI** The Bathhouse. The attractive building, dating from 1951, was once actually a neighbourhood bathhouse where the locals came to scrub up each night – you can still see the wooden lockers in the hallway where shoes would be stored before entering. Since opening as a gallery in 1993 the space has mounted exhibitions by such internationally renowned artists as Louise

Yanaka Cemetery, with its Buddha and Bodhisattva statues and leafy paths, is a resting place for many well-known Tokyo figures.

FACT

No two *rakan* (Buddhist disciple images) are alike. If you see people placing a hand, one by one on the heads of each *rakan*, this is a search to find the warmest head, the belief being that this will be the image that most resembles you.

Bourgeois, Anish Kapoor and Genpei Akasegawa. Check they are open before going, as they sometimes close for weeks at a time between major exhibitions.

Yanaka Cemetery ㉑

From The Bathhouse gallery walk up the sloped street Sanski-zaka. As it bends to the left you'll find one of the entrances to **Yanaka Cemetery** (Yanaka Reien) on the right, its grounds spread over a small raised plateau that can also be accessed from Nippori Station to the northeast. Many famous Tokyo personalities are buried here and, with its moss-covered tombs, leafy paths and time-eroded Buddha and Jizo *bodhisattva* statues, the graveyard has an almost Gothic feel about it. It's also a lovely place to linger in spring when its numerous cherry trees come into bloom.

Tenno-ji ㉒ sits in the northern corner of the graveyard, its manicured grounds filled with magnolia trees and hydrangeas, which bloom in the June rainy season. The Great Buddha of Yanaka, a seated bronze figure dating from 1690, is the temple's pride and joy.

Asakura Choso Sculpture Museum ㉓

In this district of grave-makers and stonemasons, it seems natural to come across a gallery dedicated to sculpture. The **Asakura Choso Sculpture Museum** (Asakura Chosokan), a

SHOPPING

Department Stores

Matsuzakaya
3-29-5 Ueno, Taito-ku
Tel: 03-3832 1111
www.matsuzakaya.co.jp/ueno
Split into connected north and south wings, Ueno's century-old department store has a children's play area on its top floor and stocks almost anything you could need. There is another branch in Ginza.

Markets and Shopping Streets

Ameya Yokocho
6-10-7 Ameyoko Plaza, Uneo, Taito-ku
www.ameyoko.net/e
Over 500 shops and stalls cram into the 400-metre (1,300ft) strip south of Ueno Station around and beneath the railway tracks that is Tokyo's greatest street market. You can find all kinds of goods here, including cheap clothes, shoes and many great souvenirs. The market specialises in food, in particular fish, dried fish, seaweed,

fruit, rice crackers and pickles.
Yanaka Ginza
3 Nishi-Nippori, Arakawa-ku
www.yanakaginza.com
This pedestrianised shopping strip is one of the most traditional in Tokyo and is a delight to explore. Find shops selling woven baskets, *geta* (traditional wooden sandals), pottery as well as food. Goto-no-Ame founded in 1922 (at the Nippori Station end of the street), is famous for its sweets and you can sample cheap (¥150 to ¥200) but lovely *menchikatsu* (breaded and deep-fried meat patties) at either Niku-no-Sato or Niku-no-Suzuki. About half way down the street, Kanikitien sells premium green teas, which you can sample before buying, as well as cups, teapots and other tea associated utensils. Note that many of the street's 70 shops are closed on Mondays.

Paper

Isetatsu
2-18-9 Yanaka
Tel: 03-3823 1453

This tiny, well-preserved shop has two floors with combs, dolls, crafted fans and colourful chests of paper drawers, made from *washi* (handmade paper). A hallmark of Isetatsu is its *chiyogami* – woodblock printed papers in both traditional and modern designs.

Rice Crackers

Kikumi Senbei
3-37-16 Sendagi, Bunkyo-ku
Tel: 03-3821 1215
This wonderful shop was built in 1875 and has been serving large square-shaped *senbei* (rice crackers) in various flavours ever since.

Woodcraft

Jusan-ya
2-12-21 Ueno, Taito-ku
Tel: 03-3831 3238
In the same family since it was opened by a samurai in 1736, the specialty here is finely handcrafted boxwood combs. On Shinobazu-dori, directly across from the southeast corner of the pond.

gallery exhibiting the work of Fumio Asakura, is close to the borders of the cemetery, on the left of the road that bears right after exiting Nippori Station's west exit. The museum, which comprises the artist's studio-house and a lovely courtyard garden, has been closed for a four-year renovation, but is set to reopen in mid-2013. From the museum return to the road that runs from the station, turn left and continue until you see the 'Yuyake Dandan' flight of steps leading to **Yanaka Ginza** ㉔. Along this narrow, picturesque pedestrianised shopping street are several sculptures of cats peering down from the eaves of roofs or out of the corners of shop entrances – the area is famous for its feline residents.

Hebi-michi ㉕

At the end of Yanaka Ginza turn left and continue along Yomise-dori until you arrive back at Sansaki-zaka; turn right to pass the venerable rice cracker shop **Kikumi Senbei** on the way to Shinobazu-dori and the entrance to Sendagi subway station. Alternatively, cross over Sansaki-zaka to find **Hebi-michi,** a narrow residential lane that wriggles like a snake (which is what 'hebi' means) through Yanaka towards Nezu. Around here and along Sansaki-zaka you'll find several interesting craft stores including the printed-paper shop **Isetatsu**.

Daien-ji ㉖

Opposite Isetatsu set back from Sansaki-zaka is Daien-ji, a temple that contains a monument to the charms of Osen, a tea shop girl used by the artist Harunobu as a model for several of his woodblock prints. A statue of Kannon, the Goddess of Mercy, stands next to Osen's monument and many Tokyoites, especially the elderly, make pilgrimages here to rub a spot on the statue that corresponds to the part of their body

where they are suffering an ache or pain in the hope of a cure. If this statue is anything to go by, stomach ailments and headaches are the commonest complaints among Tokyo's senior citizens.

Nezu-jinja ㉗

From Daien-ji follow Sansaki-zaka west until you reach Shinobazu-dori. Follow this south, crossing over Nichi-idai Tsutsuji-dori, and then take the next right to reach the grounds of **Nezu-jinja**. This popular shrine is known for its azalea festival in late April, when more than 3,000 bushes within the compound come into bloom. The shrine was rebuilt by Japan's fifth shogun, Tsunayoshi, in 1706. Look out for the Inari fox shrine with a row of red *torii* gates lining the approach and a stage for religious dances. The closest subway station to the shrine is Nezu at the junction of Shinobazu-dori and Kototoi-dori.

HONGO

Heading uphill west from Nezu is **Hongo**. Like Yanaka, this district

FACT

Hongo is associated with the highly gifted writer Higuchi Ichiyo, featured on the Japanese ¥5,000 note. A long-time habitué of Hongo, Higuchi, who succumbed to tuberculosis at the age of 24, chronicled the struggles of ordinary people and the city's vanishing Meiji-era districts with a rare maturity for one so young.

Azaleas at Nezu-jinja.

Tokyo University students at archery practice.

TIP

Travellers looking for cheap accommodation should bear in mind that in February, legions of young hopefuls descend from the provinces to take university entrance examinations. In many cases, budget rooms will have been booked weeks in advance.

remains stubbornly unfashionable and rather proud of the fact. Hongo's claim to have supported human settlement predating Edo is impressive. When earthen pots and other implements were found in a prehistoric mound on the high ground towards the northern section of Hongo in 1828, their design was considered sufficiently different from the preceding Jumon era to designate a new one, the Yayoi Period. The slope running down the hill from the excavation site to Nezu Station is, not surprisingly, called Yayoi-zaka.

Hongo was one of 15 wards created in 1878 for the new capital. In 1947 it was combined with the contiguous district of Koishikawa and became **Bunkyo-ku** (Culture Ward), the name reflecting its reputation as an enclave of academia and home to artists and writers. Slopes such as **Honmyoji-zaka** and **Kiku-zaka** (Chrysanthemum Slope) add interest to the Hongo district,

creating a dipping and rising urban geography.

Tokyo University ㉘

At the heart of the Hongo area is the campus of **University of Tokyo** (Tokyo Daigaku; www.u-tokyo.ac.jp/en), a pleasant place to stroll under the shade of its massive gingko trees. Founded by Imperial decree in the 1870s, this prestigious university, more popularly known as Todai, was built on the estate of the powerful Maeda feudal lords after being transplanted from Kanda in the 1880s.

Aka-mon ㉙

Just south of the main entrance to the campus on Hongo-dori is the **Aka-mon** (Red Gate) erected in 1827 by the lord to welcome his new bride. This is the only gate of its kind remaining in Japan, a symbol for the university itself, and lends a traditional touch to the otherwise mainly prewar, vaguely Art Deco-style buildings of the campus.

The main exception is the **Fukutake Hall** ㉚ (http://fukutake.iii.u-tokyo.ac.jp), designed by Tadao Ando and opened in 2008. The long, low concrete structure includes a 200-seat theatre, various meeting halls, the UT Café Berthollet Rouge (see page 181) and a shaded terrace that can also be used as a venue for art and media events.

Sanshiro Pond ㉛

Shrubbery surrounds the **Sanshiro Pond** (Sanshiro-ike) at the centre of the campus. Once the focus of what was considered one of the most beautiful gardens of Edo this artificial pond created in 1638 is shaped like the Japanese character for heart (*kokoro*), which explains its official name Yutokuen Kokoroji Ike. It's more common popular name Sanshiro comes from its depiction in a novel of the same name by the celebrated Japanese writer Natsume Soseki.

BEST RESTAURANTS, BARS AND CAFÉS

PRICE CATEGORIES

Prices for a three-course dinner per person without drinks and taxes:

¥ = under ¥2,000
¥¥ = ¥2,000–¥3,000
¥¥¥ = ¥3,000–¥5,000
¥¥¥¥ = over ¥5,000

Restaurants

Japanese

Echikatsu
2-31-23 Yushima, Bunkyo-ku. Tel: 03-3811 5293. http://r.gnavi.co.jp/g085100/lang/en
Open: D Mon–Fri. ¥¥¥¥ ⑥ p274, C3
The setting itself is beautiful – a large, atmospheric Japanese house dating from 1871. The food is delectable: *shabu-shabu* (beef dipped in broth) and *sukiyaki* (one-pot dish) – prepared with Matsuzaka beef, the best in Japan. Several of the rooms have garden views. Reservations advised.

Hantei
2-12-15 Nezu, Bunkyo-ku. Tel: 03-3828 1440. Open: L & D Tue–Sun. ¥¥¥ ⑥ p274, C2
Kushiage 'deep-fried skewers of fish, meat and vegetables) is served in a wonderful old wooden building in one of Tokyo's best-preserved downtown areas. Although there is an English menu, there is no need to order as the dishes just keep coming till you ask for them to stop.

Honke Ponta
3-23-3 Ueno, Taito-ku. Tel: 03-3831 2351. Open: L & D Tue–Sun. ¥¥ ⑥ p274, D3
Opened in 1905, this eatery serves *yoshoku*, a Japanised version of Western food introduced to Tokyo a century ago. Besides *tonkatsu* and other deep-fried breaded food (chicken, meat and seafood), there are also croquettes, stews and sautéed shellfish. Most dishes come with rice and *miso* (savoury soybean) soup.

Ikenohata Yabu Soba
3-44-7 Yushima, Bunkyo-ku. Tel: 03-3831 8977. Open: L & D Thu–Tue. ¥¥ ⑥ p274, D2

This traditional *soba* (buckwheat noodles) shop was set up by a veteran chef previously at Kanda Yabu Soba, the most illustrious soba shop in the city. Prices are very reasonable. English menu available.

Izuei
2-12-22 Ueno, Taito-ku. Tel: 03-3831 0954. Open: daily 11am–9.30pm. ¥¥¥¥ ⑥ p274, D2
Overlooking Shinobazu pond, Izuei has been dishing up succulent *unagi* (grilled eel) dishes for over 250 years. You can sit at a table on the ground floor or on tatami mats on the upper levels. Dinner courses can get expensive, but there are relatively good lunch deals to be had.

Musashino
2-8-11 Ueno, Bunkyo-ku. Tel: 03-3831 1672. Open: Daily 11.30am–9pm. ¥¥ ⑥ p274, D2
Tonkatsu (breaded and deep-fried pork cutlet) is the special here. It comes in generous, succulent portions in sets that also include a bowl of rice, bowl of miso and pickles.

Nezu Club
2-30-2 Nezu, Bunkyo-ku. Tel: 03-3828 4004. Open: D Wed–Sat. ¥¥¥¥ ⑥ p274, C1
This delightful little restaurant serves excellent Japanese cuisine that is neither casual nor formal but halfway in between. It is easiest to order the ¥7,000 set dinner, but you can nibble substantially for considerably less than that.

Sasanoyuki
2-15-10 Negishi, Taito-ku. Tel: 03-3873 1145. www.sasanoyuki.com
Open: Tue–Sun 11am–9pm. ¥¥¥ ⑥ p274, D1
Considering that this is arguably Tokyo's most famous tofu restaurant, having been in business for 315 years, the prices are reasonable and the atmosphere relaxed – despite its connections as suppliers to the royal family. The set courses here are quite filling even though tofu is generally light.

Bars and Cafés

Takioka
6-9-14 Ueno, Taito-ku
Tel: 03-3833 2777
⑥ p274, D2
A very informal *tachinomi-ya* (standing bar) full of *shitamachi* vibe that's ideal for a few cold beers, or some *sake* and *shochu*, accompanied by simple, low-cost *izakaya* fare such as delicious *yakitori* (grilled chicken skewers).

UT Café Berthollet Rouge
Fukutake Hall, Tokyo University, 7-3-1 Hongo, Bunkyo-ku
Tel: 03-5841 0211
www.reims.co.jp/UTcafe
⑥ p274, C2
Hang out with Todai students and faculty at this sleek café located in an equally sleek Tadao Ando-designed building. Its concept is a modern Parisian-style café. Closed Sunday.

The Warrior Celt
3F Ito Building, 6-9-22 Ueno, Taito-ku
Tel: 03-3836 8588
www.warriorcelt.jp
⑥ p274, D2
Offering a great range of beers and ciders, many imported from the British Isles, this foreigner-friendly bar often has live music performances. From 8pm on the first, third and fifth Wednesday of the month they also have lively Celtic music sessions where anyone can pick up an instrument and join in with the fun.

Yanaka Coffee
3-8-6 Yanaka, Taito-ku
Tel: 0120-874 877
www.yanaka-coffeeten.com
⑥ p274, C1
You'll smell the delicious scent of roasting beans well before you reach this shoebox size coffee shop and roasters situated around the corner from Yanaka Ginza. Closed the third Thursday of the month.

ASAKUSA

This earthy area, where you'll find the city's most visited temple complex, is the heart of old Tokyo; to its west is a creaky old amusement park, a drum museum and shops which sell the kitschy plastic food models often seen in Japanese restaurants.

L egend has it that on 18 March 628 two fishermen discovered a tiny image, a golden Kannon (the Buddhist Goddess of Mercy) statue in their nets in the Sumida River in the northeast of Edo. A temple – **Asakusa Kannon**, better known as **Senso-ji** – was built for the relic soon after near the river. It quickly became an important place of pilgrimage and remains Tokyo's most important Buddhist place of worship.

In his book *Tokyo Sights and Insights*, Ryosuke Kami points out that Asakusa has long been a place where worshippers came 'not just for religious purposes but for the entertainment that abounded in the temple's backyard, ranging from theatres, archery galleries, and circuses to brothels.' From the mid-1800s until World War II, Asakusa was the centre of all fine things in Tokyo, a nucleus of theatre and literature, of cuisine and other sensual delights. Its flowering, however, began with exile: first, with the banishment of the Yoshiwara, the licensed prostitution district, to Asakusa in the 1600s, and later with theatre, especially *kabuki*, in the 1800s. In the 1930s, Asakusa was the largest entertainment district in Japan, a role that was later handed to Shinjuku.

Asakusa had two prized qualities: *iki*, a sense of style and urbane polish, and *inase*, meaning chivalry or bravado, making the area, until its peak in the 1800s, *the* place to be seen in Edo Tokyo. Even samurai (banned from mixing with the lower classes) and priests (escaping strict vows of celibacy) would enter the district in disguise.

The heart of old Tokyo is still here in this quintessentially working-class

Geisha decked out in their finery at Asakusa Kannon.

The Hozo-mon gate at the Asakusa Kannon.

Gallery éf ❷

Address: 2-19-18 Kaminarimon,
Taito-ku, www.gallery-ef.com
Tel: 03-3841 0442
Opening Hours: Wed–Mon
11am–7pm
Entrance Fee: free
Transport: Asakusa

Before or after exploring Asakusa it's worth dropping by **Gallery éf.** The exhibition space that hides behind this hip café and bar (open until midnight) is inside a stonewalled *kura* (traditional storehouse) dating from 1868, which is just as interesting to view up close as is the contemporary artwork.

Senso-ji

The central compound of **Senso-ji** (www.senso-ji.jp) Asakusa's spiritual centre, is best approached through the **Kaminari-mon** ❸ (meaning 'Thunder Gate') facing onto Kaminarimon-dori, a minute's walk from the subway exit. This impressive, red-painted wooden entrance is flanked by leering, twin meteorological deities (Fujin, god of wind, on the right, and Raijin, god of thunder, on the left), and a magnificent 4-metre

Detail of the Senso-ji compound.

district. Asakusa is a vital part of the *shitamachi* – a word that translates, literally, as 'downtown', but stands more precisely for 'home of the common people' – a plebeian area synonymous in Japanese minds with hard work and equally hard play, a bustling mercantile mentality, libertine pleasures, Bohemianism and a strong sense of community. Fortunately, all these characteristics are still very much alive today.

Sumida Park ❶

As you exit Asakusa subway station, the district's temple area lies northwest, while the **Sumida River** (see page 200) and **Azuma Bridge** (Azuma-bashi) is to the east. On the Asakusa side of the river, just north of Azuma Bridge, is **Sumida Park** (Sumida Koen), a pleasant place for a stroll, especially in spring when cherry trees are in bloom. It is also one of the best spots from which to take in a view of the Philippe Starck-designed **Super Dry Hall** (see page 202) – the futuristic building of Asahi Breweries, topped by a giant gilded sculpture that is known as the 'Golden Turd' for obvious reasons – and, further away, the soaring Tokyo Skytree (see page 202), the city's communication tower across the river, which opened to the public in 2012.

ASAKUSA'S FESTIVALS

The seasons are not allowed to pass by without some festival or event of purely secular invention taking place in Asakusa – flowers in January, bean throwing in February, golden dragon dancing in March and again in October, Tokyo's largest firework display over the nearby Sumida River in late July, a white crane parade in November, a kite market in December, traditional horseback archery in April as well as a relatively new innovation – a Brazilian-style carnival in August.

The biggest event is the Sanja Matsuri (Three Shrines Festival) held on the third weekend in May. Senso-ji, and the roads and sinuous lanes that run around it provide the epicentre for this mammoth four-day spectacle, an important spring event for many Tokyoites. Dozens of intricate portable shrines are carried through the streets by young men and women, with much rough jostling and caterwauling. It is said the shrine gods enjoy being tossed around in this manner, something they get plenty of from the seething, swaying and chanting crowds at Asakusa. Picture opportunities abound as you will spot geisha and yakuza (gang members) sporting full-bodied tattoos – both rare sights in Tokyo these days.

(13ft) -tall red paper lantern with the character for 'thunder' emblazoned across it.

Nakamise-dori ❹

Stretching for about 250 metres/yds from Kaminari-mon to Senso-ji's main hall of worship is **Nakamise-dori**; a perpetually thronged avenue of around 100 colourful stalls selling an amazing variety of products from the traditional (rice crackers and paper fans) to the bizarre (clothes for dogs). If you come at night you'll see that the stall shutters are all decorated with paintings of traditional scenes.

Denbo-in ❺

To the left where Nakamise-dori crossed Denboin-dori, sits **Denbo-in** the residence of the Senso-ji's head priest. This monastery buildings date back to 1777 but its 12,200-sq-metre garden (131,320-sq-ft) created by the Zen landscape gardener Kobori

Enshu is around a century older. The complex is currently closed to the public.

Hozo-mon ❻

At the end of Nakamise-dori, pass under the grand **Hozo-mon** (Treasury Gate), with its ensemble of protective statues, to enter the main temple grounds. The upper storey of the gate contains Chinese sutras dating from the 14th century. A large bronze incense burner stands beyond the Hozo-mon where a steady stream of visitors place lighted incense sticks in the burner before offering a brief prayer. Japanese also consider it good luck to waft the incense smoke over their clothing with their hands.

Kannon Hall ❼

The legendary golden image fished out of the Sumida River all those centuries ago is supposed to be hidden from view inside the **Kannon Hall** (Kannondo), the main building

Fan shop on Nakamise.

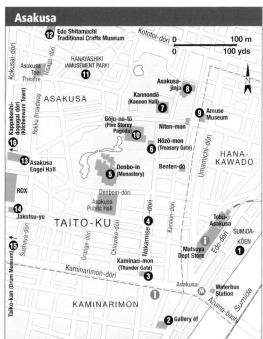

of the temple complex that has been on this spot since 645. Kannondo has been rebuilt many times since it was first erected by the third shogun Tokugawa Iemitsu in 1648; the current structure, whose most recent major renovation was completed in 2010, dates from 1958 and has reinforced concrete walls and a dramatically sloping roof covered in titanium tiles.

On busy days, the temple resounds to the clank of money as coins are tossed into the offertory box, hands are clapped and bells, attached to thick ropes, are rung. The statue of Kannon, a mere 6cm (2ins) high, is believed to be housed in a fireproof box in the inner sanctum of this large hall, behind the golden altar. Although the original has never been seen by the public a replica is taking out for viewing annually on 13 December. Three times a day, the temple's monks gather to chant sutras in its honour. The hall contains an important collection of votive paintings dating from the 18th and 19th centuries, while the altar, the centrepiece of the main hall, is jam-packed with religious objects.

Asakusa-jinja ⑧

Behind Kannondo and to the right is the shrine dedicated to the fishermen who found the Kannon image. **Asakusa-jinja** (www.asakusajinja.jp/english) is one of the few buildings in the complex to have remained more or less intact since it was built in the 17th century. The shrine, also known as the Sanja Sanma (Shrine of the Three Guardians), is popular for traditional weddings and is the starting place for Asakusa's most famous annual festival, the Sanja Matsuri (see page 183).

In front of the shrine is the **Niten-mon**, the main eastern gate to Senso-ji. Built in 1618 and a designated Important Cultural Treasure,

the gate is usually covered with votive papers left by visitors.

Japanese prayer cards (votive papers) and dolls.

Amuse Museum ⑨

Address: 2-34-3 Asakusa, Taito-ku
Tel: 03-5806 1181
Website: www.amusemuseum.com.
Opening Hours: Tue–Sun 10am–6pm
Entrance Fee: charge
Transport: Asakusa

Beside the Niten-mon is the six-storey **Amuse Museum**. A building partly filled with clothes made of ancient rags may not sound that 'amusing' but the collections on display here make this is one of the best of Asakusa's modern tourist sights. Combining articles from the 30,000 piece private collection of ethnographer, folklorist and author Chuzaburo Tanaka with digital reproductions of *ukiyo-e* prints from the Spaulding Collection at the Museum of Fine Art, Boston, the museum has been put together with great care and plenty of imagination, with everything labelled in both Japanese and English.

Patched rag clothes (*boro*) form the core of the collection. Used for many generations by the same poor

FACT

Victorian-era traveller Isabella Bird, visiting Asakusa Kannon in 1878, noted the different approaches to faith, both the intellectual and intuitive. In her book *Unbeaten Tracks in Japan*, she observed that the temple's main hall was 'full of all the mysterious symbols of a faith which is a system of morals and metaphysics to the educated and initiated, and an idolatrous superstition to the masses.'

The decorated stalls along Nakamise.

Young taiko drummers during the Sanja Matsuri festival.

families, they are displayed as if they are high fashion. Coming close up to the garments you can admire their rough beauty and the brilliance of their design. Tanaka collaborated with Akira Kurosawa to source 350 costumes for his movie *Dreams* and there's a section of the museum devoted to these.

On the top floor *orihime* (weaving girls) in kimonos sit at looms creating pieces for the museum's shop, while beside them is a café and Bar Six, which affords great views over the area. On the ground floor there's a shop, café and also a small theatre where music and dance performances are sometimes held.

Five-Storey Pagoda ❿

The western section of the Asakusa complex is dominated by the **Five-Storey Pagoda** (Goju-no-to), an impressive reconstruction dating from 1973 of the original, first built here in 942. Opposite the pagoda is the small **Yakushido**, dating from 1649 and one of the oldest structures at the temple.

Hanayashiki Amusement Park ⓫

Address: 2-28-1 Asakusa, Taito-ku, www.hanayashiki.net
Tel: 03-3842 8780
Opening Hours: times and closures vary throughout the year; see schedule on website.
Entrance Fee: charge
Transport: Asakusa

West of the temple grounds, in the direction of Kokusai-dori and the Asakusa View Hotel (see page 249), is Asakusa's main entertainment district. This is where the endearingly old-fashioned **Hanayashiki Amusement Park**, opened in 1853 and as such Japan's oldest amusement park, is located. Not surprisingly there is a vintage quality to many of the attractions in the park, including an eerie and rather run-down *obakeyashiki* – ghost house – dating from the 1950s. Visitors to the toilet at the Hanayashiki (echoes of an old Parisian *pissoir* with a dented roof) will be amused – perhaps momentarily paralysed in the vitals – by a sudden, hurtling vibration as the one-minute roller-coaster, squeezed into the confines of the park, rattles 1 metre (3ft) or so overhead.

Edo Shitamachi Traditional Crafts Museum ⓬

Address: 2-22-13 Asakusa, Taito-ku
Tel: 03-3842 1990
Opening Hours: daily 10am–8pm
Entrance Fee: free
Transport: Tsukuba Express Asakusa or Asakusa

Across the street from Hanayashiki lie the back streets of Asakusa's sprawling entertainment district, centring on **Rokku Broadway**. Lurid posters outside cinemas and fleapit clubs advertise porn and *yakuza* movies, re-runs of sentimental films and sex cabarets. This area is also known for *taishu engeki*, an enduring *shitamachi* brand of popular theatre.

At the north end of Rokku Broadway, the street becomes Hisago-dori and along here you'll find the **Edo Shitamachi Traditional Crafts Museum** (Edo Shitamachi Dento Kkogeikan) displaying around 400 items representing over 50 different crafts made in Taito Ward and elsewhere; also known as Gallery Takumi you can shop for souvenirs here, and there are usually live demonstrations by craftspeople between 11am and 5pm on Saturdays.

Asakusa Engei Hall ⑬

Address: 1-43-12 Asakusa, Taito-ku
Website: www.asakusaengei.com
Tel: 03-3841 6545
Opening Hours: daily 11.40am–10pm
Entrance Fee: charge
Transport: Tsukuba Express Asakusa or Tawaramachi

South along Rokku Broadway **Engei Hall** is Asakusa'a most prominent theatre. The daily bill here (¥2,500 for an all-day ticket) includes dozens of acts, ranging from *manzai* stand-up comedy duos and acrobats to *rakugo* storytellers and magicians. Everything is in Japanese and some of the acts so rapier even fluent Japanese speakers might struggle to keep track of the gags, but much of the slapstick humour and performances transcend language barriers. An hour or two here is a great window into Japanese culture and wit.

Jakotsu-yu ⑭

Address: 1-11-11 Asakusa, Taito-ku
Tel: 03-3841 8641
Website: www.jakotsuyu.co.jp
Opening Hours: Wed–Mon 1pm–midnight
Entrance Fee: charge
Transport: Tsukuba Express Asakusa or Tawaramachi

Continuing south along Rokku Broadway and behind the department store ROX is the traditional *sento* (bathhouse) **Jakotsu-yu**, fed by an *onsen* (hot-water spring) pumping water from a kilometre (.5 mile) beneath the ground. The mineral content of the water makes it appear

TIP

You can board waterbuses at the pier beside the Azuma Bridge in Asakusa for tours of the Sumida River. It is also possible to go beyond Hinode Pier to Rainbow Bridge, Odaiba and the bay. Departures are usually every 30 to 40 minutes from 9.50am to 3.40pm for Hama Rikyu Detached Garden; until 7.20pm to Hinode Pier; and from 10.10am to 5.20pm to Odaiba.

SHOPPING

Cosmetics

Hyakusuke
2-2-14 Asakusa,
Taito-ku
Tel: 03-3841 7058.
This establishment has supplied geisha and *kabuki* actors with cosmetics for over a 100 years. Among its refined goods is a skin cream made from the droppings of the Japanese nightingale. A block east of the northern end of Nakamise-dori.

Crafts

Bunsendo
Nakamise-dori, Taito-ku
Tel: 03-3844 9711
Stocks one of the best selections of Japanese fans in the area. On the left just beyond the Kaminari-mon gate.

Fujiya
2-2-15 Asakusa, Taito-ku
Tel: 03-3841 2283
This popular shop specialises in *tenugui* (hand-printed towels sporting original designs), which make great souvenirs. A block east of the northern end of Nakamise-dori.

Kurodaya
1-2-5 Asakusa, Taito-ku
Tel: 03-3844 7511
To the right of Kaminari-mon this business, dating back to 1856, sells traditional woodblock prints and *washi* (handmade) paper products.

Sukeroku
Nakamise-dori, Taito-ku
Tel: 03-3844 0577
This shop on Nakamise-dori is as tiny as its products: miniature handmade dolls in Edo Period costumes.

Yonoya Kushiho
1-37-10 Asakusa, Taito-ku
Tel: 03-3844 1755
Much sought out for its traditional hairpieces, ornaments and exquisite boxwood combs. On Demboin-dori.

Food

Tokiwado
1-3-2 Asakusa, Taito-ku
Tel: 03-3841 5656
www.tokiwado.com
An open-fronted store next to Kaminari-mon that specialises in *kaminari okoshi* (thunder rice crackers) and other types of *senbei*.

TIP

The Asakusa Culture Tourist Information Centre (tel: 03-3842 5566; daily 9.30am–8pm) is opposite the Kaminari-mon. Drop by to find out what's going on in the area and to join a one-hour guided walking tour of Senso-ji Temple and the surrounding area (Sun 11am and 2pm; free).

Kappabashi kitchenware.

brown. There are small outdoor baths (*rotemburo*), a main bathroom decorated with a tiled mural of Mount Fuji and baths in which a mild electric current is pulsed through the water – meant to be stimulating for the body.

Drum Museum

Address: 2-1-1 Nishi-Asakusa, Taito-ku
Tel: 03-3842 5622
Opening Hours: Wed–Sun 10am–5pm
Entrance Fee: charge
Transport: Tsukuba Express Asakusa or Tawaramachi

South of ROX department store, at the junction of Kaminarimon-dori and Kokusai-dori, is the **Drum Museum** (Taiko-kan), on the second floor above a shop that sells drums and large items like portable shrines used in Shinto festivals. Drums from all over the world are displayed here, and visitors are encouraged to try them out (a blue dot on a drum means you can play it; a red dot means you can't). Listen out for the 1-metre (3ft) -diameter

Japanese *taiko* (drum), which is popular with children.

Kappabashi-dogugai-dori

A few blocks west of the museum takes you to the kitchenware wholesale district known as Kappabashi (www.kappabashi.or.jp/en). The intersection of Kappabashi-dogugai-dori and Asakusa-dori, where the main shops start is difficult to miss: look for the building topped with a giant chef's head, replete with a white, pleated hat. One corner of the building is decorated with several tiers of coffee cups.

Wholesale merchants sell every type of restaurant and kitchen equipment imaginable – hence its English nickname 'Kitchenware Town'. It's a great place to pick up pottery, knives and other kitchen implements as well as the plastic food samples (*sampuru*) you will see in restaurant display windows all over the city.

On the left hand side of the street also look for the golden statue of a *kappa*, the water sprite of Japanese folk stories, whom the merchants have adopted as their mascot.

RYOUNKAKU

In 1890, a 60-metre (200ft) tower was erected near Senso-ji's Five-Storied Pagoda. Officially called Ryounkaku (Cloud-Surpassing Pavilion) but commonly known as Ju-ni-kai (Twelve Stories), the octagonal tower of red bricks around a wooden frame was designed by the Scottish engineer W.K. Burton. On completion Ryounkaku was the tallest building in the eastern hemisphere and only 21.6 metres (71ft) shy of being the world's loftiest tower. Privately owned, it had the first public elevator in Japan and offered visitors a view from the top, as well as shopping opportunities. Although it was later reinforced with steel, the tower was so severely damaged by the 1923 earthquake that it had to be torn down.

BEST RESTAURANTS, BARS AND CAFÉS

Restaurants

Japanese

Chinya

1-3-4 Asakusa, Taito-ku. Tel: 03-3841 0010
www.chinya.co.jp Open: L & D Mon, Wed–Fri, Sat-Sun 11.30am–9pm. ¥¥¥¥ 89 p274, E2

In business since the Edo era, diners at Chinya eat at low tables set on *tatami* mat flooring, a lovely and fittingly traditional setting for fine beef *shabu shabu* and *sukiyaki* courses.

Daikokuya

1-38-10 Asakusa, Taito-ku. Tel: 03-3844 1111. www.tempura.co.jp Open: daily 11.10am–8.30pm. ¥ 90 p274, E2

Daikokuya really only serves one main dish upon which its reputation is founded. Dig into traditional Edo Period-style *tendon* (tempura rice bowl) with authentic *shitamachi* atmosphere and surroundings to go with it. On Demboin-dori.

Hatsuogawa

2-8-4 Kaminarimon, Taito-ku. Tel: 03-3844 2723. Open: L & D daily. ¥¥ 91 p274, E2

An *unagi* (grilled eel) restaurant that captures the atmosphere of Asakusa's prewar heyday. The old wooden building has all the usual design trimmings, down to the paper screens and stands of bamboo. Boxed sets of broiled fish are the best value and worth a try, though the skewered eel is also very good.

Ichimon

3-12-6 Asakusa, Taito-ku. Tel: 03-3875 6800. Open: D daily. ¥¥ 92 p274, E1/2

This rustic *izakaya* (tavern) offers a good all-round selection of Japanese dishes and excellent range of *sake*. Note that you pay for each dish as it arrives, using wooden coupons (called *mon*), which you will be asked to buy upon arrival.

Kawakaze

3-34-11 Asakusa, Taito-ku. Tel: 03-3876 7711. Open: D Tue–Fri, L & D Sat, Sun. ¥¥¥ 93 p274, E1/2

Strictly traditional and located in one of Tokyo's most loved entertainment districts, Kawakaze has an interior that is decidedly more classy than the feisty, downtown streets of Asakusa that you have to walk to get here. Exquisite array of tofu dishes served with aplomb on tatami mats to the accompaniment of fine Japanese *sake* and the barely audible swish of kimono hems.

Komagata Dojo

1-7-12 Komagata, Taito-ku. Tel: 03-3842 4001. Open: daily 11am–9pm. ¥¥ Off map

This 210-year-old restaurant specialises in loach, a small freshwater fish similar to eel but with an earthier flavour. There are only two dishes here: *yanagawa* (loach omelette) and *dojo nabe* (loach stew). Dishes are laid on tatami mats.

Otafuku

1-6-2 Senzoku, Taito-ku. Tel: 03-3871 2521. www.otafuku.ne.jp D daily (closed Mon Mar–Oct). ¥¥¥ 94 p274, E1

Oden, a lightly seasoned broth in which vegetables and processed seafood are stewed, is the speciality here, and it's extremely good. The very filling courses, which include more than *oden*, start from ¥5,250, but if you don't have a big appetite you can eat well for less at this restaurant by going à la carte.

Sometaro

2-2-2 Nishi-Asakusa, Taito-ku. Tel: 03-3844 9502. Open: daily noon–10.30pm. ¥ 95 p274, E2

This rustic-looking eatery serves *okonomiyaki*, a flour and egg-based pancake stuffed with vegetables, shrimp and other ingredients covered with lashings of soy sauce and mayonnaise. It is sometimes called Japanese pizza, but the only resemblance to the Italian fare is its flatness. Great atmosphere.

Waentei-Kikko

2-2-13 Asakusa, Taito-ku. Tel: 03-5828 8833. www.waentei-kikko.com Open: L & D Thu–Tue. ¥¥¥¥ Off map

In a lovely wooden house between Hozo-mon and Benten-do, you can enjoy a delicious boxed bento lunch for ¥2,500 while listening to live performances on the *shamisen*, a Japanese version of a banjo. The concerts also take place at dinner, when the *kaiseki* and blowfish courses start from ¥6,825.

Bars and Cafés

Bar Six

2-34-3 Asakusa, Taito-ku
Tel: 03-5806 1181
www.amusemuseum.com
Off map

A sophisticated bar at the top of the Amuse Museum with black leather sofas and a broad balcony providing dress circle views across the grounds of Senso-ji in one direction and of the Tokyo Skytree in the other.

Kamiya Bar

1-1-1 Asakusa, Taito-ku
Tel: 03-3841 5400
Off map

This famous Asakusa bar, established in 1880 and located one minute east of Kaminari-mon on Kaminari-dori, invented the cognac-based cocktail known as *denki-bran* (translated as electric brandy), which the locals here tend to chase down with lager. Simple Japanese and European food is also served here – on the ground floor you line up to order and pay before you eat; if you sit upstairs it's regular restaurant service.

SUIDOBASHI, OCHANOMIZU, KANDA AND AKIHABARA

A fine Edo-era stroll garden, an obscure temple supposedly haunted by the spirits of foxes and a school turned into a contemporary arts centre are all found in these areas also well-known to lovers of books, electronics, *anime* and *manga*.

The east-west line of the Kanda River (Kanda-gawa) passes across a drained marshland from the districts of Iidabashi and Suidobashi and across to Kanda, Ochanomizu and Akihabara. This area of expanded flatlands cutting from the southern bluff of the Yamanote hills extending south of Yushima defines the area covered in this chapter.

Yushima, which means 'Island of Hot Water', an allusion to a prehistoric age when hot water bubbled up from the hills, is situated in the Soto-Kanda (Outer Kanda) district. Things have cooled down since then, but even in the late Edo and early Meiji periods, streams of clear water trickled down from the Yushima and Yamanote hills to the marshes and meadow land of the old riverine lower city. The incidental function of these *sakamichi* (areas of sloping roads), to provide drafts of fresh air and the occasional unimpeded view beyond the city, has largely been lost to high-rises and power lines, but the basic configuration remains.

Historically, the area not only marked the physical transition from the high city to the low, it was also the point where the residences, shops and trade districts of the townspeople mingled with zones set aside for the military class, the samurai and their households.

SUIDOBASHI AND AROUND

Koishikawa Korakuen ❶

Address: 1-6-6 Koraku, Bunkyo-ku
Tel: 03-3811 3015
Website: http://teien.tokyo-park.or.jp/en/koishikawa
Opening Hours: daily 9am–5pm
Entrance Fee: charge
Transport: Iidabashi

Office workers heading home through Kanda.

As a gentle start to your exploration of this quarter of the city pay a visit to **Koishikawa Korakuen**, one of the city's finest Edo-Period stroll gardens, the entrance of which is closest to Iidabashi station. This is all that remains of the estate of Yorifusa Tokugawa, patriarch of the powerful Mito Tokugawa clan. Work began on the garden in 1629 and was finally completed by his heir. Stroll gardens were intended for amusement as much as aesthetic contemplation. The designers of such gardens tried to incorporate scenes from the Chinese classics as well as miniaturised Japanese landscapes.

A small stream passing through the garden is called the Oikawa River and symbolises a river of the same name in Arashiyama, near Kyoto, while two small hills, each covered in dwarf bamboo, are said to represent Mount Lu, a Buddhist pilgrimage site in China. The north end of the garden provides a completely different perspective as paddy, irises and plum trees come into view. The garden also features a large lotus pond best viewed in August when the plants are in blossom, and a section with a small pond, once a place of study for the Mito family. Apart from a Chinese gate that once graced the entrance to this inner garden, all else remains unchanged, including its original stone-paved path.

Tokyo Dome City ❷

Address: 1-3-61 Koraku, Bunkyo-ku
Tel: 03-5800 9999
Website: www.tokyo-dome.co.jp
Opening Hours: daily 10am–9pm
Entrance Fee: charge
Transport: Suidobashi and Korakuen

Immediately north of Suidobashi Station but also accessible from Korakuen Station is **Tokyo Dome City**, an area that takes its name from the 55,000 capacity stadium at its centre. Affectionately known by its nickname the 'Big Egg', Tokyo Dome

is used as a venue for major rock concerts – Madonna, Britney Spears and U2 have performed here – as well as professional baseball games: it's the home base for the popular team Yomiuri Giants.

The neighbouring **amusement park** was formerly known as Korakuen after the nearby garden and some people may still call it that. Big-thrill rides, including the giant doughnut-shaped Big O Ferris wheel and the Thunder Dolphin roller-coaster which reaches speeds 130kmh (80mph), alternate with gentler attractions such as musical fountains, a carousel and a play area packed with toys for small children.

Baseball Hall of Fame and Museum ❸

Address: 1-3-61 Koraku, Bunkyo-ku
Tel: 03-3811 3600
Website: http://english.baseball-museum.or.jp
Opening Hours: Mar–Sept Tue–Sun 10am–5pm, Oct–Feb Tue–Sun 10am–6pm
Entrance Fee: charge
Transport: Suidobashi

Rich autumn leaves at Koishikawa Korakuen Garden.

The Thunder Dolphin rollercoaster goes right through the middle of the spokeless Ferris wheel.

Spa LaQua ❹

Address: 1-3-61 Koraku, Bunkyo-ku
Tel: 03-5800 9999
Website: www.laqua.jp
Opening Hours: daily 11am–9am
Entrance Fee: charge
Transport: Korakuen

At the northern end of Tokyo Dome City is the shopping mall LaQua atop of which you'll find the **Spa LaQua,** a luxurious bathhouse that uses water pumped up from a natural hot spring 1,700 metres (5,577ft) below ground. The facility – one of the best in Tokyo – features outdoor baths, massage bubble baths and various type of sauna. There are also relaxation areas where you can snooze, making this a great place to pass the night if you miss the last subway home and can't afford a taxi. The only drawback is an outdated policy many bathhouses still have from when tattoos were associated almost exclusively with yakuza: nobody with tattoos is allowed entry.

Also found within Tokyo Dome City, the dome's **Baseball Hall of Fame and Museum** offers a comprehensive, mostly visual history of Japanese baseball. There are very good English-language pamphlets at hand to steer you through almost 140 years of the game in Japan.

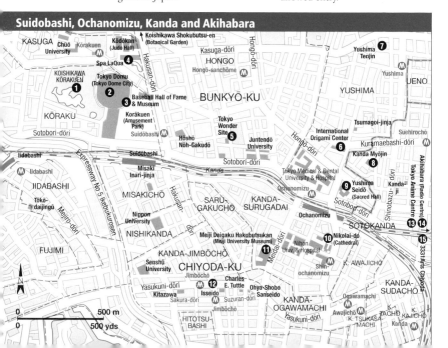

Suidobashi, Ochanomizu, Kanda and Akihabara

Tokyo Wonder Site Hongo ❺

Address: 2-4-16 Hongo, Bunkyou-ku
Tel: 03-5689 5531
Website: www.tokyo-ws.org
Opening Hours: Tue–Sun 11am–7pm
Entrance Fee: free
Transport: Suidobashi

Head east from Suidobashi Station along Sotobori-dori. Bear left just before you reach the striking Century Tower, designed by British architect Norman Foster, to find **Tokyo Wonder Site**. Set up by the Tokyo Metropolitan Government to encourage and promote exciting new works by young and up-and-coming artists, the building contains three floors of whatever is current, from paintings to video installations. If you like what you see here, check out another gallery that is part of the project, in Shibuya.

International origami centre ❻

Address: 1-7-14 Yushima, Bunkyo-ku
Tel: 03-3811 4025
Website: www.origamikaikan.co.jp/info/e_us.html
Opening Hours: Mon–Sat 9.30am–6pm
Entrance Fee: free
Transport: Ochanomizu

From Tokyo Wonder Site continue east towards Hongo-dori. Branching off from here to the north is Kurameabashi-dori that runs behind the Tokyo Garden Palace hotel. Along it is the **Origami Center** (Origami Kaikan), set up in 1859 and considered to be the birthplace of this art of folding paper. The centre holds exhibitions of origami art and there's a workshop on the top floor where you can watch paper being made, dyed and printed. In the shop selling an amazing range of papers and books

An Edo-Period bridge at the Koishikawa Korakuen Garden.

TIP

Yushima Tenjin holds its annual Plum Festival in February (its tiny garden is said to be one of the premier spots in Tokyo for plum viewing). In late October, admirers of the chrysanthemum throng to the shrine to see clever tableaux made from the imperial flower's petals.

An izakaya in Kanda.

devoted to the art, the assistants also provide free origami lessons.

Yushima Tenjin ❼

Address: 3-30-1 Yushima, Bunkyo-ku
Tel: 03-3836 0753
Website: www.yushimatenjin.or.jp
Opening Hours: daily 8am–5pm
Entrance Fee: free
Transport: Yushima

Across the road from the Origami Center, Yokomi-zaka runs north towards **Yushima Tenjin**, the city's so-called 'Shrine of Literature'

dedicated to the 9th-century statesman and poet Michizane Sugawara, deified here in the form of Tenjin, patron of learning and the arts. A steady flow of students come here to pay homage throughout the year, but spring, the traditional time for entrance exams, sees inordinate numbers flocking to the shrine to seek Tenjin's intercession on their behalf.

Kanda Myojin ❽

Address: 2-16-2 Soto-Kanda, Chiyoda-ku
Tel: 03-3254 0753
Website: www.kandamyoujin.or.jp
Opening Hours: daily 8am–5pm
Entrance Fee: free
Transport: Ochanomizu

Returning to Origami Center and Kuramaebashi-dori, a block to the east is one of Tokyo's most important places of Shinto worship. **Kanda Myojin** is a shrine dedicated to rebel general Taira no Masakado, who fought for the oppressed Kantoites against Imperial forces. There is a *taiko* (drum) troupe attached to the shrine called Masakado Taiko. The troupe's main themes celebrate the life of Masakado, but its fame comes from being one of the few all-women *taiko* groups in Japan.

The temple, a concrete reconstruction of a 1616 original, enshrines two other deities besides Masakado: Ebisu, the god of commerce, family prosperity and good marriages, and Daikoku, entrusted with the care of farmers and fishermen. Side stores sell *mikoshi* (portable shrines) used during the Kanda Matsuri, one of the city's three great festivals marked by a magnificent street procession.

Yushima Seido ❾

Address: 1-4-25 Yushima, Bunkyo-ku
Tel: 03-3201 1331
Website: www.seido.or.jp
Opening Hours: daily 9.30am–5pm
Entrance Fee: free
Transport: Ochanomizu

TAKUZOSU INARI: THE FOX SPIRIT LAIR

In the middle of a narrow backstreet, just five minutes from Kasuga Station on the Oedo and Mita subway lines, is an old tree said to be visited by an Inari fox deity. Somehow, locals have kept town planners away from this sacred spot – incredible given how often and extensively Tokyo makes itself over. Overlooking it is the former house of the well-known Taisho-era poet and author, Rohan Koda, who predominantly wrote historical and supernatural shorts set in Edo. The tree is a signpost indicating the presence a few steps away of the **Takuzosu Inari**, a shrine that is one of the spookiest spots in the city. Shoehorned into the pinched precincts of the shrine are rows of *torii* gates, Jizo and Kannon statues, and fierce-looking fox messengers. Stone steps descend under blackened trees (that seem permanently wet) to an eerie cave called the Oana, its dank rock-face the home, it is believed, of the resident white fox. Credence of this comes from author Nagai Kafu who, in his short story *Kitsune* (The Fox), relates how his father spotted the bushy-tailed messenger here one afternoon. Should you spot it, count its tails. It's said the more tails an Inari has, the more powerful and wise it is.

Just across the street from the Kanda Myojin is the **Yushima Seido**, a fascinating building and one of the few Confucian shrines left in Tokyo. Founded in 1632 by a scholar in the Tokugawa government, the centre moved to Soto-Kanda in 1691 when the hall became an academy for Edo's ruling elite. Drawn to Confucian teachings with their regard for hierarchy and obedience, the Tokugawa government happily set about adopting its more authoritarian aspects as a kind of unofficial state philosophy; this became known as neo-Confucianism.

OCHANOMIZU

Nikolai Cathedral ⑩

Address: 4-1 Surugadai, Kanda, Chiyoda-ku
Tel: 03-3295 6879
Website: www.geocities.jp/ynicojp2/english
Opening Hours: Tue–Fri 1–3.30pm (and services from 7.30am and 5pm)
Entrance Fee: charge
Transport: Ochanomizu or Shin-Ochanomizu

South of Yushima Seido, Hijiri Bridge (Hijiri-bashi) crosses the Kanda-gawa leading to one end of Ochanomizu Station. Ochanomizu, means 'Honourable Tea Water'. Water for the shogun's tea is said to have been drawn from the area's deep, and reportedly sweet, wells.

Two blocks south of Hijiri Bridge, the **Nikolai Cathedral** (Nikolai-do) is the main church of the Russian Orthodox faith in Japan. It is named after its founder St Nikolai Kassatkin, a Russian missionary who spent much of his life promoting the Orthodox Church's teachings in Japan. Designed by British architect Josiah Conder, the cathedral was completed in 1891, but lost the top of its original dome in the 1923 earthquake. Even though it was replaced with a smaller dome, the Byzantine style building stands out as an exotic addition to the area.

Meiji University Museum ⑪

Address: 1-1 Kanda-Surugadai, Chiyoda-ku
Tel: 03-3296 4448
Website: www.meiji.ac.jp/museum
Opening Hours: Mon–Sat 10am–5pm
Entrance Fee: free
Transport: Ochanomizu

East of the Cathedral, along Ochanomizu's main street, Meidai-dori, Meiji University has several buildings and departments. The **Meiji University Museum** (Meiji Daigaku Hakubutsukan) is located in the institute's University Hall, on the right as you descend the slope. The fourth-floor exhibition halls house an extensive collection of objects found on digs around Japan sponsored by the university's archaeological faculty, as well as items from China and Korea. Well labelled in English and Japanese, the museum has over 10,000 exhibits, ranging from stone tools of the Pleistocene Age to Kofun tomb (AD 250–538) clay *haniwa* figures.

Characters and games galore at Tokyo Anime Center.

Shinto priest at Yushima Tenjin Shrine.

FACT

The *pachinko* (Japanese pinball) arcade, with blaring sound and glitzy walls, is an industry in its own right. The 13,000 or so halls in Japan gross over 29 trillion yen per annum – spinning more profits than either the steel or auto industries.

Located one floor down is the best reason for a visit, a fascinating section with exhibits relating to the investigation, capture and punishment of criminals during the Edo and Meiji periods. The university, founded in 1881 as the Meiji Judicial School, draws its exhibits from a collection exceeding 250,000 objects. Woodblock prints depicting the kind of punishments given to criminals at the time hang alongside vividly real instruments of torture and execution.

Jimbocho ⑫

Continuing down Meidai-dori will lead to the intersection with Yasukuni-dori and into the heart of the area known as **Jimbocho**, named after the samurai Nagaharu Jinbo, who lived here at the end of the 17th century. In 1913, after a fire had destroyed much of the area, a

SHOPPING

In addition to checking out Jimbocho for its antiquarian books and old woodblock prints and Akihabara for its electronic goods and merchandise related to *manga* and *anime*, have a browse around the Kanda Ogawamachi area along Yasukini-dori, where there are numerous sporting goods shops mostly focused on winter sports, hiking and golf, and Ochanomizu, which has lots of musical instrument stores.

Books

Isseido
1-7 Kanda-Jimbocho, Chiyoda-ku
Tel: 03 3292 0071
www.isseido-books.co.jp
Inside this exquisite Art Deco building dating from 1931 is a gem of a family-run antiquarian bookstore for collectors of rare books and maps.

Sanseido
1-1 Kanda-Jimbocho, Chiyoda-ku
Tel: 03-3233 3312
www.books-sanseido.co.jp
Foreign language books and magazines are found on the sixth floor of this mainstay of the Jimbocho area, although you will have to pay quite a bit more for them than you would at home.

Costumes

Cospa Gee Store
2F MN Building, 3-15-5 Soto-Kanda,
Chiyoda-ku
Tel: 03-3526 6877
www.geestore.com
If you want to get in on the cosplaying (literally 'costume play') game, this is the place to come for your outfit.

Donkihote
4-3-3 Soto-Kanda, Chiyoda-ku
Tel: 03-5298 5411
www.donki.com
The Donkihote chain sells a real mishmash of goods. At this large branch on Chuo-dori, there's an entire floor here dedicated to cosplay, while other floors carry everything from sex toys to discount clothing and cosmetics. There's also a maid café and the AKB48 theatre in the building. It's *otaku* paradise.

Electronics and Computer Games

AsoBitCity
4-3-3 Soto-Kanda, Chiyoda-ku
Tel: 03-3251 3100
http://asobitcity.laox.co.jp
Electronics, cartoon character goods, a shooting gallery and model train sets.

Laox
1-2-9 Soto-Kanda,
Chiyoda-ku
Tel: 03-3253 7111
www.laox.co.jp
The largest of Akihabara's duty-free shops with an extensive line-up of electronic products plus cosmetics, handicrafts and novelty souvenir goods. Staff are multilingual.

Super Potato
3-5F Kitanayashi Building, 1-11-2 Soto-Kanda, Chiyoda-ku
Tel: 03-5289 9933.
www.superpotato.com
This store is packed with old computer games and consoles – one for diehard fans of Pac-Man, Super Mario Brothers and Donkey Kong.

Yodobashi Akiba
1-1 Kanda Hanaokacho, Chiyoda-ku
Tel: 03-5209 1010
www.yodobashi-akiba.com
This huge electronic superstore dominates the east side of the station and offers good discount prices. There are also several decent restaurants and cafés in the building, not to mention a massage chair display section where you can have a free test of the merchandise.

Woodblock Prints

Hara Shobo
2-3 Kanda-Jimbocho,
Chiyoda-ku
Tel: 03-5212 7801
www.harashobo.com
This unusual store stocks a nice selection of prints, both old and new, with a good range of prices. English is spoken.

university professor opened a bookstore in the area, which was the start of Jimbocho's association with the publishing industry. There are now stores specialising in art books, second-hand books, comic books and more, as well as *ukiyo-e* (woodblock prints) and antiques. The Japanese website http://.jimbou.info provides more information on what's available in this 'book town'.

AKIHABARA

Heading east from Ochanomizu and crossing the Kanda-gawa will soon bring you to **Akihabara** (www.e-akihabara.jp) a name which translates as 'Field of Autumn Leaves'. Today Akihabara is best known as the country's foremost commercial showcase for Japanese technology and as a mecca for those interested in *anime*, *manga* and computer games who have nicknamed the area 'Akiba'. It's here that the craze for Maid Cafés (see page 198) and the J-pop dance group AKB48 (www.akb48.co.jp) started; you'll need to be very lucky (or exceedingly unlucky, depending on your view of the group!) to find tickets to their

phenomenally popular shows which take place on the eighth floor of the Don Quixote store on Akiba's main thoroughfare Chuo-dori.

Despite its adoption by a generation of *manga*-obsessed, cosplaying *otaku*, Akihabara remains endearingly close to its low-life roots, with its strident shop assistants, all going hoarse hawking their goods to passers-by, and with a gaggle of unruly electronic stalls still huddled beneath the railway tracks. Hundreds of tax-free shops and discount stores, ranging from multistorey affairs to hole-in-the-wall businesses, are shoehorned into just a few blocks. At night, the multinational throng of shoppers, smoky food stalls and giant, neon billboards, evoke street scenes from the 1982 movie *Blade Runner*.

Tokyo Anime Center ⑬

Address: UDX Building, 4F, 4-14-1 Sotokanda, Chiyoda-ku
Tel: 03-5298 1188
Website: www.animecenter.jp
Opening Hours: daily 11am–7pm
Entrance Fee: free
Transport: Akihabara

TIP

Walking tours of Akihabara can be arranged with Japanese pop culture expert Patrick Galbraith, author of *The Otaku Encyclopedia*; see www.otaku2.com for details. Galbraith also narrates the self-guided audio tour of the area offered by Tokyo Realtime (www.tokyorealtime.com).

Poster advertising a Maid Café.

An electronics store.

Since the early 2000s there has been a great deal of property development in Akihabara focussed around the JR station where the Yamanote and Sobu lines intersect and join with the Tsukuba Express Line out to the city of Tsukuba, a 'science city' planned in the 1960s, in Ibaraki prefecture. Above the Tsukuba Express entrance is a giant branch of the electronics megastore Yodabashi Camera while

to the west, inside the Akihabara UDX building is the **Tokyo Anime Center**. This showcase for the newest and best-known *anime* (animation) work done in Japan, includes a screening room, exhibition gallery, shop and a studio where visitors can listen to voice actors recording dialogue.

Radio Centre ⑭

Akihabara's post-war black market developed into an area of stalls under the railway tracks selling radio spare parts. Those stalls still exist today in the market area known as Radio Centre, and exploring them is a fascinating way to travel back several decades to a time when things such as mobile phones and Sony PlayStations were the stuff of science fiction. In the backstreets on the other side of Chuo-dori, the main thoroughfare in the area, there are many other small stores selling everything from used video games and laptops to computer components and distressingly popular pornographic comics.

3331 Arts Chiyoda ⑮

Address: 6-11-14 Soto-Kanda, Chiyoda-Ku
Tel: 03-6803 2441
Website: www.3331.jp
Opening Hours: (gallery) Mon, Wed, Thu noon–7pm, Fri–Sun until 8pm; (main building) daily 10am–9pm
Entrance Fee: charge
Transport: Suehirocho

On the site of the former Chiyoda Rensei Junior High School tucked away in the streets west of Chuo-dori is the exciting arts centre 3331 **Arts Chiyoda**. Aiming to be a hub for artistic development in the city and fostering links with other artistic communities and projects around Japan and overseas is what this place is all about. There are usually several different exhibitions going on here as well as private gallery spaces and a studio for students working on a community TV channel.

MAID CAFÉS

Maid cafés, where young women dressed in costume (from French waitress in lacy pinafore and cap to nuns or 'beautiful boys') serve customers in an exaggeratedly formal manner. The phenomena kicked off in Akiba in 1991 at **Cure Maid Café** (www.curemaid.jp) founded by a cosplay outfitter and was embraced by the *otaku* community of young men and later by the Japanese government who saw them as a way to sell Japan as a tourist destination to a younger demographic.

There are hundreds of different types of maid cafés now in Akiba, not all of them related to serving food and drinks; getting your ears cleaned by a girl while you lay on her lap is not something everyone would choose to experience, for example. One of the most successful operations, **@home café** (Mitsuwa Building 4F-7F, Soto-Kanda 1-11-4, Chiyoda-ku, tel: 03-3255 2808, www.cafe-athome.com) has a ¥700 cover charge before you order any drinks, food or pay to play any games (like paper, scissors, rock) with the maids, but it is lively and will give you a good idea of what these cafés are all about. If there are long lines here (there often are) and/or you're looking for a quieter experience, try **Mai:lish** (2F FH Kowa Square, 3-6-2 Soto-Kanda, Chiyoda-ku, tel: 03-5289 7310, www.mailish.jp) near Suehirocho subway station. You could even try **Popopure**, which has some English-speaking maids.

BEST RESTAURANTS, BARS AND CAFÉS

Restaurants

French

Arbol

4-7 Kagurazaka, Shinjuku-ku. Tel: 03-6457 5637. Open: daily 5pm–midnight. ¥¥¥ **96** p274, A3

There are many French restaurants in Kagurazaka. This relaxed place tucked away in the district's back streets has an open-plan kitchen and a vegetable garden on their roof from which they pick ingredients for their dishes.

Italian

Canal Café

1-9 Kagurazaka, Shinjuku-ku. Tel: 03-3260 8068. www.canalcafe.jp Open: Mon–Fri 11.30am–11pm, Sat, Sun 11.30am–9.30pm. ¥¥ **97** p274, A3

The outer café section serves light snacks, while the main restaurant offers capable Italian-based meals. Just the place to relax with a nice bottle of wine, next to the old castle moat, watching waterfowl and rowing-boats.

Stefano

6-47 Kagurazaka, Shinjuku-ku. Tel: 03-5228 7515. www.stefano-jp.com Open: L & D daily. ¥¥¥ **98** p274, A3

For the price range, this is some of the best Italian food in the city. Chef Stefano Fastro serves the food of his native Veneto, including home-made pasta, tasty antipasti and satisfying main dishes. Courses from ¥5,500, but you can eat à la carte for a little less.

Japanese

Botan

1-15 Kanda-Sudacho, Chiyoda-ku. Tel:

03-3251 0577. Open: Mon–Sat 11.30am–9pm. ¥¥¥¥ **99** p274, C4

In a wooden building in a traditional neighbourhood, waitresses in kimonos bring a charcoal brazier and a small iron pan, on which you cook chicken, vegetables and tofu in a sweet-savoury sauce – it's the only dish of the house and it's delicious.

Isegen

1-11-1 Kanda-Sudacho, Chiyoda-ku. Tel: 03-3251 1229. www.isegen.com Open: L & D, Apr–Sept Mon–Fri, Oct–Mar Mon–Sat. ¥¥¥¥ **100** p274, C4

The current structure dates from the 1930s, but this historic restaurant has been in business for 180 years serving the same dish: *anko nabe*, a monkfish casserole cooked at the table. As a side dish to the *nabe*, try the delicately flavoured boiled monkfish liver, *kimosashi*.

Kandagawa Honten

2-5-11 Soto-Kanda, Chiyoda-ku. Tel: 03-3251 5031. Open: L & D Mon–Sat (closed 2nd Sat of the month). ¥¥¥¥ **101** p274, C3/4

Located near Akihabara, this 200-year-old establishment serves broiled eel. Refined and traditional in atmosphere, the restaurant prepares and cooks to order, so allow plenty of time. Reservations essential.

Kanda Yabu Soba

2-10 Kanda-Awajicho, Chiyoda-ku. Tel: 03-3251 0287. www.yabusoba.net Open: daily 11.30am–8pm. ¥ **102** p274, C4

The most illustrious noodle shop in the city, Yabu serves classic Edo-style handmade *soba* (buckwheat noodles) in a classic, tranquil setting complete with a small garden. Besides the noodles, it also has a small range of simple, tasty side dishes. Rain or shine, be prepared to queue for a table.

Konakara

1-9-6 Yushima, Bunkyo-ku. Tel: 03-3816 0997. http://konakara.com Open: D Mon–Sat. ¥¥¥ **103** p274, C3

A short walk from Ochanomizu Sta-

tion, this small restaurant specialises in *oden* – tofu, eggs, fish cake and vegetables simmered in a savoury broth flavoured with premium *shiitake* mushrooms. This warm and nourishing food is served in a wooden building designed like a Japanese country house.

Bars and Cafés

Artists Café

Tokyo Dome Hotel 1-3-61 Koraku, Bunkyo-ku
Tel: 03-5805 2243
www.tokyodome-hotels.co.jp
29 p274, B3

There are great views from this sophisticated jazz bar on the 43rd floor of the Tokyo Dome Hotel.

Devil Craft

4-2-3 Nihombashi-Muromachi, Chuo-ku
Tel: 03-6265 1779
www.devilcraft.jp
Off map

A few minutes south of Kanda Station, this brew-pub run by three expats serves up 15 craft beers from Japan and overseas on tap, but is just as popular for its handmade Chicago-style pizzas.

Gundam Café

1-1 Kanda-Hanaokacho, Chiyoda-ku
Tel: 03-3251 0078
g-cafe.jp/english
30 p274, D3

Join the *otaku* faithful of Akiba at this futuristic café themed after the famous giant robot *anime* show franchise Mobile Suit Gundam. You can enjoy food and drink named after Gundam characters and plot points such as taiyaki (sweet bean filled hot cakes) in Gundam robot shapes.

Popopure

1-8-10 Soto-Kanda, Chiyoda-ku
Tel: 03-3252 8599
www.popopure.com
31 p274, C3/D3

A maid café with a slight difference. Some of the maids here are non-Japanese and speak English.

SUMIDA RIVER

Relatively few tourists venture east across the Sumida River -- but there's much to discover in this part of Tokyo including lovely gardens, the sumo stadium, excellent museums and galleries and the soaring Tokyo Skytree.

Opposite Asakusa, on the northeast bank of the Sumida River (Sumida-gawa), it's difficult to imagine that the sprawling residential and small industry area of **Mukojima** was once farms and paddy fields providing food for Edo. It was here that the shoguns enjoyed the sport of falconry and planted cherry tree saplings along the river bank. Later famous for its temples and pleasure quarters, Mukojima's riverside teahouses were also the haunt of the literati and *demimonde*.

It remains Tokyo's largest geisha district although it's nothing like Kyoto and without an introduction to one of the closeted *okiya* (geisha houses), or outside major festivals, you're unlikely to see one of these female entertainers on the streets.

MUKOJIMA AND AROUND

Yutoriya ❶

Address: 2-38-7 Mukojima. Sumida-ku
Tel: 03-5247 2001
Website: www.yutoriya.jp
Opening Hours: daily 9am–6.30pm
Entrance Fee: free
Transport: Hikifune or Keisei Hikifune

Amid low-rise housing sprawl in the northeast corner of Mukojima is architect Hasegawa Itsuko's space-age **Yutoriya,** a planetarium, community centre, library and media centre all rolled into one. Also known as the Sumida Culture Factory and defined as a 'microcosm of the greater media city', the building rises in a series of triangulated roofing, perforated screens and has a large central dome that has to be seen to be believed.

Mukojima Hyakkaen Gardens ❷

Address: 3-18-3 Higashi-Mukojima,

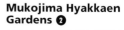

View of the Sumida River.

Sumida-ku
Tel: 03-3611 8705
Website: http://teien.tokyo-park.or.jp/
en/mukojima
Opening Hours: daily 9am–5pm
Entrance Fee: charge
Transport: Higashi-Mukojima

From Yutoriya a short walk north-west along the main road leads **Mukojima Hyakkaen Gardens**, the only Edo-era flower garden remaining in Tokyo. In the early 19th century a wealthy antiques dealer Sahara Kiku-u set up this garden with colleagues and named it Hyakkaen meaning 'a garden of a hundred flowers that is in bloom throughout the four seasons'. Covering little more than a hectare (2 acres), it is intensely planted with trees, deciduous shrubs, flowering bushes and herbaceous perennials, the most notable being a beautiful, 30-metre (100ft) tunnel of bush clover that bursts into a riot of purple-rose flowers in September.

A couple of minutes' walk west of the garden towards the river you'll come across the small shrine **Shirahige-jinja**. Although the main buildings may have been reconstructed after the air raids, memorial stones dotting the grounds suggest an older site. A plaque notes that Terajima village mostly comprised paddy fields between the years 1688–1704, its fertile soil carried over from the upstream Sumida River, also ideal for growing the aubergines popularly known as *terajima-nasu*.

Chome-ji and Kofuku-ji ❸

A short walk south of Shirahige-jinja brings you to the raised metropolitan expressway. Just before you duck under this to walk along the riverside pathway (a wonderful spot for cherry blossom viewing in spring) you'll pass **Chomei-ji** meaning 'temple of long life'. There once was a well here that a shogun is supposed to have drawn

water from and many poets, scholars and authors are also buried in the temple grounds. A few metres south from Chomei-ji, the Zen temple **Kofuku-ji** was founded in 1673. Look out for its distinctive Chinese gate and main hall. Next to Chomei-ji is the famous sweet rice dumpling shop **Chomei-ji Sakuramochi Yamamotoya**.

Ushijima-jinja ❹

Enjoy the riverside walk between the Sakura-bashi and Kototoi-bashi where you'll head back inland along Kototoi-dori through the northern tip of **Sumida Park** (Sumida Koen). Here too is **Ushijima-jinja**, a shrine dedicated to Susano-no-Mikoto, the younger brother of Japan's mythological sun goddess, Amaterasu. Ushijima means 'Cow Island', a reference that is picked up by the shrine's *Nadi-ushi* (stroking cow), a stone statue of a cow dressed in a red bib. Local folklore says the statue has the power to heal – just stroke the part of the cow's body that corresponds with the area that is troubling you.

TIP

If you happen to be in Tokyo on the last Saturday in July be sure to see the spectacular fireworks *(hanabi)* display along the Sumida River.

Flags of various sumo champions.

The Asahi Beer Company dates back to 1889, but its top-selling Super Dry only debuted in 1987. Although popular in Japan, it has received less than favourable reviews overseas.

The bush clover tunnel in the Hundred Flowers Garden.

Asahi Super Dry Hall ⑤

Exit the park to the south and head in direction of the **Azuma Bridge** (Azuma-bashi). On the left, you will see French designer Philippe Starck's **Asahi Super Dry Hall**. The corporate headquarters of the Asahi Beer Company is as striking a piece of architecture today as it was when first unveiled in 1989. The 22-storey, amber glass-covered tower is paired with a giant black, inverted pyramid topped with a giant sculpture that is officially called the *Flaming Ornament* but is universally known as the 'golden turd'. Almost as large as the building itself, the quirky hollow structure was built using submarine construction methods. The first and second floor of this building house a bar called Flamme d'Or (see page 209) while on the 22nd floor of the tower there's another bar, the Asahi Sky Room.

Tokyo Skytree ⑥

Address: 1-1-2 Oshiage,

Sumida-ku
Tel: 0570-550 634
Website: www.tokyo-skytree.jp/en/
Opening Hours: daily 8am–10pm
Entrance Fee: charge
Transport: Narihirabashi or Oshiage

Rising east of Asahi Super Dry Hall is the 634-metre (2,080ft) -tall **Tokyo Skytree**, the city's latest digital communications tower, a 21st-century successor to Tokyo Tower (see page 151), opened to the general public in 2012. Apart from having the city's highest observatory (at 450 metres/1,476ft), with dizzying panoramic views over Tokyo, the tower also has another deck at 350 metres (1,148ft) with a café and restaurant. At the base, in the Sola Machi complex (www.tokyo-solamachi.jp), there is an aquarium, restaurants, shops, and other attractions, while standing just to the east is Sky Tree East Tower, a 31-storey office building that also houses some restaurants.

Sumida River, Ryogoku and East Tokyo

RYOGOKU

National Sumo Stadium and Sumo Museum ⑦

Address: 1-3-28 Yokoami, Sumida-ku
Tel: 03-3622 0366
Website: www.sumo.or.jp/eng
Opening Hours: (Museum) Mon–Fri 10am–4.30pm
Entrance Fee: free
Transport: Ryogoku

The next area of interest east of the Sumida-gawa is **Ryogoku**, primarily known for its history of sumo wrestling. Emerging from Ryogoku Station you can't miss the green roof of the enormous **National Sumo Stadium** (Kokugikan), home to Japan's national sport. If you are not lucky enough to be in town when one of the main sumo tournaments are held in the months of January, May and September, there is always the small but intriguing **Sumo Museum** (Sumo Hakubutsukan) located on the same premises.

There are several sumo stables in the area where wrestlers work out and live. It is quite normal to see

Tokyo Skytree.

stocky wrestlers walking around Ryogoku, unmistakable with their topknots, kimonos and wooden clogs. The staple diet for sumo wrestlers is a weight-inducing and nutritious stew called *chanko-nabe*, which can be sampled at several restaurants in the area. From more information about sumo, see page 210.

Philippe Starck's distinctive design is embodied in the Asahi Super Dry Hall.

Edo-Tokyo Museum ⑧

Address: 1-4-1 Yokoami, Sumida-ku
Tel: 03-3626 9974
Website: www.edo-tokyo-museum.or.jp
Opening Hours: Tue–Fri, Sun 9.30am–5.30pm, Sat 9.30am–7.30pm
Entrance Fee: charge
Transport: Ryogoku

Behind the Sumo Stadium is the enormous **Edo-Tokyo Museum** (Edo-Tokyo Hakubutsukan), a must for anyone interested to learn how the city evolved into what it is today. The museum is housed in an ultra-contemporary building that looks

FACT

Major earthquakes are said to hit the Tokyo area every 60 to 70 years. The last, the Great Kanto Earthquake, in which over 100,000 people perished, occurred in 1923, making the next one, if predictions are correct, long overdue.

Herons can be seen at Kyu Yasuda Garden.

like the bridge of a spaceship. The designers of the museum claim that their inspiration for the massive platform, raised on concrete stilts, came from the design of old Japanese rice storehouses elevated above ground to stop rats from destroying the crop. The museum does an excellent job in evoking the merchant life and culture of people living during the Edo Period, from the common people to samurai.

To reach the start of the permanent exhibition, visitors cross a reconstruction of the original Nihombashi Bridge. Exhibitions not only cover the early life of Edo, but also the years from 1868, through the post-war reconstruction years and the 1964 Tokyo Olympics. Temporary exhibitions are held in the large basement gallery. The museum shop has a good selection of traditional crafts from the *shitamachi* area.

Kyu Yasuda Garden ⑨

Murals at the National Sumo Stadium.

Just north of the Sumo Stadium next to the Sumida-gawa is the pretty **Kyu Yasuda Garden** (Kyu Yasuda Teien; daily 9am–4.30pm; free).

This tiny, Edo-Period stroll garden and the grounds of a larger estate were acquired by banker and industrialist Yasuda Zenjiro in the 1850s. Interestingly, the late Zenjiro was the grandfather of the avant-garde artist and musician Yoko Ono.

Yokoami Park and Tokyo Ireido ⑩

Across the road is **Yokoami Park** (Yokoami Koen), a small park and austere temple-like complex of **Tokyo Ireido** dedicated to the 140,000 victims of the Great Kanto Earthquake, which struck just before noon on 1 September 1923 and destroyed over 70 percent of Tokyo. Incense is burnt before the three-storey pagoda and memorial hall not only to mark the earthquake, but also in remembrance of a second catastrophe, the same number who died in bombing raids that wiped out most of this largely residential part of Tokyo in March 1945. A small **museum** (tel: 03-3622 1208; Tue–Sun 9am–4.30pm; charge) also within the park displays remains from the fateful day.

Tabi Museum ⓫

Address: 1-9-3 Midori, Sumida-ku
Tel: 03-3631 0092
Opening Hours: Mon–Sat 9am–6pm
Entrance Fee: charge
Transport: Ryogoku

A short stroll southeast of Ryogoku Station, just past the intersection of Kiyosumi and Keiyo-dori, takes you to the quaint **Tabi Museum** (Tabi Shiryokan), one of several small, often family-run, trade and craftsmen-oriented museums that dot the Sumida Ward area. There are only a handful of places left in Tokyo that make *tabi*, the dainty little split-toe socks worn by women attired in kimonos, sumo wrestlers and practitioners of certain traditional disciplines like archery. The creation of *tabi* may not be an art, but as a quintessentially Japanese creation, this museum and factory, displaying the tools and equipment used in their making, has a certain curiosity value.

Eko-in Temple and the Site of Lord Kira's Villa ⓬

The next two sites are for history lovers. A little west along Keiyo-dori from the Tabi Museum is **Eko**-in.

FUKAGAWA HISTORY

The area gets its name from the late 16th-century local leader Fukagawa Hachiroemon who was granted the land by Tokugawa Ieyasu and charged with draining and filling in the swamp that once existed here. In the late 17th century, following one of Tokyo's perennial disastrous fires, the area began to boom as lumberyards were relocated here and new bridges over the Sumida River facilitated commerce between the two sides of the city. At the same time the area also became one of the city's 'unlicensed' quarters where brothels, masquerading as teahouses, plied their business – a trade that continued right up to and a few years beyond World War II.

Rebuilt in a fairly uninspiring modern form after it was destroyed in World War II, the appeal of this small temple is its historical significance not its design, because after the devastating Long Sleeves Fire of 1657, it was here where the ashes of the estimated 100,000 victims (almost a third of Tokyo's population at the time) were interned. In the backstreets immediately east of Eko-in there is another historical site of note, one that played a part in the story of the 47 **ronin** (see page 164). The remains of the **villa of Lord Kira** now form part of a small, not particularly interesting park, but this is where the 47 *ronin* took their vengeance on Lord Kira, the man who had caused the death of their master. You can still see the well in which the *ronin* are said to have washed Kira's decapitated head before they took it to Sengaku-ji temple and placed it on their master's grave.

Re-creation of ancient Tokyo at the Edo-Tokyo Museum.

Japanese-style split-toe socks ('tabi') – on display at the Tabi Museum – are made with the 'seta' (wooden Japanese sandals) in mind.

TIP

The Tokyo Mizube Line (tel: 03-5608 8869; www.tokyo-park.or.jp/english/business/index.html) waterbuses along the Sumida River, out into Tokyo Bay and over to Odaiba (see page 217) can be caught from opposite the National Sumo Stadium.

KIYOSUMI-SHIRAKAWA AND AROUND

Basho Memorial Hall ⑬

Address: 1-6-3 Tokiwa, Koto-ku
Tel: 03-3631 1448
Opening Hours: Tue–Sun 9.30am–5pm
Entrance Fee: charge
Transport: Morishita

Take the subway one stop south from Ryogoku to Morishita (or just keep following the river south) from where you'll head towards the river to find the next sight, just south of the Shin-Ohashi Bridge. **Basho Memorial Hall** (Basho Kinenkan) stands on the very spot from where the great *haiku* poet Matsuo Basho set off in 1689 for a five-month hike that would result in his masterpiece, *Narrow Road to a Far Province*. The museum contains original manuscripts and objects from the poet's journeys but you'll need to understand Japanese to get the most out of it as there is no English labelling.

Kiyosumi galleries ⑭

Address: 1-3-2 Kiyosumi, Koto-ku
Tel: see below
Opening Hours: Tue–Sat noon–7pm
Entrance Fee: free
Transport: Kiyosumi-Shirakawa

Continue along the river to the blue-painted Kiyosu-bashi, a handsome suspension bridge built in 1928. Around the corner, an ageing but still functioning warehouse now provides the home for six commercial art galleries spread across its three uppermost floors, including **Tomio Koyama Gallery** (www.tomiokoyama gallery.com; tel: 03-3642 4090) and

SHOPPING

Antiques

On the first and second Sunday of the month an antiques market is held in the grounds of Tomioka Hachiman-gu (see page 208), while the same location hosts a flea market on the 15th and 28th days of most months from 8am to sunset.

Clothing

Lion-Do
4-30-10 Ryogoku, Sumida-ku
Tel: 03-3631 0650
www.liondo.co.jp
Off map
If you're a plus-size male then this store specialising in clothing for sumo giants is a good place for items such as *yukata* (cotton robes) and *jimbei* (pyjama-style outfits).

Confectionary

Chomei-ji Sakuramochi Yamamotoya
5-1-14 Mukojima, Sumida-ku

Tel: 03-3622 3266
www.sakura-mochi.com
Off map
Beside the temple of the same name, this 300-year-old shop is supposed to be where **sakuramochi**, a sweetened rice cake wrapped in a cherry leaf, was invented. The best way to try the **mochi** is with a good green tea, which you can enjoy together here for a bargain ¥250.

Kototoi Dango
5-5-22 Mukojima, Sumida-ku
Tel: 03-3622 0081
www.kototoidango.co.jp
Off map
If you like *mochi* (pounded glutinous rice cake) then you should try the *dango* (mochi balls) here flavoured with red bean paste, white bean paste and *miso*. Kototoi is the old name for the neighbourhood.

Crafts

Musashiya Hozan
1-28-3 Ishiwara,

Sumida-ku
Tel: 03-3622 0262.
www.hagoita.co.jp
Off map
This workshop by the north end of Kyu Yasuda Garden specialises in *Hagoita*; cloth-covered cardboard paddles that were originally used for a game of battledore but are now just purely decorative pieces.

Sumo-wrestling Goods

Ryogoku Takahashi Company
4-31-15 Ryogoku,
Sumida-ku
Tel: 03-3631 2420
http://edo-sumo.d.dooo.jp
Off map
This long-established bedding, sheets and towel business also sells sumo-related goods and souvenirs. As a special order, you can buy a mini-*mawashi*, the decorative aprons worn by wrestlers.

Shugo Arts (www.shugoarts.com; tel: 03-5621 6434) both specialising in contemporary art (ranging from painting to sculptures to video installations), and **Taka Ishii Gallery** (tel: 03-5646 6050; www.takaishiigallery.com) which usually displays photographic works. All the galleries here attract major Japanese and international artists, but also give exposure to up-and-coming talent.

Kiyosumi Garden ⑮

Address: 3-3-9 Kiyosumi, Koto-ku
Tel: 03-3641 5892
Website: http://teien.tokyo-park.or.jp/en/kiyosumi
Opening Hours: daily 9am–5pm
Entrance Fee: charge
Transport: Kiyosumi-Shirakawa

A short walk east from the galleries is the spacious **Kiyosumi Garden** (Kiyosumi Teien), a typical *kaiyushiki teien* or 'pond walk around garden'. Fed by water from the Sumida River, the garden was first built in 1688 by a rich lumber merchant named Kinokuniya Bunzaemon. During the Meiji era, it was bought by another wealthy businessman, Yataro Iwasaki,

The Fukagawa Edo Museum.

the founder of the Mitsubishi Group of companies, who had the grounds restored to his own liking.

Apart from a beautiful teahouse set serenely beside the pond, a special feature of the garden is the 55 rare stones, brought from all over Japan by Mitsubishi's steamships. Stone lanterns, miniature islands, stepping stones and many species of flower, including Japanese quince, azaleas and hydrangeas, dot the grounds. In one corner of the garden is an almost separate iris garden that is absolutely beautiful in June.

Fukagawa Edo Museum ⑯

Address: 1-3-28 Shirakawa, Koto-ku
Tel: 03-3630 8625
Opening Hours: daily 9.30am–5pm (closed 2nd and 4th Mon of month)
Entrance Fee: charge
Transport: Kiyosumi-Shirakawa

A few blocks east of the subway station follow a charming traditional shopping street (along which you'll

---

ANCIENT ART OF TATTOOS

Strongly identified with the *yakuza*, Japan's organised crime syndicates, tattoos *(irezumi)* were once also popular among the working class and groups like firemen, carpenters and sushi chefs. Tattooing in Japan is age-old – the indigenous Ainu used it for decorative and social purposes. In the Edo Period, skin decoration started to be influenced by *ukiyo-e* (woodblock prints) in their design and technique. The firemen of Edo probably had the first full-body tattoos, covering all but the hands, feet and head, as a form of spiritual protection. During the Fukagawa Hachiman Matsuri and Sanja Matsuri festivals, men with such tattoos can be seen hoisting the shrines along the streets surrounding the temples.

TIP

For an audience with Mukojima's geisha book one of the special tours offered by Hato Bus (www.hatobus.com/en/course/16j.html) that includes dinner and geisha entertainment at the *ryotei* (banqueting restaurant) Sakura-Chaya (www.sakurajaya.jp).

Dramatic entrance to the Tokyo Museum of Contemporary Art.

pass an award-winning public toilet with an Edo-era facade) to find the **Fukagawa Edo Museum** (Fukagawa Edo Shiryokan). Built on a small and intimate scale, it nevertheless has 11 original buildings, all taken from the Fukagawa district in around 1842, including homes, shops, a theatre, a boathouse tavern and even a 10-metre (33ft) fire tower.

Tokyo Museum of Contemporary Art ⑰

Address: 4-4-1 Miyoshi, Koto-ku
Tel: 03-5245 4111
Website: www.mot-art-museum.jp
Opening Hours: Tue–Sun 10am–6pm
Entrance Fee: charge
Transport: Kiyosumi-Shirakawa or Kiba

Tomioka Hachiman-gu

Roughly a kilometre (.5 mile) east of the Fukagawa Edo Museum, it is back to the present with the **Tokyo Museum of Contemporary Art** (Tokyo-to Gendai Bijutsukan) in the north section of Kiba Park (Kiba Koen). This excellent museum features art from a stock of over 4,500 items in its permanent collection as well as new work by both Japanese and foreign artists. There are plenty of experimental and interactive displays, an extensive database in both Japanese and English, and a couple of good restaurants.

MONZEN-NAKACHO

Fukagawa Fudoson ⑱

Return to Kiyosumi-Shirakawa Station and go one stop more south to **Monzen-Nakacho**, a busy commercial strip, which retains the atmosphere of Old Tokyo. Off it, is **Fukagawa Fudoson**, a well patronised temple of the Shingon sect of Buddhism. The original early 18th-century temple was destroyed in World War II; this one, dating from 1862, was relocated from its original home in Chiba prefecture outside of Tokyo. The narrow shopping street leading to the temple from exit 1 of Monzen-Nakacho Station is lined with small restaurants and stalls selling senbei (rice crackers).

Tomioka Hachiman-gu ⑲

A minute's walk east of the temple is the **Tomioka Hachiman-gu** (www. tomiokahachimangu.or.jp) the shrine that is the focus of one of Tokyo's greatest festivals, the Fukagawa

Hachiman Matsuri. Held in mid-August every three years (next is 2015), the frenetic festival sees over 100 portable shrines paraded around the streets amid a massive, unrelenting water fight. A 1968 reconstruction of the 17th-century original, the current shrine has impressive prayer and spirit halls and a towering, green, copper-tiled roof. It is dedicated to eight deities, including Benten, the popular goddess of beauty and the arts.

The shrine is strongly associated with sumo wrestling and in the Edo era was the official venue for the sport. Walk to the back of the shrine and you will see the **Yokozuna Monument**, engraved with the names of long-departed sumo wrestlers who reached the rank of *yokozuna*, the highest in the sumo world.

BEST RESTAURANTS, BARS AND CAFÉS

PRICE CATEGORIES

Prices for a three-course dinner per person without drinks and taxes.
¥ = under ¥2,000
¥¥ = ¥2,000–¥3,000
¥¥¥ = ¥3,000–¥5,000
¥¥¥¥ = over ¥5,000

Restaurants

Japanese

Chanko Kawasaki
2-13-1 Ryogoku, Sumida-ku
Tel: 03-3631 2529
Open: D Mon–Sat
¥¥¥ ⑩ p274, E4
Like many others in the area, this restaurant specialises in *chanko-nabe* stews, but it has the edge because of its location in a charming post-World War II wooden house and its friendly owners. A set meals starts at ¥3,050 and bookings are advised as it's pretty small.

Kintame
1-14-3 Tomioka, Koto-ku
Tel: 03- 3641 4561
www.kintame.co.jp
Open: Tue–Sun 11am–5pm
¥¥ Off map
Opposite the Fukagawa Fudo in Monzen Nakacho, this appealing place serves tasty Kyoto-style fish marinated in sake lees (rice mash) and a variety of pickles.

Masago Sushi
4-27-3 Ryogoku, Sumida-ku
Tel: 03-3632 0011

Open: L & D Sun–Fri.
¥¥ ⑮ p274, E4
Good value traditional sushi shop that specialises in Yohei-zushi, the style invented in the early 19th century by local sushi chef Hanaya Yohei that led to the hand-pressed fingers of rice topped with fish and seafood that are most popular today.

Tomoegata
2-17-6 Ryogoku, Sumida-ku
Tel: 03-3632 5600
www.tomoegata.com
Open: L & D daily (closed Mon June–Aug)
¥¥¥ ⑯ p274, E4
Colourful banners mark the exterior of this restaurant, with branches either side of the road. Sample the sumo wrestlers' favourite stew *chanko-nabe*, which can be ordered in a variety of courses and with a choice of four stocks.

Southeast Asian

Cafe Hai
2F Tokyo Metropolitan Museum of Contemporary Art, 1-1 Miyoshi, Koto-ku
Tel: 03-5620 5962
Open: Tue–Sun 11am–5.30pm
¥¥ Off map
Just as good a reason for visiting this museum as the art is its on-site restaurant serving exceptionally tasty Vietnamese and other Southeast Asian-style dishes in a cleverly designed space. The pho and baguettes are the standouts on the menu.

Bars and Cafés

La Flamme d'Or
Super Dry Hall, 1-23-1 Azumabashi, Sumida-ku
Tel: 03-5608 5381
www.asahibeer.co.jp/restaurant/azuma/flamdoll1.html
Off map
See inside one of Tokyo's strangest buildings by visiting this Asahi beer hall where the ceiling seems to be held up by giant skittles.

Popeye
2-18-7 Ryogoku, Sumida-ku
Tel: 03-3633 2120
www.40beersontap.com
㉜ p274, E4
Three minutes' walk south of Ryogoku Station in the street behind the Hotel Bellegrand you'll find this great bar serving over 70 beers on tap, all top microbrews from around Japan overseas. This place fills up quickly, so it's best to call ahead and ask Aoki-san, the owner (and one of Japan's most respected hopheads) to reserve you a seat.

Skytree Cafe
Tokyo Sky Tree, 1-1-2 Oshiage, Sumida-ku
Tel: 0570-550 634
www.tokyo-skytree.jp
Off map
You will struggle to get a better view with your coffee than at this café on the lower of Tokyo Skytree's two decks, 350 metres (1,148ft) above ground. Opens from 8am until 9.45pm, so you have the choice of daytime or night views across the city.

THE SPORT OF SUMO

The apprenticeship of a sumo wrestler is long and hard, but the rewards are great for those who reach the top.

Professional sumo is run by the Japan Sumo Association who organise the six annual *basho* (tournaments) held across Japan, plus other events, and oversee the 50 odd *beya* (stables) in which wrestlers or *rikishi* live and train together. In most *beya* the day typically begins at 6am with several hours of practice. Harsh and tedious exercises work to develop the wrestlers' flexibility and strength, followed by repetitive practice matches amongst the *beya's* wrestlers (the only time they wrestle one another, as wrestlers of the same *beya* don't compete during actual tournaments).

Practice ends around noon, when the wrestlers bathe. Lower ranked wrestlers are expected to scrub the backs of the higher ranked *ozeki* and *yokozuna* (grand champion, the highest rank and rarely achieved). They will also serve meals and run errands. The food staple of the stable is *chanko-nabe*, a high-calorie, nutritious stew of chicken, fish or beef with *miso*. Side dishes of fried chicken, steak and bowls of rice – and even salads – fill out the meal.

Apprentice wrestlers receive no salary as such, only a small living allowance. A wrestler's first break comes when he reaches the *makushita* level, comprised of about 200 wrestlers from all over Japan, and begins to receive a more generous allowance. When a wrestler makes the next step up and reaches the *juryo* level, he becomes a *sekitori*, or ranked wrestler, and earns a salary of around US$11,000 a month. An *ozeki*, the second-highest rank in the uppermost *makuuchi* level, receives about US$25,000 monthly, and a *yokozuna*, US$30,000. The winner of one of six annual tournaments receives up to US$100,000.

The dohyo ring is carefully prepared ahead of a Grand Tournament.

A wrestler squats, wearing a ceremonial apron, before the bout begins.

Few people know that the sumo practice tournament at Tokyo's Kokugikan arena in the district of Ryogoku, is open to the public.

The outfits sumo wrestlers wear are dictated by strict tradition.

Sumo wrestlers enjoy the bulk-building stew chanko-nabe after a training session.

AN ANCIENT SHINTO SPORT

Sumo has been around for at least 2,000 years. Japanese mythology relates an episode in which the destiny of the Japanese islands was once determined by the outcome of a sumo match between two gods. The victorious god started the Yamato imperial line.

Ancient sumo painting.

While wrestling has always existed in nearly every culture, the origins of sumo as we know it were founded on Shinto rituals. Shrines were the venue of matches dedicated to the gods of good harvests. In the Nara and Heian Periods, sumo was a spectator sport for the imperial court, while during the militaristic Kamakura Period, sumo was part of a warrior's training. Professional sumo arose during the 1700s and is quite similar to the sumo practised in today's matches.

Shinto rituals punctuate the sumo match. The ritual stomping before a match *(shiko)* drives evil spirits from the ring (not to mention loosening the muscles) before a match. Salt is tossed into the ring for purification, as Shinto beliefs say that salt drives out evil spirits. Nearly 40kg (90lbs) of salt is thrown in one tournament day.

The oiled hair of sumo wrestlers is shaped into the form of an icho, or gingko leaf, before they participate in a bout.

TOKYO BAYSIDE

From a bustling fish market to serene gardens and a zippy monorail out to an artificial island stacked with futuristic architecture, plus mammoth shopping malls, a giant bathhouse and Ferris wheel – bayside Tokyo offers all this and more.

If the inlets of the Tokyo Bay area and the bluffs between them were the cradle of old Edo – the site for its great castle and the flatlands that accommodated the bustling merchant classes east of the Sumida River – then the shoreline was the crucible for newer developments. Even today, the area continues to expand. Landfills have been adding new dimensions to Tokyo's urban compression for over 400 years. Tokyo Bay is home to the euphemistically named Dream Island (Yume-no-shima), composed entirely of rubbish – an ingenious solution to dealing with the mountains of garbage generated by millions of citizens. Started in the 1960s, Yume-no-Shima has since been covered by topsoil and now hosts a sports park, tropical greenhouse and waste facility.

TSUKUDAJIMA

At the mouth of the Sumida River, a series of interlocking islands appear, the first in a number of landfills reclaimed from mudflats in the bay. The most interesting is the northern section of **Tsukudajima**, which can be reached on foot by crossing Tsukuda Bridge from Tsukiji, or by walking north from Tsukishima Station on the Yurakucho and Oedo subway lines. Meaning 'Island of Cultivated Rice Fields' the island's name is a reference to the rural outskirts of Osaka, from where its first settlers came in the 17th century to work as fishermen, supplying the shogun's kitchens with fish as well as keeping an eye on movements in Edo's bay.

By the early Meiji Period, Tsukudajima has been combined with the reclaimed islands of Ishikawajima to the north and Tsukishima to the

Apartment blocks on Tsukuda Island.

south into one contiguous landfill. Spared the great fires of Edo and the earthquake that struck Tokyo in 1923, the island's cosy huddles of housing blocks, narrow alleyways full of potted plants and old-fashioned street corner lift-pumps (some still in use), lend Tsukudajima its distinct character. Many of the houses have traditionally crafted features, including black ceramic roofs, oxidised copper finials of an ancient, green patina and well-seasoned wood walls. A prime example is the shop **Tenyasu Honten**, which can be found facing the Sumida-gawa, after crossing the Tsukuda Bridge (Tsukuda-Ohashi). You'll also see here a replica of an Edo-period lighthouse.

Sumiyoshi-jinja ❶

Less than a minute's walk to the left after crossing Tsukuda-Ohashi is the area's venerable **Sumiyoshi-jinja**. Vestiges of the shrine's role as a protector of sea travellers, fishermen and sailors can be seen in carvings on beams and transoms covering some of the small outer buildings. One particularly realistic relief on the roof of the well beside the shrine's *torii* (gate) shows fishermen in a skiff, with firewood burning in a metal basket as they cast their nets in the bay at night.

A few steps beyond the shrine, **Tsukudako-bashi** is an attractive bridge with a red handrail that spans a narrow, tidal inlet where you can get a modest insight into the former life of this quarter. The fishermen's shacks and boathouses are less charmingly dilapidated than they were just a few years ago and the number of their vessels is depleted.

TSUKIJI AND AROUND

Retrace your steps over Tsukuda Bridge and drop back down to the river promenade on the left-hand side fronting St Luke's Hospital and continue towards the Kachidoki Bridge.

One road in from the river is the entrance to **Tsukiji Jisaku**, an exclusive and expensive banqueting restaurant in the former home of Mitsubishi group founder Iwasaki Yataro. The lush entranceway is a foretaste of the traditional gardens that several of the mansion's rooms overlook.

Tsukiji Hongan-ji temple.

Tsukiji Hongan-ji ❷

Address: 3-15-1 Tsukiji, Chuo-ku
Tel: 03-3541 1131
Website: www.tsukijihongwanji.jp
Opening Hours: daily 7am–6pm
Entrance Fee: free
Transport: Tsukiji

From Tsukiji Jisaku turn right onto Harumi-dori and walk northwest towards Shin-Ohashi-dori. To the right of here is the area's most imposing building, **Tsukiji Hongan-ji**. Founded in Asakusa in 1617, the original temple was destroyed by fire. The current structure, a stone building designed by the architect Chuta Ito, was built in 1935. Ito, a student

Tsukudajima has an enormous market, the main produce being fish.

Tokyo Bayside

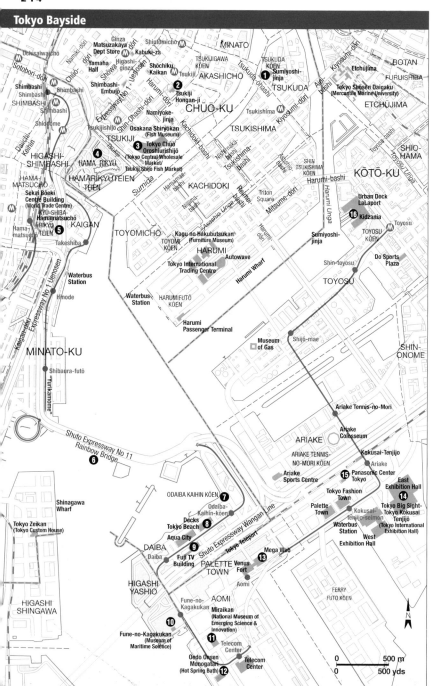

of Tatsuno Kingo, who designed Tokyo Station, travelled extensively in the Hindu and Buddhist countries of Asia. Many of the motifs incorporated into this extraordinary building, especially its lotus-shaped main facade and domes, reflect these foreign influences. Take a peek into the interior, with its opulent gold altar and elaborately carved transoms, which can seat up to 1,000 people.

Tokyo Central Wholesale Market ❸

Address: 5-2-1 Tsukiji, Chuo-ku
Tel: 03-3542 111
Website: www.tsukiji-market.or.jp
Opening Hours: Mon–Sat 3am–noon but check website for occasional holidays
Entrance Fee: free
Transport: Tsukiji-Shijo

Six days a week, close on 3,000 tonnes of seafood from all around the world arrive at **Tokyo Metropolitan Central Wholesale Market**, better known as **Tsukiji Market**, for sorting, auctioning and dispatching. Wholesalers start laying out their stalls at 3am and then begin preparing for the famous tuna auctions that start at 5.25am. The best cuts of these rock-hard fish, lined up like frozen sputniks, labelled and marked in red paint with their country of origin and weight, sell wholesale for as much as ¥10,000 per kilo, several times the price of the most expensive prime beef. The first auction of the year traditionally sees the first tuna go for ridiculous sums, as restaurants compete for the publicity that comes with the annual marquee purchase. In 2013, a chain of budget sushi restaurants stumped up a record-breaking ¥56.49 million (US$736,000) for a single 269kg (593-pound) bluefin tuna. At 7am the fruit and vegetable auctions start, and Tsukiji keeps buzzing up until noon as vendors hawk some 450 different types of fish.

With all this fresh seafood on tap, Tsukiji is an excellent place to indulge in a sushi breakfast: in the outer market (jogai-shijo) you'll find a cluster of stalls selling sushi and other dishes made with seafood. One of the best is **Sushi Bun** or you could try a seafood *donburi* (rice bowl) at **Kanno**.

TIP

Tsukiji has become so popular that only 120 visitors, divided into two groups, are allowed to watch the famous tuna auctions which kick off at 5.25am. Registration for a place starts at 5am. If you do plan to attend an auction be aware that this is a place of business so be respectful and follow the rules which include no flash photography.

Fresh tuna ready for auction at Tsukiji Fish Market.

Hama Rikyu Detached Garden.

An assortment of knives on sale at Tsukiji.

Hama Rikyu Detached Garden ❹

Address: 1-1 Hama-Rikyu Teien, Chuo-ku
Tel: 03-3541 0200
Website: http://teien.tokyo-park.or.jp/en/hama-rikyu
Opening Hours: daily 9am–5pm
Entrance Fee: charge
Transport: Shiodome or Tsukiji-Shijo

Exiting the market on to Shin-Ohashi-dori, turn left and work your way around to the entrance to the expansive *Hama Rikyu Detached Garden* (Hama Rikyu Teien), just a 10-minute walk south. Developed in the 1650s as grounds for the Hama Palace (an estate owned by Matsudaira Tsunashige, a lord from Kofu Province), they passed into the hands of the sixth shogun, Ienobu, who turned the grounds into landscaped gardens and a duck shooting site. The present garden, reached by crossing the Nanmon Bridge, or by

waterbus from Asakusa (see page 182), were opened to the public in 1945. The highlight is a large tidal pond, with a small tea pavilion at its centre and islets connected by wooden bridges, behind which the glistening skyscrapers of the Shiodome area dominate the skyline.

Kyu-Shiba Rikyu Garden ❺

Address: 1-4-1 Kaigan, Minato-ku
Tel: 03-3434 4029
Website: http://teien.tokyo-park.or.jp/en/kyu-shiba
Opening Hours: daily 9am–5pm
Entrance Fee: charge
Transport: Hamamatsucho

If you have a taste for formal gardens, there is another one just a few minutes' walk south of Hama Rikyu, opposite Hamamatsucho Station. Arranged around a large pond, the **Kyu-Shiba Rikyu Garden** (Kyu-Shiba Rikyu Teien) is, along with Koishikawa Korakuen Garden (see page 190), one of the few classic stroll gardens in Tokyo to have survived intact from the feudal era. It was created in the late 17th century by Okubo Tadatomo, an official of the ruling Tokugawa shogunate.

ODAIBA

South of the garden are the dock areas of Takeshiba, Hinode and Shibaura. **Hinode Station** on the Yurikamome monorail is a convenient spot to board the rail crossing over the bay to **Odaiba**. The name of this man-made island comes from the cannon emplacements placed in Tokyo Bay in 1853 to defend the city against any attack by Commodore Perry's Black Ships (see page 35). Odaiba's fortunes began to take off in the bubble years of the 1980s when the vast tracts of landfill here were used as an urban laboratory for construction projects requiring more space than downtown Tokyo can conceivably spare.

Rainbow Bridge ❻

The remains of two of the Tokugawa's cannon emplacements can still be seen south of the multi-decked **Rainbow Bridge** that links Odaiba to the city. It's possible to walk across the 918 metre (3,000ft) -long suspension bridge in around 30 minutes rather than take the monorail – either way you get superb views of the city that really give an incredible sense of its vast scale. If you plan to walk, alight the monorail at Shibaura-Futo and climb up to observation gallery from where the pedestrian walkway starts.

Odaiba Kaihin Park ❼

Alight at Odaiba Kaihin-koen Station where **Odaiba Kaihin Park** (Odaiba Kaihin Koen) offers a pleasant swathe of green abutting an artificial sandy beach that gets very busy on hot days. Although the beach is pretty on the eyes, it is best to avoid paddling in the water, as it has a reputation for being heavily polluted.

Decks Tokyo Beach and Joypolis ❽

Across the road from Odaiba Kaihin-koen are restaurants and cafés at **Sunset Beach Restaurant Row**. The line of eateries is the

View of Tokyo from Odaiba.

KASAI RINKAI KOEN

East of Odaiba, beyond several more man-made islands, is **Kasai Rinkai Park** (www.tokyo-park.or.jp/english/park/detail_02.html#kasairinkai), the largest public recreational area in Tokyo's central 23 wards. Divided into several zones, the park includes a giant Ferris wheel, a large bird sanctuary, cycle tracks, barbecue areas and a breezy beach front. Its highlight is **Tokyo Sea Life Park** (www.tokyo-zoo.net/english; Thu–Tue 9.30am–5pm; charge) one of the area's best aquariums, home to a massive donut-shaped tank teeming with fish and other sea creatures. Take the ferry from Ariake on Odaiba (or from Hinode Pier or Hamamatsucho on the mainland) or the Keiyo Line from Tokyo Station to Kasai Rinkai-koen.

exterior part of the shopping mall Decks Tokyo Beach where you'll also find the state-of-art video game arcade **Joypolis** (daily 10am–11.30pm; charge), which offers the latest in virtual reality machines alongside all manner of cutting-edge gaming cabinets. More shops and a multiplex cinema can be found next door at **Aqua City**; on the beachside of this mall a small-scale replica of the Statue of Liberty adds a surreal element to the view of the city skyline.

Fuji TV Building

Address: 2-4-8 Daiba, Minato-ku
Tel: 03-5500 8888
Website: www.fujitv.co.jp/en
Opening Hours: Tue–Sun 10am–8pm
Entrance Fee: charge
Transport: Daiba

Opposite the shopping malls is the unmissable **Fuji TV Building** headquarters of Fuji Television, a popular commercial TV channel, and one of the most futurist-looking structures on Odaiba. Yet another Kenzo Tange design, its two 25-storey blocks are connected by a lattice of girder-like sky corridors some of which suspend a 32-metre (105ft) -diameter, titanium-panelled sphere containing both a restaurant and an observatory.

Museum of Maritime Science ⑩

Address: 3-1 Higashi-Yashio, Shinagawa-ku, www.funenokagakukan.or.jp
Tel: 03-5500 1111
Opening Hours: Tue–Sun 10am–5pm
Entrance Fee: charge
Transport: Fune-no-Kagakukan

You can either walk or hop back on the monorail to the next station for the **Museum of Maritime Science** (Fune-no-Kagakukan) which bears the unmistakable shape of an ocean liner. Exhibits here trace the history of shipping and commercial transportation. Bringing the whole subject alive are two actual ships, the *Soya*, once used for expeditions to the Antarctic, and the *Yoteimaru*, one of a fleet of now almost obsolete ferries that carried passengers between Honshu and Hokkaido islands.

National Museum of Emerging Science and Innovation ⑪

Address: 2-41 Aomi, Koto-ku
Tel: 03-3570 9151
Website: www.miraikan.jst.go.jp
Opening Hours: Wed–Mon 10am–5pm
Entrance Fee: charge
Transport: Fune-no-Kagakukan or Telecom Centre

A short walk further south will bring you to the fascinating **National Museum of Emerging Science and Innovation** also known as the **Miraikan**. Tokyo's best science museum, this is where you can learn all about robotics (including seeing a demonstration of the Honda's Asimo humanoid robot), space travel, genetics, the internet and other miracles of

Get tickets to the observation deck of the Fuji TV Building.

modern technology. All the displays have English explanations and almost everything is made accessible to kids, who are given free rein to run about and bash many of the exhibits.

Oedo Onsen Monogatari

Address: 2-57 Aomi, Koto-ku
Tel: 03-5500 1126
Website: www.ooedoonsen.jp/english
Opening Hours: daily 11am–9am
Entrance Fee: charge
Transport: Telecom Centre

If the past has more appeal than the future, walk over to the extraordinary **Oedo Onsen Monogatari**, a traditional hot spring bathing complex designed along theme park lines. Sample outdoor and indoor tubs, saunas and a foot massage bath made of sharp pebbles. Massages, spa treatments, hot sand baths and a pedicure performed by tiny 'doctor

fish' who nibble the dead skin off your feet all cost extra. There are also plenty of stalls and restaurants to grab a good lunch, dinner or snack. The entrance fee to this fun complex includes towels and a choice of colourful patterned *yukata* (lightweight dressing gown). Be sure to observe local bath etiquette.

Mega Web

Address: 1 Aomi, Koto-k
Tel: 03-3599 0808
Website: www.megaweb.gr.jp
Opening Hours: daily 11am–9pm
Entrance Fee: free
Transport: Aomi

Return to Telecom Centre station and go one more stop east to reach the next major commercial complex **Palette Town**. On the east side of this is **Mega Web** which includes the **Toyota City Showcase**, where

Pop art sculpture near Tokyo Big Sight in Odaiba.

SHOPPING

Apart from the places listed below, the outer market of Tsukiji Market (see page 215) is a good place to hunt for culinary-related souvenirs, such as knives and pottery, and even items such as T-shirts and hats.

Food and Drink

Tenyasu Honten
1-3-14 Tsukuda, Chuo-ko
Tel: 03-3531 2351
p278, D4/D5
Dating back to 1837, this charming shop sells *tsukudani* – seaweed and fish preserve in a preparation of salt, soy sauce and sugar. A sampler box of six types of *tsukudani* is ¥2,000.

Uogashi Meicha
4-10-1 Tsukiji, Chuo-ku
Tel: 03-3541 3396
www.uogashi-meicha.co.jp
p278, D4
A venerable tea merchant's shop that specialises in various green and Chinese brews. It's possible to

sample the teas before you buy. Located between Tsukiji Market and Hongan-ji.

Shopping Malls

Aqua City
1-7-1 Daiba, Minato-ku
Tel: 03-3599 4700
www.aquacity.jp/en
Off map
This large bayside mall includes plenty of well-known overseas brands, including Adidas, Gap and Lacoste, as well as several floors of restaurants, a multiplex cinema and the island's only Shinto shrine.

Decks Tokyo Beach
1-6-1 Daiba, Minato-ku.
Tel: 03-3599 6500
www.odaiba-decks.com
Off map
There are plenty of opportunities to buy the latest fashions here as well as cruise a section of the mall designed to evoke the retro-glam days of 1960s Japan.

Urban Dock LaLaport Toyosu
2-4-9 Toyosu, Koto-ku.
Tel: 03-6910 1234
www.toyosu.lalaport.jp
Off map
Offering nearly 200 stores, ranging from fashion to toys to interiors and including branches of Uniqlo, Muji and Tokyu Hands, this mega mall is a handy one-stop shopping experience with the usual extras of restaurants, multiplex cinema and a couple of cultural sights thrown in.

Venus Fort
Palette Town, 1 Aomi, Koto-ku.
Tel: 03-3599 0700
www.venusfort.co.jp.
Off map
Few Tokyo shopping malls have been designed with such élan as Venus Fort, which features a level that would not look out of place in the shopping piazza of an Italian city. There's also one level packed with 50 discount outlet shops and another that focuses on items for the family, selling everything from toys to pets.

TIP

The best way of getting around Odaiba is to use the Yurikamome monorail (www.yurika mome.co.jp) which connects with Tokyo's metro at Shimbashi and Toyosu stations. An ¥800 one-day ticket (¥400 for kids) allows you to hop on and off at will.

simulated as well as real rides on the latest models can be enjoyed, the **History Garage** and its collection of classic cars from around the world, and a giant candy-coloured Ferris wheel (charge); on the west side is the giant mall Venus Fort, part of which is lit by an artificial sky that changes back and forth throughout the day, simulating sunset, sunrise and midday.

Tokyo Big Sight ⓮

Address: 3-11-1 Ariake, Koto-ku
Tel: 03-5530 1111
Website: www.bigsight.jp/english
Opening Hours: daily 9am–9pm
Entrance Fee: free
Transport: Kokusai Tenjijo Seimon

Take a short walk along the track to the next massive chunk of futurism – the Tokyo International Exhibition Center, better known as **Tokyo Big Sight**. Housing exhibition halls, meeting rooms, restaurants and cafés, it is used for major events such as Tokyo International Anime Fair and Comiket (see page 25). It is marked by four giant inverted pyramids and is fronted by an amusing sculpture of a huge red-handled saw sticking out of the ground.

Panasonic Center Tokyo ⓯

Address: 3-5-1 Ariake, Koto-ku
Tel: 03-3599 2600
Website: panasonic.net/center/tokyo
Opening Hours: Tue–Sun 10am–6pm
Entrance Fee: free
Transport: Ariake

Like the Sony Building in Ginza (see page 99) this is a giant showcase for the electronics manufacturer's latest products including Nintendo games and audio visual equipment. It's not all about selling as there is also the quite educational **Risupia** (10am–5pm; charge) 'digital network museum' where you can learn about science and mathematics using high-tech displays.

Kidzania ⓰

Address: 2-4-9 Toyosu, Koto-ku
Tel: 0120-924 901
Website: www.kidzania.jp
Opening Hours: Tue–Fri noon–7pm, Sat, Sun 11am–7pm
Entrance Fee: charge
Transport: Toyosu

From Ariake, the Yurikamome monorail continues east to the terminus at Toyosu. Two minutes' walk north of here facing Tokyo Bay is another mammoth 21st-century Tokyo retail experience – **Urban Dock LaLaport Toyosu**. Besides the many shops, restaurants and the multiplex cinema inside the complex, there is also **Ukiyo-e Tokyo** (Tue–Sun 11am–6pm; charge), a small exhibition of traditional woodblock prints, and **Kidzania Tokyo**, an interior theme park where children (from ages 2 to 12) get to run a small fantasy town, play-acting in roles ranging from a bank teller or fire fighter to a burger flipper. Reservations are essential (and ideally well in advance) and kids really need to understand some Japanese to get the most out of a trip here.

TSUKIJI ON THE MOVE

The name Tsukiji means 'reclaimed land'. The shogun ordered a landfill to be made there in 1657 after that year's disastrous Long Sleeves Fire. During the early Meiji years, some vaguely European-looking wooden houses were built at Tsukiji for the foreigners who worked in the newly opened legations, trading houses and missionary enterprises.

The market moved from its former home in Nihombashi to Tsukiji in 1935. Since the current location has become outdated, another move is planned, currently slated for 2015, to a new facility being built on contaminated reclaimed land in Toyosu, across Tokyo Bay. There's already a stop on the Yurikamome Line called Shijo-mae ('beside the market').

The giant Ferris wheel at Mega Web.

BEST RESTAURANTS, BARS AND CAFÉS

PRICE CATEGORIES

Prices for a three-course dinner per person without drinks and taxes:

¥ = under ¥2,000
¥¥ = ¥2,000–¥3,000
¥¥¥ = ¥3,000–¥5,000
¥¥¥¥ = over ¥5,000

Restaurants

Chinese

Lijiang
1-6-7 Tsukuda, Chuo-ku. Tel: 03-3531 6631. Open: L & D daily. ¥ 107 p278, D3
Look for the ceramic pickling jars lined up outside this cosy Chinese restaurant beside the Tsukudako-bashi bridge and Tsukudashima. They have a variety of lunch sets for around ¥1,000.

Indian

Khazana
5F Deck's Tokyo Beach, 1-6-1 Daiba, Minato-ku. Tel: 03-3599 6551. www.maharajagroup.com Open: daily 11am–11pm. ¥¥ Off map
All the usual North Indian staples are found at this place which offers a very affordable all-you-can-eat lunch (until 4pm) plus outside tables with great "views of the Rainbow Bridge especially when it's illuminated in the evening.

Japanese

Edogin
4-5-1 Tsukiji, Chuo-ku. Tel: 03-3543 4401. www.tsukiji-edogin.co.jp Open: daily L & D. ¥¥ 108 p278, C4
Despite the cavernous interior, this sushi place is always packed. The fish is super fresh – much of it is taken from tanks in the middle of the dining room. The portions are generous, and the restaurant's location just around the corner from Tsukiji Fish Market ensures that quality is good.

Kanno
4-9-5 Tsukiji, Chuo-ku. Tel: 03-3541 9191. Open: daily 5am–3.30pm. ¥¥ 109 p278, D4

Facing Shin-Ohashi-dori, this simple stall with roadside seating, dishes up *donburi* (rice bowls) topped with creamy *uni* (sea urchin), *ikura* (salmon roe) and *maguro* (tuna) at bargain prices.

Oshio
1-21-5 Tsukishima, Chuo-ku. Tel: 03-3532 9000. Open: daily 11am–10pm. ¥ 110 p278, D4
The Tsukishima area is famous for its simple eateries serving the savoury pancakes *okonomiyaki* and *monjayaki* (a particular Tokyo speciality. This is a reliable place to sample these dishes in a variety of flavours including the classic pork and *kimuchi* combination and less orthodox *mentaiko* (cod roe) with cheese.

Sushi-Bun
5-2-1 Tsukiji, Chuo-ku. Tel: 03-3541 3860. www.tsukijinet.com/tsukiji/kanren/sushibun/eng.html Open: Mon–Sat 6am–2.30pm. ¥¥ 111 p278, C4
The original Sushi Bun opened over 150 years ago when the fish market was at Nihombashi. The same family still run it in its present location within the market complex. There's an English menu and set menus start from ¥2,625.

Takeno
6-21-2 Tsukiji, Chuo-ku. Tel: 03-3541 8698. Open: Mon–Fri 11am–9pm, Sat 11am–8pm. ¥¥ 112 p278, D4
This simple Japanese diner used to be patronised only by workers from the Tsukiji Fish Market. But since it got discovered by the rest of Tokyo, it now stays open till dinner time. Mixed platters of sashimi and tempura are terrific value. Cash only.

Tsukiji Jisaku
14-19 Akashicho, Chuo-ku. Tel: 03-3541 2391. www.jisaku.co.jp Open: D Mon–Fri, L & D Sat, L Sun. ¥¥¥¥ 113 p278, D4.
If you have guests to impress this elegant traditional mansion with manicured garden views and waitresses in kimonos serving *kaiseki ryori* – Japanese haute cuisine – is the place to come. Just be pre-

pared for a hefty bill, as the courses start from ¥21,000 per person.

Tsukiji Sushiko
4-7-1 Tsukiji, Chuo-ku. Tel: 03-3547 0505. www.tsukiji-sushiko.com Open: L & D daily. ¥¥ 114 p278, D4
This is a spacious and elegantly designed sushi spot. The restaurant is close to the market, so you can expect freshness and good quality. There are many other branches around Tokyo, including in Odaiba and Ginza.

Korean

Yakiniku Sabo Tenten
Urban Dock Lalaport Toyosu, 2-4-9 Toyosu, Koto-ku. Tel: 03-3532 8929. www.foodies.co.jp Open: daily 11am–11pm. ¥¥¥ Off map
High-quality meat, a good range of Korean side dishes, plus dark modern decor, make this place in Lalaport Toyosu a good option for *yakiniku* (Korean barbecue).

Bars and Cafés

The Canteen
2-7-4 Aomi, Koto-ku. Tel: 03-5330 0261. Off map
On the waterfront next to the Miraikan, this hip café-restaurant serves a fusion of Japanese and Continental cuisines along with a nice selection of cakes and sweets.

Les Deux Bleue
Urban Dock LaLaport Toyosu, 2-4-9 Toyosu, Koto-ku. Tel: 03-3536 8326. Off map
Facing the bay at the back of this mega mall is this pleasant café that's a good spot to catch the breeze and watch the patrons who fawn over their pampered pooches (dog snacks are on the menu).

Nandeya
Aqua City, 1-7-1 Daiba, Minato-ku. Tel: 03-5564 3160. Off map
A row of dangling *aka-chochin* (red lanterns) greets patrons. This old-fashioned and relaxed *izakaya* on the ground floor of the mall offers small plates; wash it down with your beer, *shochu* or *sake*.

EXCURSIONS

An efficient rail system makes nearby getaways easily accessible if you want to escape Tokyo: choose from rambunctious Tokyo Disney Resort, old-world Kawagoe, laid-back Yokohama, Zen-like Kamakura, majestic Mount Fuji and temple-crammed Nikko.

Tokyo's congestion and big city attractions may be interesting for a short period, but even after a few days the most seasoned travellers may find themselves itching to get away. And the good news is, Japan's well-established rail system makes escaping a breeze. An hour or so by rail (see page 233) is all you need before arriving at some of the country's most famous sights – the temple town of Nikko, the Edo-Period merchant enclave of Kawagoe, cosmopolitan Yokohama, coastal Kamakura, or exploring Mount Fuji and Hakone. Most of the attractions listed in this section can be done as day trips. However, getting out of the city can be challenging – especially on weekends, when it may seem as if all of Tokyo has the same idea.

Chiba Prefecture

The neighbouring prefecture to the east of metropolitan Tokyo is **Chiba** (www.chiba-tour.jp) and it's usually the first place visitors to Japan see since this where Narita International Airport is located. Closer into Tokyo you'll find the fairy-tale castle and thrill rides of Tokyo Disney Resort, while slightly further out are the old castle town of Sakura and the surf

beaches and rural delights of the Boso Peninsula.

Tokyo Disney Resort ❶

Address: 1-1 Maihama, Urayasu-shi, Chiba-ken
Tel: 045-683 3333
Website: www.tokyodisneyresort.co.jp
Opening Hours: daily but hours vary depending on season and special events
Entrance Fee: charge
Transport: Maihama
Hundreds of millions of visitors

Main Attractions
Tokyo Disney Resort
Ichiban-gai
Kita-in
Minato Mirai 21
Kamakura
Enoshima
Mount Fuji
Hakone
Tosho-gu
Lake Chuzenji

Maps and Listings
Map, page 224

Tokyo Disney Resort.

Excursions

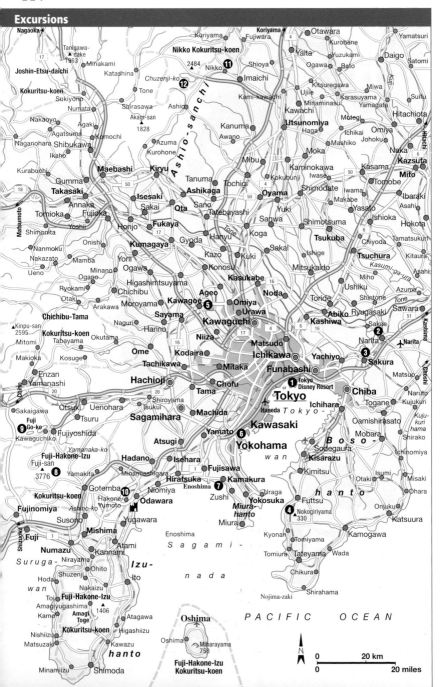

Nagaoka

Koriyama

Koriyama
Fujiwara

Otawara
Kurobane

Yamatsuri

Tanigawa-dake 1963
Minakami

Nikko Kokuritsu-koen

Yuzukami

Yaita

Daigo

Satomi

Joshin-Etsu-daichi

Katashina

2484
Nikko

Shioya

Ogawa

Bato

Kokuritsu-koen

Chuzenji-ko

Imaichi

Ujiie

Karasuyama
Yamagata

Suifu

Sukiyono

Tone

Ashio

Kami-kawachi

Miwa

Hitachiota

Numata

Shirasawa

Minaminasu

Kawachi

Motegi

Omiya

Nakaoyo

Akagi-san
1828

Azuma

Utsunomiya

Haga

Ichikai
Johoku

Naka

Kazsuta

Agaki

Komochi

Kanuma

Mashiko

Agatsuma
Shibukawa

Kurohone

Awano

Mibu

Kaminokawa

Iwase

Makabe

Kasama

Mito

Naganohara

Ikaho

Mibu

Kokubunji

Iwama

Yasato

Tomobe

Ibaraki

Kurabuchi

Maebashi

Kiryu

Tanuma

Tochigi

Shimodate

Iwata

Makabe

Asahi

Gumma

Takasaki

Isesaki

Ashikaga

Sano

Oyama

Shimotsuma

Ishioka

Hokota

Annaka

Fujioka

Sakai

Ota

Tatebayashi

Yuki

Sanwa

Tsukuba

Chiyoda

Tamatsukuri

Tomioka

Yoshii

Honjo

Fukaya

Gyoda

Koga

Sakai

Ishige

Tsuchura

Kitaura

Asahi

Shimonita

Onishi

Kumagaya

Hanyu

Tone

Kazo

Kuki

Mitsukaido

Miho

Azuma

Nanmoku

Nakazato

Yorii

Ogawa

Konosu

Kasukabe

Toride

Ushiku

Shintone

Sawara

Ueno

Minano

Higashimtsuyama

Noda

Abiko

Ryugasaki

Sakae

Ryokami

Chichibu

Moroyama

Ageo

Omiya

Kashiwa

Narita

Kinpu-san 2595

Arakawa

Naguri

Sayama

Urawa

Matsudo

Kashiwa

Sakura

Chichibu-Tama

Okutama

Hanno

Kawaguchi

Ichikawa

Funabashi

Chiba

Kokuritsu-koen

Tabayama

Niiza

Kodaira

Mitaka

Naruto

Mitomi

Kosuge

Ome

Tachikawa

Tokyo
Disney Resort

Ichihara

Togane

Kujukuri

Makioka

Enzan

Hachioji

Chofu

Tokyo

Kuju-kuri hama

Yamanashi

Tama

Haneda

Tokyo-

Shirako

Sakaigawa

Otsuki

Uenohara

Shiroyama

Machida

Kawasaki

Boso-

Tsukui

Sagamihara

Yamato

Yokohama

wan

Ichinomiya

Fuji Go-ko

Tsuru

Kisarazu

Kawaguchiko

Fujiyoshida

Atsugi

Isehara

Fujisawa

Kimitsu

Otaki

Isumi

Misaki

Yamanaka-ko

Hadano

Hiratsuka

Kamakura

hanto

Ohara

Fuji-Hakone-Izu

Fuji-san 3776

Yamakita

Minamiashigara

Niomiya

Enoshima

Zushi

Yokosuka

Uraga

Futtsu

Onjuku

Katsuura

Fujinomiya

Gotemba

Odawara

Miura-hanto

Kokuritsu-koen

Ashino-ko
Yumoto

Yugawara

Miura

Susono

Mishima

Yugawara

Enoshima

Kyonan

Tomiyama

Kamogawa

Fuji

Numazu

Kannami

Atami

Sagami-

Tomiura

Tateyama

Wada

Suruga-

Nirayama

Izu-

nada

wan

Shuzenji

Ohito

Ito

Chikura

Hoda

Nakaizu

Shirahama

Toi

Fuji-Hakone-Izu

Atagawa

Nojima-zaki

Amagiyugashima

Amagi Toge
1406

Kamo

Higashiizu

PACIFIC OCEAN

Kokuritsu-koen

Nishiizu

Kawazu

Oshima

Matsuzaki

hanto

Oshima

Minarayama
758

Minamiizu

Shimoda

Fuji-Hakone-Izu
Kokuritsu-koen

N

0   20 km

0   20 miles

have passed through the gates of Tokyo Disney Resort since it opened in 1983. As well as the original Disneyland park, a fair copy of the original in California, there's also the neighbouring DisneySea Park with attractions designed along aquatic themes. Avoid visiting on weekends and holidays when the lines for the most popular rides are invariably enormous.

Narita-san (Shinsho-ji)

Address: 1 Narita,Naritasa-shi, Chiba-ken
Tel: 0476-22 2111
Website: www.naritasan.or.jp
Opening Hours: daily 24 hours
Entrance Fee: free
Transport: JR Narita or Keisei Narita

But there is much more to the prefecture than the Magic Kingdom. Most people are in a hurry to leave Chiba's Narita area after arriving at Narita Airport, which is a shame as the area has much to offer. In **Narita** town ❷ is the venerable temple complex of Narita-san Shinsho-ji, a 15-minute walk from either of the town's train stations, which are themselves little more than 10 minutes from the airport. Dating back to AD 940, it is one of the most important in the entire Kanto region, drawing worshippers especially over the first three days of the New Year.

There are several reasons for Narita-san's popularity. Foremost is its image of Fudo, the Buddhist 'god of fire', said to have been carved by Kobo Daishi, the saint who founded the Shingon sect in the 9th century. The complex, with the 58-metre (190ft) -tall Great Pagoda of Peas – a beautiful three-storeyed carved pagoda that's an Important Cultural Property – and a spacious landscaped park packed with blossoming trees and a calligraphy museum is also highly attractive.

The three-tiered pagoda of Narita-san.

National Museum of Japanese History

Address: 117 Jonai-cho, Sakura-shi, Chiba-ken
Tel: 043-486 0123
Website: www.rekihaku.ac.jp
Opening Hours: Tue–Sun 9.30am–4.30pm
Entrance Fee: charge
Transport: Keisei Sakura

An overview of the nation's history can be enjoyed in the former castle town of **Sakura** ❸, on the Narita Keisei and JR Sobu lines. Within the extensively landscaped former castle grounds is the **National Museum of Japanese History** (Kokuritsu Rekishi Minzoku Hakubutsukan), which presents Japanese history from an anthropological point of view with the aid of some 200,000 well-presented artefacts.

Nokogiri-yama ❹

The hilly Boso Peninsula (Boso Hanto), shaped like a pelican's craw

TIP

Other easily accessible places of interest in Chiba are the historic towns of Sawara and Itako (www.suigosanto.com/en) built on canals that meander through thousands of hectares of marshland. Tours using poled boats take visitors along the waterways, and usually include a 'traditional lunch' and even a spot of fishing.

Participants at the Kawagoe Festival.

The carefully preserved old godowns of Kawagoe today house shops and restaurants.

the rock face near the top of the mountain, and a cluster of 1,553 stone statues of *rakan* (disciples of the Buddha). Descend a long flight of steps to visit the Yakushi Nyorai Buddha, Japan's largest figure of the Buddha. The base to the tip of the giant lotus bud that stands behind the statue's head like a stone anti-macassar measures an impressive 31 metres (100ft). The Buddha image was originally built in 1783.

Easily accessed from Chiba city, the east coast of the peninsula has some of the most underrated beaches in the Tokyo area – although Tokyo's surfing enthusiasts have certainly discovered them. **Onjuku,** with white sand, palm trees and beach-front cafés, is the most pleasant, though **Katsuura** and **Kamogawa,** both south of Onjuku, are also good for swimming. Kujukuri-hama, north of Onjuku, has over 60km (37 miles) of black, volcanic beach.

separating Tokyo Bay from the Pacific, is also easily accessed from Tokyo by train lines. On the penin-sula's southwest coast is Nokogiri-yama (translated as 'saw-tooth mountain'). A short ropeway (daily 9am–4pm; charge) takes visitors half-way up the mountain, which affords a fine panorama of Tokyo Bay and Mount Fuji. Just as interesting is a 33-metre (110ft) image of Kannon, the Goddess of Mercy, carved into

Kawagoe ❺

Saitama prefecture, to the north of Tokyo, doesn't have an abundance

An ornate float at the Kawagoe Festival.

The wooden bell tower of Toki-no-Kane is a distinctive landmark in old-world Kawagoe.

includes a cup of tea and a traditional Japanese sweet (okashi).

Continuing down Ichiban-gai, on the left inside an old tobacco wholesaler's is the **Kurazukuri Shiryokan** (tel: 049-222 5399; www.kawagoe.com/kzs; Tue–Sun 9am–4.30pm; charge). This is one of the first *kurazukuri* to be rebuilt after the great fire of 1893, which wiped out over a third of the city. The displays give a good idea of what it used to be like to live in such houses.

Across the road, and down a lane to the right, is the **Toki-no-Kane**, a three-storey wooden bell tower that has become synonymous with Kawagoe. The tower was originally constructed in the 17th century and has since been through four editions, the most recent being this one dating from after the 1893 fire. Listen out for the bell, which tolls four times daily: at 6am, noon, 3pm and 6pm. The sound of the bell has been designated by the government as one of the (oddly named) '100 best sound scenes of Japan'.

Back on the Ichiban-gai, **Osawa Jutaku,** dating from 1792, is Kawagoe's oldest *kurazukuri*. It's now a handicraft shop selling traditional

of tourist offerings but one great one that it does have is the former castle town of **Kawagoe** (www.koedo.or.jp). Less than an hour northwest of Tokyo, discover this 'Little Edo' famed for its historic core of *kurazukuri* – black-walled merchant houses, some dating from the 18th century – and the transported remains of Edo castle.

Ichiban-gai

From Kawagoe Station it's about a 15-minute walk to reach the town's historical core, first along Crea Mall and then Taisho-roman-dori. At the end of this street, the *kurazukuri* immediately in front of you used to house the Kameya sweet shop and factory and is now the **Yamazaki Museum of Art** (open Fri–Wed 9.30am–4.30pm; charge) displaying screen paintings by the 19th-century artist Gaho Hashimoto. Entry

Yokohama's Chinatown is the largest in Japan.

all that remains of the old castle – the entrance and main visitors' hall of the palace **Honmaru** Goten (tel: 049-224 6015; Tue–Sun 9am–5pm; charge) built by a local lord Matsudaira Naritsune in 1848. Now a museum containing beautifully painted screens and waxwork dummies of samurai and lords of old.

A 10-minute walk south back towards the station brings you to **Kita-in,** (www.kawagoe.com/kitain; daily 9am–4.30pm; charge) an important Buddhist temple-museum dating back to AD 830. After a major fire in 1638, the third shogun Tokugawa Iemitsu ordered that parts of the original Edo castle be transported here to aid in the temple's reconstruction. From these historic wooden buildings – the likes of which do not exist in Tokyo itself – you can admire a traditional Japanese garden planted with plum, cherry and maple trees as well as hydrangea and azaleas.

products like Japanese masks and dolls. Opposite is the **Kawagoe Festival Museum** (tel: 049-225 2727; daily Apr–Sept 9am–6pm, Oct–Mar 9am–5pm, closed 2nd and 4th Wed of the month; charge) in which you can view two more of the ornate floats paraded around in the Kawagoe festival, along with videos of past events.

At the next main intersection after the Kawagoe Festival Museum turn left and walk a block to reach the narrow stone-paved lane on the left that is **Kashi-ya Yokocho,** or Confectioners' Row. Souvenirs and trinkets have been added to the 22 nostalgically old-fashioned shops selling traditional candies, crackers and other sweet treats such as purple sweet potato ice cream.

Honmaru Goten and Kita-in

Returning to the bell tower, a 10-minute walk east brings you to

TIP

Yokohama's oldest Western-style accommodation, the New Grand Hotel (tel: 045-681 1841; www. hotel-newgrand.co.jp), was built in 1927. Its second-floor lobby is a marvellous time capsule of old Yokohama.

Ferris wheel in Minato Mirai.

Kita-in's other crowd-pleaser is the **Gohyaku Rakan**, a grove of stone statues carved between 1782 and 1825. The name means 500 statues, though there are actually 540 depictions of the disciples of the Buddha; no two are alike. One figure scratches his head, a couple get drunk on wine, others meditate, rub a sore foot or beat drums.

Yokohama ❻

West of the capital is Yokohama (www. city.yokohama.lg.jp/en) capital of Kanagawa prefecture. An integral part of the Greater Tokyo area, it is also a major urban centre in its own right, with a population of 3.6 million, as well as one of Asia's greatest seaports. Easily covered on foot, it has relatively uncrowded streets (except on weekends) and a laid-back atmosphere.

Minato Mirai 21 and around

The central bay area is dominated by **Minato Mirai 21** (www.minato-mirai21.com) a massive development made from reclaimed land and historic disused dock buildings. Sights here include the 70-storey Landmark Tower (www.yokohama-landmark.jp) with its Sky Garden observation deck on the 69th floor (charge), the handsome 1930s tall ship *Nippon Maru* (www.nippon-maru. or.jp; charge) and the **Yokohama Museum of Art** (Yokohama Bijutsukan; tel: 045-221 0300; www. yaf.or.jp/yma; Fri–Wed 10am–6pm; charge), with its excellent collection of modernist sculpture.

Walk through the Nippon-Maru Memorial Park and across the Kisha-Michi Promenade to **Shinko Pier,** a man-made island housing the Akarenga Park (www. yokohama-akarenga.jp). The island's old red-brick custom houses have been renovated and now serve as fashionable shops, restaurants and boutiques. Shinko Pier is also home to the **Cosmo World** amusement

Skyscrapers overlook the waterfront.

park (www.senyo.co.jp/cosmo), which boasts among its many attractions two roller-coasters and the 112.5-metre (369ft) -high 'Cosmo Clock' Ferris wheel.

The other side of the Okagawa River from Sakuragicho Station is an area of old government buildings, banks and other institutional structures. Further on is a charming tree-lined street with red-brick pavements called Basha Michi-dori (Street of Horse Carriages). The interesting **Kanagawa Prefectural Museum of Cultural History** (Kanagawa Kenritsu Kindai Bijutsukan; tel: 045-201 0926; www. ch.kanagawa-museum.jp; Tue–Sun 9.30am–5pm; charge) is located here. The stately building, erected in 1904 as a bank, is one of the best surviving examples of the city's old commercial architecture.

Along the waterfront

In Yokohama's early days Honcho-dori became the centre of commercial activities. The wide street is still bracketed with banks and office buildings like the handsome red-brick clock tower of the **Yokohama Port Opening Memorial Hall** (Yokohama-shi Kaiko Kinen Kaikan), which miraculously survived the 1923 earthquake and World War II fire bombings.

EAT

No visit to Yokohama would be complete without a meal in Chinatown (Chuka-gai), tucked back from the waterfront. Founded in 1863, these dozen or so blocks contain the largest and best Chinatown in Japan.

One of numerous shrines tucked in the verdant hills of Kamakura.

Also in this area are numerous prefectural offices, and near the waterfront, the Yokohama Custom House (Yokohama Zeikan). **The Yokohama Archives of History** (Yokohama Kaiko Shiriokan; tel: 045-201 2100; www.kaikou.city.yokohama.jp; Tue–Sun 9.30am–5pm; charge), on the site of the former British consulate, houses a museum with various exhibits about Yokohama's fascinating history, and a library with related audio-visual materials.

Opposite is the Yokohama Port Opening Square, where Japan and the United States signed the Treaty of Peace and Amity in 1854. A little bit farther down the same road is the 106-metre (348ft) **Marine Tower** (tel: 045-664 1100; http://marinetower.jp; daily 10am–10pm; charge for observation deck), which was reopened in 2009 after a major renovation, and the **Yokohama Doll Museum** (Ningyo no Ie; tel: 045-671 9361; www.yokohama-doll-museum.

com; daily 10am–4.30pm; charge), which displays some 3,500 dolls from Japan and around the world. **Yamashita Park** (Yamashita Koen) along the waterfront is well worth a visit. The former passenger liner and hospital ship *Hikawa-Maru* (www.nyk.com/rekishi/e; Tue–Sun 10am–5pm; charge) is permanently moored here and can be visited.

Yamate area

Southeast of Yamashita Park is Yamate, where the foreign merchants used to live in palatial homes. Before exploring Yamate, pause for a spectacular view of the bay and bridge from Harbour View Park (Minato-no-Mieru Oka Koen) at the top of the hill called France Yama. In the rose garden beside the park's gate, you can visit the **British House Yokohama** (Yokohama-shi Igurisu-kan; tel: 045-623 7812; daily 9am–5pm; July–Aug until 6pm; charge) home to the city's first British legation. Cross the road opposite the gates and go straight ahead. At the Foreigners' Cemetery (Gaijin Bochi), around 4,200 foreigners are buried. The adjacent **Yamate Museum** (Yamate Shiriokan; tel: 045-622 1188; daily 11am–4pm; charge), with quaint displays on the life of early foreign residents, sits near where Japan's first brewery was located. Immediately west of Yamate, on the way to Chinatown, is the lively shopping street of Motomachi (www.motomachi.or.jp).

About two kilometres south of Yamate, and best reached via bus from Yokohama Station, is **Sankei-en** (www.sankeien.or.jp; daily 9am–5pm; charge), a traditional Japanese garden built in 1906 by a local silk merchant. Its extensive grounds have a number of historical buildings, including a farmhouse and three-storey pagoda.

Kamakura ❼

Kamakura (www.kcn-net.org/kamakura) lies cradled in a spectacular natural amphitheatre, flanked on three sides by wooded mountains and on the fourth by the blue Pacific. For roughly 150 years from 1192, Kamakura was the de facto political and cultural capital of Japan, during which time a warrior administration based here built impressive temples and commissioned notable works of art, a great deal of it Zen-influenced.

Kamakura has no less than 65 Buddhist temples and 19 Shinto shrines, interspersed with walks through quiet surrounding hills. Most visitors customarily begin their sightseeing from Kita-Kamakura Station, nearest to the great Zen Buddhist temples of **Engaku-ji** (tel: 0467-22 0478; daily 8am–4pm; Apr–Oct until 5pm; charge), **Tokei-ji** (tel: 0467-22 1663; daily Nov–Feb 8.30am–4pm, Mar–Oct until 5pm; charge) and **Kencho-ji** (tel: 0467-22 0981; daily 8.30am–4.30pm; charge).

Wakamiya-dori

On the east side of Kamakura Station, where you'll also find the tourist office, is the broad boulevard of Wakamiya-dori. Parallel is pedestrian-only Kamachi-dori, a lane full of trendy shops and eating places.

Kamakura is also known for Kamakura-*bori* (lacquerware), first appearing in the 13th century as utensils used in religious ceremonies. Learn more about this art at the

Statue at the entrance to the Wakamiya-dori boulevard.

Entrance to the Wakamiya-dori boulevard.

Kamakurabori Kaikan (tel: 0467-25 1502; www.kamakuraborikaikan.jp; daily 9am–5pm; charge) on the right along Wakamiya-dori.

Tsurugaoka Hachiman-gu

The approach to Kamakura's main shrine, **Tsurugaoka Hachiman-gu** (www.tsurugaoka-hachimangu.jp; daily Oct–Mar 6am–8.30pm, Apr–Sept 5am–8.30pm) at the end of Wakamiya-dori, crosses a steep, half-moon bridge. Behind the shrine's Heike Pond is the **Kanagawa Prefectural Museum of Modern Art** (Kanagawa Kenritsu Kindai Bijutsukan; tel: 0467-22 5000; www.moma.pref.kanagawa.jp; Tue–Sun 9.30am–5pm; charge), with changing exhibitions by contemporary Japanese and foreign artists.

A little past the Genji Pond is the **National Treasure Hall** (Kamakura Kokuhokan; Tue–Sun 10am–4.30pm; charge) where the 2,000 treasures from the various temples of Kamakura are displayed.

Continuing up the avenue, cross a 25-metre (82ft) dirt track, along which every 16 September mounted archers gallop and unloosen their

Lake Ashino with the snow-capped Mt Fuji in the background.

Racks of padlocks near the bell tower in Enoshima.

arrows at targets in an ancient samurai ritual. Then you reach an open area below the steps to the shrine's Main Hall. Most of the present shrine buildings are reconstructions, but the red-painted halls, lively souvenir stalls and ebullient flow of visitors make it one of Kamakura's most earthy pilgrimage spots.

The Great Buddha

Back at Kamakura Station take the Enoden Line to Hase Station, which is closest to Kamakura's famous Daibutsu (Great Buddha) in the grounds of **Kotoku-in** (www.kotoku-in.jp; daily Oct–Mar 8am–5pm, Apr–Sept 6am–5.30pm; charge). At 11 metres (40ft) in height and weighing 94,000kg (93 tons), the Daibutsu is unlikely to get lost in the crowd. Stand a few metres in front of the statue to get the full impact of this

artwork cast in 1252. Astonishingly, the statue has survived some massive typhoons and tsunami – one in 1495 ripped away the wooden building then enclosing it – as well as earthquakes.

On the way back to the station, to the right, it's worth climbing up to the hillside temple **Hase-dera** (tel: 0467-22 6300; www.hasedera.jp; daily Mar–Sept 8am–5pm, Oct–Feb until 4.30pm; charge) with its 9-metre (30ft), 11-headed Hase Kannon statue, along with thousands of small Jizo statues decked out in colourful bibs and bonnets.

Enoshima

Board the Enoden train again and get off at Enoden Enoshima Station. It's a 15-minute walk from here across the 600-metre/yd causeway to the tiny sacred island of **Enoshima,** its hilly slopes plastered with an extraordinary collection of shrines, grottos and souvenir shops. Local fishermen traditionally came to Enoshima to pray for a bountiful catch. Escalators take the faithful to higher reaches, but it's not difficult to follow the old pilgrim routes as

they wind up through this island of the gods. Apart from its shrines and sacred caves, the island boasts a yachting harbour, a botanical garden (charge) containing more than 300 species of tropical plants and several cafés with fine views of Mount Fuji.

MOUNT FUJI AND HAKONE

It would be hard to find a mountain more highly praised for its beauty than Fuji, or a lake more often photographed than Hakone's Ashi-no-ko. Most of the region is designated a 'national park', but due to Japan's rather weak laws at protecting and restricting commercial exploitation of such assets, national parks are more often than not considered 'nature' amusement parks.

Climbing Mount Fuji

Sweeping up from the Pacific to form a nearly perfect cone, 3,776 metres (12,388ft) above sea level, **Mount Fuji** ❶ (Fuji-san) is said to watch over Japan and her people. Like many natural monuments held to be sacred and imbued with a living spirit, Fuji was considered off

A 'forest of sculptures' in the foothills of Mount Fuji are part of the Hakone Open Air Museum.

Climbing Mount Fuji.

GETTING THERE FROM TOKYO

Tokyo Disney Resort: 15-minute train ride from Tokyo Station on the JR Keiyo Line to Maihama, or take the Tozai Line (subway) to Urayasu, and then catch a shuttle bus.
Nokogiri-yama: 90 minutes from Tokyo Station to Hamakanaya on the JR 'Sazanami' express.
Kawagoe: The Tobu Tojo Line express from Ikebukuro takes 30 minutes to JR Kawagoe. JR trains also run on the same route, but take slightly longer.
Yokohama: Take the Tokyu Toyoko Line train (25 to 35 minutes) from Shibuya, or the JR Tokaido Line (25 minutes) from Tokyo Station to Yokohama.
Kamakura: An hour's journey from Tokyo Station (or 30 minutes from Yokohama) on the JR Yokosuka Line to Kita-Kamakura or Kamakura.
Mount Fuji and Hakone: The Odakyu Line from Shinjuku serves Hakone. JR Pass holders can access the area from Odawara on the *shinkansen* (bullet train) line.
Nikko: A two-hour train ride to the north of Tokyo – by direct local or Tobu Line express train from Asakusa to Tobu Nikko.

Heavily gilded rooftop of Toshogo-jinja in Nikko.

TIP

See www.odakyu.jp/global_ site for details about Odakyu Electric Railway's two and three-day Hakone Passes (¥5,000/¥5,500) both of which cover a return trip on the Odakyu Line from Shinjuku to Odawara, plus unlimited use of the Hakone Tozan Railway, the Sounzan funicular, Hakone Ropeway, boats on Ashi-no-ko, and most local buses. It also gets you discounts at many of Hakone's attractions.

limits to women until 1867, when an English woman broke the taboo and scaled the mountain.

According to a Japanese saying, there are two kinds of fools: the ones who never climb Mount Fuji and the ones who climb it twice in a lifetime. The ascent to Mount Fuji's summit can take anything from five to ten hours, depending on the route, so don't attempt the climb unless you are reasonably fit.

For those who wish to see the rising sun from Fuji's peak, start in the afternoon, stay overnight at one of the cabins near the top, and complete the climb while it is still dark. Or start at about 9pm and climb through the night. On a mountain this high you need to be prepared for extreme changes of temperature and rain, so bring along a sweater, gloves and a waterproof jacket, plenty of water and a torch.

Fuji Five Lakes ❾

The Fuji Go-ko (Five Lakes) district skirts the northern base of Mount Fuji and provides an ideal year-round resort, offering a range of outdoor recreational activities such as camping and water sports during the summer months, and skiing and skating in the winter.

From east to west, the lakes are Yamanaka-ko, Kawaguchi-ko, Sai-ko, Shoji-ko and Motosu-ko. Yamanaka-ko, which is the largest in the group, and the picturesque Kawaguchi-ko, are the most frequented of the five, but some of the most picturesque and tranquil spots are hidden near the smaller and more secluded three other lakes.

Hakone ❿

Hakone, set against the backdrop of Mount Fuji, has long been a popular place for rest and recreation. Tours usually start at Hakone-Yumoto Station, where the Hakone Tozan Railway begins its 9km (6-mile) zigzag route up all the way to the terminus at Gora. The gateway to Hakone's 16 hot springs, Hakone-Yumoto nestles in a shallow ravine where the Hayakawa and Sukumo rivers flow together. If on a day trip, the luxurious *onsen* complex **Tenzan Tohji-kyo** (tel: 0460-86 4126; www.tenzan.jp; daily 9am–11pm; charge), a five-minute taxi ride from Hakone-Yumoto Station, provides an exquisite hot spring treat.

Some 20 minutes from Hakone-Yumoto on the Hakone Tozan lies **Miyanoshita**, the oldest and most thriving of the spa towns. Miyanoshita is home to the famous **Fujiya Hotel** (tel: 0460-82 221; www.fujiyahotel.jp). Opened in 1878, it is a veritable time capsule, with a 1930s-style wood-panelled dining room, a library full of old books and waitresses in Agatha Christie-period uniforms. Look out for the guest book with comments from personalities like Margaret Thatcher, John Lennon and Yoko Ono, among others.

The Hakone Tozan train also stops at **Hakone Open Air Museum** (Chokoku no Mori Bijutsukan; tel: 0460-82 1161; www.hakone-oam.or.jp; daily 9am–5pm; charge) an outdoor sculpture garden that has few parallels elsewhere in the world. The works of Picasso, Rodin, Leger, Takamura Kotaro and many others are on display at this stunning location.

At the Gora terminal, change over to the funicular to Mount Soun (Soun-zan) and transfer to the cable car headed for Togendai, which lies on the shore of **Ashi-no-ko**, a beautiful caldera lake crisscrossed by pleasure boats. On the way up is **Owakudani** (Valley of the Greater Boiling) in the old crater of Mount Kami. It is an interesting place but the sulphurous fumes coming out of the lunarscape can be overwhelming.

Nikko ⓫

A couple of hours north of Tokyo is the delightful mountain town of Nikko, a treasure house of religious art and architecture produced during the Tokugawa era and set among dense cedar forests. In 1617 Nikko

TIP

The ¥1,000 *nisha-ichiji* combination ticket sold at booths in Nikko outside Rinno-ji's Sanbutsu-do Hall and Tosho-gu's Omote-mon, will save you some money. It covers entry to Rinno-ji, Futarasan-jinja and most of Tosho-gu. Add ¥520 if you wish to tag on entry to see Tosho-gu's sleeping cat carving and Ieyasu's tomb.

Lake Chuzenji.

was chosen by the Tokugawa as the burial place of their first shogun, Ieyasu. **Tosho-gu**, an astonishingly elaborate memorial shrine, was completed in 1636.

The ideal way to approach the complex is via the steps opposite the vermillion bridge **Shinkyo** (daily 9am–4pm; charge), spanning the Daiya River at the top of the main street, around a 20-minute gentle uphill walk from both the JR and Tobu Nikko stations. From there, follow the cedar avenue to the temple **Rinno-ji** (daily Apr–Oct 8am–5pm, Nov–Mar until 4pm; charge). Rinno-ji's Sanbutsudo Hall houses three gigantic images: Bato Kannon (protector of horses), Amida, and the thousand-armed Kannon, the Goddess of Mercy.

Continue along the main Omotesando path towards the Five Storey Pagoda (Goju-no-to). Just before the main entrance to the **Tosho-gu** (www.toshogu.jp; daily Nov–Mar 8am–4pm, Apr–Oct until 5pm; charge), the Buddhist-style gate Omote-mon is guarded by two mythical kings. The adjacent Sacred Horse Stable is

carved with scenes illustrating the life cycle of humanity. Past the *torii* gate at the top of the stone steps is Tosho-gu's most famous feature, the Yomei-mon, beyond which only the highest-ranking samurai could once pass. Standing 11 metres (35ft) high, this gate is covered with hundreds of intricate carvings – children at play, clouds, pine trees, bamboo and animals – all painted in a riot of brilliant colours.

More treasures await inside: the east and west corridors surrounding the main building are also covered with carvings, among them the celebrated but difficult to find Nemuri-Neko, or Sleeping Cat, on the side of the Sakashita-mon gate. Beyond this gate are the 200-odd steps to Tokugawa Ieyasu's mausoleum (charge).

Retrace your route to the exit of Tosho-gu, bear right at the pagoda and walk along a path lined with stone lanterns, to reach the grounds of **Futarasan**-jinja (daily Apr–Oct 8am–5pm, Nov–Mar until 4pm; charge). Dedicated to nearby Mount Nantai, the simplicity of this red-lacquered shrine, and its pleasant garden, is a welcome relief after the highly accomplished but ostentatious Tosho-gu shrine.

Lake Chuzenji ⑫

From Nikko take the 30-minute bus ride up the winding mountain road to **Lake Chuzenji**, (Chuzenji-ko) 1,270 metres (4,170ft) above sea level. From there, savour the clear air and lakeside scenery: a sightseeing boat leaves the pier just across the road from the bus stop, for a one-hour tour of the lake.

Five minutes' walk in the opposite direction is the observatory of the 100-metre (320ft) -high **Kegon Falls** (Kegon no Taki; charge); a lift descends right to the bottom of the gorge where a platform allows views of the thundering falls.

Torii gate and Five-Storey Pagoda at Nikko.

The mighty Kegon Falls.

東京ミッドタウンは、おかげさまで開業5周年

Tokyo Midtown
5th Anniversary

INSIGHT GUIDES TRAVEL TIPS
TOKYO

TRANSPORT

GETTING THERE AND GETTING AROUND

GETTING THERE

By Air

Tokyo is served by two main airports: **New Tokyo International Airport** (Narita) about 66km (41 miles) east of the city; and the **Tokyo International Airport** (Haneda), 20km (12 miles) to the south of the city centre. The airports are usually simply referred to as Narita and Haneda.

Traditionally most international flights to Tokyo arrive at Narita, while Haneda is primarily for domestic flights. However, with the addition of a terminal and an extra runway, there is now an increasing number of international flights to Haneda, too.

Narita Airport

Although rather inconveniently located, Narita is an efficiently run airport with two terminals and two runways. Both terminals have currency exchange counters, restaurants and cafés, internet facilities, post offices, health clinics, and a range of shops. Terminal 2 has a children's playroom, day rooms for taking a nap and showers.
General and Flight Info: 0476-34 8000; www.narita-airport.jp/en
Tourist Info: 0476-34 5877

(Terminal 2); 0476-30 3383 (Terminal 1)

Haneda Airport

Haneda Airport is Tokyo's main hub for domestic flights including those of the main domestic airlines – Japan Air Lines (JAL; www.jal.com) and All Nippon Airways (ANA; www.ana.co.jp).

The addition of a runway and terminal has also seen more international flights operating at Haneda. A regular shuttle bus service links the international terminal to the domestic terminal.

Haneda's three terminals are comfortable and well designed, with many restaurants, cafés, shops, post offices and information desks.
Airport Info: 03-5757 8111; www.tokyo-airport-bldg.co.jp.

Flying from UK and US

The four big-name airlines serving Tokyo from the UK are British Airways, JAL, ANA and Virgin Atlantic. Flying time direct from London is 11 to 13 hours.

Coming from the US or Canada, you are spoiled for choice. Besides JAL and ANA, among the better known airlines that fly the Tokyo route are American Airlines, Delta and United Airlines. Flying time from the US west coast is 12 to 13 hours; from the east coast it's 18 to 20 hours, including stopovers.

Tokyo is an increasingly important transportation hub for direct flights to major destinations like Beijing, Shanghai, Hong Kong, Bangkok and farther afield to Singapore, Bali and Sydney.

KEY AIRLINES

Air China
2-5-2 Toranomon, Minato-ku
Tel: 03-5251 0711
www.airchina.com.cn
American Airlines
2-2-3 Uchisaiwai-cho,
Chiyoda-ku
Tel: 03-4550 2111
www.aa.com
British Airways
3-5-1 Toranomon, Minato-ku
Tel: 03-3298 5238
www.britishairways.com
Qantas Airways
3-5-1 Toranomon, Minato-ku
Tel: 03-3593 7000
www.qantas.com.au
Singapore Airlines
1-10-1 Yurakucho, Chiyoda-ku
Tel: 03-3213 3431
www.singaporeair.com
United Airlines
3-1-1 Marunouchi, Chiyoda-ku
Tel: 0120-226 688
www.united.com
Virgin Atlantic Airways
3-9-19 Higashi, Shibuya-ku
Tel: 03-3499 8811
www.virgin-atlantic.com.

While fares vary from airline to airline, late April to early May, August and December tend to be the most expensive times to fly to Japan from the UK or US as they coincide with the country's Golden Week, O-bon and Year End-New Year holidays. Flying even a few days on either side of these peak periods can result in huge savings.

By Road

The expressways that connect major cities throughout Japan are of extraordinarily high quality. Like the British, the Japanese drive on the left, and the signs are generally self-explanatory. All major expressways charge a toll fee, so apart from traffic-congested roads, the option of using a train or bus is much more appealing. See 'Driving' (page 243) for details on car hire.

Japan has an excellent system of inter-city buses. They offer a comfortable and sometimes cheaper alternative to trains. Buses often include destinations not covered by trains, and many operate direct services, unlike trains. Night buses are cheaper than trains, but leave late and arrive in the early hours.

The main **JR bus office** is located on the south side of Tokyo Station (tel: 03-3215 1056). **The Tokyo Bus Association** (tel: 03-5360 7111) has information on buses arriving and departing from the city. A good discount long distance bus service is **Willer Express** (willerexpress.com).

By Sea

Although few people arrive by sea, Japan's ferry services are quite extensive, at least in their connections with South Korea and China.

There is a regular boat service between South Korea's port of Pusan and Shimonoseki in Japan. A hydrofoil also plies between Pusan and Hakata in Japan.

Ferries from China (Shanghai and Tanggu) arrive in Osaka and Kobe respectively, from where

passengers travel either by rail or air to Tokyo.

By Train

The majority of train lines entering Tokyo from major Japanese cities, whether JR or *shinkansen* (bullet train), terminate or make a stop at Tokyo Station on the JR Yamanote Line. Travelling to places like Hakone and Nikko usually involves taking a private line. Major non-JR line terminals are Asakusa, Shibuya and Shinjuku stations, and these last two on the useful Yamanote Line.

Information on train connections to the places of interest outside Tokyo are found on page 233.

GETTING AROUND

From Narita Airport

Because of its distance from Tokyo, you should allow at least one hour to reach the city centre, depending on the time of day and your mode of transport.

There are basically three ways to get into Tokyo: taxi; limousine bus; and train – either express trains such as JR's Narita, Express or Keisei Railway's Sky Access, or the slower regular trains.

By Taxi

This is most expensive option, and usually the slowest. The fare to or from downtown Tokyo is ¥20,000 to ¥30,000 and one is often sitting in a traffic jam, watching the meter spin inexorably higher. The rides are strictly metered, and have no extra surcharges.

Expect the 66km (41-mile) ride to central Tokyo to take anywhere between 1.5 and three 3 hours depending on traffic density. Signs indicating taxi ranks are clearly indicated at exit points throughout the terminals.

By Limousine Bus

Convenient, frequent and comfort-

able airport 'limousine' buses are much cheaper than taxis. However, they are also subject to traffic jams. These buses connect Narita Airport with most parts of the city, including major hotels and railway stations as well as Haneda Airport, Tokyo Disneyland and Y-CAT (Yokohama City Air Terminal). Tickets (around ¥3,000, depending upon destination) can be bought in the arrival lobby after clearing immigration and customs. Buses are boarded outside the terminal at the curb, and will carry any amount of luggage at no extra charge. Estimated travel time to central Tokyo: 1 hour and 15 minutes, barring major traffic jams.

For enquiries, call 03-3665 7220 (www.limousinebus.co.jp).

By Train

Between the two express trains – **JR's Narita Express** and **Keisei's Sky Access** – the Keisei service is the fastest, taking just 36 minutes to reach the city centre. Both train companies also offer slower and cheaper train services into Tokyo. The stations for both lines are found on the basement level of each of the two terminal buildings.

Narita Express connects with the JR railway network at Tokyo, Shinagawa, Shinjuku, Ikebukuro, Omiya, Yokohama and Ofuna stations. It takes one hour to travel to Tokyo Station, and costs ¥2,940 (¥4,430 for first class; although the seats are more than comfortable enough in standard class).

For JR train information (in English), call 03-3423 0111; www.jreast.co.jp/e.

Keisei's Sky Access runs to Tokyo's Ueno Station, stopping first at nearby Nippori; you can connect with JR lines at either station, as well as the subway at Ueno. It takes 41 minutes to Ueno (36 to Nippori) and costs ¥2,400. Contact Keisei Ueno Information Centre at tel: 03-3831 0131; www.keisei.co.jp.

Note: Using the train and subway can involve long walks. If you have more baggage than you can carry, make use of the fast and reliable baggage delivery services at the airport. Look for counters in the arrival lobby. JAL's ABC service is recommended (tel: 03-3545 2800 or 0120-919-120). For about ¥1,500 to ¥2,500 per piece, they deliver your baggage by the following day to anywhere in Japan. Similarly, they pick up bags from anywhere and deliver to Narita.

T-Cat Departures

Passengers of selected airlines taking the airport limousine bus to Narita can complete check-in and passport control procedures at **Tokyo City Air Terminal** (T-CAT) in downtown Tokyo. To find out if your airline offers this service, call T-CAT at 03-3665 7111, www. tcat-hakozaki.co.jp/eng. T-CAT can be accessed by taxi (most taxi drivers know it just as Hakozaki) or by subway from Suitengumae Station on the Hanzomon Line.

From Haneda Airport

By Taxi

By taxi, it should take about 30 minutes to central Tokyo, and cost around ¥5,000, but expect to encounter traffic congestion.

By Limousine Bus

An airport limousine bus service connects Haneda with central Tokyo. Fares range from ¥1,000, depending on which part of the city you're heading to. There is also a service from Haneda to Narita that takes about 75 minutes and costs ¥3,000.

By Train

Most people opt for the cheaper, slower trains. Frequent services run from the Keihin Kyuko Railway Station in the airport basement. The train takes 13 to 25 minutes to Shinagawa Station, depending on the exact service, and costs ¥400.

By Monorail

If travelling light, another alternative is the Tokyo Monorail, which connects Haneda with Hamamatsucho Station on the JR Yamanote Line. It takes only 14

ASKING FOR HELP

Japanese people are generally very helpful when quizzed about addresses and, if nearby, may even on occasion escort you to your destination. When in doubt, ask at the local koban (police box). The police are generally very helpful and will consult maps on your behalf and even phone to confirm an address.

minutes and costs ¥470, but can be very crowded during rush hour.

Orientation

Central Tokyo is divided into 23 ku (wards), which are sub-divided into cho (districts), then numbered chome (blocks) – see page 260. Japanese people tend to think in terms of city blocks, often finding their way from one block to the next by using landmarks such as shops, restaurants and architectural features as markers. Even taxi drivers get confused once they depart from the main thoroughfares and sights. Maps are essential for navigating the city. Good English-language city maps which show major landmarks along with railway and subway lines can be picked up for free from major hotels or Tourist Information Centre (TIC) offices (see page 267).

Exits at train stations are usually clearly signposted overhead. Landmarks like museums, department stores and government offices are marked in English on yellow boards, which should be visible as you exit the ticket barriers. Train stations usually have maps near their exits. Though often in Japanese, they provide some sense of orientation.

Public Transport

The public transport system in Tokyo is unrivalled anywhere in the world. A sophisticated and highly efficient network of railway lines, subways and bus routes serves the city. During rush hour, services

run every one to two minutes on some lines, at a degree of reliability inconceivable elsewhere.

Both trains and subways are notoriously crowded during the morning and evening rush hour, and sometimes run at 300 percent of the seating capacity.

Major roads can be even more congested. For that reason, taxis are only useful if you are travelling routes not served by a subway.

Subway (Metro)

The subway system is clean, safe and convenient. It is also the fastest and most economical means of getting across town. There are 13 lines crisscrossing central Tokyo, nine operated by Tokyo Metro and four by Toei Subway.

Subways run to precise schedules, indicated on timetables posted at each station. Services run from 5am to around 12.30am at intervals of two to three minutes during rush hours, with frequencies dropping to around every five to ten minutes at off-peak periods. The frequency is slightly reduced on weekends.

All subway and train stations have a route map indicating fares for each stop near the ticket machines, usually in English.

The fares for both subways and trains are regulated on a station-to-station basis, so if you cannot determine the fare required, just purchase the cheapest ticket available (¥160 for Tokyo Metro lines, ¥180 for Toei lines) at the ticket machine. If you have not paid the correct fare, simply top up the difference on arrival – either at designated fare adjustment machines or at the station office.

PASMO magnetic smart cards (www.pasmo.co.jp), valid for any public transportation line in Tokyo can be bought at subway stations (¥500 deposit), and recharged when depleted. These are simply passed over sensors of the automated ticket gates as you enter, with the fare deducted at your destination. Japan Railway's **Suica** cards act in exactly the same way and both this and PASMO cards can be used on subways, trains and buses. If you are going to be out and about a lot, it's well worth getting one these cards to avoid the hassle of fare adjusting and fiddling with ticket machines.

Train

Above ground, **Japan Railways** (JR) operates an equally efficient service, with equivalent frequency and operating hours (5am–1am) on commuter lines. Like the subways, the lines are colour coded.

The **Yamanote Line** (green) makes a long, 35km (21-mile) oval loop around central Tokyo, with other lines branching out to the suburbs. These are either JR lines or several private train lines, like Keio and Tobu, radiating out to the suburbs from hubs situated around the Yamanote Line.

JR fares start at ¥130. Suica and PASMO magnetic smart cards can also be used in place of tickets. A one-day ticket for unlimited train travel in central Tokyo (the 'Tokunai' pass) costs ¥730. Other passes are available for travelling out of Tokyo or in combination with the subway and buses (see: www.jreast.co.jp/e/pass).

Station arrivals are announced in Japanese and sometimes English on the trains. There is usually a map or electronic display above the train doors indicating the stops on the line and the connecting lines. Station names are written in Japanese and English.

Taxis

Taxis are a convenient but pricey way of getting around town. The standard flagfall is ¥710 for the first 2km (1.2 mile) and ¥80 for every 275 metres/yds after that. Short trips typically run to ¥2,000. No tipping is expected.

Taxis are readily available on almost every street corner, and at every major hotel and railway station. A red light in the front window signifies that the taxi is available. Roads are narrow and rush hour traffic appalling – especially on Fridays or before a holiday.

Most taxi drivers speak only

TAXIS' AUTO DOORS

There is no need to touch the doors at all when getting in or out of a taxi. The doors are opened and closed by the driver, who operates a lever at the front. After hailing a taxi, wait for the door to open; on arrival, the door will be opened again for you.

Japanese, so it can be helpful to have your destination written out in Japanese. Many drivers are not native Tokyoites, and are only familiar with central Tokyo and the main landmarks. Having the address of your destination handy also means they can input it into their car navigation systems and avoid getting lost! Do not be surprised if taxis fail to stop when you hail them, particularly at night. Drivers will be looking for profitable long runs out to the suburbs rather than stranded foreigners wanting to return to their hotels. Recommended taxi operators are: **Hinomaru**: tel: 03-3212 0505; www.hinomaru.co.jp/taxi **Nihon Kotsu**: tel: 03-5755 2336 (English language); www.nihon-kotsu.co.jp/en.

Buses

There are no English signs on Tokyo buses, but imminent stops are announced by a recorded voice. Passengers pay on entry, dropping the flat fare (usually ¥200) into a box located next to the driver; there's a machine in the box for changing notes if you don't have the coins. Tourist information centres and hotels can give you bus maps with the major routes marked. Buses generally run from 5.30am to midnight.

River Buses

For river cruises, enquire at **Tokyo River Buses**, tel: 0120-977 310; www.suijobus.co.jp. The most popular itinerary is the trip up the Sumida River to Asakusa from Hinode (or vice versa; 40 minutes). Other routes include a 45-minute cruise around Tokyo Harbour, starting at

Hinode and going past the Rainbow Bridge and the Odaiba area to Kasai Sealife Park (55 minutes); and to the Shinagawa Aquarium (35 minutes). Hinode Pier is near Takeshiba and Hinode stations on the Yurikamome New Transit System (five and seven minutes from Shimbashi, respectively). River buses can be boarded at Hama Rikyu Garden (near Shimbashi Station), Asakusa, and Odaiba.

Look out for the striking, *Himiko* vessel, designed by *manga* artist Leiji Matsumoto, which morphs into the floating bar Jicoo at night (www.jicoofloatingbar.com).

Driving

Tokyo is not an easy place to drive in, even when you know the city layout. Except on the crowded expressways, there are few road signs in Romanised Japanese. For getting out of town, it is usually faster to take public transport. If you do need to hire a car try **Toyota Rent-a-Car** (http://rent.toyota.co.jp/en), which has branches at the airports and across the city.

Cycling

Intrepid travellers may want to try cycling around Tokyo. Major roads can be perilous, but if you stick to the back roads bikes offer a great way to get intimate with the city at surface level. Some hotels provide free bike rental, while rental shops vary in price from as little as ¥1,000 up to ¥4,000 a day. A good website for locating a handy rental shop and for other cycling information is Cycle Tokyo (http://cycle-tokyo.cycling.jp).

TRAVEL PASSES

Active sightseers can save by buying a Tokyo Furii Kippu, a one-day pass that entitles you to use all JR, subway and bus lines in the Tokyo region. Pass offices (look out for a triangle symbol on subway maps) at major stations sell the tickets for ¥1,580.

ACCOMMODATION

SOME THINGS TO CONSIDER BEFORE YOU BOOK THE ROOM

Choosing a Hotel

There is never a shortage of places to stay in Tokyo. Accommodation ranges from deluxe Western-style hotels and no-frills business lodgings to budget 'capsule hotels'. Tokyo's top hotels are among the finest in the world in terms of facilities and service. The older establishments especially exude a distinctive Japanese ambience. Business hotels target Japanese salarymen rather than foreign businessmen, providing bedrooms that are clean and functional, but barely big enough to contain the bed.

Traditional Japanese inns, or *ryokan*, provide a very different experience. At their best (and most expensive), they epitomise the essence of Japanese hospitality. You sleep on *futon* mattresses on *tatami* mats, bathe in a traditional bath, and are served exquisite *kaiseki ryori* meals in your room by attendants in kimono.

On an altogether different level, there are budget Japanese-style inns (*minshuku*) that give a taste of the traditional but at a fraction of the cost of a top *ryokan*. These simple family-run lodgings offer personalised service and simple accommodation, and give a close-up view of how many Japanese live.

Capsule hotels offer basic bunk-style accommodation in enclosed cabins just big enough to sit up in. They are not an option for long-term stays (you can't store luggage), but are good in an emergency. There are capsule hotels in most areas where salarymen go carousing. Most are for men only, but a few have floors reserved for women.

Hotel Areas

For the sake of simplicity, many visitors choose to stay at places close to the circular Yamanote Line, where many of the main sights are located. Many of the bigger Yamanote stations like Shinjuku, Ikebukuro and Tokyo are transportation hubs linked to overground and subway lines that will take you to other sights within or outside the city.

Stations like these are mini-cities in their own right, offering a vibrant package of activities that include shopping, restaurants and nightlife. Each has its own distinctive character. While you may choose an area for a notable feature that interests you (Ueno for museums, Shibuya for fashion, Roppongi for nightlife), these micro-cities work hard at providing something for everyone. Central Tokyo (Roppongi, Akasaka, Nihombashi and Ginza) tends to

be more expensive and cater to the business market, while areas such as Shinjuku, Shibuya, Ueno and Ikebukuro tend to have a greater choice.

Prices and Bookings

Western-style hotels charge on a per-room basis, but at traditional *ryokan* inns and pensions, customers are charged per person, with the rate usually including dinner and breakfast. Many larger hotels also offer non-smoking rooms and women-only floors. All hotel rates include 5 percent consumption tax. Luxury hotels may impose a 10 to 15 percent service charge. If your room costs over ¥10,000 per person per night, there's also a Tokyo Metropolitan Government tax of ¥100 per person per night (¥200 per person if the room costs over ¥15,000).

Useful websites include **Japan Hotel Association** (www.j-hotel.or.jp), **Japanican** (www.japanican.com), **Japan Ryokan Association** (www.ryokan.or.jp), **Japan Ryokan and Hotel Association** (www.nikkanren.or.jp) and **Japan Guest Houses** (www.japaneseguesthouses.com)

Note: budget travellers should book in advance for February, when thousands of students descend on the city for university entrance exams.

IMPERIAL PALACE AREA, YURAKUCHO AND GINZA

Luxury

Imperial Hotel
1-1-1 Uchisaiwai-cho, Chiyoda-ku
Tel: 03-3504 1111
www.imperialhotel.co.jp
① p278, C3
Japan's first Western-style hotel (built in 1890 and now in its third incarnation), offers top service and restful rooms. Its central location opposite Hibiya Park makes it a favourite of both travellers and business people. (1,058 rooms)

Mandarin Oriental, Tokyo
2-1-1 Nihombashi Muromachi, Chuo-ku
Tel: 03-3270 8800
www.mandarinoriental.com/tokyo
② p278, D1
Handily situated near Nihombashi Station, this five-star hotel mixes sumptuous contemporary designs award-winning restaurants, top service, and one of the city's best spas. (178 rooms)

The Peninsula Tokyo
1-8-1 Yurakucho, Chiyoda-ku
Tel: 03-6270 2888
www.peninsula.com/tokyo
③ p278, C3
A branch of the Hong Kong flagship, the Peninsula's superb location and high-class style is hard to match. Try to get one of the middle- or upper-level rooms, from where the views are outstanding. (314 rooms)

Tokyo Station Hotel
1-9-1 Marunouchi, Chiyoda-ku
Tel: 03-5220 1112
www.tokyostationhotel.com
④ p278, C2
Located inside the old red-brick Tokyo Station Building, the addition of this classically designed hotel was part of the station's make over. (150 rooms)

Expensive

Hotel Com's Ginza
8-6-15 Ginza, Chuo-ku
Tel: 03-3572 4131
www.hotelcoms.jp/english/ginza
⑤ p278, C3
Part of a classy business hotel chain, right in the backstreets of

Tokyo Station Hotel.

Ginza. Quite comfortable if you don't mind foregoing some of the frills. Single room prices from ¥14,000. Nearest station: Shimbashi. (267 rooms)

Diamond Hotel
1-10-3 Kojimachi, Chiyoda-ku
Tel: 03-3263 2211
www.diamond-hotel.co.jp
⑥ p278, A2
There's an old-fashioned grace to this hotel, in a quiet area just minutes from the Imperial Palace, the British Embassy and Hanzomon Station. The hotel's Chinese restaurant serves authentic favourites like Peking duck. (204 rooms)

Mitsui Garden Hotel Premier
8–13-1 Ginza, Chuo-ku
Tel: 03-3543 1131
www.gardenhotels.co.jp/ginza
⑦ p278, C3
Close by the Shiodome development, the Mitsui Garden Hotel's rooms may not be overly large, but with sleek, modern interiors created by Italian designer Piero Lissoni and dazzling views, you're sure to nestle in. (361 rooms)

Moderate

Ginza Mercure
2-9-4 Ginza, Chuo-ku

Tel: 03-4335 1111
www.mercureginza.jp
⑧ p278, C3
This stylishly decorated hotel, occupying a former office building, is centrally located but on a quiet backstreet. It offers dedicated ladies' rooms with a boutique hotel feel. (208 rooms)

Yaesu Fujiya Hotel
2-9-1 Yaesu, Chuo-ku
Tel: 03-3273 2111
www.yaesufujiya.com
⑨ p278, C2
A short walk from Tokyo Station, this long-running hotel has some elegant touches like its majestic, red-carpeted staircase descending into the lobby. Rooms are small, but well equipped; there are a few Japanese-style rooms, too. (377 rooms)

Yaesu Terminal Hotel
1-5-14 Yaesu, Chuo-ku
Tel: 03-3281 3771
www.yth.jp/english
⑩ p278, D2
The rooms in this business hotel are far from spacious, but they are clean and reasonable value for the location. Good amenities, including flat-screen TV. The location, close to Tokyo Station, is a big plus. (117 rooms)

IKEBUKURO, MEJIRODAI AND SHINJUKU

Hotel Chinzan-so
2-10-8 Sekiguchi,
Bunkyo-ku
Tel: 03-3943 1111
http://hotel-chinzanso-tokyo.jp
⑪ p272, D2
Western luxury is combined with
Japanese attention to detail at
this superlative property in an
unparalleled setting, overlooking
the beautiful Chinzan-so garden
with its pagoda, waterfall and
Buddhist statuary. A 10-minute
walk from Edogawabashi Station.
(283 rooms)

Park Hyatt Tokyu
3-7-1 Nishi-Shinjuku, Shinjuku-ku
Tel: 03-5322 1234
www.tokyo.park.hyatt.com
⑫ p276, B1
Made famous when the movie
Lost in Translation was shot here,
this de luxe property has a fantastic setting on the upper 14 floors
of the 52-storey Park Tower.
Expect top-class facilities and
superb service. Home to the
excellent New York Grill restaurant and adjoining New York Bar.
(178 rooms)

Hilton Tokyo
6-6-2 Nishi-Shinjuku, Shinjuku-ku
Tel: 03-3344 5111
www.hilton.co.jp/tokyo
⑬ p272, B4
Set among the skyscrapers of
west Shinjuku, the rooms are
Western in style, but with Japanese accents, all with modem
lines and cable TV. The closest
subway station is Tochomae, but
it's also easy walking distance
from Shinjuku. (806 rooms)

Hyatt Regency Tokyo
2-7-2 Nishi-Shinjuku, Shinjuku-ku
Tel: 03-3348 1234
http://tokyo.regency.hyatt.com
⑭ p272, B4
In the heart of West Shinjuku, this
is one of Tokyo's most praised
hotels, though you wouldn't realise it from the outside. The posh
executive floors are exclusive,

with separate facilities and king-
sized beds. (744 rooms)

Keio Plaza Hotel
2-2-1 Nishi-Shinjuku, Shinjuku-ku
Tel: 03-3344 0111
www.keioplaza.co.jp
⑮ p276, B1
Located directly above Tochomae
station, this 45-storey skyscraper
on the west side of Shinjuku, is an
older, established property but
well maintained. It offers a gym,
business facilities, outdoor swimming pool and good selection of
restaurants and bars. (1,450
rooms)

The b Ikebukuro
1-39-4 Higashi-Ikebukuro, Toshima-ku
Tel: 03-3980 1911
www.theb-hotels.com
Off map
Just a three-minute walk from
Ikebukuro Station, The b Ikebukuro offers stylish contemporary rooms and efficient service.
There's also a good, low-cost
izakaya in the basement. (175
rooms)

Shinjuku Prince Hotel
1-30-1 Kabuki-cho, Shinjuku-ku
Tel: 03-3205 1111
www.princehotels.com/en/shinjuku
⑯ p272, B4
Look down from your room at the
goings-on in Kabuki-cho, the
heart of Shinjuku nightlife. The
hotel has renovated rooms and
good facilities, including a 25th-
floor restaurant with the best
views this side of Shinjuku. (571
rooms)

Sunshine City Prince Hotel
3-1-5 Higashi-Ikebukuro, Toshima-ku
Tel: 03-3988 1111
www.princehotels.com/en/sunshine
Off map
Efficient, well-run and well
equipped with business facilities.
This Prince hotel is conveniently
located in the Sunshine City complex, which is a hive of activity
with its array of shops, restaurants and amusements. JR Ikebukuro Station is an eight-minute

*View from the Park Hyatt Hotel,
Shinjuku.*

walk away. (1,166 rooms)

Hotel Villa Fontaine, Shinjuku9
2-40-9 Kabuki-cho, Shinjuku-ku
Tel: 03-5292 3330
www.hvf.jp/eng/shinjuku
Off map
Opened in 2008, this branch of
the Villa Fontaine chain, which
has 13 other properties in Tokyo,
has smart rooms and a good
range of amenities that include
94cm (37in) flat-screen TVs in
each room. In Kabuki-cho, a ten-
minute walk from Shinjuku Station. (66 rooms)

Green Plaza Capsule Hotel
1-29-2 Kabuki-cho, Shinjuku-ku
Tel: 03-3207 5411
www.hgpshinjuku.jp
⑰ p272, B4
Claiming to be Tokyo's very first
capsule hotel, this men-only
operation is one of the best and

PRICE CATEGORIES

**Price categories are for a
double room without breakfast
and taxes:**
Luxury = over ¥30,000
Expensive = ¥20,000–¥30,000
Moderate = ¥10,000–¥20,000
Budget = under ¥10,000

biggest of its kind. Located in the heart of Kabuki-cho, the capsules are surprisingly comfortable and even come with their own TVs. There's also an outdoor bath. (600 capsules)

Kimi Ryokan
2-36-8 Ikebukuro, Toshima-ku
Tel: 03-3971 3766
www.kimiryokan.jp
Off map
This homely *ryokan* is one of

Tokyo's best-loved budget places with helpful English-speaking staff. It is very popular, so book in advance. Located in a quiet back-street, a 10-minute walk to JR Ikebukuro Station. (38 rooms)

SHIBUYA AND AOYAMA

Luxury
Cerulean Tower Tokyu Hotel
26-1, Sakuragaoka-cho, Shibuya-ku
Tel: 03-3476 3000
www.ceruleantower-hotel.com
Off map
Shibuya's most upmarket hotel covers the 19th to 37th floors of a tower offering splendid views. Spacious, fully equipped and tastefully decorated rooms. On the premises are bars and several Japanese and Western eating options, including a modern *kaiseki* restaurant, and *noh* theatre. (411 rooms)

Expensive
Hotel Floracion
4-17-58 Minami-Aoyama, Minato-ku
Tel: 03-3403 1541
www.floracion-aoyama.com
Off map
Aoyama is short on hotels but this one, tucked away in the back streets off Omotesando, is worth

seeking out. Good quality Western-style rooms, a selection of even nicer Japanese-style rooms and pleasant service. (189 rooms)

Granbell Hotel, Shibuya
15-17 Sakuragaoka-cho, Shibuya-ku
Tel: 03-5457 2681
www.granbellhotel.jp
Off map
Decorated in hip boutique hotel-style, with Ray Lichtenstein prints in some rooms and natural wood tones in others. It's in a quiet area a short walk south of Shibuya Station. (105 rooms)

Shibuya Excel Tokyu
1-12-2 Dogenzaka, Shibuya-ku
Tel: 03-5457 0109
www.tokyuhotelsjapan.com
⑱ p276, B4
Aimed at businesspeople and those who want to be in the thick of Shibuya. The Excel Tokyu occupies part of the Mark City complex attached to JR Shibuya Station.

There are two floors for women only. (408 rooms)

Moderate
Shibuya City Hotel
1-1 Maruyamacho, Shibuya, Shibuya-ku
Tel: 03-5489 1010
www.courthotels.co.jp/shibuya
⑲ p276, B4
This small, functional business hotel seven minutes from Shibuya Station and opposite the Bunkamura is ideally located for the arts, shopping and nightlife of Shibuya. (57 rooms)

Tokyu Stay Shibuya
8-14 Shinsencho, Shibuya-ku
Tel: 03-3477 1091
www.tokyustay.co.jp/e/hotel/SIB
Off map
One of a chain of appealing apart-hotels around the city. All the rooms have self-catering and laundry facilities and offer more space and style than the average business hotel. (120 rooms)

ROPPONGI AND AKASAKA

Luxury
ANA InterContinental Tokyo
1-12-33 Akasaka, Minato-ku
Tel: 03-3505 1111
www.anaintercontinental-tokyo.jp
⑳ p276, E3
A few minutes' walk from the Tameike-Sanno subway station, this popular hotel offers large rooms with those on the upper storeys having great views. Top-grade facilities include a great selection of restaurants including an outpost of Michelin-starred chef Pierre Gagnaire. (843 rooms)

Grand Hyatt Tokyo
6-10-3 Roppongi, Minato-ku

Tel: 03-4333 1234
http://tokyo.grand.hyatt.com
㉑ p276, D4
Truly spectacular, but in an under-stated manner. Wood, glass and marble in the public areas form clutter-free and contemporary lines. Bedrooms feature flat-screen TVs (including one in the bathroom), CD players and high-speed internet, plus capacious bathrooms. There's also a great range of fine restaurants and bars. Roppongi Station is a three-minute walk away. (387 rooms)

New Otani
4-1 Kioi-cho, Chiyoda-ku

Tel: 03-3265 1111
www.newotani.co.jp/en/tokyo
㉒ p276, E2
A massive complex with many restaurants and extensive Japanese gardens that are worth seeing in their own right. On the boundary with Akasaka, but within a 10-minute walk of the Imperial Palace, the location is ideal for both sightseeing and nightlife. Free entry to the New Otani Art Museum for guests. (1,600 rooms)

Hotel Okura
2-10-4 Toranomon, Minato-ku
Tel: 03-3582 0111

www.hotelokura.co.jp/tokyo/en
㉓ p278, A3
Long held to be one of Japan's
great hotels, the Okura offers an
atmospheric blend of traditional
Japanese decor and 21st-century
facilities including an excellent
range of restaurants. A five-minute walk from Roppongi-Itchome
Station. (858 rooms)

The Prince Park Tower Tokyo
4-8-1 Shibakoen, Minato-ku
Tel: 03-5400 1111
www.princehotels.com/en/parktower
Off map
The flagship of the Prince Hotel
group, this 33-floor tower is right
up against Tokyo Tower. Rooms
with balconies are a plus as are
top-notch facilities including a
pool, a spa and bowling alley. A
short walk from Shiba-koen subway station. (673 rooms)

Ritz Carlton
Tokyo Midtown, 9-7-1 Akasaka, Minato-
ku
Tel: 03-3423 8000
www.ritzcarlton.com
㉔ p276, E4
Occupying the top nine floors of
the 53-storey Midtown Tower is
this ultra-luxury hotel. Beautifully
decorated and spacious rooms
are complemented by the Ritz's
famous afternoon teatime service, with bird's-eye views of
Tokyo from The Lobby Lounge and
Bar on the 45th floor. (248 rooms)

Akasaka Excel Hotel Tokyu
2-14-3 Nagatacho, Chiyoda-ku
Tel: 03-3580 2311
www.tokyuhotelsjapan.com
㉕ p276, E2
Reliable quality and efficient service, with reasonable rates compared with the deluxe hotels
nearby. Rooms away from the
road are quieter. Good shops and
restaurants in the downstairs
mall, and bars up on the upper
levels. (293 rooms)

Akasaka Yoko Hotel
6-14-12 Akasaka, Minato-ku
Tel: 03-3586 4050
www.yokohotel.co.jp

Roppongi Hills.

Off map
Midway between Roppongi's
restaurants, galleries and night-
time entertainment, and Akasaka's famous Shinto shrines,
Nogi and Hie, the Yoko is in a
convenient location. Though
quite small and somewhat
dated, the rooms are affordable
and clean, and come with
internet connection. (241
rooms)

The b Roppongi
3-9-8 Roppongi, Minato-ku
Tel: 03-5412 0451
www.theb-hotels.com
㉖ p278, A4
Branch of a business hotel-cum-
boutique hotel with stylish interiors, good service and a location
that's an easy walk from Roppongi's nightlife, Tokyo Midtown,
Roppongi Hills and other top
attractions. (76 rooms)

Hotel Ibis
7-14-4 Roppongi, Minato-ku
Tel: 03-3403 4411
www.ibis-hotel.com
㉗ p276, E4
A good, mid-range option in the
heart of the Roppongi area and
right above all the action. Well-
designed, if smallish rooms. Good
business facilities, including
modem ports and multilingual
staff. Good value for this part of
Tokyo. (182 rooms)

Hotel Villa Fontaine Roppongi
1-6-2 Roppongi, Minato-ku
Tel: 03-3560 1110
www.hvf.jp/eng
㉘ p276, E4
One in a chain of excellent value,
stylish business hotels, which has
13 other branches around the city.
Offers rooms larger than most in
this category, a complimentary
buffet breakfast and discounted
rates at weekends. (300 rooms)

Asia Centre of Japan Hotel
8-10-32 Akasaka, Minato-ku
Tel: 03-3402 6111
www.asiacenter.or.jp
㉙ p276, D3
Book well ahead for this popular
lodging for low-budget travellers.
Rooms in the newer wing are a
notch up from the older, cramped
ones. A few minutes' walk from
the subway, the location is good
for both Roppongi and Aoyoma
areas. (173 rooms)

PRICE CATEGORIES

Price categories are for a
double room without breakfast
and taxes:
Luxury = over ¥30,000
Expensive = ¥20,000–¥30,000
Moderate = ¥10,000–¥20,000
Budget = under ¥10,000

SHINAGAWA, MEGURO AND EBISU

The Claska
1-3-18 Chuo-cho, Meguro-ku
Tel: 03-3719 8121
www.claska.com
Off map
A sleek boutique hotel that combines contemporary Scandinavian interiors with traditional Japanese design sensibilities. It includes a hip café-bar and art gallery. (18 rooms)

Meguro Gajoen
1-8-1 Shimo Meguro, Meguro-ku
Tel: 03-5434 3837
www.megurogajoen.co.jp
Off map
Staying at this famous wedding and function hall is a pricey treat but well worth it if you want to experience top-grade *ryokan*-style service and facilities. Both European and Japanese-style rooms are available, but ask for the latter. Only a three-minute walk from Meguro JR Station. (23 rooms)

Westin Hotel Tokyo
1-4-1 Mita, Meguro-ku
Tel: 03-5423 7000
www.westin-tokyo.co.jp
Off map

This hotel offers spacious guest rooms, sophisticated interiors and personalised service, and is in a handy location for Yebisu Garden Place. The Westin models itself after grand European-style hotels, with gracefully designed rooms, an elegant lobby and tastefully decorated public spaces. (438 rooms)

Grand Prince Hotel Takanawa
3-13-1 Takanawa, Minato-ku
Tel: 03-3447 1111
www.princehotels.com/en/takanawa
Off map
The pick out of a complex of three Prince hotels surrounding the same beautifully landscaped gardens. The facilities here are uniformly good and both the Japanese- and Western-style rooms are well presented and spacious. It's five minutes' walk from JR Shinagawa Station. (414 rooms)

Sheraton Miyako Hotel Tokyo
1-1-50 Shiroganedai, Minato-ku
Tel: 03-3447 3111
www.miyakohotels.ne.jp/tokyo/english
Off map

Located in a pleasant, quiet neighbourhood near the Happoen Garden and the National Park for Nature Study, this is a lovely retreat, with super comfortable beds clothed in Frette sheets. (492 rooms)

Hotel Excellent Ebisu
1-9-5 Ebisu-Nishi, Minato-ku
Tel: 03-5458 0087
www.soeikikaku.co.jp
Off map
Though it has plain, rather small rooms and only basic facilities, this business hotel's helpful staff, attractive rates and handy location near Ebisu Station make it a popular choice. (127 rooms)

Sansuiso Ryokan
2-9-5 Higashi-Gotanda, Shinagawa-ku
Tel: 03-3441 7475
www.sansuiso.net
Off map
Cosy *ryokan* just a five-minute walk from the Gotanda station. Japanese-style rooms, with private or shared facilities. (10 rooms)

UENO, YANESEN AND ASAKUSA

Asakusa View Hotel
3-17-1 Nishi-Asakusa, Taito-ku
Tel: 03-3842 2117
www.viewhotels.co.jp/asakusa
30 p274, E2
Well situated for sightseeing and shopping in downtown Asakusa. The rooms are Western-style and offer good views as does the bar on the 28th floor. (337 rooms)

Ryokan Katsutaro Annex
3-8-4 Yanaka, Taito-ku
Tel: 03-3828 2500
www.katsutaro.com/annex_index
31 p274, C3

This modern *ryokan* combines the best of Japanese decor with tatami flooring and paper screen windows, private bathrooms and broadband internet access in each room. Free internet and coffee in the entrance area. Just around the corner from Yanaka Ginza, a lively street with craft and tea shops. (11 rooms)

Ryokan Shigetsu
1-31-11 Asakusa, Taito-ku
Tel: 03-3843 2345
www.shigetsu.com
32 p274, E2
Steps away from Nakamise-dori, this is one of Asakusa's nicest *ryokan* offering both small Western- or Japanese-style rooms, all

en suite. The top floor bath offers views over the nearby temple roofs. (22 rooms)

Hotel Sardonyx Ueno
6-6-7 Ueno, Taito-ku
Tel: 03-3833 7200
www.hotel-sardonyx.com/ueno
33 p274, D2
Comfortable and well-priced business hotel, where each room is equipped with broadband internet access and an LCD television. Within walking distance of three JR stations and a 10-minute walk to Ueno Park. (181 rooms)

Sukeroku-no-yado Sadachiyo
2-20-1 Asakusa, Taito-ku
Tel: 03-3842 6431

www.sadachiyo.co.jp
34 p274, E2
Close by Senso-ji, this is atmospheric *ryokan* where the traditions of old Edo are maintained. All the tatami rooms have en-suite bathrooms but there are also traditional-style larger communal baths. (20 rooms)
Ueno First City Hotel
1-14-8 Ueno, Taito-ku
Tel: 03-3831 8215
www.uenocity-hotel.com
35 p274, D3
This smart business hotel with a

red-brick facade prides itself on its comfort and efficiency. Within walking distance of both Ueno and the area around the Yushima Tenjin Shrine. (77 rooms)

K's House Tokyo
3-2-10 Kuramae, Taito-ku
Tel: 03-5833 0555
http://kshouse.jp/tokyo-e
36 p274, E3
Clean, friendly hostel with a mix of dorms and private rooms. Internet access and shared kitchen

facilities. Near Kuramae Station. (18 rooms and dorms)
Sawanoya Ryokan
2-3-11 Yanaka, Taito-ku
Tel: 03-3822 2251
www.sawanoya.com
37 p274, C1
Small but comfortable rooms with tatami mats in this friendly *ryokan* in a residential neighbourhood close to the old quarter of Yanaka. The ¥315 self-service breakfast is good value. A short walk from the Nezu subway station. LGBT friendly. (12 rooms)

SUIDOBASHI, OCHANOMIZU, KANDA AND AKIHABARA

Expensive
Hotel Metropolitan Edmont
3-10-8 Iidabashi, Chiyoda-ku
Tel: 03-3237 1111
www.edmont.co.jp
38 p274, B3
A five-minute walk west of JR Suidobashi Station (or east of Iidabashi), this large hotel is efficiently run with comfortable, well-equipped rooms. Outside the mainstream area – thus few foreign tourists – but still within walking distance of the Yasukuni Shrine, the Tokyo Dome area and the Kanda-Jimbocho bookstore district. (665 rooms)

View from the InterContinental Tokyo Bay

Yama-no-ue (Hilltop) Hotel
1-1 Surugadai, Kanda, Chiyoda-ku
Tel: 03-3293 2311
www.yamanoue-hotel.co.jp
39 p274, C4
Five minutes southwest of JR Ochanomizu Station, this secluded hotel has genuine period charm. A favourite of writers and artists, the service is impeccable and the quality of the ten restaurants and bars is of a high standard. (74 rooms)

Moderate
Tokyo Green Hotel Korakuen
1-1-3, Koraku, Bunkyo-ku

Tel: 03-3816 4161
www.greenhotel.co.jp/en
Off map
Good value given its central location, next to Suidobashi Station and Tokyo Dome. The natural tone interiors create a tranquil setting, and there's a cheap café and free Wi-fi. (207 rooms)

Budget
Capsule Inn
6-9 Akihabara, Taito-ku
Tel: 03-3251 0841
www.capsuleinn.com
Off map
It's a fun experience to stay in a capsule hotel for one night (any longer and it's not so fun). This modern place with capsules for just ¥4,000 is in a great location and has separate floors for men and women. (169 capsules)
Sakura Hotel
2-21-4, Kanda-Jimbocho, Chiyoda-ku
Tel: 03-3261 3939
www.sakura-hotel.co.jp

PRICE CATEGORIES

Price categories are for a double room without breakfast and taxes:
Luxury = over ¥30,000
Expensive = ¥20,000–¥30,000
Moderate = ¥10,000–¥20,000
Budget = under ¥10,000

Room at the Grand Pacific Le Daiba

40 p274, B4
This popular centrally located budget hotel offers all non-smoking private rooms, which are tiny, as well as cheaper dorm accommodation. It has friendly English-speaking staff who will help you make the most out of your stay. There are other branches in Asakusa, Ikebukuro and Shinjuku. (43 rooms)

Tokyo International Youth Hostel
Central Plaza, 18F, 1-1 Kagurakashi, Shinjuku-ku
Tel: 03-3235 1107
www.jyh.gr.jp/tcyh
Off map

The city runs this spick-and-span youth hostel (open to everyone) in a skyscraper, which is fine if you don't mind sharing a room. It's right next to JR Iidabashi Station. There is an 11pm curfew to bear in mind and other hostel rules. (Dorms can accommodate 179 people)

SHIODOME AND TOKYO BAYSIDE

Luxury

Conrad Tokyo
1-9-1 Higashi-Shimbashi, Minato-ku
Tel: 03-6388 8000
www.conrad.co.jp
41 p278, C4
Shiodome's high-end accommodation doesn't come more luxurious than this. Immaculate service from a multi-lingual staff, designer rooms with hardwood finishing, private cedar baths, views across the Hama-Rikyu Garden and Tokyo Bay, and two Michelin-starred restaurants are just part of the pampering environment this hotel offers. (290 rooms)

Grand Pacific Le Daiba
2-6-1 Daiba, Minato-ku
Tel: 03-5500 6711
www.grandpacific.jp
Off map
The traditional European style of this luxury hotel's interior jars with the futuristic architecture of Odaiba, but the rooms are pleasant and there are plenty of facilities available, including indoor and outdoor swimming pools. (884 rooms)

Expensive

InterContinental Tokyo Bay
1-16-2 Kaigan, Minato-ku
Tel: 03-5404 2222
www.interconti-tokyo.com
Off map
All the spacious, stylishly appointed rooms here have panoramic views across Tokyo Bay towards Odaiba and the Rainbow Bridge. It's part of a complex that faces the east exit of Takeshiba Station and is a short walk to the pleasant Hama-Rikyu landscaped garden. (336 rooms)

Hotel Nikko Tokyo
1-9-1 Daiba, Minato-ku
Tel: 03-5500 5511
www.hnt.co.jp
Off map
Smack bang in front of Odaiba Station on the Yurikamome Line, the Nikko has one of the best views of the waterfront, offering a romantic setting for its comfortable rooms, first-rate service and top-quality food. (453 rooms)

Moderate

Tokyo Bay Ariake Washington Hotel
3-7-11Ariake, Koto-ku
Tel: 03-5564 0111
http://tokyobay.washington-hotels.jp
Off map
A comfortable business hotel on Odaiba, this has the same facilities found in the other branches of the Washington chain. It's popular with those attending exhibitions at the Tokyo Big Sight venue next door. Located a short walk away from Ariake Station. (830 rooms)

ACTIVITIES

THE ARTS, NIGHTLIFE, SPORTS, SIGHTSEEING TOURS AND CHILDREN'S ACTIVITIES

THE ARTS

Classical Music

Bunkamura Orchard Hall
2-24-1 Dogenzaka,
Shibuya-ku 150
Tel: 03-3477 9111
www.bunkamura.co.jp
One of Tokyo's first retail and culture complexes, Bunkamura includes Orchard Hall for symphonic concerts, ballets and operas, and the smaller Theatre Cocoon for chamber music and theatre.

Casals Hall
1-6 Kanda-Surugadai,
Chiyoda-ku
Tel: 03-3294 1229
www.nu-casalshall.com
Hosts piano recitals and other intimate classical music performances.

NHK Hall
2-2-1 Jinan, Shibuya-ku
Tel: 03-3465 1751
www.nhk-c.or.jp/nhk_hall
Catch concerts here by the NHK Symphony Orchestra.

Suntory Hall
1-13-1 Akasaka, Minato-ku
Tel: 03-3505 1001
www.suntory.com/culture-sports/suntoryhall
Renowned for its excellent acoustics, beer-maker Suntory's hall in Akasaka's Ark Hills complex was built with the advice of renowned maestro Herbert von Karajan.

Tokyo Bunka Kaikan
5-45 Ueno Park, Taito-ku
Tel: 03-3828 2111
www.t-bunka.jp
With two halls, this was for decades post-war Japan's premier classical music venue and has been refurbished. A wide-ranging programme of symphonic and opera concerts, and home to the Tokyo Ballet. Thanks to a late

Tokyo - the city that never sleeps.

1990s refurbishment it is still a pleasant place to take in a wide-ranging programme of symphonic and opera concerts, as well as performances by the Tokyo Ballet.

Tokyo Opera City
3-20-2 Nishi-Shinjuku, Shinjuku-ku
Tel: 03-5353 0770
www.operacity.jp
The home of the superb New National Theatre (see page 254) and its opera company, which stages Mozart concerts. Smaller adjoining theatres offer ballet and drama.

Tokyo Symphony Orchestra
www.tokyosymphony.com/en
Arguably Tokyo's finest orchestra. Although it stages concerts of world classics, it tries to highlight recent work by contemporary Japanese composers as well.

Rock and Pop

Japan, one of the world's largest music markets, has been an essential port of call for Western rock groups since the Beatles played at the Budokan back in the mid-1960s. While the best-known performers can sell out at mega-venues such as the Tokyo Dome at the drop of a hat, it is often possible to catch big names playing at relatively intimate settings.

Akasaka Blitz
5-3-2 Akasaka, Minato-ku

BUYING TICKETS

The major ticketing companies have outlets in all shopping areas and department stores. Most tickets for concerts and other events can also be purchased at convenience stores such as Lawson, 7-Eleven and Family Mart.

Ticket Pia
Tel: 0570-029 111
http://t.pia.jp
CN Playguide
Tel: 03-5802 9999
www.cnplayguide.com
Lawson
http://l-tike.com

Tel: 03-3584 8811
www.tbs.co.jp/blitz
A 2,000-capacity concert hall boasting an advanced lighting and sound system. Part of the Tokyo Broadcasting System complex in Akasaka. Has a sister venue in Yokohama.

Billboard Live
4F Tokyo Midtown, 9-7-4 Akasaka, Minato-ku
Tel: 03-3405 1133
www.billboard-live.com
Licensed by the American music industry trade magazine *Billboard*, this glistening international jazz and pop supper club is a centrepiece of the Midtown development.

Nippon Budokan
2-3 Kitanomaru-Koen, Chiyoda-ku
Tel: 03-3216 5100
www.nipponbudokan.or.jp
Built to hold martial arts competitions, this historic venue has also welcomed chart-topping acts from The Beatles to Destiny's Child.

O-East
2-14-8 Dogenzaka, Shibuya-ku
Tel: 03-5458 4681
http://shibuya-o.com
This mid-sized hall is part of a two-building, multistorey venue for live domestic and international concerts in the youth culture mecca of Shibuya. The acts here range from J-pop and K-pop to indie rock.

Tokyo Dome (Big Egg)
1-3-61 Koraku, Bunkyo-ku
Tel: 03-5800 9999
www.tokyo-dome.co.jp
Also home to baseball's Yomiuri Giants, this vast covered dome is notorious for its poor acoustics. Past visitors include the Red Hot Chili Peppers and The Police.

Tea Ceremonies

Matcha, the frothy, slightly bitter green brew served as part of the proceedings in *chanoyu*, the tea ceremony, can be sampled at several international hotels in Tokyo, or among the tea-green foliage of some of the city's Japanese gar-

Powdered green tea.

dens such as Happo-en (see page 161), Hama-Rikyu Detached Garden (see page 216) and Shinjuku Gyoen (see page 120). Other places to try (advance reservations required; expect to pay between ¥1,000 to ¥1,500) are:

Imperial Hotel (Toko-an)
1-1-1 Uchisaiwai-cho, Chiyoda-ku, (4F of Main Wing)
Mon–Sat 10am–4pm. Fee charged for 20-minute session.

Hotel New Otani (Seisei-an)
4-1 Kioi-cho, Chiyoda-ku, (7F of Tower Building)
Tel: 03-3265 1111
Thu–Sat 11am–4pm. Fee charged for 15 to 20 minute sessions.

Hotel Okura (Chosho-an)
2-10-4 Toranomon, Minato-ku, (7F of the main building)
Tel: 03-3582 0141
Mon–Sat 11am–noon, 1–4pm. Fee charged for 15 to 20 minute sessions.

Theatre and Dance

Asakusa Engei Hall
1-43-12 Asakusa, Taito-ku
Tel: 03-3841 6545
www.asakusaengei.com
Daily revues featuring *manzai* stand-up comedy, *rakugo* story-telling and other traditional comic acts.

Bunkamura Theatre Cocoon
2-24-1 Dogenzaka, Shibuya-ku
Tel: 03-3477 9111
www.bunkamura.co.jp

TRANSPORT

ACCOMMODATION

ACTIVITIES

A – Z

LANGUAGE

A highly regarded dance venue, the Cocoon stages lively international acts from flamenco to modern experimental dance.

Imperial Theatre
3-1-1 Marunouchi, Chiyoda-ku
Tel: 03-3213 7221
www.toho.co.jp/stage
Long-established venue for everything from Ibsen to Yukio Mishima's noh dramas and even J-pop boy band revues.

Meiji Theatre (Meiji-za)
2-31-1 Nihombashi-Hamacho, Chuo-ku
Tel: 03-3660 3939
www.meijiza.co.jp/en
Modern plays as well as samurai costume dramas are staged here.

New National Theatre
1-1-1 Honmachi, Shibuya-ku
Tel: 03-5351 3011
www.nntt.jac.go.jp/english
Divided into the Opera House, Playhouse and Pit: the first is for modern dramas by both Japanese and foreign playwrights, the latter two are modern dance venues.

Suehirotei
3-6-12 Shinjuku, Shinjuku-ku
Tel: 03-3351 2974
One of Tokyo's last remaining theatres for rakugo, a genre of humorous storytelling.

Takarazuka Theatre
1-1-3 Yurakucho, Chiyoda-ku
Tel: 03-5251 2001
kageki.hankyu.co.jp/english
Campy dramas and musicals from an all-women troupe who cross-dress to extraordinary effect.

Tokyo International Players
Mobile tel: 090-6009 4171
www.tokyoplayers.org
Very professional performances in English of contemporary and older plays from members of the foreign and Japanese communities. The venues change regularly. Check the website.

Traditional Theatre

Cerulean Tower Noh Theatre
26-1 Sakuragaoka-cho, Shibuya-ku
Tel: 03-3476 3000
www.ceruleantower.com

This beautiful noh theatre hosts professional as well as amateur noh and kyogen performances (without English translations).

Kabuki-za
4-12-15 Ginza, Chuo-ku
Tel: 03-3541 3131
www.kabuki-za.co.jp
Reopened in a new building in spring 2013, after a three-year hiatus Kabuki-za is once again Tokyo's premier venue for kabuki. English audio guides available.

National Noh Theatre
4-18-1 Sendagaya, Shibuya-ku
Tel: 03-3423 1331
www.ntj.jac.go.jp
Noh performances are given about once a week, usually starting in the afternoon. A short English programme is available.

National Theatre
4-1 Hayabusa-cho, Chiyoda-ku
Tel: 03-3265 7411
www.ntj.jac.go.jp
Two auditoriums. The Large Hall stages kabuki for eight months of the year. Bunraku performances are given in the Small Hall for the remaining months. English-language summaries of the plot are included in the programmes; earphone guide available.

Shimbashi Embujo
6-12-2 Ginza, Chuo-ku
Tel: 03-3541 2600
www.shochiku.co.jp/play/enbujyo
A major venue for kabuki performances in Tokyo. You can also see here 'Super-Kabuki', by star performer Ichikawa Enosuke – a high-octane version of the original, kabuki drama – and occasional dances by troupes of geisha.

Jazz and Live Music

There is an enthusiastic and knowledgeable audience for jazz in Tokyo – and some excellent clubs to enjoy it in – like the sophisticated and world-class Blue Note. At the other end of the spectrum are 'live houses', where rock bands are the mainstay.

B-Flat Akasaka
Akasaka 6-6-4, Minato-ku
Tel: 03-5563 2563

KABUKI-ZA

Kabuki-za, Tokyo's largest and most famous kabuki theatre was demolished in 2010 to make way for a tower block and more modern theatre that reopened in April 2013. The 1,800-seat theatre holds regular kabuki performances with English guidance available. www.kabuki-za.co.jp.

www.bflat.biz
A classic jazz club in the nightlife district of Akasaka. Features top local acts and the occasional international artiste.

Blue Note Tokyo
6-3-16 Minami-Aoyama, Minato-ku
Tel: 03-5485 0088
www.bluenote.co.jp
Top international acts appear in this sophisticated venue. The ambience is much like that at the original venue in the US, and the performances are top notch. Despite the high entrance fees, the club is always full.

Blues Alley Japan
1-3-14 Meguro, Meguro-ku
Tel: 03-5496 4381
www.bluesalley.co.jp
Basement jazz and blues venue (with a focus more on the jazz side) that attracts local and international acts.

Body and Soul
B1, 6-13-9 Minami-Aoyama, Minato-ku
Tel: 03-5466 3348
www.bodyandsoul.co.jp
A favourite with music industry folk, the vibes here are exclusively jazz.

Club Quattro
Parco Quattro, 5F, 32-13 Udagawacho, Shibuya-ku
Tel: 03-3477 8750
www.club-quattro.com
Located inside the Parco department store – you need to take the lift to reach it. International rock and world music bands as well as local groups play on what is one of Tokyo's most storied stages.

Izakaya bars in Shimbashi.

Crocodile
B1, 6-18-8 Jingumae, Shibuya-ku
Tel: 03-3499 5205
One of the oldest live houses in Tokyo, Crocodile has expanded its repertoire over the years to include not just rock, but whatever happens to be hip, including rap bands, Latin combos and jazz. You can also see Tokyo Comedy Store performances here once a month.

Eggman
1-6-8 Jinnan, Shibuya-ku
Tel: 03-3496 1785
eggman.jp/venue
Talent spotters come here to see and sometimes sign up local acts.

NIGHTLIFE NEWS

The weekly free magazine *Metropolis* (www.metropolis.co.jp) has good nightlife listings, while the monthly *JSelect* (www.jselect.net) and free *EL Magazine* (www.elmagazine.com) also cover the city's music scene.

Cyber Japan (www.cyberjapan.tv) follows the club scene as well as street fashion.

Time Out Tokyo (www.timeout.jp) has event and gig reviews, as well as extensive nightlife listings.

Many have gone on to greater things in the world of Japanese rock and J-Pop. Centrally located in the trendy Jinnan district.

Hibiya Kokaido
1-3 Hibiya-Koen, Chiyoda-ku
Tel: 03-3591 6388
hibiya-kokaido.com
A variety of music, including jazz, classical, traditional and pop, is staged at this hall, which dates back to 1929.

JZ Brat
2F Cerulean Tower Tokyu Hotel, 26-1 Sakuragaoka-cho, Shibuya-ku
Tel: 03-5728 0168
www.jzbrat.com
Top-name international and home-grown acts at this small but acoustically perfect venue.

La.Mama Shibuya
Premier Dogenzaka Building, B1F, 1-15-3, Dogenzaka, Shibuya-ku
Tel: 03-3464 0801
www.lamama.net
A longtime feature of Shibuya's vibrant music scene, La.Mama has moved away in recent years from hardcore rock and punk acts to the softer world of J-Pop.

Liquid Room
3-16-6 Higashi, Shibuya-ku
Tel: 03-5464 0800
www.liquidroom.net
This live house, one of Tokyo's most popular, also offers the Time

Out lounge bar (www.timeoutcafe.jp). Features an excellent lineup of rock concerts and DJ events.

Tokyo International Forum
3-5-1 Marunouchi, Chiyoda-ku
Tel: 03-5221 9000
www.t-i-forum.co.jp
An architecturally inspired grouping of elegant concert halls in various sizes, which play host to anything from pop to jazz and classical.

NIGHTLIFE

Clubs

Japanese youth are amazingly well clued in to the latest music styles, and Tokyo has developed a vibrant club scene.

Ageha
2-2-10 Shin-Kiba, Koto-ku
Tel: 03-5534 1515
www.ageha.com
Ageha is the name that Studio Coast adopts on weekends, when it transforms itself into Tokyo's biggest dance club bar, with three separate dance rooms and a poolside bar. Clubbers are bussed in from Shibuya and Shinjuku by the thousands for massive parties.

Air

2-11 Sarugaku, Shibuya-ku
Tel: 03-5784 3386
www.air-tokyo.com
Situated in between Shibuya and trendy Daikanyama, Air is a comfortable, mid-sized dance club that competes with Tokyo's leading venues for young clubbers looking to dance to house, trance, drum and bass, and hip-hop.

Club Asia

1-8 Maruyama-cho, Shibuya-ku
Tel: 03-5458 2551
www.clubasia.co.jp/asia
The dance floors and bars on different levels make for an interesting design, though the music can get warped in the process. The club gets booked up for a lot of private events, so it's always best to check it is open in advance.

Eleven

1-10-11 Nishi-Azabu, Minato-ku
Tel: 03-5775-6206
www.go-to-eleven.com
Once home to famed club Yellow, this incarnation is still strong on techno music.

Fai Aoyama

B2F, 5-10-1 Minami-Aoyama, Minato-ku
Tel: 03-3486 4910
www.fai-aoyama.com
An eclectic range of music rules here, from classic disco to the latest breakbeats and electro pop.

Microcosmos

2-23-12 Dogenzaka, Shibuya-ku
Tel: 03-5784 5496
http://microcosmos-tokyo.com
Chilled out café-bar by day that turns into a hip dance venue at night.

Super Deluxe

B1F 3-1-25 Nishi-Azabu, Minato-ku
Tel: 03-5412 0515
www.super-deluxe.com
Arty salon hosting Tokyo's best range of events (practically every night of the week) from live music to the monthly Pecha Kucha show-and-tell for Tokyo creatives.

Womb

2-16 Maruyama-cho, Shibuya-ku
Tel: 03-5459 0039
www.womb.co.jp

This cavernous club has established itself as one of Tokyo's serious dance culture venues. Top DJs play here on a regular basis.

Gay and Lesbian Venues

Although gays and lesbians do not promote themselves as much as they do in other international cities, there is a very real gay scene in Tokyo – mainly centred in the Shinjuku Ni-chome district, close to Shinjuku-Sanchome Station where there are around 300 or so tiny gay bars, clubs and restaurants; all the following places are located there and are welcoming to non-Japanese. For more information see www.utopia-asia.com/tipsjapn.htm.

Advocates

2-18-1, Shinjuku, Shinjuku-ku
Tel: 03-3358 8638
Highly popular spot among the expat and local gay crowd who gather on the pavement outside the tiny bar creating a street party atmosphere every night.

Arty Farty

2F Dai 33 Kyutei Building, 2-11-7 Shinjuku, Shinjuku-ku
Tel: 03-5362 9720
Foreigner-friendly gay bar and dance club where guys and girls mingle and bop around to disco tunes. Gets busy after midnight,

Experimental music at Super Deluxe.

while its sister bar Annex around the corner is the place for earlier drinks.

GB

Business Hotel T Building, B1F, 2-12-3, Shinjuku, Shinjuku-ku
Tel: 03-3352 8972
Well known among Tokyo's gay community as a hotspot for hook-ups between foreigners and locals. Attached to a business hotel that offers short-stay terms. Men only.

Kinsmen

2F, 2-18-5, Shinjuku
Tel: 03-3354 4949
www11.ocn.ne.jp/~kinsmen
Another long-running Anglo-phone-friendly venue with a classy, cocktail bar ambience. Both men and women are welcome.

Kinswomyn

Daiichi Tenka Building, 3F, 2-15-10, Shinjuku, Shinjuku-ku
Tel: 03-3354 8720
Long-running lesbian bar. A relaxed, easy-going place that sticks to its women-only rule.

New Sazae

Ishikawa Building, 2F, 2-18-5, Shinjuku, Shinjuku-ku
Tel: 03-3354 1745
There's little that's new about this old workhorse of Ni-chome, which gives off a very 1970s vibe and is popular with cross-dressers and drag queens.

SPORTS

Participant Sports

Fitness Centres

There are gyms in most of the major hotels that are open (for a fee) for non-guests and tourist information centres will be able to direct you to the nearest municipal gyms.

Chiyoda Ku Sports Centre
2-1-8 Uchi-kanda, Chiyoda-ku
Tel: 03-3256 8444
A decent-sized gym and pool for local residents, which visitors can use for a small fee. Open daily 9am–9pm. Closed 1st and 3rd Mondays.

Minato-ku Sports Centre
3-1-19 Shibaura, Minato-ku
Tel: 03-3452 4151
A reasonable admission fee allows for use of a good swimming pool, gym and sauna. Open daily 9am–9pm. Closed first and third Mondays.

Golf

Driving ranges can be found all over the city, even on some department store roofs; there's a good one in Meiji-Jingu Outer Garden (www.meijijingugaien.jp/english/golf.html). There are also several hundred golf courses within a couple of hours from central Tokyo, and while prices for a round are still relatively high compared with the UK or US, prices (especially on weekdays) have dropped considerably. The majority of courses are also now open to non-members. For information on ranges and courses, see www.golf-in-japan.com.

Tokyo Metropolitan Golf Course
1-15-1 Shinden, Adachi-ku
Tel: 03-3919 0111
Tokyo's cheapest public course with 18 holes. You will be lucky to get on this course at the weekend, but weekdays are usually less busy. Open daily, dawn to twilight.

Ice-skating

Ice-skating is a popular spectator event among the Japanese, with exhibition shows and tournaments held at the National Stadium.

Meiji Jingu Ice Skating Rink
Gobanchi, Kasumigaoka, Shinjuku-ku
Tel: 03-3403 3458
www.meijijingugaien.jp/english/ice-skating

Yoga

Ashtanga Yoga Japan
5-30-6 Ogikubo, Suginami-ku
Tel: 090-4956 7996
www.ashtanga.jp/en
Specialises in Ashtanga yoga. Offers single sessions and classes.

Sun and Moon Yoga
Meguro Eki Mae Mansion, Higashi Guchi Building, 3-1-5 Kami Osaki, Suite 204, Shinagawa-ku
Tel: 03-3280 6383
http://sunandmoon.jp
Beginners to advanced classes taught by American writer and yoga specialist Leza Lowitz.

Spectator Sports

Baseball

Japan's 'second national sport' maintains its appeal across the generations. Tokyo has two home teams: the Yomiuri Giants (in the Central League) and the Yakult Swallows (Central League). The season runs from April to October, culminating in the best-of-seven Japan Series between the pennant winners of the Central and Pacific leagues.

Jingu Stadium
13 Kasumigaoka, Shinjuku-ku
Tel: 03-3404 8999
www.jingu-stadium.com
Most baseball fans prefer the atmosphere at the Jingu ballpark (built as part of the 1964 Olympic complex) to the Big Egg. It's the home ground of the Swallows, and draws big crowds for the games against the Giants and the Hanshin Tigers (from Osaka).

Tokyo Dome
1-3-61 Koraku, Bunkyo-ku
Tel: 03-5800 9999
www.tokyo-dome.co.jp
Japan's first sports dome, nicknamed the Big Egg, is the home ground of the Yomiuri Giants, historically Japan's most successful team and one that non-Giants fans love to hate.

Horse Racing

Horse racing has become a fashionable spectator sport, offering one of the few chances people have to gamble. Schedules in English are available from the Japan Racing Association's English-language website: japanracing.jp/en.

Tokyo Racecourse
1-1, 1-2 Hiyoshi-cho, Fuchu City
Tel: 042-363 3141
jra.jp/facilities/race/tokyo

Martial Arts

Judo, karate, aikido, kyudo (archery) and kendo all have championships or demonstration events on a regular basis. These are usually held at the Nippon Budokan.

All-Japan Judo Federation
1-16-30 Kasuga, Bunkyo-ku
Tel: 03-3818 4172
www.judo.or.jp

All-Japan Kendo Federation
Nippon Budokan, 2-3 Kitanomaru-Koen, Chiyoda-ku
Tel: 03-3211 5804
www.kendo-fik.org

International Aikido Federation
17-18 Wakamatsucho, Shinjuku-ku
Tel: 03-3203 9236
www.aikido-international.org

Japan Karate Association
2-23-15 Koraku, Bunkyo-ku
Tel: 03-5800 3091
www.jka.or.jp

Nippon Budokan
2-3 Kitanomaru-Koen, Chiyoda-ku
Tel: 03-3216 5100
www.nipponbudokan.or.jp

Motorboat Racing

Popular among Tokyoites, *kyotei* as this sport is known, is usually

TRANSPORT
ACCOMMODATION
ACTIVITIES
A – Z
LANGUAGE

held between six motorboats that can reach speeds of 80kmh (50mph). This is one of the few chances people have to place bets.

Edogawa Kyotei
3-1-1 Higashi-Komatsugawa, Edogawa-ku
Tel: 03-3656 0641
www.edogawa-kyotei.co.jp

Rugby

As the strongest rugby nation in Asia, Japan regularly qualifies for the Rugby World Cup. There is a keen following at the universities and a thriving corporate league. For information on the game in Japan and where to watch it, visit the Japan Rugby Football Union's website, http://jrfu.org.

Soccer

Soccer now competes with baseball for the most popular sport slot, with the J-League and both the men's and women's national teams (the latter the current world champions) getting widespread coverage on TV. The J-League season runs from March to October, with a special Emperor's Cup event in December. Regular J-League games are played at the National Stadium, as are some international fixtures (some are also held in Yokohama). The capital's two top teams, Tokyo FC and Verdy, play at the Ajinomoto Stadium, in Chofu City, western Tokyo. Check www.j-league.or.jp and www.jfa.or.jp for the latest info.

Ajinomoto Stadium
376-3, Nishimachi, Chofu City
Tel: 0424-40 0555
www.ajinomotostadium.com

National Stadium
Kasumigaoka, Shinjuku-ku
Tel: 03-3403 1151
http://naash.go.jp/kokuritu

Sumo

Three of sumo's six annual 15-day tournaments are held in Tokyo in January, May and September. Junior wrestlers begin their bouts at about 10am; senior wrestlers start at 3pm on the first

Sumo wrestlers.

and the last days, and at 3.30pm on other days.

Tickets for the Tokyo tournaments are sold at the office of the Nihon Sumo Kyokai at National Sumo Stadium (nearest station is JR Ryogoku) as well as from ticket agencies throughout Tokyo. Box seats are usually monopolised by corporate season ticket holders, but it is not usually too difficult to snag one of the limited number of tickets for unreserved seats that go on sale each day of a tournament at 8am (one per person). Tickets are priced from ¥2,100 to ¥10,500.

National Sumo Stadium
1-3-28 Yokoami, Sumida-ku
Tel: 03-3623 5111
www.sumo.or.jp

SIGHTSEEING TOURS

If your time is limited, the best way to see the highlights of the city is on a tour. These vary from buses to individual taxis and even helicopters. The Japan Guide Association (tel: 03-3863 2895; www.jga21c.or.jp/index_e.html) can put you in touch with an accredited tour guide. You can then negotiate the fee and itinerary with the guide.

Bus Tours

Bus tour options include half-day, full-day and evening tours. Prices range from ¥2,500 for a morning

tour to in excess of ¥10,000 for a full-day out and about with meals. English-language tours can be booked from major hotels in downtown Tokyo or directly with the tour company.

Hato Bus Tokyo
Tel: 03-3435 6081
www.hatobus.com/en
This long-established sightseeing tour company offers a variety of day and night tours. Half-day tours start from ¥2,600. All tours depart from the Hamamatsucho Bus Terminal, but pick-ups from designated hotels are also available.

Japan Gray Line Company
Tel: 03-5275 6525
www.jgl.co.jp/inbound
Gray Line of Japan offers a small selection of morning, afternoon and full-day tours to the main sights for between ¥4,000 and ¥9,700. Pick up from major hotels available.

Sky Bus
Tel: 03-3215 0008
www.skybus.jp
Open-top double-decker buses are the mode of transport on tours around the Imperial Palace grounds and through Ginza (¥1,500; 50mins); from Tokyo Tower to the Rainbow Bridge (¥1,700; 1hr); or over to Odaiba at night (¥2,000; 2hr), amongst other low-cost tour options.

Sunrise Tours
Tel: 03-5796 5454
www.jtb-sunrisetours.jp
This company (operated by the reputable Japan Travel Bureau)

provides the widest range of tours in and around Tokyo. There are day and overnight tours to sights outside the city, like Kamakura and the Mount Fuji area, as well as to places farther afield like Kyoto and Osaka.

River Tours

Tokyo River Bus
Tel: 03-5733 4812
www.suijobus.co.jp
The Sumida River Line waterbus plies the route from Asakusa, past a series of old bridges, to Hama-Rikyu Detached Garden and Hinode Pier. In addition, there are vessels that depart regularly from Hinode Pier to Odaiba, Palette Town, Tokyo Big Sight and Kasai Sealife Park.

Walking Tours

Mr. Oka's Walking Tours of Tokyo
http://mroka.homestead.com
Run by an enthusiastic retired tour guide and historian, this offers a chance to see aspects of the city not covered by conventional tour companies. The highly informed Oka san's main interest is social history, a field he explains very engagingly in English.
Tokyo Tour Guide Services
www.tourism.metro.tokyo.jp/english/tourists/guideservice/guideservice
The Tokyo Metropolitan Government offer a series of walking tours, a few of which are free. They all depart from the tourist information centre in the Metropolitan Government Office in Shinjuku. Reservations should be made online.

CHILDREN'S ACTIVITIES

There's plenty to keep children amused in and around Tokyo. There are samurai-era relics to explore, river buses and streetcars to ride on, parks to run

around in and more – plus, of course, there's always Tokyo Disneyland. Here are some possibilities; for more options see www.tokyowithkids.com, a site packed with practical suggestions such as babysitting services, entertainment options and links to seasonal festivals that would appeal to kids.
Fukugawa-Edo Museum
1-3-8 Shirakawa, Koto-ku
www.kcf.or.jp/fukagawa/english.html
Explore a 19th-century Edo neighbourhood in a wonderfully realistic reproduction complete with lighting and sound effects.
Hakuhinkan Toy Park
8-8-11 Ginza, Chuo-ku
www.hakuhinkan.co.jp
Tokyo's top toy store gives kids a chance to play with the goods, both Japanese and imported.
Hanayashiki Amusement Park
A few minutes west of Senso-ji temple in Asakusa
www.hanayashiki.net
A small amusement park full of retro rides that are great fun for small kids.
Joypolis
1-6-1 Daiba, Minato-ku
Tel: 03-5500 1801
http://tokyo-joypolis.com
A three-storey indoor amusement park packed with the latest virtual reality machines and arcade games that make for a great rainy day alternative for parents at a loss as to how to entertain restless children.
Kiddyland
6-1-9 Jingumae, Shibuya-ku
www.kiddyland.co.jp
Four floors of toys, games, novelties and the latest electronics gadgets aimed at older children (and many adults too).
Kidzania
Lalaport Toyosu 3F, Urban Dock, 2-4-9 Toyosu, Koto-ku
Tel: 0570-064 646
www.kidzania.jp
A role-playing theme park where children get to try their hands at more than 80 jobs, including pilot and TV anchor, and get paid in 'Kidzos'. It's most recommended

for kids with some understanding of the Japanese language. Reservations are essential.
Sanrio Puroland
1-31 Ochiai, Hijimachi
Tel: 042-339 1111
www.puroland.co.jp
Puroland, the home of Sanrio's Hello Kitty character, is the perfect place for small kids with an obsession for all that is pink and sparkly. The highlights here are the daily musical revues that see Kitty-chan (as Hello Kitty is affectionately known) shimmy and shout with the help of other Sanrio characters. There are also a few simple rides, shops and Hello Kitty's extravagantly designed mansion to explore.
Shinagawa Aquarium
3-2-1 Katsushima, Shinagawa-ku
Tel: 03-3762 3433
www.aquarium.gr.jp
Adjacent to Tokyo Bay this is one of the city's best aquariums, including a giant Tunnel Water Tank with a walk-through tunnel affording overhead views of stingrays and giant groupers; a Dolphin and Sea Lion Stadium, with shows of charming marine-mammal antics; and a Touching Pool where children can gently slide their hands along the backs of starfish and other sea creatures.
Tama Zoo
7-1-1 Hodokubo, Hino-shi
042-591 1611
www.tokyo-zoo.net/english/tama/main.html
A spacious 'natural habitat' zoo, complete with safari-park rides.
Tokyo Disney Resort
1-1 Maihama, Urayasu-shi, Chiba Prefecture
045-683 3333
www.tokyodisneyresort.co.jp
Home to both Tokyo Disneyland and DisneySea Park. Buy a one-day passport to each of the parks or a two-day passport for both.
Toshimaen
3-25-1 Koyama, Nerima-ku
www.toshimaen.co.jp
Amusement park with roller coasters and other rides, plus seven swimming pools complete with convoluted water slides.

A – Z

AN ALPHABETICAL SUMMARY OF PRACTICAL INFORMATION

A

Addresses

Tokyo is one of the most complex cities in the world. Even the Japanese get confused when trying to get from A to B, which is why businesses often print little maps out on cards, websites and advertisements.

However, with a little knowledge of how the streets are laid out and numbered, you should be able to negotiate the city without too much frustration. Apart from main roads, very few streets have names. Addresses traditionally follow a big-to-small system, with the *ku* (ward) listed first, then the *cho* or *matchi* (district) and then the *chome* (an area of a few blocks), the block itself and the number of the building within that block. A typical address rendered in Japanese might read like this: Minato-ku, Hamamatsucho, 3-8-12, Riverfield Hotel, 4F. However, the English rendition of Japanese addresses often follows a different order, most commonly the one used throughout this guide: Riverfield Hotel, 4F, 3-8-12 Hamamatscho, Minato-ku; here, 3 is the number or the *chome*, 8 is the number of the block and 12

is the number of the building within that block.

Note: in Japan the ground floor equals the first; also look out for floor numbers often shown on the outside of the building.

Admission Charges

Practically all museums and public galleries in Tokyo charge an admission fee – anything from ¥200 to ¥1,500 depending on the size and nature of the institution. If you are planning on visiting a lot of museums then investing in the GRUTT Pass (www.museum.or.jp/grutto) is recommended. This ¥2,000 ticket provides free or discounted entry to 75 public, national and private institutions, including all of Tokyo's major museums. It is valid for two months after first being used and can be bought at participating venues and the Tokyo Metropolitan Government tourist information centre in Shinjuku (see page 267).

Age Restrictions

The age of consent is 18, the same age it is legal to drive. If you are hiring a car in Japan, though, you must be over 21 and have an international driving licence. The legal age for drinking alcohol is 20, but this is not strictly

enforced. For smoking the legal age is also 20.

B

Budgeting for Your Trip

Tokyo has a reputation for being one of the most expensive cities in the world, but after over 15 years of economic stagnation, the cost of living index in capitals like London and Paris have caught up, and in some cases exceeded, that of Tokyo. Compared with other Asian capitals though, Tokyo remains the most costly.

Accommodation can run from as little as ¥2,000 in a dorm bed at a hostel, ¥5,000 in a modest inn, to over ¥50,000 in one of its top-class hotels. Food is better value than you would think, especially lunch sets, where there is fierce competition for customers. A lunch set at a decent restaurant can be had for as little as ¥800. Japanese fast food restaurants have all-hours fixed sets from only ¥500. Expect to pay ¥2,000 to ¥3,500 for a two–three-course dinner without drinks. Drinking alcohol, though, can boost the bill substantially. Reckon on ¥500 to ¥700 for the cheapest beer or glass of house wine at a good restaurant or bar. Cheaper izakaya, however, often have beer for as low as ¥200.

Public transport is inexpensive with single metro tickets starting off at ¥160. Taxis have a base fare of ¥710 but rise quite quickly if you get stuck in a traffic jam.

C

Children

Tokyo may be crowded, but with a little forward planning, travelling with children is both feasible and enjoyable, and the options, ranging from science and nature museums to amusement parks, toyshops, aquariums and zoos, are quite broad.

On trains, buses and subways, children up to age 12 travel for half-fare; those under six ride for free. Try to avoid trains during rush hour, especially when using strollers.

Department stores and malls usually have family rooms or areas set aside for mothers to nurse infants or change nappies. The malls are also good places to eat, since their restaurant floors offer a variety of food, often with child-size portions. Many restaurants, especially those in malls, offer good value set meals for kids (ask for okosama setto).

Some of the larger hotels offer babysitting services. Several have outdoor swimming pools that are open to the public at specific hours during summer.

See also Children's Activities (page 259).

Climate

In Tokyo, spring is ushered in with the cherry blossoms in early April, and the temperature starts to rise. By May, the weather will become warm and pleasant, still without any great humidity. June brings rather grey, drizzly weather, known poetically as

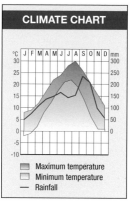

CLIMATE CHART

■ Maximum temperature
□ Minimum temperature
— Rainfall

tsuyu (dew), a rainy spell that lasts about a month.

Midsummer is hot and sticky, with the mercury rising to around 35°C (100°F) – up to 40°C in the especially hot summer of 2004 – and hovering overnight at around an uncomfortably sticky 25°C (72°F). Typhoons (tropical storms) occur between August and October (though Tokyo is affected far more rarely than Okinawa and western Japan).

From mid- to late September, there is usually a late summer, with hot days that cool when the humidity level drops at night.

During October and early November, there are many mellow autumn days – this is the Tokyoites' favourite time of the year.

After a month or so of rainy, changeable weather, winter arrives, with clear blue skies and low humidity. The harshest cold sets in in January and February, although Tokyo only receives occasional snowfalls. The weather in March is usually chilly, overcast and changeable.

All this, naturally, is subject to global climate change.

Periods to Avoid

There are three times in the year when almost all of Japan is on holiday and travelling en masse. It is unwise to pass through Narita Airport or plan any train trips during these periods:

New Year Around 28 December – 4 January
Golden Week 29 April – 5 May (avoid weekends at either end)
Obon Seven to 10 days centring on 15 August.

What to Wear

Japanese people place importance on appearance and dress accordingly. For visitors, casual clothes are acceptable in almost all situations, except in business, for which a suit is de rigueur.

The weather is relatively predictable, so dress for the season. Bring a thick jacket or overcoat for winter weather in January and February; in summer, wear light fabrics (cotton or linen); in spring and autumn, a light jacket will prove handy as will waterproof clothing and an umbrella for showers. At any time of year you'll be walking a lot to see the city, so wear comfortable shoes.

Crime and Safety

For a city its size, Tokyo has a low incidence of petty theft, and personal security is far higher than in most cities in Europe and North America. Theft of luggage and money is rare, though not unheard of in Tokyo.

Organised crime is another matter, and it can turn violent. The police try to keep a lid on prostitution, gambling, ticket touting, illegal immigration and the protection

Cycle police on patrol.

TRANSPORT

ACCOMMODATION

ACTIVITIES

A – Z

LANGUAGE

rackets operated by the *yakuza* gangs, conducting sporadic crackdowns only when inter-gang warfare spills onto the streets.

However, visitors need never come into contact with the underbelly of Japanese society. If an incident occurs, report it to the nearest *koban* (police box). These are located in every neighbourhood, especially in busy areas and outside major railway stations. If possible, go with an eyewitness or a Japanese speaker. For police contact details, see 'Emergencies'.

Customs Regulations

Non-residents entering the country are given a duty-free allowance of 400 cigarettes or 500 grams of tobacco; three 760ml bottles of alcohol; 2oz of perfume; and gifts and souvenirs whose total value is not more than ¥200,000. If you are carrying the equivalent of over ¥1 million, you must declare it.

Japan bans the import and use of illegal drugs, firearms and ammunition, as well as swords – and strictly punishes anyone caught with the above items. Pornographic magazines and videos showing pubic hair are also forbidden in Japan. It is also illegal to bring in endangered species or products containing them.

For further information, see www.customs.go.jp.

D

Disabled Travellers

Although Tokyo is still behind most Western cities in wheelchair accessibility, major strides have been taken over the past decade to improve access and facilities for the disabled.

Wide doors and special toilets are being designed into new buses and trains, including the Narita Express, *shinkansen* bullet trains and some local commuter lines. Most major JR stations have elevators and/or escalators with special attachments for wheelchairs.

Similarly, consideration is given to those with visual impairments in some parts of the city, with markers built into the pavements, braille signs on newer JR ticket machines and speakers emitting jingles at pedestrian crossings.

Nevertheless, it is still a struggle for the disabled to get around Tokyo, and don't contemplate using a wheelchair in trains or subways during rush hours from 7.30 to 10am and 5 to 7.30pm.

It is possible to reserve a special seat for wheelchairs on the *shinkansen*. For more information, call the JR English InfoLine at 050-2016 1603.

Find out up-to-date information at http://accessible.jp.org/tokyo/en, the website of the **Japanese Red Cross Service Volunteers**, 1-1-3 Minato-ku, Shiba Daimon; tel: 03-3438 1311. The 24-hour Japan Helpline is also be a great source of information and is able to help out in emergencies (tel: 0570-000 911).

E

Electricity

Japan's power supply is 100 volts AC. Tokyo and Eastern Japan run on 50 cycles (Western Japan uses 60 cycles). Plugs are two-pin. Most hotels have adaptors.

Embassies and Consulates

Embassies and consulates open Monday through Friday. Call ahead to find out the hours, as these vary.
Australia: 2-1-14 Mita, Minato-ku; tel: 03-5232 4111; www.australia.or.jp
Canada: 7-3-38 Akasaka, Minato-ku; tel: 03-5412 6200;

EMERGENCIES

Police: 110
Fire/ambulance: 119
Japan Helpline: 0570-000 911 (24 hours); www.jhelp.com
Tokyo Police Information: 03-3501 0110. A service that provides information and answers queries in English.
Tokyo English Life Line: 03-5774 0992; www.telljp.com Counselling service. Daily 9am–11pm.

www.canadanet.or.jp
UK: 1 Ichiban-cho, Chiyoda-ku; tel: 03-5211 1100; http://ukinjapan.fco.gov.uk
US: 1-10-5 Akasaka, Minato-ku; tel: 03-3224 5000; http://tjapan.usembassy.gov

Etiquette

There are points of etiquette for doing just about everything in Japan (blowing your nose in public for instance, especially at high volume is considered rude). Although as a visitor you may be blissfully unaware of most of them (and will be immediately forgiven for almost any faux pas anyway), the cardinal rule is to try to be courteous at all times.

At work and in most formal situations, the Japanese may seem reticent and lacking in spontaneity. But when drinking and having a good time, Japanese, especially the men, can become very raucous and often let out their real opinions and feelings.

Bathhouses

Whether at a hot spring resort, a local *sento* (bathhouse) or a traditional inn, the procedure is the same. Disrobe, enter the bathroom (in public you hide your modesty with a small washcloth), and wash and rinse off thoroughly under a shower before easing into the hot bath – which is for soaking, not washing yourself. Do not pull the plug after you've finished: others will use the same water.

Dining

Drinking: When having beer or *sake*, one always pours for the other party, who will hold up the glass while it is filled. It is polite to keep the glasses filled; if you have had enough, leave your glass full.

Eating: Soup is sipped directly from the bowl in which it is served. So is the broth of hot noodles, except for *ramen*, which comes with a spoon. When sipping soup, tea or other hot liquids, it is customary to draw in a good amount of air at the same time. Slurping sounds for noodles and other soup dishes are quite acceptable, but should be kept to a minimum in polite company.

Footwear

There is a strong distinction in Japan between the areas inside and outside the home. Just inside the entrance to homes (and many restaurants and ryokan and some museums and galleries) is an area where you are expected to remove your shoes. From here, you step up into the living area either wearing the slippers provided or in your stockinged feet. This keeps the house clean and increases the amount of useable space, since you can sit on the floor without worrying about getting dirty. (Men sit cross-legged and women sit with their legs tucked under.) Slippers are never worn on tatami mats. Go barefoot or in socks instead. Note that there will be a separate pair of slippers to be used in the toilet.

Invitations

It is rare to be invited to someone's home. Most people live too far out of town or find their homes too cramped to invite guests. If you receive an invitation, take along a small gift with you: flowers, a food item or something from your own country.

Trains/Subway

On rush-hour trains you may find yourself being pushed and bumped around. You do not need to be polite here; just push along with everyone else.

G

Gay and Lesbian

Despite the presence of a few token transvestite personalities on prime-time television, the gay scene in Japan has a low profile. In Shinjuku's Nichome district there are around 300 bars and clubs catering to all age groups and sexual preferences (see page 256). For information see:

Gay Net Japan (www.gnj.or.jp), a support and friendship group that has several discussion groups on its website.

Tokyo Wrestling (www.tokyo wrestling.com) for the latest information on Tokyo's lesbian scene.

Utopia (www.utopia-asia.com/tipsjapn.htm): an Asian site with Tokyo contacts and information.

H

Health and Medical Care

No vaccinations are required before entering Japan, except if arriving from certain countries in Africa, Asia or South America. Hygiene levels are high, and you are unlikely to become ill as a result of eating or drinking. Tokyo's tap water is safe to drink.

Hospitals/Clinics

Although some doctors speak English, it is likely the receptionist and nursing staff will not. When seeking medical aid, go with a Japanese-speaking companion. **Tokyo Medical Information Service** (tel: 03-5285 8181; www.himawari.metro.tokyo.jp/qq/qq13enmnlt.asp; daily 9am–8pm) can provide emergency medical translation services over the phone and can help you find

English-speaking doctors and dentists.

Most hospitals and clinics do not have an appointment system for outpatient treatment, and visits usually entail a long wait. The following facilities are accustomed to dealing with foreign patients.

Japanese Red Cross Medical Centre, 4-1-22 Hiro-o, Shibuya-ku; tel: 03-3400 1311; www.med.jrc.or.jp

St Luke's International Hospital, 10-1 Akashicho, Chuo-ku; tel: 03-3541 5151; www.luke.or.jp

Tokyo British Clinic, 2F Dai-kanyama Y Bldg, 2-13-7 Ebisu-Nishi, Shibuya-ku; tel: 03-5458 6099; www.tokyobritishclinic.com

Tokyo Medical and Surgical Clinic, 2F 32 Shiba-koen Bldg, 3-4-30 Shiba-koen, Minato-ku; tel: 03-3436 3028; www.tmsc.jp.

Pharmacies

The American Pharmacy (B1F, Marunouchi Building, 2-4-1 Marunouchi, Chiyoda-ku; Mon–Sat 10.30am–9pm, Sun 10am–8pm; prescriptions filled until 6.30pm daily; tel: 03-5220 7716) has English-speaking pharmacists. Alternatively, try one of the Koyasu pharmacies: in the Hotel Okura (tel: 03-3583 7958), Roppongi (tel: 03-3401 8667) and Hiroo (tel: 03-3446 4701).

Travel Insurance

All Japanese subscribe to national or company health insurance schemes, and charges for hospitals, consultations and drugs are high. Make sure you buy a travel health insurance policy.

I

Internet

Broadband and/or Wi-fi internet access is common at Tokyo's hotels and either free or available for a charge of around ¥1,000 a day. You can also get online at the 24-hour *manga* cafés found

TRANSPORT
ACCOMMODATION
ACTIVITIES
A – Z
LANGUAGE

around the capital such as the chains **Gera Gera** (www.geragera.co.jp) and **Gran Cyber Cafe Bagus** (www.bagus-99.com/net-cafe). Other places include: **Apple Ginza Store,** 3-5-12 Ginza, Chuo-ku: daily 10am–9pm **Marunouchi Café Seek,** 2F, Shin Tokyo Building, 3-3-1 Marunouchi, Chiyoda-ku: Mon–Fri 9am–8pm, Sat and Sun 11am–6pm; www.marunouchi cafe.com **Wired Cafes** (www.cafecompany.co.jp/brands/wiredcafe).

L

Left Luggage

There are 24-hour counters offering storage facilities in both Terminals 1 and 2 at Narita Airport (tel: 0476-34 5000) and in the arrival lobby of the international terminal at Haneda Airport. There's also a baggage room at Tokyo Station (daily 9am–8pm).

Lost Property

JR trains and subways: Items left behind on trains and subways are usually kept for a few days at the station where they were

The Japanese postal system is efficient but expensive.

handed in. After that, they are sent to one of the major stations where they are stored for another five days. Call any of the following for help:

JR English-language infoline at tel: 050-2016 1603; Tokyo Metro, tel: 03-3834 5577; Toei trains and buses don't have a lost and found number: report any lost items to your nearest station.

Police: The Tokyo Metropolitan Police Department, tel: 03-3814 4151 (lost and found centre).

Taxis: All taxi companies in Tokyo report unclaimed items to the **Tokyo Taxi Kindaika Centre,** tel: 03-3648 0300.

M

Maps

Tourist offices provide adequate maps of Tokyo for free. Visitors requiring more in-depth coverage will find Tuttle's Getting Around **Tokyo: Pocket Atlas and Transportation Guide** very useful.

Media

Newspapers/Magazines
There are two daily newspapers in English: the *Japan Times* (www.japantimes.co.jp) and the *Daily Yomiuri* (www.yomiuri.co.jp/dy). The *Nikkei Weekly* (www.nikkei.com) is a financial digest.

The quality of the English-language magazines in Japan isn't great, but the free weekly *Metropolis* (metropolis.co.jp) sometimes includes interesting features and reviews and also has up-to-the-minute listings. Also look out for the quarterly *Tokyo Journal* (www.tokyo.to) and the monthly *JSelect* (www.jselect.net).

Radio
Tokyo's main foreign language radio station is **Inter FM** (76.1 MHz; www.interfm.co.jp), which broadcasts news and music

mainly in English. **J-Wave** (81.3 MHz; www.j-wave.co.jp) also has some shows in English. Try also **Radio Japan Online** (www.nhk.or.jp/nhkworld/english/radio/program), which streams programmes in 17 languages from Japan's national broadcaster NHK.

Television

There are seven terrestrial TV channels. Two are from the quasi-national **Japan Broadcast Corporation (NHK)** and the other five are private-sector commercial networks. NHK also broadcasts on two satellite channels. A small percentage of the programmes – including news bulletins such as NHK's 7pm and 9pm broadcasts – is bilingual, offering English on the sub-channel. Ask your hotel reception which button to press to see if the programme has a bilingual service.

Overseas networks, such as CNN and BBC, are available on satellite and cable TV at most large hotels.

Money

The unit of currency is the yen (indicated as ¥). Coins are issued in denominations of ¥500, ¥100, ¥50, ¥10 and ¥1. There are bank notes for ¥10,000, ¥5,000, ¥2,000 and ¥1,000.

Cash Machines
Major credit cards and cash cards linked to Cirrus, PLUS, Maestro and Visa Electron networks can be used at post office ATMs. Most ATMs of Seven Bank (located at 7-Eleven stores) also accept these cards.

Changing Money
Yen can be purchased at branches of major Japanese banks and authorised money-changers on presentation of your passport. Besides the airport, authorised moneychangers can be found in the major hotels. At Narita Airport, bank counters remain open during airport

Carry some cash as credit cards are not always accepted.

hours. International transactions (eg remittances) are best conducted at major branches of Japanese banks, which have English-speaking staff.

Credit Cards

Major credit cards (eg American Express, Diners Club, Visa, MasterCard) are accepted at most establishments in and around Tokyo without surcharges. However, credit cards are not accepted in some restaurants and small bars.

Credit cards issued by foreign banks cannot be used to make cash withdrawals, except at a few selected ATMs around central Tokyo. Check with your card issuer.

American Express: 0120-020 120
Diners Club: 03-3406 7031
MasterCard: 03-5728 5200
Visa: 0120-133 173.

Tipping

'No tipping' remains the rule in Japan, except for unusual or exceptional service. At more upmarket restaurants, a service charge of 10 to 15 percent is included on the bill.

Traveller's Cheques

Traveller's cheques can be used only at a very limited number of hotels, restaurants and souvenir shops, but can be cashed at banks.

O

Opening Hours

Standard business hours for government offices and private sector companies are Mon–Fri, 9am–5pm. They are closed on national holidays. Banks are open 9am–3pm. Department stores and larger shops usually operate from 10am–8pm (sometimes later); all are open on Sundays and perhaps closed another day of the week. Convenience stores are open 24 hours. Most restaurants serve lunch from 11.30am–2pm and dinner from 6–9.30pm. Pubs, bars and izakaya usually remain open much later. Museums often close on Mondays.

P

Photography

Although there are no restrictions on what you can photograph, use your discretion in religious places. Millions of Japanese are avid amateur photographers so camera stores are plentiful everywhere. The best prices for cameras and film are found at discount chains such as **Bic Camera** (www.biccamera. com), **Sakuraya** (www.sakuraya. co.jp), Laox (www.laox.co.jp) and **Yodobashi** (www.yodobashi.co. jp). The main stores for these are in Akihabara and Shinjuku, with outlets in the other main shopping districts.

Postal Services

Post offices are open Mon–Fri 9am–5pm; some are also open Sat 9am–3pm. For English-language information about postal services, including postal fees, call tel: 0570-046 111 or go to www.post.japanpost.jp.

Express Mail/Courier

Larger post offices offer express mail services. International parcel post cannot exceed 30kg per package to any international destination. For heavier packages use a commercial courier service.
Federal Express: tel: 0120-003 200, fedex.com/jp
Yamato Transport: tel: 0120-008 008, www.kuronekoyamato. co.jp/english.

R

Religious Services

Most Japanese follow both the indigenous animist religion

PUBLIC HOLIDAYS

1 January Ganjitsu (New Year's Day)
January, 2nd Monday Seijin-no-Hi (Coming of Age Day)
11 February Kenkoku Kinen-no-Hi (National Foundation Day)
Around 21 March Shumbun-no-Hi (Vernal Equinox Day)
29 April Showa-no-Hi (Showa Day)
3 May Kenpo Kinenbi (Constitution Memorial Day)
4 May Midori-no-Hi (Greenery Day)
5 May Kodomo-no-Hi (Children's Day)
July, 3rd Monday Umi-no-Hi (National Maritime Day)
September, 3rd Monday Keiro-no-Hi (Respect for the Aged Day)
Around 23 September Shubun-no-Hi (Autumnal Equinox Day)
October, 2nd Monday Tai-iku-no-Hi (Sports Day)
3 November Bunka-no-Hi (Culture Day)
23 November Kinro Kansha-no-Hi (Labour Thanksgiving Day)
23 December Tenno Tanjobi (Emperor's Birthday).

TRANSPORT

ACCOMMODATION

ACTIVITIES

A – Z

LANGUAGE

Shinto as well as Buddhism, which was imported to Japan from Korea around the 6th century. About 1 percent of the population is Christian (with a higher percentage in Tokyo).

Catholic

Azabu Church: 3-21-6 Nishi-Azabu, Minato-ku, tel: 03-3408 1500, www.azabu-catholic.org.
Franciscan Chapel Centre: 4-2-37 Roppongi, Minato-ku, tel: 03-3401 2141, www.tokyofcc.com.

Jewish

Jewish Community of Japan: 3-8-8 Hiroo, Shibuya-ku, tel: 03-3400 2559, www.jccjapan.or.jp.

Muslim

Islamic Centre Japan: 1-16-11 Ohara, Setagaya-ku, tel: 03-3460 6169, http://islamcenter.or.jp.

Protestant

United Church of Christ in Japan, Ginza Church: 4-2-1 Ginza, Chuo-ku, tel: 03-3561 0236, www.ginza-church.com.
International Christian University Church: 3-10-2 Osawa, Mitaka-shi, tel: 0422-33 3323, www.icuchurch.com.

S

Smoking

Smoking is banned on all public transport and in most public buildings. There are sometimes separate smoking sections in bars and restaurants but few eating and drinking places are fully smoke free and many do not police their policies too strictly. Smoking on the street is being clamped down on in certain central wards such as Chuo-ku, Chiyoda-ku and Shinjuku-ku – you'll see smokers in these places clustered in designated smoking spots.

Student Travellers

If you have an International Student Identity Card (ISIC) you will usually qualify for the student discount at sights.

T

Taxes

At present a consumption tax (VAT) of 5 percent is applied to all retail transactions (including at hotels and restaurants). There is a good chance this may rise to closer to 10 percent in the near future.

Telephones

Public phones are available throughout Tokyo, though the number is dropping because of the prevalence of mobile phones. The minimum cost of a local call is ¥10 per minute. Telephone cards – not coins – are the primary form of payment for public phones, though you can still find machines that accept ¥10 and ¥100 coins. Be aware that change isn't given if you use a ¥100 coin to make a short call.

Area Codes

Tokyo 03
Yokohama 045
Narita 0476
Fukuoka 092
Hiroshima 082
Kagoshima 099
Kyoto 075
Nagasaki 0958
Nagoya 052
Naha 098
Osaka 06
Sapporo 011
Sendai 022
Note: Local telephone numbers that begin with 0120, 0088 or 0053 are toll-free calls that can be dialled only within Japan.

Directory Assistance

Local: 104. Ask for an English-speaking operator.

International: (English-speaking) 0057.

Domestic Calls

Long-distance domestic calls (over 60km/37 miles) are cheaper after peak hours by up to 40 percent. If calling from one province to another in Japan, be sure to dial the area code first (including the zero) before the phone number. When calling within Tokyo, do not dial the city's area code.

International Calls

International Dialling Code for Japan is 81: if calling Tokyo from overseas, dial +81-3 and then the local number.
International operator, dial 0051 to make a person-to-person, collect, or credit-card call from anywhere in Japan.
To make overseas calls from Tokyo, first dial the access code of one of the international call service providers (they each have their own cards which can only be used at the appropriate telephone booth), then the country code and the number.
KDD 001
NTT 0033
Softbank Telecom 0041
    International calls are possible from some grey and green public telephones; look for the globe logo.

Mobile Phones

Japan uses two mobile phone systems: PDC and CDMA. If you come from a country that uses the more common GSM system found in Asia, UK, Europe, Australia and New Zealand, your phone will most likely not work. Check with your home service provider if unsure, as you will have to rent a handset, which can be done most easily at one of the international airports. Buying a prepaid phone in Japan requires you to show proof of local residency.
    The major mobile phone operators are **NTT Docomo** (www.ntt-docomo.co.jp) and **Softbank** (www.softbank.jp/en).

Most mobile phone numbers begin with 090 or 080.

Time Zone

Tokyo (like the rest of Japan) is +9 hours GMT; +14 hours EST (New York); and +17 PST (Los Angeles). Japan does not have summer daylight savings time.

Toilets

Public toilets are reasonably common on Tokyo's streets, in its parks and most of its subway and railway stations. People use the facilities in department stores, convenience stores or coffee shops, too. Most toilets are Western style but you'll also come across the traditional squatting type, too. Carry tissues, as toilet paper isn't always available. The same goes for soap in public toilets in parks and stations.

Tourist Information

The Japan government is vigorously implementing advertising and other programmes aimed at attracting more tourists to the country. This has resulted in more information available on the Internet, and at tourism offices both within the country and overseas.

The **Tourist Information Centres (TIC)** run by the **Japan National Tourism Organisation (JNTO)**, not only have massive amounts of information on Tokyo, but can also organise hotel reservations. The multilingual counter staff found in the tourism offices are exceedingly well trained and helpful. The main one in Tokyo is at 3-3-1 Marunouchi, Chiyoda-ku, tel: 03-3201 3331, www.jnto.go.jp.

For Tokyo-specific tourist information the best office to head for is **Tokyo Tourist Information Centre** (1F Tokyo Metropolitan Government No. 1 Building, 2-8-1 Nishi-Shinjuku; tel: 03-5321 3077; daily 9.30am– 6.30pm). It has branches at

REST ROOM
WESTERN STYLE
洋式公衆便所

A bilingual sign.

Haneda Airport (tel: 03- 6428 0653; daily 9am –11pm) and in the Keisei Line station at Ueno (tel: 03-3836 3471; daily 9.30am –6.30pm).

Overseas Tourist Offices

See JNTO's website (www.jnto. go.jp) for a full list of overseas offices.
Australia
Suite 1, Level 4, 56 Clarence Street, Sydney NSW 2000, tel: 02-9279 2177, www.jnto.org.au
Canada
481 University Avenue, Suite 306, Toronto, ON M5G 2E, tel: 416-366-7140, www.ilovejapan.ca
UK
5th Floor, 12/13 Nicholas Lane, London, EC4N 7BN, tel: 020-7398 5670, www.seejapan.co.uk
US
New York: 11 West 42nd Street, 19th Floor, New York, NY 10036, tel: 212-757-5640, www.japantravelinfo.com
Los Angeles:
340 East Second Street, Little Tokyo Plaza, Suite 302 Los Angeles, CA 90012, tel: 213-623-1952, www.japantravelinfo.

Visas and Passports

Visas are required only for visitors from some countries; most may stay for up to 90 days with just a valid passport. A visa is necessary for foreigners living in Japan and engaged in business or study. Check with the Japanese embassy or consulate in your

own country, or go to the website www.mofa.go.jp, before making travel plans.

Extension of Stay

Anyone wishing to extend their stay should visit the Tokyo Regional Immigration Bureau office (5-5-30 Konan, Minato-ku; tel: 5796 7111; www.moj.go.jp).

Weights and Measures

Japan follows the metric system, except in cases governed by strong tradition. For example, rice and *sake* are measured in units of 1.8 litres and rooms are measured by a standard *tatami* mat size.

Women Travellers

Tokyo is not a dangerous place for women on their own. However, instances of harassment do occasionally occur, and incidents of women being groped on crowded trains are not uncommon. Western women, while less likely to be targeted, are not completely exempt.

The idea of the independent career woman has slowly gained acceptance over the past two decades, however, a deep, occasionally aggressive streak of sexism still runs through Japanese society. This is evidenced in degrading TV shows (not all latenight), tabloid 'sports' newspapers featuring explicit pictures, plus thinly veiled ads for prostitution services and cartoon books which glorify sexual violence towards women.

That said, it is safer to walk, travel, eat and drink anywhere in Tokyo than it is in most world cities. Areas like Shinjuku's Kabukicho are not advisable if you are alone, but two women together will generally suffer nothing more unpleasant than leering.

TRANSPORT

ACCOMMODATION

ACTIVITIES

A – Z

LANGUAGE

LANGUAGE

UNDERSTANDING THE LANGUAGE

General

Japanese is the main language, but in the conduct of international business, English is used. Signs on streets, stations and public buildings in Tokyo are generally written in Roman letters as well as Japanese text, sometimes with English translations. The level of spoken English is generally poor.

Japanese uses three different forms of writing (four, including Roman letters): two simple homegrown syllabaries (phonetic scripts) known as *hiragana* and *katakana*, each of which consist of 46 basic characters plus the Chinese characters (*kanji*). Knowledge of just under 2,000 of these (plus their numerous compounds) is required to read a daily newspaper.

While it is unnecessary to memorise more than a very few simple *kanji* characters (those for 'man' and 'woman' are useful at hot spring resorts and public toilets), it is not so daunting to learn the two *kana* scripts. This will help you read station names and some menu listings.

Hiragana is used for transliterating most *kanji* and for connectors that cannot be written with *kanji*. *Katakana* is used primarily for representing foreign names and loan words (eg *takushi*/taxi).

Pronunciation Tips

Apart from a few consonants, Japanese is easy to pronounce. The vowels in standard Japanese are always regular. The most important aspect is to give each syllable equal stress and to avoid the intonation patterns of English and other Western languages.

Consonants do not exist on their own, with the exception of 'n', which only follows a vowel, but are always accompanied by one of the five basic vowel sounds. These are pronounced much as they would be in English, with the following notes:
chi – as in cheese
g – always hard (as in get)
ji/ju/jo – as in jeans/June/joke
n – pronounced like m before b or p (*tenpura* is read tempura; *shin-bun* (newspaper) is pronounced shimbun)
tsu – like 'it's' (without the i)
The basic vowel sounds are pronounced much as in Spanish.
a – like the a in about
e – like the e in egg
i – like the i in ink
o – like the o in orange
u – like the u in butcher
In combination the vowels are pronounced as follows:
ai – like 'eye'
ae – almost the same as ai, but with a slight e sound at the end
ao – like the ow in cow

TERMS OF ADDRESS

Japanese do not usually use first names, but the family name, followed by '-san,' which can stand for Mr, Mrs, Miss or Ms. The suffix '-chan' may be used by close friends, or the suffix '-kun' when talking to boys or close mal friends.

au – almost the same as ao, but with a slight u sound at the end
ei – like the ay in way
io – like an elision 'ee-yo'
iu – like an elision 'ee-yu'
ue – like an elision 'oo-e'
uo – like an elision 'oo-oh'
When i and u occur in the middle of words, they are sometimes almost silent. For example, *shitamachi* (Tokyo's 'low city') is actually pronounced 'sh'ta-machi', while *sukiyaki* sounds more like 's'kiyaki'. A final u is also pronounced so imperceptibly as to be unnoticeable: thus *desu* is always pronounced 'dess'.

Vowels are sometimes elongated (doubled), and this is indicated in Roman letters by a macron (a line over the said vowel), by an extra h (after o), or by writing a double vowel (in the case of i). The spelling in English, however, does not always reflect the double vowel.

Words and Phrases

Essential Phrases

Do you speak English? *eego ga dekimasu ka?*
Please write it down *kaite kudasai*
Pardon? *sumimasen*
I understand *wakarimashita*
I don't understand/I don't know *wakarimasen*
Yes/No *hai/iie*
OK *ookee*
Please *onegai shimasu*
Thank you (very much) *(doomo) arigatoo*

Greetings

Good morning *ohayoo gozaimasu*
Hello (afternoon) *kon-nichi-wa*
Good evening *konban-wa*
Good night *oyasumi nasai*
Goodbye *sayoonara (shitsure shimasu for formal occasions)*
How are you? *ogenki desu ka?*
My name is... *...to moshimasu*
I'm Mr/Ms Smith *watashi wa Smith desu*
Are you Mr/Ms Honda? *Honda-san desu ka?*
I'm American *Amerika-jin desu*
I'm British *Igirisu-jin desu*
I'm Australian *Osutoraria-jin desu*
I'm Canadian *Kanada-jin desu*

Asking for Directions

Excuse me, where is the toilet? *sumimasen, toire wa doko desu ka?*
Excuse me, is there a post office near here? *sumimasen, kono chikaku ni, yubin-kyoku wa arimasu ka?*
on the left/right *hidari/migi ni*
bakery *pan-ya*
stationer's *bunboogu-ya*
pharmacy *yakkyoku*
bookshop *hon-ya*
supermarket *suupaa*
department store *depaato*
restaurant *resutoran*
hotel *hoteru*
station *eki*
taxi rank *takushii noriba*
bank *ginkoo*
hospital *byooin*
police station *kooban*

Out Shopping

This one *kore*
That one *(near the other person) sore*
That one *(near neither of you) are*
Do you have...? *...(wa) arimasu ka?*
How much is it? *ikura desu ka?*
I'll take this *kore o kudasai*

Boarding the Train

Ticket (office) *kippu (uriba)*
reserved seat *shitei seki*
unreserved seat *jiyu seki*
first-class car *guriin sha*
Which platform does the train for Nagoya leave from? *Nagoya yuki wa namban sen desu ka?*
Thank you (very much) *(doomo) arigato gozaimasu (informally, doomo is enough)*
Don't mention it *doitashimashite*
Thanks for the meal *gochisosama deshita*
Here you are *doozo*
After you *doozo*

Days/Time

Sunday *nichi-yoobi*
Monday *getsu-yoobi*
Tuesday *ka-yoobi*
Wednesday *sui-yoobi*
Thursday *moku-yoobi*
Friday *kin-yoobi*
Saturday *do-yoobi*
Yesterday *kino*
Today *kyo*
This morning *kesa*
This evening *konya*
Tomorrow *ashita*

Months/Seasons

January *ichi-gatsu*
February *ni-gatsu*
March *san-gatsu*
April *shi-gatsu*
May *go-gatsu*
June *roku-gatsu*
July *shichi-gatsu*
August *hachi-gatsu*
September *ku-gatsu*
October *juu-gatsu*
November *juu-ichi-gatsu*
December *juu-ni-gatsu*

At the Hotel

Western-style hotel *hoteru*
business hotel *bijinesu hoteru*
love hotel *rabu hoteru*

Japanese-style inn *ryokan*
guesthouse *minshuku*
temple accommodation *shuku-boo*
youth hostel *yuusu hosuteru*
I have a reservation *yoyaku shite arimasu*
Do you have a room? *heya wa arimasu ka?*
I'd like a single/double room *shinguru/daburu ruumu o onegai shimasu*
I'd like a room with ...... *tsuki no heya o onegai shimasu*
twin beds *tsuin beddo*
double bed *daburu beddo*
bath/shower *furo/shawa*
air-conditioning *eakon*
TV/telephone *terebi/denwa*
How much is it? *ikura desu ka?*
Can I see the room please? *heya o misete kudasai*

At the Restaurant

A table for two, please *futari onegai shimasu*
The bill, please *o-kanjoo onegai shimasu*
tsukemono **pickled vegetables**
sashimi **raw fish with soy sauce and Japanese horseradish**
sushi **rice balls topped with fish/seafood**
tempura **battered vegetables, fish or seafood**
okonomiyaki **pizza/savoury pancake**
gyoza **meat/veg dumplings**
soba **buckwheat noodles**
udon **thick wheat-flour noodles**
tonkotsu ramen **pork broth-based dish with Chinese (ramen) noodles**
tonkatsu **breaded deep-fried pork**
yakitori **grilled chicken skewers**
sukiyaki **thin slices of beef and vegetables in aromatic sauce**
shabu-shabu **slices of beef or pork cooked in broth**
karee raisu **Japanese curry on rice**
teppanyaki **griddled meat/fish**
kamameshi **rice casserole**
biiru **beer**
ocha **green tea**
o-sake/nihonshu **sake**
mizu **water**
mineraru wootaa **mineral water**

FURTHER READING

Food and Drink

Drinking Japan, by Chris Bunting. An entertaining and detailed look at everything on the bar menu in Japan, from sake and shochu to Japanese whiskey and wine.

The Insider's Guide to Sake, by Philip Harper. A foreigner, who has become a full-time sake brewer, explains what makes the trade so special.

Izakaya: The Japanese Pub Cookbook, by Mark Robinson. Profiling some of the author's favourite izakaya in Tokyo with over 60 associated recipes.

The Sake Handbook, by John Gauntner. Explains the intricacies of Japan's national tipple, and includes favourite Tokyo drinking holes.

What's What in Japanese Restaurants, by Robb Satterwhite. Invaluable for deciphering menus.

History and Culture

Embracing Defeat, by John Dower. Pulitzer prize-winning study of Japan under the American Occupation.

Inventing Japan, by Ian Buruma. Looks at the period 1853 to 1964 and how Japan changed itself after opening up to the outside world.

Low City, High City: Tokyo From Edo to the Earthquake, by Edward Seidensticker. The best history of how the city changed from shogun's capital to a modern metropolis.

My Asakusa: Coming of Age in Pre-War Tokyo, by Sadako Sawamura. A delightful and frank memoir of one of the city's best-loved districts by the late actress-writer Sawamura.

Speed Tribes, by Karl Taro Greenfeld. Profiles of Tokyo's subterranean youth culture.

Tokyo: 29 Walks in the World's Most Exciting City, by John H. Martin and Phyllis G. Martin. Guided walks around Tokyo and its environs that delve deep into the city's history and development.

Tokyo Megacity, by Donald Richie and Ben Simmons. Thirty-one fascinating essays on Tokyo, accompanied by slick photography, by one of the city's foremost expat writers.

Tokyo Underworld, by Robert Whiting. Fascinating biography of an American gangster in the post-war era.

Tokyo Vice, by Jake Adelstein. An entertaining and revealing account by an American journalist about his years on the crime beat for the Yomiuri Shimbun, Japan's top-selling newspaper.

Wrong About Japan, by Peter Carey. Tokyo as seen through the eyes of the Australian author who visits with anime-obsessed 12-year-old son

Literature

Blind Willow, Sleeping Woman, by Haruki Murakami. Twenty-four stories by Japan's best-known author, several of them set in Tokyo.

Green Tea to Go: Stories from Tokyo, by Leza Lowitz. Superior stories of Tokyo life, love and cultural orientation.

Idoru, by William Gibson. Futurist fantasy but strangely accurate rendering of Japanese youth in the digital age. Parts of his novel *Pattern Recognition* are also set in Tokyo.

Number9Dream, by David Mitchell. Booker Prize-nominated novel that is partly set in Tokyo and paints a vivid picture of the contemporary city.

Out, by Natsuo Kirino. Slick thriller about a group of women who commit murder and how they go about covering it up. If you like this also check out the follow-up novel Grotesque, about the deaths of two Tokyo prostitutes.

Samurai Boogie, by Peter Tasker. Private eye Kazuo Mori investigates the underbelly of the city in Tokyo-based Tasker's *noir* novel. Check out also the more recent *Dragon Dance*, also set in Tokyo.

Tokyo Stories: A Literary Stroll, translated and edited by Lawrence Rogers. An anthology of stories by Japanese writers with Tokyo settings. Many appear for the first time in English.

A View from the Chuo Line, by Donald Richie. Minimalist stories set in Tokyo from the master observer.

Misc

A Flower Lover's Guide to Tokyo, by Sumiko Enbutsu. Includes 40 walks that take advantage of all seasonal blooms.

Twenty-first Century Tokyo: A Guide to Contemporary Architecture, by Julian Worrall and Erez Golani Solomon. Illustrated survey of some of the city's most striking modern buildings and structures.

Other Insight Guides

Among nearly 200 companion books to this one are several titles covering Japan, including *Insight Guide Japan, Smart Guide Tokyo, Step-by-Step Tokyo* and *Fleximap Tokyo*, an indispensable map of the city.

TOKYO STREET ATLAS

The key map shows the area of Tokyo covered by the atlas section. An index of street names and places of interest shown on the maps can be found on the following pages. For each entry there is a page number and grid reference

Map Legend

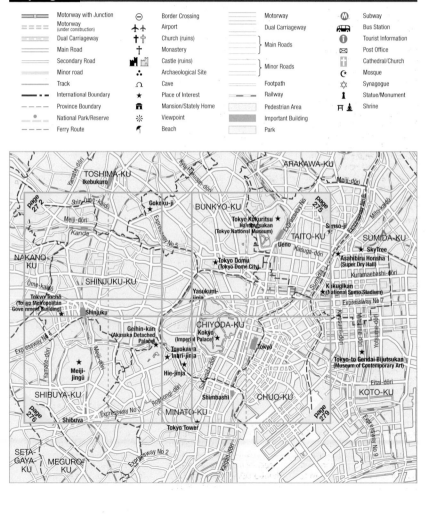

▭ Motorway with Junction	⊖ Border Crossing		Motorway	Ⓜ Subway
Motorway (under construction)	✈ Airport		Dual Carriageway	🚌 Bus Station
Dual Carriageway	✝ Church (ruins)		Main Roads	❶ Tourist Information
Main Road	✝ Monastery			✉ Post Office
Secondary Road	Castle (ruins)		Minor Roads	Cathedral/Church
Minor road	Archaeological Site			Mosque
Track	∩ Cave		Footpath	Synagogue
International Boundary	★ Place of Interest		Railway	Statue/Monument
Province Boundary	🏠 Mansion/Stately Home		Pedestrian Area	Shrine
National Park/Reserve	Viewpoint		Important Building	
Ferry Route	Beach		Park	

ARAKAWA-KU

TOSHIMA-KU
Ikebukuro

Gokoku-ji

BUNKYO-KU

Tokyo Kokuritsu ★
Hakubutsukan
(Tokyo National Museum)

TAITO-KU

Senso-ji

SUMIDA-KU

★ SkyTree

Asahibiru Honsha
(Super Dry Hall)

Kuramaebashi-dori

NAKANO-KU

SHINJUKU-KU

Tokyo Domu
(Tokyo Dome City)

Ueno

Kikugikan
(National Sumo Stadium)

Tokyo Tochō
(Tokyo Metropolitan
Government Building)

Shinjuku

Yasukuni-jinja

CHIYODA-KU

Geihin-kan
(Akasaka Detached
Palace)

Kokyo
(Imperial Palace) ★

Tokyo

Toyokawa
Inari-jinja

Meiji-jingū ★

Hie-jinja

Tokyo-to Gendai Bijutsukan
(Museum of Contemporary Art)

Eitai-dori

KOTO-KU

SHIBUYA-KU

Shimbashi

CHUO-KU

Shibuya

MINATO-KU

Tokyo Tower

SETA-GAYA-KU

MEGURO-KU

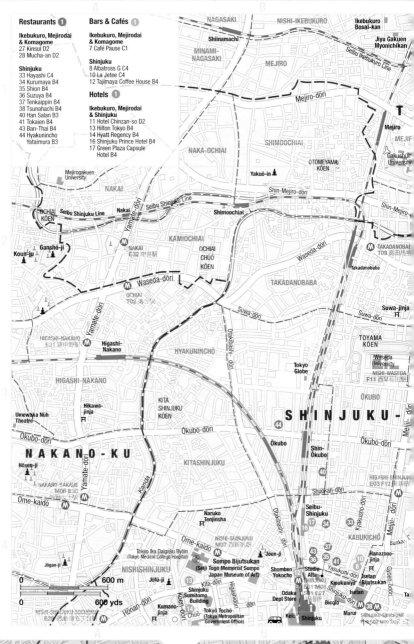

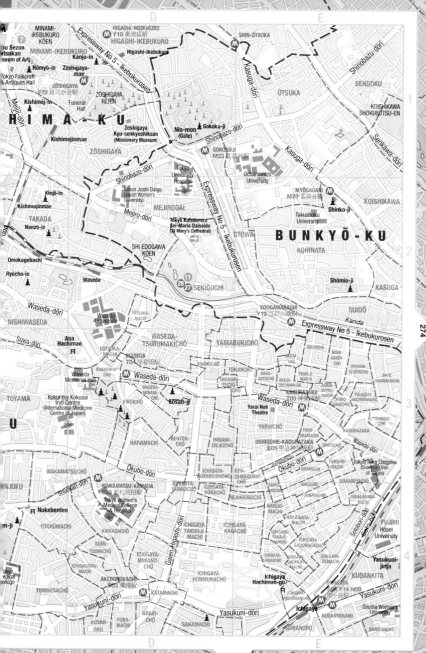

MINAMI-IKEBUKURO KŌEN

ou Sezon
otsukan
seum of Art)

MINAMI-IKEBUKURO

Expressway No 5 - Ikebukurosen

HIGASHI-IKEBUKURO
Y10 東池袋駅

HIGASHI-IKEBUKURO

Ⓜ

Higashi-Ikebukuro

SHIN-ŌTSUKA

Shinobazu-dōri

Kanju-in

Tokyo Folkcraft
& Antiques Hall

Hōmyō-in

Zōshigaya-
mae

ZŌSHIGAYA
F10 雑司か谷駅

Ⓜ

ZŌSHIGAYA
REIEN

Funeral
Hall

Nio-mon
(Gate)

Gokoku-ji

GOKOKUJI
M23 護国寺駅

Ⓜ

Shinobazu-dōri

Kasuga-dōri

ŌTSUKA

Senkawa-dōri

SENGOKU

KOISHIKAWA
SHOKUBOTSU-EN

HIMA-KU

Meijiro-dōri

Kishimoj-in

Zōshigaya
Kyu-senkyoshiksan
(Missionary Museum)

ZŌSHIGAYA

Shinobazu-dōri

Kishimojinmae

Ochanomizu
University

Nihon Joshi Daigu
(Japan Women's
University)

Tokyo
University
Hospital

Kasuga-dōri

MYŌGADANI
M23 茗荷谷駅

Ⓜ

Shinko-ji

KOISHIKAWA

Kinjō-In

Kishimojinmae

TAKADA

Mejiro-dōri

MEJIRODAI

Tōkyō Katedoraru
Sei-Maria Daiseido
(St Mary's Cathedral)

Takushoku
University

BUNKYŌ-KU

Nanzo-in

SHI EDOGAWA
KŌEN

OTOWA

KŌHINATA

Shōmio-ji

KASUGA

Omokagebashi

Ryocho-in

Waseda

Kanda

SUIDŌ

NISHIWASEDA

Waseda-dōri

Waseda
University

TOTSUKA-
MACHI

SEKIGUCHI

Ⓜ

EDOGAWABASHI
Y12 江戸川橋駅

Expressway No 5 - Ikebukurosen

NISHI-
GOKEN-
CHŌ

HIGASHI-
GOKENCHŌ

SHIN-
OGAWAMACHI

Suwa-dōri

Ana
Hachiman

Waseda
Memorial Hall

TOTSUKA-
MACHI

WASEDA
T04 早稲田駅

WASEDA-
TSUBUMAKICHŌ

YAMABUKICHŌ

KIKUICHŌ

WASEDA-
MINAMI-
CHŌ

ENOKICHŌ

TENJINCHŌ

HIGASHI-
ENOKI

IKUTA-
CHŌ

NAKA-
ZATOCHŌ

TSUKI-
JI-
MACHI

AKAGI-
MOTO-
MACHI

SHINO-
HACHIMANCHŌ

TSUKUDO-
CHŌ

TOYAMA

Kokuritsu Kokusai
Iryō Centre
(International Medicine
Centre of Japan)

HARAMACHI

Sōsan-ji

Yarai Noh
Theatre

YARAICHŌ

Waseda-dōri

Ⓜ

KAGURAZAKA

U

BENTEN-
CHŌ

MINAMI-
ENOKICHŌ

YOKO-
TERAMACHI

USHIGOME-KAGURAZAKA
E05 牛込神楽坂駅

FUKURO-
MACHI

IWATOCHŌ

Waseda-dōri

Tokyo Rika Daigaku
(Science Univ
of Tokyo)

WAKAMATSUCHŌ

Ōkubo-dōri

Ⓜ

Suaruka-dōri

Ⓜ

WAKAMATSU-KAWADA
E03 若松河田駅

ICHIGAYA-
YAMABUSHICHŌ

ICHIGAYA-
YANAGICHŌ

KITA-
YAMABUSHI-
CHŌ

Ōkubo-dōri

NAKACHŌ

SAIKU-
CHŌ

NANDO-
MACHI

WAKAMIYACHŌ

INJUKU

Tokyo Women's
Medical College
& Hospital

ICHIGAYA-
KŌRACHŌ

NIJUKKIMACHI

MINAMICHŌ

FUNAGAWARA-
MACHI

Nukebenten

YOCHŌMACHI

KAWADACHŌ

Galen Higashi-dōri

ICHIGAYA-
YAKUOJI
MACHI

ICHIGAYA-
KAGACHŌ

HARAIKATA-
MACHI

FUJIMI

Hōsei
University

en-ji

SUMI-
YOSHICHŌ

ICHIGAYA-
NAKANO-
CHŌ

ICHIGAYA-
TAKAJO-
MACHI

ICHIGAYA-
SADOHARACHŌ

ICHIGAYA-
TAMACHI

Yasukuni-
jinja

okyo
edical
ollege

ICHIGAYADAI-
MACHI

AKEBONOBASHI
S03 曙橋駅

Ⓜ

ICHIGAYA-
HONMURACHŌ

KATAMACHI

Ichigaya
Hachiman-gū

ICHIGAYA-
SANAICHŌ

ICHIGAYA
TSUKIMI-
CHŌ

Sokubo-dōri

Yasukuni-dōri

KUDANKITA

Ōzuma Women's
University

TOMISACHŌ

AIZUMI-
CHŌ

FUNA-
MACHI

ARAKI-
CHŌ

SAKAMACHI

Yasukuni-dōri

GOBANCHŌ

Ichigaya

Ⓜ

ICHIGAYA
Y14 N09 市ヶ谷駅

Yasukuni-dōri

KUDANMINAMI

SANBANCHŌ

274

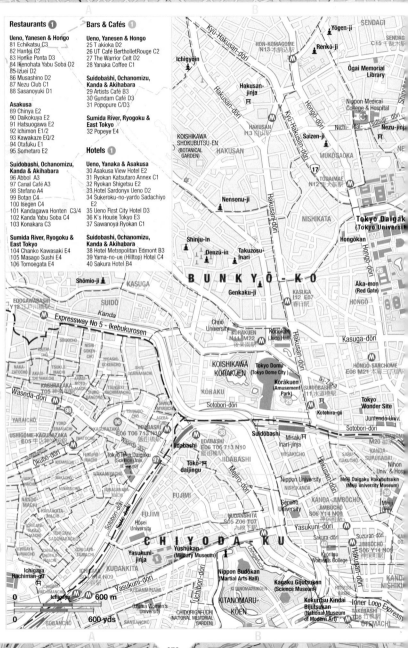

Restaurants ①

Ueno, Yanesen & Hongo
81 Echikatsu C3
82 Hantei C2
83 Honke Ponta D3
84 Ikenohata Yabu Soba D2
85 Izuei D2
86 Musashino D2
87 Nezu Club C1
88 Sasanoyuki D1

Asakusa
89 Chinya E2
90 Daikokuya E2
91 Hatsuogawa E2
92 Ichimon E1/2
93 Kawakaze EQ/2
94 Otafuku E1
95 Sometaro E2

Suidobashi, Ochanomizu, Kanda & Akihabara
96 Abbol A3
97 Canal Café A3
98 Stefano A4
99 Botan C4
100 Isegen C4
101 Kandagawa Honten C3/4
102 Kanda Yabu Soba C4
103 Konakara C3

Sumida River, Ryogoku & East Tokyo
104 Chanko Kawasaki E4
105 Masago Sushi E4
106 Tomoegata E4

Bars & Cafés ①

Ueno, Yanesen & Hongo
25 T akioka D2
26 UT Café BertholletRouge C2
27 The Warrior Celt D2
28 Yanaka Coffee C1

Suidobashi, Ochanomizu, Kanda & Akihabara
29 Artists Café B3
30 Gundam Café D3
31 Popopure C/D3

Sumida River, Ryogoku & East Tokyo
32 Popeye E4

Hotels ①

Ueno, Yanaka & Asakusa
30 Asakusa View Hotel E2
31 Ryokan Katsutaro Annex C1
32 Ryokan Shigetsu E2
33 Hotel Sardonyx Ueno D2
34 Sukeroku-no-yardo Sadachiyo E2
35 Ueno First City Hotel D3
36 K's House Tokyo E3
37 Sawanoya Ryokan C1

Suidobashi, Ochanomizu, Kanda & Akihabara
38 Hotel Metropolitan Edmont B3
39 Yama-no-ue (Hilltop) Hotel C4
40 Sakura Hotel B4

ARAKAWA-KU

Asakura Chosokan
(Asakura Choso Museum)
Daien-ji
Zensho-en
YANAKA
YANAKA
REIEN
NEGISHI

Nippori

SHITAYA

RYUSEN

SENZOKU

Kokusai-dori

Showa-dori

Kan'ei-ji
Onoterusaki-jinja
Ōtori-jinja

Zuirin-ji
SCAI The
Bathhouse
Jomyo-in
Yoshidaya
Sake-ten
Uguisudani
Eishin-ji
IRIYA
IRIYA
HJ8 入谷駅

ASAKUSA

Gyokurin-ji
TOKUGAWA
SHOGUN
GRAVEYARD
Tokyo Kokuritsu
Hakubutsukan
(Tokyo National Museum)
Kishimoj-in
Kototoi-dori

Tokyo Geijutsu Daigaku
(Tokyo National University
of Fine Arts & Music)
Honnen-ji
Banryuji
Taito Traditional
Crafts Museum

Gokoku-in

Tokyo-to Bijutsukan
(Tokyo Metropolitan
Art Museum)
Ryō-daishi
TAITŌ-KU

Kokuritsu Kagaku Hakubutsukan
(National Science Museum)
KITA-UENO
NISHI
ASAKUSA HANAYASHIKI
(AMUSEMENT PARK)

UENO ZOO
UENO-KOEN
UENO-KOEN
Gojūnō-to
(Five-Storey
Pagoda)
Kokuritsu Seiyo Bijutsukan
(National Museum of Western Art)
MATSUGAYA
Tengaku-in
Gojūnō-to
(Five Storey Pagoda)

Shōkei-ji
IKENOHATA
Tokyo Bunka Kaikan
(Tokyo Metropolitan
Festival Hall)
Ueno
Asakusa Kōgei-kan
(Handicraft Museum)
Denbō-in

Bojo Tenjinsha
Kiyomizu
Miyamoto
Unosoke Shoten
(Drum Museum)
ROX
Kaminari-
mon

Yokoyama
Taikan Kinenkan
(Yokoyama Taikan
Memorial Hall)
Benten-
dō
Kannon-dō
Saigō
Takamori
INARICHO
G17
Tokyo
Hongan-ji
Kaminarimon-dori
Kaminarimon-dori

Shinobazu-
no-ike
Asakusa-dori
TAWARAMACHI
G18

Shitamachi
Fuzoku Shiryokan
UENO
G16 H17
Shitaya-jinja
Asakusa-dori

KYU IWASAKI-TEI GARDENS
Shinobazu-dori
HIGASHI-UENO
MOTO-ASAKUSA
KAMINARIMON
G19 A18

Tokudai-ji
UENO-OKACHIMACHI
E09
Kinryū-ji
KOMAGATA

Yushima
Tenjin
G15
Kasuga-
dori
Okachimachi
SHIN-
OKACHIMACHI
F10
Kasuga-dori
Kurofune-
jinja
YUSHIMA
C13
Matsuzakaya
NAKA-OKACHIMACHI
H16
KOJIMA
KOTOBUKI

YUSHIMA
UENO
TAITO
MISUJI

Tsumagoi-jinja
SUEHIROCHO
G14
Kaya-dera
KURAMAE
36
Umaya-
bashi

Kanda Myojin
Kanda-ji
TORIGOE
Torigoe-jinja
KURAMAE
A17 E11

Yushima
Seido
Akihabara
UDX
Building
ASAKUSABASHI
Kuramaebashi-dori
Kuramaebashi-dori
Sumida

Tokyo Anime
Centre
SOTOKANDA
KANDA
IZUMICHO
Sakaki-jinja
Edo-dori
YOKOAMI

ikolai-do
athedral)
101
1. KANDA-NERIBEICHO
2. K.-AIOICHO
3. K.-MATSUNAGACHO
4. K.-HANAOKACHO
5. K.-HIRAKAWACHO
6. K.-SAKUMAGASHI
YANAGIBASHI
ASAKOSABASHI
A16
KYU YASUDA
TEIEN

SHIN-OCHANOMIZU
C12
99
102
KANDA
SUDACHO
KANDA
SAKUMACHO
Kanda
Kokugikan
(National
Sumo Stadium)
Ryōgoku

AWAJICHO
M19
Akihabara
AKIHABARA
H15
Sumo
Hakubutsukan
RYOGOKU
E12

IWAMOTOCHO
S08
Yasukuni-dori
NIHOMBASHI-
BAKUROCHO
RYOGOKU
105

Kanda
Kandahei-sei-dori
UCHIKANDA
Sotobori-dori
Chuo-dori
7. K.-SARAYACHO
8. KANDA-IWAMOTOCHO
9. K.-KITANORICHO
10. K.-KON'YACHO
11. K. NISHIFUKUDACHO
12. K.-MIKURACHO
13. K.-HIGASHI
MATSUSHITACHO
Bakurochō
HIGASHI-
NIHOMBASHI
Ryogoku-
bashi
Ryōgoku-
bashi
Keiyo-dori

HIGASHI-NIHOMBASHI
A15 S09
CHŪŌ-KU
Eshima-
sugiyama-
jinja
SUMIDA-KU
RYOGOKU

BAKURO-
YOKOYAMA
KODENMACHO
KODENMACHO
KODEMMACHO
H16
Yoshin-ji
CHITOSE

279

272

NISHISHINJUKU
Ome-kaidō
NISHI-SHINJUKU M07 西新宿五丁目
KABUKICHŌ
Shomben
Yokochō
Hanazono-jinja
Yasuk

Jōgan-ji
Yamate-dōri
Tokyo Ika Daigaku Byōin
(Tokyo Medical College Hospital)
Shinjuku Kita-dōri
Studio
Alta
Yasukuni-dōri
Kinokuniya

Jōfū-ji
Shinjuku
Sumitomo
Building
E28 都庁前
SHINJUKU
E01 M08
S01 M07
新宿
Isetan

NISHI-SHINJUKU GOCHŌME
E29 西新宿五丁目
TOCHŌMAE
Chūō
dōri
Odaku
Dept Store
Bicqlo
新宿
Marui
SHINJUKU
E01 M08
S01 E27
Jokaku-ji
Taisi

HONAN-DŌRI
Honan-dōri
Kumano-H
jinja
Tokyo Tochō
(Tokyo Metropolitan
Government Office)
Highway
Bus Terminal
15
Plaza-dōri
32
Shinjuku
39
Tenryū-ji

Yamate-dōri
SHINJUKU
CHŪŌ-KŌEN
Fureai-dōri
SHINJUKU
SHINJUKU

SHINJUKU-KU
Honan-dōri
NS Building
Minami-dōri
Kōshū-kaidō
SHINJUKU
SHINJUKU
Takashimaya
Times Square
30
SHINJI

HONMACHI
Minami-dōri
Shinjuku
Park Tower
29 12
Bunka Women's
University
Meiji-dōri
Yoyogi

Fudō-dōri
Sūidō-dōri
Bunka Gakuen
Fukushoku Hakubutsukan
(Bunka Costume Museum)
YOYOGI

Tokyo
Opera City
Minami-Shinjuku
42

Sūidō-dōri
Shin-Kokuritsu Gekijō
(New National Theatre)
Expressway No 4 Shinjukusen
Odakyū Line
Kokuritsu Noh-Gakudō
(National Noh Theatre)

HATSUDAI
初台駅
Tōken Hakubutsukan
(Japanese Sword Museum)
SENDAGA

HATSUDAI
Keiō Line
Hōmotsuden Honkan
(Meiji-jingū Treasure House)
KITA-SANDŌ
Hatomori-jin

HATAGAYA
幡ヶ谷駅
Sangūbashi
MEIJI-JINGŪ
(INNER GARDEN)
Meiji-dōri

NISHIHARA
National
Olympic Memorial
Youth Centre
Meiji-jingū

MOTO-
YOYOGICHŌ
YOYOGI-
KAMIZONOCHŌ
JINGŪ NAIEN
(INS GARDEN)
Hōmotsu-Tenjishitsu
(Treasure Museum Annex)
63
JINGŪMAE

Yoyogi-Hachiman-
jinja
YOYOGI-
SHIBUYA-KU
KŌEN
Harajuku
Takeshita-dōri
18
Tōgō-jinja

Yoyogi-Uehara
Yoyogi-Hachiman
Ukiyo-e Ōta Kinen
Bijutsukan
(Ukiyo-e Ōta Memorial
Museum of Art)

YOYOGI-UEHARA
C01 代々木上原駅
Inokashira-dōri
YOYOGI-KŌEN
C02 代々木公園駅
MEIJI-JINGŪMAE
C03 F15
明治神宮前
Ōmo
sar
Omotesandō

UEHARA
Kokuritsu Yoyogi Kyōgijō
(Yoyogi National Stadium)

TOMIGAYA
NHK Hall
JIN'NAN
Kitatani
Inari-jinja
Chōsen-ji

Tokai
University
NHK Hoso
(NHK
Broadcasting
Centre)
NHK
Studio Park
Onden-jinja

KAMIYAMACHŌ
Shibuya
Ward Hall
UDAGAWA
CHO
Bastille-
dōri

KOMABA
KŌEN
Toritsu Kindai Bungaku Hakubutsukan
(Tokyo Metropolitan Museum
of Modern Japanese Literature)
Toguri Bijutsukan
(Toguri Museum
of Art)
Kanze
Nōh-Gakudō
Tabako to Shio no
Hakubutsukan
(Tobacco & Salt Museum)
Kodomo no Shiro
(National
Children's Castle)

Nihon Mingeikan
(Japan Folk Craft
Museum)
Tokyo
University
SHŌTŌ
58
Kanze
Nōh-Gakudō
55
AB-dōri
Marui
Dept Store
Seibu Dept
Store
SHIBUYA
17
54
Aoyama-dōri
60

MEGURO-
KU
KOMABA
NAGESHIMA
SHŌTŌ
KŌEN
Shōtō Bijutsukan
(Shōtō Museum
of Art)
Bunkamura
Tōkyū Dept
Store
109 Building
DŌGEN-
ZAKA
Dōgen
59
SHIBUYA
C01 F16 G01
渋谷駅
Hachikō
Mark
City
SHIBUYA
Miyamasu-zaka
Shibuya
Hikarie
Kokuren Dai
(United Nati
Universit
62
Tōfuku-ji

0 ———— 600 m
0 ———— 600 yds

A   B

61

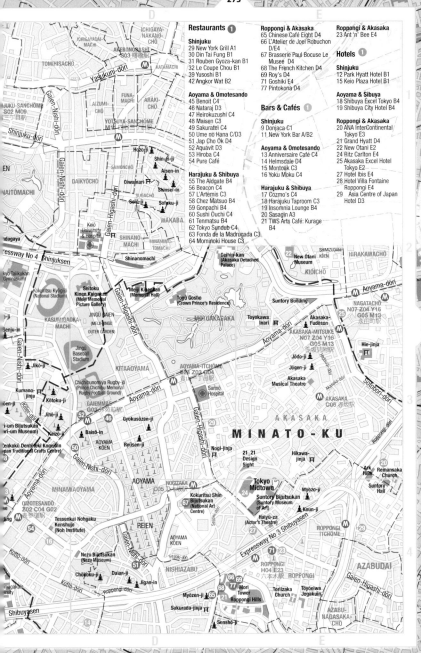

Restaurants ❶

Shinjuku
29 New York Grill A1
30 Din Tai Fung B1
31 Rouben Gyoza-kan B1
32 Le Coupe Chou B1
39 Yusoshi B1
42 Angkor Wat B2

Aoyama & Omotesando
45 Benoit C4
46 Nataraj D3
47 Heirokuzushi C4
48 Maisen C3
49 Sakuratei C4
50 Ume no Hana C/D3
51 Jap Cho Ok D4
52 Aquavit D3
53 Hiroba C4
54 Pure Café

Harajuku & Shibuya
55 The Aldgate B4
56 Beacon C4
57 L'Artemis C3
58 Chez Matsuo B4
59 Gonpachi B4
60 Sushi Ouchi C4
61 Tenmatsu B4
62 Tokyo Sundub C4
63 Fonda de la Madrugada C3
64 Mominoki House C3

Roppongi & Akasaka
65 Chinese Café Eight D4
66 L'Atelier de Joel Robuchon D/E4
67 Brasserie Paul Bocuse Le Musee D4
68 The French Kitchen D4
69 Roy's D4
71 Goshiki E4
77 Pintokona D4

Bars & Cafés ❶

Shinjuku
9 Donjaca C1
11 New York Bar A/B2

Aoyama & Omotesando
13 Anniversaire Café C4
14 Helmsdale D4
15 Montoak C3
16 Yoku Moku C4

Harajuku & Shibuya
17 Cozmo's C4
18 Harajuku Taproom C3
19 Insomnia Lounge B4
20 Sasagin A3
21 TWS Arts Café: Kurage B4

Roppongi & Akasaka
23 Ant 'n' Bee E4

Hotels ❶

Shinjuku
12 Park Hyatt Hotel B1
15 Keio Plaza Hotel B1

Aoyama & Sibuya
18 Shibuya Excel Tokyo B4
19 Shibuya City Hotel B4

Roppongi & Akasaka
20 ANA InterContinental Tokyo E3
21 Grand Hyatt D4
22 New Otani E2
24 Ritz Carlton E4
25 Akasaka Excel Hotel Tokyo E2
27 Hotel Ibis E4
28 Hotel Villa Fontaine Roppongi E4
29 Asia Centre of Japan Hotel D3

Restaurants

Imperial Palace, Marunouchi & Nihombashi
1 Salt C2
2 Signature D1
3 Locanda Elio A2
4 Breeze of Tokyo C2
5 Kizushi D1
6 Kurosawa A3
7 Muromachi Sunaba D1
8 Ten-mo D1
9 Yukari C3

Yurakucho, Ginza & Shiodome
10 Hei Fung Terrace C3
11 Aux Amis des Vins C3
12 Gordon Ramsay at the Conrad C4
13 Cardenas Ginza C3
14 Dhaba India C2
15 Ajioka C3
16 Bird Land C3
17 Little Okinawa C3
18 Ohmatsuya C3
19 Rangetsu C3
20 Robata C3
21 Sakyo Higashiyama C3
22 Shin Hinomoto C3
23 Ten-Ichi Deux C3
24 Tonton Honten C3
25 Yukun Sakagura B3
26 Aronya Tabeta C2

Roppongi & Akasaka
70 Fukuzushi A4
72 Hassan A4
73 Inakaya East A4
74 Ninja A2
75 Nobo Tokyo A 3/4
76 Nodaiwa A4
78 Tofuya Ukai B4
79 Tokya Curry Lab A4
80 Daigo B4

Tokyo Bayside
107 Lijiang D3
108 Edogin C4
109 Kanno D4
110 Oshio D4
111 Sushi-Bun C4

112 Takeno D4
113 Tsukiji Jisaku D4
114 Tsukiji Sushiko C4

Bars & Cafés

Imperial Palace, Marunouchi & Nihombashi
1 100% Chocolate Café C2
2 Marunouchi House C2
3 Old Imperial Bar C3
4 Towers C2

Yurakucho, Ginza & Shiodome
5 Lion Beer Hall C3
6 The Lobby C3

Roppongi & Akasaka
22 Agave A4
24 The Pink Cow A4

Hotels

Imperial Palace, Yurakucho & Ginza
1 Imperial Hotel C3
2 Mandarin Oriental, Tokyo D1
3 The Peninsula Tokyo C3
4 Tokyo Station Hotel C2
5 Hotel Com's Ginza C3
6 Diamond Hotel A2
7 Mitsui Garden Hotel Premier C3
8 Ginza Mercure C3
9 Yaesu Fujiya Hotel C2
10 Yaesu Terminal Hotel D2

Roppongi & Akasaka
23 Hotel Okura A3
26 The b Roppongi A4

Shiodome & Tokyo Bayside
41 Conrad Yokyo C4

STREET INDEX

ZONES

ART AND PHOTO CREDITS

INDEX

RESTAURANTS

BARS AND CAFÉS

INSIGHT GUIDES
TOKYO

ABOUT THIS BOOK

Project Editor
Rebecca Lovell
Series Manager
Tom Stainer
Art Editor
Ian Spick
Map Production
original cartography Berndtson
& Berndtson, updated by Apa
Cartography Department
Production
Tynan Dean and Rebeka Ellam

Distribution

UK
Dorling Kindersley Ltd
A Penguin Group company
80 Strand, London, WC2R 0RL
customerservice@dk.com

United States
Ingram Publisher Services
1 Ingram Boulevard, PO Box 3006,
La Vergne, TN 37086-1986
ips@ingramcontent.com

Australia
Universal Publishers
PO Box 307
St Leonards NSW 1590
sales@universalpublishers.com.au

New Zealand
Brown Knows Publications
11 Artesia Close, Shamrock Park
Auckland, New Zealand 2016
sales@brownknows.co.nz

Worldwide
**Apa Publications GmbH & Co.
Verlag KG (Singapore branch)**
7030 Ang Mo Kio Avenue 5
08-65 Northstar @ AMK
Singapore 569880
apasin@singnet.com.sg

Printing

CTPS-China

© 2013 Apa Publications (UK) Ltd
All Rights Reserved

First Edition 1991
Sixth Edition 2013

What makes an Insight Guide different? Since our first book pioneered the use of creative full-colour photography in travel guides in 1970, we have aimed to provide not only reliable information but also the key to a real understanding of a destination and its people.

To achieve this, our books rely on the authority of locally based writers and photographers.

This new edition of *City Guide Tokyo* was commissioned by **Rebecca Lovell** and supervised by series editor **Tom Stainer**. The book was thoroughly updated by travel writer **Rob Goss** who lives in Tokyo. He has also written several other books for Insight, including *Insight Guide: Japan*. This edition builds on the success of earlier editions produced by **Simon Richmond, Francis Dorai** and **Low Jat Leng**. The text of writers who contributed to previous editions has been updated for this book. They include **Stephen Mansfield**, who wrote the history and architecture chapters, and compiled the restaurant listings; **Angela Jeffs,** who wrote the Tokyoites chapter; **Alexandra Waldman** who penned the chapter on Fashion and Design; **Mark Schreiber** who contributed the feature box entitled Encounters with "Janglish"; **Dan Grunebaum** who wrote the Tokyo After Dark chapter; and **Robbie Swinnerton** who wrote the chapter on Japanese cuisine.

Among the prominent photographers whose images bring Tokyo to life are **Richard Nowitz, Chris Stowers** and **Ming Tang-Evans**.

The book was copy-edited by **Alyse Dar.**

SEND US YOUR THOUGHTS

We do our best to ensure the information in our books is as accurate and up-to-date as possible. The books are updated on a regular basis using local contacts, who painstakingly add, amend, and correct as required. However, some details (such as telephone numbers and opening times) are liable to change, and we are ultimately reliant on our readers to put us in the picture.

We welcome your feedback, especially your experience of using the book "on the road". Maybe we recommended a hotel that you liked (or another that you didn't), or you came across a great bar or new attraction that we missed.

We will acknowledge all contributions, and we'll offer an Insight Guide to the best letters received.

Please write to us at:
Insight Guides
PO Box 7910, London SE1 1WE
Or email us at:
insight@apaguide.co.uk

Travel guides, ebooks, apps and online
www.insightguides.com

AQUA LUNA 99P.
鴨脷仔

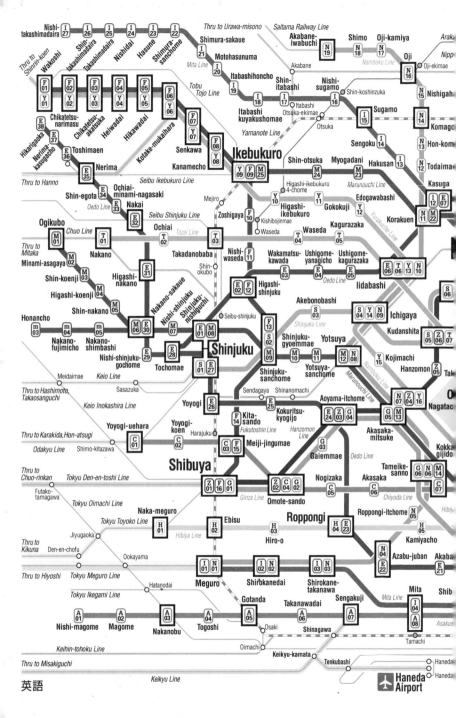